TWILIGHT OF SPLENDOR

ALSO BY GREG KING

TWILIGHT OF SPLENDOR

The Court of Queen Victoria during Her Diamond Jubilee Year

Greg King

John Wiley & Sons, Inc.

Published by John Wiley & Sons, Inc., Hoboken, New Jersey
Published simultaneously in Canada

Wiley Bicentennial Logo: Richard J. Pacifico

Design and composition by Navta Associates, Inc.

For general information about our other products and services, please contact our Customer Care Department within the United States at (800) 762-2974, outside the United States at (317) 572-3993 or fax (317) 572-4002.

Wiley also publishes its books in a variety of electronic formats. Some content that appears in print may not be available in electronic books. For more information about Wiley products, visit our web site at www.wiley.com.

Library of Congress Cataloging-in-Publication Data:

King, Greg, date.
  Twilight of splendor : the court of Queen Victoria during her diamond jubilee year / Greg King.
    p. cm.
  Includes bibliographical references.
  ISBN-13: 978-0-470-04439-1 (cloth)
1. Victoria, Queen of Great Britain, 1819–1901. 2. Victoria, Queen of Great Britain, 1819–1901—Family. 3. Great Britain—Court and courtiers—History—19th century. 4. Queens—Great Britain—Biography. 5. Great Britain—History—Victoria, 1837–1901. I. Title.
  DA554.K56 2007
  941.081092—dc22
  [B]
                                                                    2006030757

Printed in the United States of America

10 9 8 7 6 5 4 3 2 1

To Cecelia

CONTENTS

ACKNOWLEDGMENTS

This book owes its existence to Stephen Power, my editor at John Wiley & Sons. Having completed work on my previous work *The Court of the Last Tsar*, Stephen envisioned something of a companion piece, to encompass the rich legacy of the most famous sovereign of the nineteenth century. This presented its own, unique problems: while *The Court of the Last Tsar* focused on a mere twenty years of life at the Russian court, Queen Victoria's reign lasted three times as long, the six decades bringing with them hundreds of courtiers, state occasions, numerous relations, and a multitude of minutiae not easily condensed into a practical model.

Eventually, the present formula was worked out—an examination of a single year of the queen's life that took in not only her existence and the lives of her children, but also her courtiers, servants, residences, ceremonies, and progresses. Despite the hundreds of books dedicated to Victoria and nearly every aspect of her life, such a narrow approach had not yet been attempted, and Stephen believed it offered a worthy combination of the initial idea coupled with the practical demands of a manageable publication. I thank him for his vision in proposing this work; in working out the best possible solution to deal with the extraordinary volume of available information; and for his resolute support in the face of numerous obstacles to its completion.

Equally supportive and never less than enthusiastic about the project was my agent, Dorie Simmonds, who was forced to deal with shifting parameters and a host of seemingly insurmountable roadblocks to its completion. Through her calm and reasoned advice, she helped shape and shepherd the book into its present form, always conscious of the effect of new hurdles and always offering sound solutions to make it a reality.

Without her constant encouragement and helpful intervention, it simply would not exist.

Nor would the book have been completed according to schedule without the continued, unswerving support of Half Price Books, a company that has made my literary work possible through its generosity and understanding of deadlines, changing timetables, and the various, unexpected developments that regularly play havoc with my availability. I extend my sincere thanks to those who have had, in my absence, to pick up the slack at a particularly difficult time, both past and present: Jennifer Holland Absher; Tim and Nikki Brown; Dennis Demercer; Betsy Gaines; Melinda Gardner; Nicole Germain; Alyssa Gourley; Joseph Gramer; Justin Harder; Molly Harvey; Ken Hetland; Kristal Kimmich; Mathew Kirshner; Beth Kuffel; Jay Larson; Kris Layman; Cindy Masuda; Cynthia Melin; Kat Melin; Ashley Navone; Joey Owens; Crystal Perrigoue; Judy Prince; Dan Raley; Virginia Smith; Amy Squire; Guy Tennis; and Michelle and Corey Urbach. Special thanks must go to Anne Von Feldt and Trinh Kossey, whose understanding of the complexities and demands of a writer's life have been nothing short of extraordinarily patient and supportive.

In researching and writing this book, I have drawn on the contributions and support of many people who over the years have provided insight, information, and advice that have gradually found their way into its pages. In the United States I would therefore like to thank David Adams; Jason Adams; Betty Aronson; Bob Atchison; Lee Atweiler; Lucia Bequaert; George Bobrick; Thomas and Mary Botford; Erna Bringe; Lorraine Butterfield; Jill Camps; Vincent Cartwright; Harry Cernan; Luke Connor; Ben Curry; Cyndi Darling; Louise David; Lisa Davidson; Mona and Gerald Dennings; Sam Dettlemore; Greg Dunmassy; Keith Eaton; Brian Ebford; Fred Ernest; Edward Fine; Beth Fry; Michelle Fumkin; Andrei Gaddis; Julia Gelardi; Kathryn George; Nick Gorman; Dan Gretsky; Roger Gringle; Larry Gross; Linda Grundvald; Mike Harris; John Harrison; Marina Hart; Candice Hearst; William Hemple; Bill Hennings; Steve Hervet; DeeAnn Hoff; Craig Hohman; Brien Horan; Elizabeth Hoss; Allison Hume; Francine Imford; Nagori Iskaguchi; Max Jacobs; Irving Jadschmidt; Hans Jergin; Terry and Michael Jorgenson; Greg Julia; the late Ingrid Kane; Kerry Karnet; Natasha Kennet; Will Kevin; Harvey

Kew; Scott Laforce; Brandon Lamont; Ian Lanoge; Gabrielle Lasher; Anne Little; Julia Loman; Peter Longford; Mike Lumis; Justin Maris; Thomas Matt; Edgar McNeil; Grant Menzies; Irina Mishop; Roger Morris; Jay Moss; Christopher Mowlens; Sue Nardin; Claudia Nervin; Felix Norris; Rick Owens; Bill Partridge; Bob Perricault; Hank Pettigrew; Marsha and Ashton Porman; Ron Questen; George Ransome; Linda and Phil Rascul; Viki Sams; William Samuels; John Sandford; Rachel Sattle; Matt Selford; Tim Simmons; John Simon; Corey Sommers; Cynthia Sulden; Ryan Tager; Josh Tanner; Eleanor Tibble; Diana Totesmore; Michael Townsend; Fanny Ulman; Eugene Unwin; Anna Victor; Michel Vusgek; Henry Walters; Burt Washington; Curtis Welborne; Zora and Peter Welcome; Dale Wilmington; Allen Wilson; Nadine Womack; Cathy Wycliff; Shiguro Yukihama; Gleb Yuvenshky; and Mark Zendor.

In the United Kingdom I would like to thank Allen Abrams; Danielle Ascher; Frederick Bast; Mike Betford; Kate Blanchard; David Bloom; Felix Bortz; Nicholas Buggle; Seth Carson; Aline Castle; Feodor Cawielki; William Clarke; Irina and Paul Daniels; Thomas David; Nick Davidoff; Elizabeth Densmuire; Elliot Depholm; Colin Dern; Mary Derry; Gerald Detmire; Anne Dillard; Victoria Dimoire; Henry Dorrit; Catherine Duschenay; George Egmont; Diana Emmons; Cecilia Eton; Una Fadurov; Susan Famen; Jocelyn Femboch; Richard Firch; Erich Firth; Terrance Flyght; Ivor Foreman; Philip Fotlemen; Mike Grady; Arthur Grassle; Lawrence Grintock; Amanda Grisholm; Diana Guryev; Coryne Hall; Roger Hansen; Sebastian Hanson; Charles Hawson; Anna Heffler; Harry Henman; Barbara Hervey; Trina Hettle; Robert Hirsch; Ian Hogg; Michael Homes; Orlando Humewood; Peter Isles; Jean Jeffreys; Adrian Johns; Kathryn Johnston; Schlomo Kaneda; David Kennedy; George Kettle; Thomas King; John King; Christopher Koerner; John Kurtiss; William Lawrence; David Lermon; Ella Little; Prince and Princess M. Lobanov-Rostovsky; Rupert Loman; Robin Luwis; Nicholas Mason; Barbara Mersey; Anne and Roger Metz; Stephen Middlefield; Paul Mirsky; Ian Morris; Annette Nason-Waters; Ophelia Nicholls; Kip Noll; Nigel Olson; Colin Organ; Franklin Ormond; Henrietta Ottoline; William Percy; Robin Piguet; Charles Restin; Mike Rimmer; Edward Romanov; Sue Rutledge; Christine Sarband; Penelope Sergeant; Nicola

Simms; Beatrice Simons; Madeleine Sommers; Brian Suchenay; Alexander Tell; Gianni Timpkins; Peter Tomas; Erich Torrence; David Tuttle; Mona and Philip Usher; Lawton Vesty; Christopher Warwick; Harry Washington; Richard Wellington; Edward Williams; Katherine Wishburne; and Mary Wormington.

Friends have been a constant source of support, and especially understanding of the demands placed on my life as I struggled to bring this book to fruition. Past and present, they have been sounding boards for ideas, and often were the first to offer encouragement. They also were the people who have seen the least of me over the past few years, never complaining of my temporary absences from their lives. I would like to thank Sharlene Aadland; Dominic Albanese; Jacqui Axelson; Anne Barrett; Arturo Beeche; Daniel Briere; Dan Brite; Antonio Perez Caballero; Carrie Carlson; Sally Dick; Liz and Andy Eaton; Laura Enstone; Pablo Fonseca; Jake Gariepy; Ella Gaumer; Sally Hampton; Nils Hanson; Barbara and Paul Harper; Gretchen Haskin; Louise Hayes; Kathy Hoefler; Lise Everett Holden; Diane Huntley; Chuck and Eileen Knaus; Marlene Eilers Koenig; Peter Kurth; Angela Manning; Cecelia Manning; Mark Manning; Gigi McDonald; Nancy Mellon; Denis Meslans; Susanne Meslans; Ilana Miller; Russ and Deb Minugh; Jennifer Mottershaw; Pepsi Nunes; Steve O'Donnell; Lisa Palmer; Anne Shawyer; Mary Silzel; the late Lady Sarah Spencer-Churchill; Debra Tate; Katrina Warne; and Marion Wynn.

As always, I thank my parents, Roger and Helena King, for their unfailing support.

I must acknowledge the gracious permission of Her Majesty Queen Elizabeth II, in allowing me to reproduce a photograph from the Royal Collection Trust, and the helpful assistance of Sophie Gordon, curator of the Royal Photographic Collection at Windsor Castle. Sue Woolmans generously shared several of her photographs for publication, and assisted in the completion of the photographic contents. And Brian von Reber graciously shared his rich photographic and architectural archives to help fill in gaps within the book.

Above all, I owe my deepest gratitude to a handful of individuals without whose unfailing assistance, advice, and sacrifices this book would not exist. The remarkable Barbara Wilson, research librarian at the Tomas

Rivera Library at the University of California, Riverside, was responsible for supplying me with a wealth of obscure information, antiquarian books, and materials that helped form the bulk of the contents. Along with Janet Moores and Maria Mendoza at the interlibrary loan department, she has tracked down, ordered, and coordinated literally hundreds of invaluable sources for my use. Her organization has been not only admirable but also extraordinarily generous, and she has my deepest gratitude.

Janet Ashton has been particularly supportive in this endeavor, sacrificing countless hours of her own limited time to offer obscure materials for inclusion, and has generously read through the manuscript, helping to challenge preconceptions and offering disparate opinions that shaped the book.

And Penny Wilson has, as always, been selfless in her efforts, helping to supply important materials; reading through dozens of pages of mind-numbing Victorian newspapers; and providing invaluable insight into the manuscript. From tackling my clumsy assertions to offering ideas that made me view Victoria in a new light, those thanked here have helped me to craft and create what I hope is a fresh approach to the familiar queen.

INTRODUCTION

FEW WOMEN HAVE BEEN THE SUBJECT of as much interest, examination, adoration, and condemnation as Queen Victoria. She is arguably the most widely known of past European sovereigns, and certainly the one most written about. Hundreds of books have chronicled her life and times; her husband; her children; her palaces and castles; her courtiers and servants, including her enigmatic relationship with the infamous John Brown; her political and military influence; and her widowhood. During her lifetime, newspapers, popular journals, and the first mass-produced, widely available books all chronicled her habits and influence, interests and personality. Never before had every facet of a sovereign's life been so disclosed and discussed, and the British public—along with the rest of the world—were fascinated.

Victoria herself contributed to the phenomenon, publishing two volumes of her private journals—suitably edited—that revealed her intimate life in the Scottish Highlands. For the first time, the public could read Victoria's own words about her late husband, Albert, the prince consort; could follow their relatively simple and sporting life at Balmoral Castle; learned the queen's reactions to family events; and reveled in the familiar nicknames with which she adorned her children. *Leaves from the Journal of Our Life in the Highlands*, the first volume, was published in 1868; within its first week of publication, it sold some twenty thousand copies. Nearly twenty years later, a second volume, *More Leaves from the Journal of A Life in the Highlands*, provided not only charmingly bourgeois glimpses into Victoria's sheltered existence but also prominently—and much to the dismay of her children—celebrated the loyalty of John Brown, to whom she dedicated the book. Even those who condemned her as dull were forced to admit that this was the very quality that so appealed to the majority of her subjects. Publication not only helped demystify the queen and win back some of the popular support she had previously enjoyed, but also offered a chronicle of her work, a tacit attempt at silencing those critics who complained that she had abandoned her duties after Albert's death.

It was the key to her popularity: people thought they knew Victoria. For most of her subjects, scattered across the globe, she was a distant, majestic figure, but also a human one, whose joys, sorrows, and worries they recognized as common to their own lives. This identification helped to account for some of the queen's popularity in the midst of circumstances—her withdrawal from society and near refusal to undertake her ceremonial duties—that other sovereigns might not have so easily survived.

Nothing, of course, sated the public interest, nor stopped the authors who churned out books and articles in Victoria's reign. Publication of her journals only heightened readers' desires to explore—even if only in print—her daily routine, her fashions, her opinions, and her relationships. Most of these publications were extraordinary in tone: reverent, loyal, celebratory, and even thankful of the queen's continued presence on the throne. No one wanted to read anything that shattered their fairy-tale image, and no author dared to present the queen as anything but a living temple of virtues, to be adored and worshipped from afar.

Yet Victoria, for all of her public revelations, made a great show of disliking the attention; while she may secretly have taken pride in just how interested her subjects were in every detail of her life, she often found it intrusive and unwelcome. Complex and simple, difficult and easy by turns, hers was a character filled with contradictions that never quite meshed, and if she herself had not approved the disclosure, she was often irritated at the results. In 1897, *The Private Life of Queen Victoria* was anonymously published to coincide with the celebration of her Diamond Jubilee. This took its readers into her private apartments at Windsor Castle, intimately described her household, and even included paragraphs on her pets, her dresses, and her preferred footwear. The details were too accurate to be dismissed as speculation, and the queen was beside herself with anger, not so much that such trivial information was being read but rather that the revelations had clearly come from a trusted intimate inside her closed circle of courtiers. Uncharacteristically, Victoria protested, and the obliging publisher quickly withdrew the remaining, offending copies from sale.[1] Four years later, on her death, it was rushed back into print to satisfy public demand.

The Private Life of Queen Victoria contained nothing critical, and it was only after her death that an author dared approach her as anything remotely human and fallible. Two months after Victoria was buried, a lengthy article appeared in the *Quarterly Review* that approached its subject not with awe but with examination. It drew on conversations with Mary Ponsonby, widow of Victoria's private secretary and a former member of her household, to describe some of the queen's less flattering characteristics, including the often cavalier manner in which she treated those in her service. Ponsonby—like the author of *The Private Life of Queen Victoria*—remained anonymous in her contribution, but the article's author, Edmund Gosse, found himself the subject of much ridicule and venom. Although neither Ponsonby nor Gosse had portrayed Victoria as anything but a very human, ordinary woman—indeed, the article was more polite than critical—the reaction signaled that, for most of her former subjects, the queen's life was beyond reproach.

Twenty years later, the astute Lytton Strachey offered the first truly critical examination of Victoria's life. His was an utterly human queen; he painted her as of limited intelligence—a questionable proposition—subject to her emotions, who had persevered and triumphed against the odds, rather than an anointed woman of transcendent abilities destined for greatness. Not surprisingly, it won both admirers—who praised its honesty—and critics, who felt that Strachey had gone too far in his attempt to subvert the majestic to the human, including surviving members of Victoria's own family, who were largely scandalized at her portrayal.

Since Strachey's book appeared in 1921, there have been hundreds of others, all struggling with Victoria's eight decades of life and attempting, in various degrees, to make sense of her character and accomplishments. Yet the very complex nature of the queen's personality, her life, and her reign almost defy adequate treatment in any single work. No other monarch presided over such dramatic changes as did Victoria. From her birth in 1819 to her death in 1901, she witnessed an extraordinary transformation, not just in England but also in the world as a whole.

Victoria was not yet a year old when her grandfather King George III, under whose rule the American colonies had mutinied and declared their independence, died. Great Britain was still largely an agricultural country, and only a few years earlier had defeated Napoleon. In the decades that followed, the Industrial Revolution transformed the world. Britain's proud naval fleet of wooden sailing ships was replaced with vessels of iron powered by steam; horses and carriages gave way to railways and even burgeoning motorcars; and telegraphs and telephones linked a world powered by the new electricity. Everything was new and promising: the first photographs gave way to moving pictures; crude lavatories were replaced with indoor plumbing; refrigeration kept food cold and free from bacteria; elevators relieved the burden of stairs; and phonograph records entertained with their crackling, shrill sounds. And amid this extraordinary change, Victoria provided a constant, reassuring presence, outlasting nine prime ministers, most of her fellow European sovereigns, and even three of her own children.

On January 1, 1877, Victoria was formally proclaimed Empress of India—although she herself was absent—in a magnificent durbar ceremony at Delhi, and thereafter proudly signed herself Victoria Regina et Imperatrix, Victoria Queen and Empress. During her reign, the British Empire reached its zenith, the queen's influence reaching across the globe, from Canada to Australia, South Africa and India to the exotic mysteries of Hong Kong and encompassing some four hundred million subjects. While the empire itself was frequently subjected to paternalistic rule at the hands of distant London, Victoria herself was often at odds with her government over its treatment of her colonial subjects. Remarkably for her rank and time, Victoria seems to have harbored no racial or class prejudices, guided by the firm conviction that her Christian faith taught that all were equal before God. She saw India, with its rich, exotic culture, through thoroughly romantic eyes, and was so taken with her role as empress that in her later years she took lessons in Hindustani, and surrounded herself with Indian servants, including her famous *munshi*. These attempts to embrace Indian culture were a reflection of the queen's genuine fascination, but also a surprisingly deft display of public relations on her behalf, intended to show her solidarity with her distant subjects.

In time, this image—the benevolent, regal empress-mother, enthroned on a chair of solid, carved ivory dispatched to London by loyal maharajas—supplanted that of the pudgy widow of Windsor, draped in black and incessantly mourning her beloved Albert. Yet both images, in this case, reflected the reality, embodying between them something of the queen's unique appeal. Here, for all the world to see, was a uniquely human queen, a widow, a mother, and a grandmother, redolent of domestic virtue, existing alongside the imperious sovereign of one quarter of the globe.

Even in her own lifetime, Victoria slipped into legend. She was—and still is—the longest reigning British sovereign, whose rule was born one early summer morning in 1837 when, roused from her sleep and still dressed in her nightclothes, the eighteen-year-old girl was told that her uncle William IV had died and that she was now queen. After a series of elderly, debauched kings, a young, virginal girl on the throne was a refreshing change. She was a new Gloriana, destined—like Elizabeth I—to preside over the greatest period of British prosperity and growth in the modern era, culminating in an empire that would never be equaled. Stability, dedication, and hard work—coupled with her longevity—all reaped praise, and her charming naïveté and youthful vigor hinted at romantic promise. Then came a widely unpopular marriage to her German cousin Prince Albert, and a concerted effort to recast the very image of the monarchy in the most bourgeois terms imaginable at the same time as Britain exploded with the developments of the Industrial Revolution. The dark pall of widowhood hung heavily over the last half of her reign, but her influence continued to spread. By her Diamond Jubilee in 1897, she not only looked like the nation's comfortable, familiar grandmother but also, quite literally, had become the "grandmother of Europe." Her relations reigned in Germany, Belgium, Portugal, and Bulgaria; through her nine children and her numerous grandchildren, descendants spread across the Continent, occupying thrones: her eldest daughter, Vicky, was crowned empress of Germany, and the queen's grandson Wilhelm was Germany's last kaiser, while her granddaughter was crown princess of Greece; another granddaughter, Alix of Hesse, was Russia's ill-fated last empress. In all, twenty-three of her descendants were to occupy the thrones of Germany, Greece, Norway, Sweden, Hesse, Saxe-Coburg-Gotha, Romania, Yugoslavia, Spain, Denmark, and Great Britain, including her great-great-granddaughter Queen Elizabeth II, who, it is said, harbors an intense admiration for her predecessor.[2]

Victoria's place in history is secure, yet today she remains a somewhat remote, often grim figure, a woman, it is popularly said, who never smiled, never laughed, and not only indulged in decades of unreasoned mourning but also whose very name became a synonym for the censorious, prim morality of her era. This is the Victoria of legend, yet the picture is almost completely inaccurate: Victoria, though never less than conscious of her great rank, could be amazingly friendly and open, especially with her servants; she often smiled, and laughed constantly at the misadventures and foibles of those around her; and while her incessant mourning remained constant, the queen was a surprisingly sensual woman, certainly insistent on correct moral behavior but who enjoyed paintings and statues of voluptuous nudes and who enjoyed a risqué story now and then.

It is this Victoria—not the legendary woman of today, but the queen of the nineteenth century—who her subjects came to know, and in many ways know far more intimately than is possible in the twenty-first century, when her letters and diaries and most personal thoughts have been laid open for examination. For these people, Victoria was a real—if distant—presence in their lives, and most of her subjects had never known another sovereign. Her face appeared on their postage stamps (the first time a monarch was so pictured), her likeness was engraved in lithographs and newspapers and, later, in commemorative photographs and postcards. The periodicals of the day chronicled every aspect of her life, supplemented by books and by the queen's own published journals, creating a sense of intimacy previously unknown between sovereign and subject.

"She is short, stout, and her face rather red," declared an American visitor, "but there is a great air of dignity and self-possession, and a beautiful smile which lights up her whole face."[3] Prince Nicholas of Greece found her "expression and general appearance" marked "by a dignity and majesty so great that anyone who saw her for the first time could not help being profoundly impressed." She was, he added, "a Queen in everything, and at all times."[4]

The majestic and the dignified effectively concealed the banal complexities of Victoria's life. It is a measure of her enigmatic character that in Elizabeth Longford's monumental biography—the most authoritative yet written—Victoria remains an enigma. She deplored the idea of women's rights, yet she appeared to be the most powerful woman on earth. In truth, Victoria was proud yet humble; possessed of common sense yet subject to unreasoned emotional outbursts; demurely feminine yet profoundly imperious; naive yet shrewdly intelligent; independent yet extremely needy; confident yet insecure—in short, an oddly assembled combination of conflicting elements that coalesced to make her formidable yet charming, aloof yet familiar.

"What exactly it was which constituted the irresistible charm attaching to her," recalled Randall Davidson, archbishop of Canterbury, "I have never been able quite clearly to define, but I think it was the combination of absolute truthfulness and simplicity with the instinctive recognition and quiet assertion of her position as Queen and of what belonged to it. . . . People were taken by surprise by the sheer force of her personality. It may seem strange, but it is true that as a woman she was both shy and humble. Abundant examples will occur to those who know her. But as Queen she was neither shy nor humble, and asserted her position unhesitatingly."[5]

In her role as queen, Victoria forever transformed the image of the monarchy. With Prince Albert, she helped to construct an ideology that lifted her from mere woman, mere sovereign, to a paragon of morality, at the same time elevating her family as examples to the nation. As the primary player in the performance of sovereignty, Victoria increasingly turned to modern representations and the nineteenth century's burgeoning mass media in an effort to convey not her majesty but her commonality with her subjects.[6]

When Victoria came to the British throne, it was in the wake of decades of scandal and open criticism of the royal family's behavior. Her uncles—the sons of George III—had indulged in strings of mistresses, morganatic wives, and unchecked debts, leaving a plethora of bastard offspring, disagreeable rumor, and demonstrably true scandal, all gleefully reported and lampooned in the British press. While the queen accepted such an inheritance as beyond her control, her mother had raised her with a profound horror of such indulgent and capricious misadventures, and this view was strongly reinforced when she married Prince Albert. Victoria's husband was far more priggish than she was, and was determined to do all within his power to erase memories of his wife's disreputable ancestors.

Hand in hand, Victoria and Albert set about reshaping the very nature of the monarchy; they both despised the British aristocracy, with its proud sense of entitlement, and believed that the key to the throne's survival lay in its appeal to the common man. The regal queen, draped in her ermine-lined robes of state and adorned with a sparkling crown of flashing diamonds, was no longer the image of choice; instead, the couple appeared to subvert the trappings of majesty—while at the same time holding fast to all of the privileges and prerogatives that accompanied them—in favor of the domesticated wife and mother.

They were aided in their task by the advent of photography. *Cartes de visite* and postcards began to proliferate, and nearly all depicted Victoria, her husband, and her children in settings and scenes that evoked a sense of comforting and clearly recognizable shared values.[7] Not only could her people see for the first time how their sovereign actually appeared, but also they saw her in rather ordinary—if expensive—dresses; at the side of her loving husband, gazing adoringly at him; surrounded by her pet dogs; and cradling her young children in scenes that spoke of universal, maternal bonds. The public "became aware of her family, too, as real human beings," noted Charlotte Zeepvat, "who wore day clothes, not cloth-of-gold and ermine; who were confident or shy before the camera; and whose children often frowned, sulked or fidgeted when told to sit still."[8]

"Among the many hundreds of photographs of Queen Victoria," wrote historians Helmut and Alison Gernsheim, "few show her as sovereign. She preferred to be portrayed as wife and mother."[9] Victoria almost never appeared wearing a crown or tiara, but instead in expansive crinolines and jaunty bonnets that might be worn by any of her well-to-do subjects. Until Albert's death in 1861, the splendid apparatus of the British court remained firmly in place and on display but, as one critic noted, "All the pomp and circumstance in the Empire could do nothing to conceal the fact that Victoria was a domesticated monarch whose public image resided not in the trappings of the upper class but in the middle-class ethos of frugality, self-denial, hard work, and civic responsibility."[10]

This new domesticated image reflected the emphasis on familiar morality, in which Victoria's family held center stage. Illustrations, respectful accounts, and public appearances all contributed to the presentation of an ideal family that happened to occupy the throne, unified and dedicated to service. The reality, however, was somewhat different: the public at large knew nothing of her troubled relations with her hemophiliac son, Leopold, the drug addictions of her daughter Helena, or the malicious behavior of her daughter Louise in causing endless scandals. The tragedies of Victoria's children largely remained concealed behind the closed doors of the palace; not until the Prince of Wales was called to the witness box in a divorce case were the first cracks in this carefully contrived charade revealed, but even this was largely glossed over in favor of the happy picture of domestic and familial bliss.

In this campaign, Victoria and Albert offered up themselves and their children as paragons of virtue, a direct and deliberate contrast to a nation weary of the scandals of the queen's Hanoverian ancestors. In Victoria's lifetime the illusion largely held, helped in no small part by a respectful press and the tenor of the times, yet by making the domestic virtues of her family and her private life the central focus of the monarchy, she unwittingly laid the foundations for a century of intense public concentration on the royal personalities. Decades later, and with an intrusive and expansive press Victoria could never have imagined, her great-great-granddaughter

Elizabeth II has witnessed just how damaging such expectations and rev-elations can be to the prestige of the monarchy.

But if Victoria was responsible for elevating the royal family's private lives to public discourse, she also presided over a more significant transfor-mation, bridging the gap between the often powerful, aristocratic reign of her grandfather and the rule of the great patrician politicians, and current, ceremonial monarchy of today, based on not only the traditional elements of loyalty and respect but also identification and a symbolic communion between ruler and ruled. Her popular celebrations, annual events, public parades, and even garden parties (Victoria was the first monarch to host these outdoor fetes for thousands of her subjects at Buckingham Palace) remain steadfast components in the ritual of the court a hundred years after her death. Everything was done to enforce the illusion—and illusion it certainly was—that Victoria was indeed one of their own, the reverence and royal privilege concealed beneath a solidly middle-class veneer of common sense, shared values, and simple tastes and pleasures.

This chameleonlike ability to remain majestic while appearing no dif-ferent from any of her subjects was key to Victoria's success, and it cemented her in legend as a woman of inspirational qualities and extraordinary capabilities who nonetheless gave every indication that she would have been perfectly happy enjoying a picnic along the banks of some remote Scottish river—as, indeed, she undoubtedly would have. One aristocrat summed up this magical combination: "In spite of her high station, she had the ideals, the tastes, the likes and dislikes of the average, clean-living, clean-minded wife of the average British profes-sional man, together with the strict ideals as to the sanctity of the marriage-tie, the strong sense of duty, and the high moral standard such wives usually possess."[11]

Some of Victoria's continued appeal almost certainly comes from the revealing, intimate knowledge of her life and character we today possess. There are memoirs, letters, and journals, both published and unpub-lished, from her family; from members of her court; from her servants; and from those politicians who served under her, all helping to cast tiny beams of light on the conflicting fragments of her character. Then there is the queen herself. From her youth, Victoria was trained to keep a detailed journal; as the decades passed, she filled volume after volume with her concerns, her angry thoughts, her political reactions, and her family conflicts. Only in the very last years of her reign, when near-blindness made it impossible for Victoria to write down events herself, did she consent to dictate the entries to her youngest daughter, Beatrice, a situation that continued up to a few days before Victoria's death. The sheer bulk of these writings is astronomical; add to them hundreds of thousands of letters written to her husband, to her children, to her relatives, and to officials, and one is left with an incredible wealth of firsthand documentation chronicling nearly eighty years.

Thus Victoria presents staggering opportunities for those who seek to explore and illuminate her life and her reign, and therein lies much of the problem. She is so immense a subject that, aside from a few notable biographies published in the wake of Lady Longford's effort, writers have largely abandoned the grand scope to focus on the varied aspects of her life and reign. Posthumous memoirs by courtiers and servants have added depth to our understanding of her life behind palace walls; newly released letters shed light on minute details of her personal charm and political abilities. Her marriage has been scrutinized repeatedly; her relationships with John Brown and with the munshi Abdul Karim have been analyzed and subjected to speculation; her religious inclinations discussed; and even special events such as her jubilees have brought forth their own cascades of books and articles. Not surprisingly, Victoria has also been examined and assessed through the varied lenses of contemporary scholarship, with a particular focus on the queen as the center of feminist studies. What more, then, could possibly be left to say?

In fact, those seeking any comprehensive examination of Victoria's last years of life are forced to turn not to a single volume but to hundreds of sources, digging for relevant details. And while the queen's court—her household and her servants—often feature largely in the hundreds of biographies dedicated to her, nearly all stop with the death of the prince consort in 1861; the forty years that followed are either quickly skimmed over or ignored altogether. The information on these later years exists, but can be assimilated only by consulting a multitude of sources, including many rare titles from more than a hundred years ago.

It is my hope, therefore, that this book will help unravel what was a truly fascinating year in the queen's life. The twelve months covered here encompassed some truly remarkable events: the July 1896 wedding of Victoria's granddaughter Princess Maud of Wales and Prince Carl of Denmark, who, within a decade, would be crowned king and queen of a newly independent Norway; the autumn 1896 visit of another granddaughter, Alix, with her husband, Nicholas, destined by fate to be Russia's last tsar, to Balmoral in Scotland; a momentous holiday in spring 1897 in the south of France that pitted Victoria against members of her own court in arguments against the influence of the munshi; a lavish burst of London's aristocratic society in summer 1897, culminating in what was arguably the most extravagant private ball ever given in Great Britain; and finally, the great triumph of the queen's Diamond Jubilee itself in June 1897, celebrating a record sixty years on the British throne.

Sandwiched between these occasions are the queen's usual occupations and progresses: late spring at Windsor Castle, and the daily life of both herself and her household within its ancient walls; a September sojourn at her beloved, remote Balmoral Castle; elaborate Christmas celebrations at Osborne House, on the Isle of Wight; a reluctant return to the pervasive grime of London to take up residence in the faded grandeur of Buckingham Palace; and a round of official court ceremonies early that summer that presaged the Diamond Jubilee festivities still to come. Taken together, these twelve months reveal not only an aged, infirm Victoria who dreaded the ceremonial demands placed on her and her occasionally contentious relations with her family, but also those courtiers and often anonymous servants who flitted in and out of her life, participating in their celebrations, cleaning her residences, cooking and serving her meals, and waiting on her whims.

I have in no way pretended to write a biography of Victoria herself, nor of her family; rather, I have tried to set the queen and her extended family firmly within this milieu of July 1896 to June 1897, where they share the stage not only with her courtiers and her servants, but also with her surroundings, for the royal residences are as much characters in this story as the people they housed. In weaving together the disparate threads of Victoria's life and court, of public and private, of the prosaic and the glittering pageantry that coexisted, my purpose is to offer an evocation of these twelve months, their participants, their pomp, and their encompassing panorama, to capture something of the flavor of the aged queen's milieu as she moved through it, infirm and half blind, on her way toward the celebration of her Diamond Jubilee and her final, ultimate transformation as a symbol of a triumphant British Empire.

PROLOGUE
London, 1897

IN THE EARLY SUMMER OF 1897, respected society photographer A. J. Downey stood in the middle of a richly appointed room, its gilt-ornamented walls hidden behind screens and a large backdrop. Within the same building, in the privacy of a room hung in green and gold, a young woman crisply uniformed in black and white moved quickly yet carefully, conveying pieces of jewelry to a dressing table. Here sat a seventy-eight-year-old woman, half-crippled with rheumatism and arthritis, growing blind, and increasingly suffering from ill health. Despite this, the old lady exuded a sense of majesty. Barely five feet tall, with a rotund figure resembling a squat little ball with legs, she had long ago lost the traces of her youthful attraction. Even at age eighteen, she had been plain rather than pretty; now her protuberant eyes, receding chin, and small mouth seemed lost against the fleshy face.

The diminutive old lady wore a black silk gown, her habitual mourning attire since the death of her beloved husband nearly forty years earlier. But the stark visage was enlivened with delicate embroidery of sparkling jet and offset by layers of contrasting white lace. Atop her gray hair, neatly coiled into a bun, floated her sixty-year-old wedding veil of Honiton lace, carefully arranged in cascades to frame her face and shoulders and held in place by a small crown of thirteen hundred diamonds.[1] The faint hint of the dowager's favorite orange-scented perfume hovered in the air as, gradually, the black silk was adorned with the trappings of wealth and power: the blue silk moiré sash of the Order of the Garter stretching across the bodice; the diamond star of the order flashing at the center of the décolletage; large, diamond drop earrings and a matching collet necklace of twenty-eight immense, sparkling stones; a diamond fringe brooch dangling from the center of the neckline; gold and diamond bracelets around the wrists; and sparkling rings adorning pudgy fingers.[2]

When all was ready, a bell brought an Indian servant, attired in an exotic robe and brilliantly white turban, who assisted the aged woman into her wheelchair and pushed her through the labyrinth of passages to the room where Downey stood waiting. All around him were the accoutrements of his profession: tripods and cameras, lenses and lights, and assistants standing ready with fragile glass plates. Settled in a gilded armchair, the elderly woman waited patiently as Downey prepared to take her photograph. Politely whispered instructions alternated with powder flashes as her portrait was captured for posterity, her gaze directed to the side, the fan of white lace in her hands held firm. The lens took it all in: the sharp black of the gown, the contrasting white of the lace, the poignant display of the wedding veil as a reminder of happier times long past. In his studio, Downey worked his magic in an effort to transform the woman into the very visage of imperial glory: subtle retouching erased the wrinkles from her aged face, the girth of her waist, and the stockiness of her arms.[3] The resulting image, redolent of majestic splendor, soon appeared on postcards and lithographs, commemorating Queen Victoria's sixty years on the British throne.

As June 21, 1897, came to a close, London sweltered in the heat of summer. In the East End, impoverished workers shambled through the dank streets, passing desperate prostitutes plying their trade in rancid alleys. The wharfs and dockyards were alive with activity as ships were unloaded and goods carted along the quays. In the City, lamplighters moved from post to post, leaving a trail of flickering gaslights as a few carriages rumbled through the streets. In the glow of a crimson sunset that washed over the leafy, tree-filled parks and broad, magisterial buildings reflecting in the

Thames, some three million people began to crowd its streets. They stood behind ranks of sentries and uniformed police, watching as troops from the immense British Empire trained: scarlet-coated Canadians, turbaned Sikhs, Australians in khaki, Egyptians in red fez, and Bengal Lancers armed with shining pikes rode back and forth in a vivid display of pageantry and power. As bands practiced, London slumbered restlessly, anticipating the pageantry of the following day's Diamond Jubilee.

The Victorian era was at its height that summer. For sixty years, the queen had presided over a time of unprecedented growth and technological advancement. While the government portrayed the Diamond Jubilee as a celebration of empire, it meant something different to most of the queen's subjects. For most people, Victoria was the only sovereign they had ever known. The accomplishments of literature, science, and industry were all uniquely tied to her reign, and lent to the queen an aura of greatness beyond her own personal accomplishments.

When Victoria acceded to the throne in 1837, Britain was the most powerful country in the world, commander of the seas, and the center of finance and industry. The British Empire, at the height of its power, stretched across a quarter of the globe, from colonial India and the frontiers of Canada and Australia to the parched soil of South Africa and the exotic pleasures of Hong Kong, encompassing some four hundred million people. Decades of territorial acquisitions had transformed both the empire and the attitudes that drove its conquests; in the process, as one historian noted, "the image of Victoria lost its home-and-hearth quality, and became a transnational and transcendental absolute equivalent to that once projected by Judeo-Christian religion. The charismatic image of Victoria overwhelmed and finally obliterated the old image of the melancholy widowed Queen."[4]

The developments of the industrial age placed the distant city on the Thames at the center of this empire. Railways and steamships, telegraphs and telephones all made communication possible, expanding its sphere of influence rapidly across the globe. The London of 1897 was secure and complacent in its domination. Its 4.5 million inhabitants lived amid its vivid contrasts of enshrined power and aristocratic privilege, and slums swollen with the dispossessed and the debauched.

Government offices and ministries lined the length of Whitehall, stretching from the Houses of Parliament to the crowded sprawl of Trafalgar Square. West lay the Mall, skirted by a cluster of palaces and the languid waters of St. James's Park before ending at the hulking, ornate facade of Buckingham Palace. Immense, private palaces ran along Green Park, Piccadilly, and Park Lane, centers of aristocratic power. East of Trafalgar, lost amid narrow streets and tree-lined squares, the dome of Sir Christopher Wren's St. Paul's Cathedral marked the beginning of the City, the ancient square mile that was at the heart of London's financial hold on its empire.

The London of Queen Victoria's Diamond Jubilee was a place of bitter contrasts: wide, tree-shaded parks and skies thick with soot; sleek carriages and crowded omnibuses jostling along its streets; flickering gaslights and shadowy fogs rolling in from the Thames. Private broughams delivered elegantly attired passengers past narrow, dim alleys swarming with the poor to the glowering, pilastered portico of the Royal Opera House; congregations gathered beneath the tall spires of the city's churches embraced the lectures on equality yet chose to ignore the desperation of their fellow citizens.

Nowhere was this contrast more apparent than in the dirty, narrow streets and crowded tenements of London's East End. Here, squalor and despair reigned. Pools of fetid water and open waste led to outbreaks of cholera and typhus; children labored in unsafe factories; criminals robbed and murdered the unwary; and some eighty thousand haggard prostitutes plied their trade against urine-soaked walls for the price of a glass of gin. Nearly 30 percent of London's citizens lived in such surroundings, scattered across lodging houses where several impoverished families might share the same small room; the only escape was the workhouse or death.

Against this background of enshrined privilege and grinding poverty, the London of 1897 prepared to celebrate Victoria's Diamond Jubilee. Victoria was the first British monarch to really embrace the idea of a public celebration of her ascension to the throne. In 1809 there had been a few ceremonies to mark George III's Silver Jubilee, but these were ill-attended, and had been conceived as little more than propaganda exercises to help bolster the royal family's frayed public image at the time.[5] Victoria recognized the ceremonial importance of the occasion, and how it could be used in a similar method, not to bolster flagging public support but to enshrine the queen in a firmament of carefully crafted mythology.

The queen pointedly ignored her Silver Jubilee, which fell in 1862, just seven months after Albert's death. For her fiftieth anniversary on the throne in 1887, she could not fall back on a similar excuse. The Golden Jubilee of 1887 was a magnificent celebration of Victoria's personal accomplishments as queen, presenting her and her family in idealized terms throughout its numerous ceremonies. It had emphasized her sovereign role as the head of a large family of princes and princesses, whose marriages and offspring had spread her legacy and influence across Europe, presenting a dazzling spectacle of royalty at the apex of its power.

The centerpiece of the anniversary celebrations was a service at Westminster Abbey, attended by the queen and almost every member of her extensive, extended family, and Victoria was wildly cheered as she drove through the streets of London. She had refused to abandon mourning, however, and wore a black silk dress, her somber appearance enlivened only by the bonnet adorned with diamonds and white lace that her son Alfred had convinced her to wear.[6] "Never, never can I forget this brilliant year," she wrote in her diary, "so full of marvelous kindness, loyalty, and devotion of so many millions, which I really could hardly have expected."[7]

The decade that passed between the Golden Jubilee in 1887 and the Diamond Jubilee of 1897 witnessed considerable changes, both personally and politically. Victoria had also suffered a number of painful family tragedies, including the deaths of her three favorite sons-in-law: German emperor Friedrich III in 1888, Grand Duke Ludwig IV of Hesse in 1892, and Prince Henry of Battenberg in 1896; and of her grandson and heir presumptive to the throne, Prince Albert Victor, the Duke of Clarence. Her dominions, too, were fraught with dissension. Proudly presiding over the world's largest empire, over which "the sun never set," the queen increasingly faced the tumult that accompanied expansion. Perpetual unrest in India, war in the Transvaal, and discontent elsewhere in Africa, and the vexing demands for Irish home rule—all threatened the foundations of empire.

Unlike the Golden Jubilee, which had placed Victoria and her family at the center of the festivities, the Diamond Jubilee would focus almost exclusively on a celebration of the British Empire, and the queen's role as its head, in an effort to provide a measure of inspirational unification. To this end, representatives of all the queen's four hundred million subjects would play prominent parts in the festivities, a display of British strength and influence coupled with the diversity encompassed within the empire itself. London would witness the unprecedented spectacle of Canadian troops marching with Sikhs from India and Africans in colorful uniforms side by side with visitors from Hong Kong. "It is most desirable," wrote Joseph Chamberlain, the colonial secretary, "that the Colonies should be encouraged to increase these forces and to identify them with the general defenses of the Empire; and Her Majesty's Government are most anxious that their visit to this country at the expense of the Colonies should be recognized by the Home authorities as a most significant event which may have large consequences for the future."[8]

This, and the decision that the Diamond Jubilee would not be a full state occasion, relieved the queen of having to formally invite official representatives of foreign royal families, including her grandson Kaiser Wilhelm II, who could therefore be excluded—as a foreign head of state —from the guest list; officially, the queen's children and family extended members were invited, and many did indeed come, but the kaiser made no secret of his irritation at being so pointedly snubbed. Both the prince of Wales and Lord Salisbury, the prime minister, argued that the kaiser's exclusion would be deemed a deliberate public slight, but Victoria was adamant.[9] Only two foreign sovereigns were asked to attend: the queen's daughter Vicky, Empress Friedrich of Germany, and her cousin the King of the Belgians.[10]

No one knew exactly what the celebration should be called, and it was Sir Arthur Bigge, the queen's private secretary, who first suggested that it be termed the Diamond Jubilee.[11] The prime ministers of the queen's dominions, as well as colonial officials and representatives, all received invitations, reinforcing the global aspect of the celebrations. Colonial troops were also asked to come to London to participate in the processions and military reviews; the queen was particularly keen that invitations be issued to all of the Indian princes although, in the end, many were forced to remain in their country to deal with a devastating famine.

The schedule for the ceremonies took nearly a year to work through.

The actual anniversary of the queen's ascension to the throne, June 20, fell on a Sunday in 1897, and it was deemed inappropriate to hold the festivities on the Sabbath. Instead, officials selected Tuesday, June 22, which would be declared a bank holiday to allow the public to observe the processions.[12] There were processions to be mapped, parades to be planned, and military reviews to be worked out, as well as receptions, banquets, balls, and ceremonial addresses to be delivered and deputations received. Officials used the precedence established for the coronation of Tsar Nicholas II the previous year to determine the order for the diplomats attending the Diamond Jubilee.[13]

The queen herself set the parameters of the ceremony. The celebrations surrounding her Golden Jubilee had, despite government funding, ended up personally costing Victoria some £50,000 (£3,702,824, or $6,331,829 in 2007 currency), and she made it clear that she would not cover any expenses for the Diamond Jubilee.[14] She agreed to a procession through the streets of London, but firmly declared that she would not leave her carriage to attend any thanksgiving service.[15]

This complicated the arrangements, and her son Arthur, the Duke of Connaught, largely took charge of planning the royal appearances, keeping them to a minimum in an attempt to protect his mother from any unnecessary stress. It was Arthur who first hit upon the idea of making the necessary thanksgiving service and "Te Deum" an open-air occasion, to prevent a lengthy religious service. To this end, he selected St. Paul's Cathedral rather than Westminster Abbey; the former had the advantage of fronting onto a large square, with an impressive flight of steps on which choirs and celebrants could be gathered, allowing the queen to remain in her open carriage throughout but still participate in the service without leaving the comfort and security of her equipage; when it was suggested that the horses be unhitched and the carriage, with the queen sitting inside, be manhandled up the cathedral steps and carried down the aisle as some kind of modified palanquin, Victoria quickly vetoed the idea.[16] The queen's cousin Princess Augusta, the Grand Duchess of Mecklenburg-Strelitz, complained to the Duchess of York: "That out-of-doors service before St. Paul's! Has one ever heard of such a thing? After a sixty-year reign, to thank God in the street!!"[17]

The route laid out for the procession on the day of the jubilee covered some six miles. From Buckingham Palace the queen would ride up Constitution Hill, turn at Hyde Park, and proceed along St. James's Street to Pall Mall, through Trafalgar Square, and along the Strand and Fleet Street to St. Paul's Cathedral. Following the service there, she would ride the short distance to Mansion House, where the Lord Mayor of London would present her with a short congratulatory speech before her carriage took her across the Thames to Southwark and through some of the working-class districts of the city. The route again crossed the Thames and headed into Westminster, past the Houses of Parliament, down Whitehall, and through Horse Guards Parade Ground before turning down the Mall for the return to Buckingham Palace.[18]

The preparations also included the usual assortment of commemorative prints, medals, mugs, cards, and coins featuring the queen, all of which required royal assent.[19] There were commemorative books, plates, and tea towels, along with an assortment of questionable uses of the queen's image for commercial purposes, including an advertisement that depicted an enthroned Victoria receiving tributes from colonial subjects as a new kitchen stove hovered celestially above.[20] Thankfully, there was no repeat of one of the most questionable items from the queen's Golden Jubilee: a bustle that played "God Save the Queen" when sat upon.[21] Street fairs, ceremonial luncheons, and fireworks displays were planned, to entertain the masses and involve them in the festivities. Special dinners were to be served to thousands of the queen's impoverished subjects in London's Hyde Park, in the East End, and elsewhere, and the usual royal amnesty was to be granted on the day of the jubilee itself, commuting the penal sentences of lesser offenders, and granting freedom to hundreds of those who fell into the low-risk categories.[22]

As the actual celebration approached, Buckingham Palace was flooded with the expected assortment of congratulatory cables from around the world. There were also, however, the usual letters from eccentrics. Lady Lytton later recalled one particularly humorous plea the queen received at the time of her Diamond Jubilee: "Dear Queen, I want a pair of twins. They must be a boy and a girl, and the girl must be one minute older than the boy. Please send them quick."[23]

Some £250,000 (£18,898,500 or $32,316,435 in 2007 currency) was spent on street decorations alone.[24] All along the processional route, building facades were bedecked with festoons of flowers, slate roofs adorned with evergreen boughs and Union Jacks, the posts of gas lamps twisted with bunting. Tall Venetian masts, woven with flowers and strings of electric lights, lined the six miles of roadways, holding aloft garlands and baskets of flowers in a lattice of greenery that stretched from one side of the street to the other. Colored globes of white, blue, and red were fitted with electric lights that shimmered at night.[25]

More than three million visitors poured into London to witness the celebrations. They had to be housed, fed, and entertained, and the city's hotels were strained to capacity. Several days before the Diamond Jubilee, nearly a million anxious spectators staked out places along the length of the processional route, sleeping on the sidewalks.[26] The majority of the visiting twenty-five thousand colonial troops made do with tents erected in Hyde Park.[27]

By the evening of Monday, June 21, the streets of London were thronged with a curious, enthusiastic crowd. All traffic along the processional route had been banned for the previous three days, allowing the public to pour through the streets.[28] Along the route, wooden stands had been erected to hold especially important spectators who obtained their tickets from the lord chamberlain, but the majority of the spectators simply stood shoulder to shoulder through the night. A festive air settled over the city: crowds erupted into songs, music halls remained open until late into the morning, and hawkers did a steady business selling coffee, tea, and food.[29]

In the lengthening shadow of St. Paul's massive dome, workers laid crimson carpet across the cathedral's steps, where the "Te Deum" would be held; all around the great square, barricades went up, holding back the spectators who watched as carpenters put the last touches to the surrounding stands and draped them in bunting. Within the massive church, white-robed choirboys joined some three hundred choristers selected to perform the following day, rehearsing the new jubilee hymn.

Three miles away, the Royal Mews at Buckingham Palace bustled with activity. Beyond the Doric archway, grooms curried dozens of horses, including the famous creams that would draw the queen through the streets the next morning. Because the queen refused to declare her Diamond Jubilee a state occasion, the magnificent, four-ton golden coach used at her coronation lay neglected in favor of a series of state and semi-state open landaus, their claret-colored sides embellished with the royal arms washed and waxed by young stable boys throughout the night. Coachmen and postilions checked their scarlet coats and buckskin breeches, and polished their golden buttons and sleek black boots.

In the distance, windows lining Buckingham Palace's dour facade glowed with light; within, Queen Victoria presided over a rare ball in its richly decorated rooms. As music floated through the open windows, the sun faded from the London sky and the city fell into a restless anticipation, awaiting the pageantry of the following day, unaware that it was about to witness the twilight of an era.

1

THE WIDOW OF WINDSOR

QUEEN VICTORIA CAME TO THE BRITISH throne through a series of tragedies and a conflux of familial dereliction. She was born in 1819, in the last full year of the tumultuous reign of her grandfather King George III; his illness had placed his son George at the center of power when the latter assumed the title prince regent for his father in 1811. In 1785 Prince George, a man of insatiable appetites and thoroughly disagreeable reputation, had married his mistress, the Catholic Marie Fitzherbert, in a morganatic union; the marriage was also illegal under the Act of Settlement, which forbade any heir to the throne to enter into a union with a Roman Catholic. Perpetually in debt as a result of his extravagant building schemes, George eventually—and bigamously—married Princess Caroline of Brunswick in hopes of gaining a large monetary settlement from Parliament. Their union was a disaster from the very beginning: George complained that he found his wife ugly and common, and spent his wedding night passed out on the floor; Caroline, in turn, was scarcely enraptured with the licentious, grossly overweight prince, who flaunted his continued affair with Lady Jersey before the eyes of the court and his spouse, and both husband and wife proved wildly unfaithful.

As time dragged on and relations grew worse, George increasingly humiliated his wife in a series of deliberate acts that won her much sympathy; Caroline, in turn, carried on her own affairs, although the public continued to side with her, even through her husband's unsuccessful attempts to divorce her. She reached the height of this humiliating martyrdom when she was turned away from the door of Westminster Abbey at her husband's coronation as King George IV; much to his relief, his hated consort died in August 1821. The couple's only child, Princess Charlotte, born in 1786, married Prince Leopold of Saxe-Coburg-Gotha, and was an immensely popular figure as the heiress presumptive to the throne. Her death in childbirth in 1817 left the succession to the throne in a tangled, dynastic mess.

With Princess Charlotte's death, the court suddenly realized that George IV had no direct heir: in the event of his death, the throne would pass to his brothers in order of primogeniture, yet none of these men had any legitimate children who might inherit after them. The Duke of Wellington once described these princes as "the damnedest millstone around the necks of any government that can be imagined."[1] Corrupt, dissolute, and perpetually broke, they caused scandal after scandal, tainting the image of the British monarchy in the eyes of the public.

In 1791 Prince Frederick, Duke of York, the next in line to the throne, had married his cousin Princess Frederica, daughter of King Friedrich Wilhelm II of Prussia, who found her new husband so disagreeable that she promptly retired to a house in the country, leaving her husband free to carry on with his numerous mistresses. One of these women attempted to ruin the duke when their affair ended by claiming that she had influenced military appointments; although an inquiry conducted by Parliament found the prince innocent, his reputation was irreparably damaged, and he died in 1827 with no legal issue.

For George III's other sons, however, Charlotte's death meant a mad marital dash to provide legitimate heirs to the throne. Prince William, Duke of Clarence, had lived with his mistress, the actress Dorothy Jordan, for more than two decades, and she bore him ten children; these royal bastards, christened with the surname of Fitzclarence, were ineligible for the throne, and William, in exchange for a large grant from Parliament to pay off his debts, agreed to marry a suitable bride, Princess Adelaide of Saxe-Coburg and Meiningen, twenty-seven years his junior.[2] The couple's hopes to provide an heir to the throne were dashed, however; both of their daughters died in infancy.

Prince Ernst August, the Duke of Cumberland, was a thoroughly disreputable man, called "the Hanoverian Ogre," with no living children by his equally disagreeable wife, Princess Frederica of Mecklenburg-Strelitz, who was popularly believed to have murdered both of her previous husbands.[3] Society whispered that the duke himself had murdered his own valet in a fit of rage after a homosexual affair, and that he had fathered his own sister Sophia's bastard child.[4]

In 1793, another brother, Prince Augustus, had married Lady Augusta Murray, daughter of the fourth Earl of Dunmore, while on holiday in Rome, in direct contravention of the Royal Marriages Act of 1772, which decreed that those in the line of succession had to obtain the prior consent of the sovereign and of the Privy Council before entering into any union. Although two children were born of the marriage, George III had it annulled when he learned that Augustus was amenable to abandoning his wife and offspring in exchange for the title Duke of Sussex and an increased allowance from Parliament. Thus styled, the prince promptly fathered an illegitimate daughter with a young woman whose parents owned an inn near Windsor Castle; in 1831, Sussex again contracted a morganatic marriage, this time with the daughter of the second Earl of Arran. Only George III's youngest son, Prince Adolphus, Duke of Cambridge, had contracted an equal marriage, with Princess Augusta of Hesse-Kassel, but no children had as yet been born of the union.

This left George III's third son, Prince Edward, Duke of Kent. A military man of no great distinction, he was a martinet whose love for corporal punishment and even executions earned him the animosity of his men. For three decades he had lived with his mistress, Thérèse-Bernadine Mongenet of Besançon, a woman seven years older than he, who went by the name of Julie de St. Laurent.[5] On learning of Princess Charlotte's death, the Duke of Kent reluctantly abandoned his mistress and sought out a suitable wife who would provide him with a legitimate heir. At forty-nine years of age, corpulent and balding, the duke was no longer a prize catch, and his opportunities were thus considerably reduced. Eventually he settled on Victoire, Dowager Princess of Leiningen, whose husband, Duke Emich Karl, had died in 1814 after eleven years of marriage. At thirty-one the widowed Victoire had two young children, Karl and Feodora, to raise; she spoke no English and was something less than an ideal consort, but she was of equal rank and had produced healthy children, the two factors seemingly most important to the Duke of Kent.[6] She was also the sister of the late Princess Charlotte's husband, Prince Leopold of Saxe-Coburg, a tenuous tie that seemed redolent of fate, and the Duke of Kent married her in May 1818.

A year later, on May 24, the new Duchess of Kent gave birth to a girl at Kensington Palace in London. "Look at her well," her father presciently commented, "for she will be Queen of England."[7] Christened Alexandrina Victoria, the baby knew nothing of her father, who died of pneumonia seven months after her birth and just six days before his father, King George III. With the accession of the prince regent as George IV, the infant Alexandrina Victoria was suddenly second in line to the throne.

This marked a sharp downturn in the fortunes of the Duchess of Kent. Her husband's death had left her saddled with debts, and she was forced to rely on George IV for her future welfare. The king allowed her to live at Kensington Palace, but it was money from her brother Leopold that helped finance the lives of the duchess and her children.[8] George IV refused his sister-in-law's continual requests for a suitable allowance, and eventually Parliament had to step in and offer the duchess an annual income from the Civil List.[9]

The young Victoria lived a stifled existence at Kensington Palace. The duchess refused to allow her daughter her own room, and Victoria slept on a cot near her mother's bed. Despite her extraordinary possessiveness, the duchess found her daughter's nervous and contradictory temperament a burden to which she was unequal. Once, when her music teacher told her that she must practice, Victoria responded by slamming the lid of the piano, saying, "There! You see there is no must about it!"[10] Such outbursts were common: Victoria could behave with startling willfulness, accompanied by bursts of temper, screams, and floods of hysterical tears.[11]

The young Victoria also lived an isolated existence at Kensington Palace. Although her half brother, Karl, occasionally came to England on holiday, as the future ruling prince of Leiningen, he was expected to remain in Germany and continue his education. His relationship with Victoria was always tenuous at best, and they only occasionally saw each other during their youths. Victoria's only real companion was her half sister, Feodora, although, with a twelve-year age difference, the two girls initially had little in common except their mother. The widowed Duchess of Kent kept her daughter secluded at Kensington Palace, away from members of her late husband's family and from the public at large. The duchess, with her censorious tales of Victoria's "wicked" uncles, did all within her power to inculcate in her daughter a horror of the king and the royal family, with their numerous bastards, flaunted mistresses, and constant scandals; she was particularly offended that the Duke of Clarence's illegitimate children, endowed with the surname of Fitzclarence, were seen openly at court, and she harbored an abiding hatred of the Duke of Cumberland; the young Victoria heard all manner of stories about him, including warnings that he was not above assassinating her so that he could himself take the throne. As the heiress presumptive to the throne, her mother warned, Victoria must do all in her power to distance herself from her Hanoverian relatives.

Relations with her mother worsened as the Duchess of Kent relied more and more upon her husband's former equerry John Conroy, who attempted to control the duchess and, through her, the presumptive queen.[12] For solace, Victoria turned to her governess, the German Louise Lehzen, who, though devoted to her young charge, proved a rather disastrous influence on her impressionable character. The Duchess of Kent had never got on well with the imperious Lehzen, who in turn did all in her power to undermine the mother in the daughter's eyes.[13] Lehzen also encouraged in her young charge an almost preternatural sense of her own superiority and future position.

Conroy was responsible for the Kensington System, an education program he designed to help train Victoria for her role as future queen; at the same time, it carefully secluded her from any outside influences. Victoria was a good student, intelligent and generally diligent in her studies. Her favorite subjects were history and geography; she did well in German and French, and despite her dislike of music lessons could play competently. She took an early interest in art, making delightful sketches and watercolors, and had a fine soprano voice when she sang.[14]

King George IV died on June 26, 1830, and the Duke of Clarence took the throne as William IV, but the Duchess of Kent's relations with the new king were scarcely better than those with his predecessor, and a number of petty quarrels over money, titles, and precedence soured any lingering vestiges of familial affection. When the king refused to give Victoria precedence at his coronation over his brothers, the duchess refused to allow her to attend.[15] The duchess objected to the fact that the king had moved his illegitimate children into Windsor. "I never did, neither will I ever, associate Victoria in any way with the illegitimate members of the Royal Family," the duchess declared. "Did I not keep this line, how would it be possible to teach Victoria the difference between virtue and vice?"[16] Victoria herself later recalled: "It was dreadful . . . always on pins and needles, with the whole family hardly on speaking terms. I (a mere child) between two fires—trying to be civil then scolded at home."[17]

The worst incident took place in August 1836. Victoria and her mother were at Windsor Castle to celebrate the king's birthday, but William IV was in a foul mood, having learned that, contrary to his instructions, the Duchess of Kent had commandeered an additional suite of apartments at Kensington Palace for her own use. At the birthday luncheon, with seventeen-year-old Victoria opposite him and her mother seated next to the king, William loudly declared, as the guests listened in shocked silence, "I trust in God that my life may be spared for nine months longer, after which period, in the event of my death, no regency would take place. I should then have the satisfaction of leaving the royal authority to the personal exercise of that young lady, the heiress presumptive of the crown, and not in the hands of a person now near me, who is surrounded by evil advisors and who is herself incompetent to act with propriety in the station in which she would be placed. I have no hesitation in saying that I have been insulted—grossly and continually insulted—by that person, but I am determined to endure no longer a course of behavior so disrespectful to me." Victoria burst into tears, while her mother, embarrassed at so public a rebuke, was shocked into uncharacteristic silence.[18]

William IV was genuinely fond of his niece, and she of him. In the spring of 1837, in anticipation of her eighteenth birthday, the king wrote to Victoria, suggesting an increase in her allowance and the right to appoint her own household. Conroy intercepted the letter and took it to the duchess, who, acting on his instructions, ordered Victoria to write a reply dictated to her: "I wish to remain in every respect as I am now in the care of my mother. Upon the subject of money I should wish that whatever may be necessary to add may be given to my dear mother for my use, who always does everything I want in pecuniary matters."[19]

The king was not fooled, and guessed that his niece had been forced to write this reply; indeed, Victoria had at first refused to do so, and only gave in after repeated scenes with both her mother and Conroy. Concerned about this growingly distasteful turn of events, the Duchess of Kent's brother Leopold, who in 1830 had accepted the offer of the Belgian throne, dispatched his personal physician, Baron Christian Stockmar, to Kensington Palace to report on what was taking place. Stockmar found Victoria angry and alienated from her mother, and blaming Conroy for her untenable position.[20]

Within days, the situation at Kensington Palace took another, unforeseen turn. William IV had been ill for some time though, as he had hoped, he lived to see Victoria's eighteenth birthday, on May 24, 1837. Just after two on the morning of June 20, he died. The Archbishop of Canterbury and Lord Conyngham, the lord chamberlain, arrived at Kensington Palace soon after the sun had risen, and demanded to see the princess, who was asleep, at once. She appeared before them in her dressing gown and listened as they told her of her uncle's death. That night, the new, eighteen-year-old queen had her bed moved from her mother's room and dined alone in triumph.

Queen Victoria had always been a woman of immense contradiction. She could be charming and unassuming, yet she was also stubborn, impulsive, and capable of violent emotions when challenged. "Mama," her son Arthur once complained, "will always look at everything in her own light, and will not allow anybody else to have *any views* of their own."[21] Victoria was somewhat plain, not unattractive but certainly no great beauty, with the wide face, weak chin, and protuberant eyes of her Hanoverian ancestors framed by a head of luxuriant golden hair. She stood just four feet, ten inches tall—a perpetual source of worry to the royal family—and even at eighteen she was plump, a tendency that only increased with the passage of time; by the 1880s she weighed 170 pounds, and her short stature only increased the impression of ever-expanding girth.[22] "I noticed when she left her bath chair," remembered one visitor of the elderly queen, "that she was no taller standing than she was sitting down."[23]

Though somewhat dour in her later years, Victoria could also be quite entrancing. She delighted in humorous anecdotes, and possessed a strong liking for stories that revealed human foibles. Her laughter was frequent: "I have seen the Queen's lips quivering with suppressed laughter," recorded Frances, Countess of Warwick, "and, if it were not an un-courtier-like thing to say, I might go so far as to state that I have seen Her Most Gracious Majesty shaking like an agitated jelly."[24] To the end, her voice was enchanting, "like a silver stream flowing over golden stones."[25]

Queen Victoria was a curious amalgam of beliefs and prejudices, her character complex and enigmatic. Although she appeared to be one of the most powerful women in the world, Victoria firmly opposed the rights of women; she deemed universal suffrage a hideous idea, once declaring that Lady Amberley, one of its proponents and mother of Bertrand Russell, "ought to get a good whipping."[26] She harbored certain political and national prejudices, yet seemingly she was without any class or racial prejudices. She insisted on the rights and the deference due her position, yet for much of her life she happily surrounded herself with powerful men who were allowed to dictate to her and in many cases order her around, including her first prime minister, Lord Melbourne; her husband, Albert; and later, the ghillie John Brown and the munshi Abdul Karim. (A ghillie is a Scottish estate worker; munshi is the Hindu word for teacher.) Benjamin Disraeli was one of the few prime ministers she liked, and he knew how to win her over. "Everyone likes flattery," he once explained, "and when you come to royalty, you should lay it on with a trowel."[27]

Filled with high ideals, the new queen was a young woman of immense contradiction. Victoria adored gaiety, dancing, and parties, yet she was at least determined to be diligent in her work as queen. She understood her basic position, but the first years of her reign were marked with occasional missteps, including scandals, accusations of political favoritism, and her tendency to let personal prejudice dictate her policies. She could be charming, unassuming, and friendly with her servants, yet she was capable of violent displays of arrogance, insisting on every prerogative due to her as sovereign, and conscious of any perceived slight. A member of her household recalled that Victoria "bore no resemblance to an aristocratic English lady, she bore no resemblance to a wealthy middle-class English-woman, nor to any typical princess of a German court. . . . Never in her life could she be confused with anyone else, nor will she be in history. Such expressions as 'people like Queen Victoria,' or 'that sort of woman,' could not be used about her."[28]

Victoria, having been raised in isolation and alienated from her mother, had no emotional center on which to draw. She was susceptible only to her moods and feelings, and frequently gave way to excessive emotional displays when challenged or displeased. Stubborn and often impulsive in her decisions, Victoria was frequently intolerant of those around her, their circumstances, and their own concerns. She was undoubtedly remarkable, with a quick mind and a determination to rule not only her country and empire, but her extended family as well. Her grandson Kaiser Wilhelm II recalled: "She has been a very great woman. I have never been with her without feeling that she was in every sense my Grandmama and made me love her as such. And yet the minute we began to talk about political things she made me feel we were equals and could speak as sovereigns. Nobody had such power as she."[29]

The queen possessed a profound, unquestioning belief that hers was a position ordained by God, even as she presided over a democratic country and an increasingly powerful Parliament. As a constitutional monarch, what she lacked in real power she possessed in symbolic authority, and she relished her role as the nation's moral compass. She diligently read through official papers that arrived each morning in dispatch boxes, signing them with her firm "Victoria R" as a signal of the required royal assent, and the prime minister regularly briefed her on both domestic and foreign affairs. But these obligations were little more than time-consuming formalities as the government grew stronger and the monarchy weaker.

Victoria had been reluctant to wed, and it was her uncle King Leopold of the Belgians who finally pressed the issue, recommending his nephew Prince Albert of the German Duchy of Saxe-Coburg. Born in 1819 at

Schloss Rosenau in the Thuringen Forest, Albert had suffered through a tormented childhood that shaped his character. His father, Duke Ernst (brother of Victoria's mother, the Duchess of Kent), was, wrote Sir Roger Fulford, "not a pleasant character, for he was fired with political ambition which he lacked the capacity to realize and in personal habits he was selfish and extravagant."[30] Nor was he an ideal husband, which may have been one reason why his wife, Louise of Saxe-Coburg-Altenburg, left him; after her divorce in 1826, Albert never saw her again, and she died five years later of cancer. The scandalous, absent mother and the morally erratic father seared Albert's childhood; he was a deeply emotional, melancholy boy, and there were frequent outbursts and tears.[31] He had a horror of anything that smacked of impropriety, and brought these attitudes with him to England when he married. Unable to cope with his conflicted feelings, he repressed them, leading to deep bouts of depression coupled with symptoms that manifested themselves in poor health, including fainting spells and frequent headaches.

Albert impressed everyone with his studious nature and strength of character, though with his high-minded ideals and distaste for frivolity and moral impropriety, he had little in common with other young princes. He was awkward in social settings; disliked balls and receptions as a waste of time; and with his stiff, somewhat formal manner, often unwittingly gave offense. On meeting her cousin, Queen Victoria initially found his intensely serious character less than appealing; by October 1839, however, the queen was positively gushing in her impressions, writing: "Albert really is quite charming, and so extremely handsome, such beautiful blue eyes, an exquisite nose, and such a pretty mouth with delicate moustachios & slight but very slight whiskers: a beautiful figure, broad in the shoulders & a fine waist; my heart is quite going."[32] Feeling that Albert himself would never be so bold as to propose, she took the matter into her own hands, confiding to him in German, as she wrote in her diary, that "it would make me too happy if he would consent to what I wished (to marry me); we embraced each other over and over again, and he was so kind, so affectionate; Oh! To feel I was, and am, loved by such an Angel as Albert was too great delight to describe! He is perfection; perfection in every way—in beauty—in everything!"[33]

Victoria and Albert were married on February 10, 1840, in the Chapel Royal, St. James's Palace. Victoria appeared in a gown of white satin sewn by two hundred women, her veil of Honiton lace held in place by a wreath of orange blossoms.[34] After the wedding breakfast at Buckingham Palace, the couple departed for Windsor, where they were to spend their honeymoon. The next morning, Victoria confided to her journal: "I never, never spent such an evening! My dearest, dearest dear Albert sat on a footstool at my side, and his excessive love and affection gave me feelings of heavenly love and happiness I could never hoped to have felt before! He clasped me in his arms, and we kissed each other again and again."[35]

Albert was far from a popular choice as consort to the queen. Many still despised his uncle Leopold, blaming him for the death of Princess Charlotte in childbirth, and saw his hand in the union of his niece and nephew. There was grumbling, too, about a foreigner coming to England, and the royal family, on the whole, disliked him intensely. But Albert had the good sense to ignore most of the sniping and often rude behavior toward him; in many cases he actually interceded with the queen to grant an occasional concession to them, hoping to achieve some measure of familial harmony. He befriended the widowed Queen Adelaide, one of the few members of the royal family of whom Victoria herself approved, and he made great pains to win over the Duchess of Kent, acting as a liaison to smooth over their past difficulties. Under his influence, Victoria eventually came to forgive her mother for all she believed she had suffered in her childhood.

The queen, consumed as she was by her duties, had little time for her husband by day; unaccustomed to sharing her power or influence, she treated him as something of a nonentity, and Albert in turn was frustrated, lonely, and often bored at the insignificance of his life. When the queen received officials or the prime minister, Albert was asked to leave them alone, nor was he allowed to see any state papers. "I am happy and contented," he confided, "but the difficulty in filling my place with the proper dignity is that I am only the husband, and not the master of the house."[36]

With no official position or responsibilities, and condemned to a life lived in his wife's shadow, Albert struggled to maintain some semblance of self-worth and dignity. Eventually he channeled his energies into the role of her unofficial adviser. He recognized that Victoria's education, while exceptional for a lady of her day, had been far from comprehensive, and he sought to train her in areas that lay beyond the realm of her own interest. He helped her understand the changes wrought by the Industrial Revolution and their effect on her subjects; exposed her to diverse literature and art; and devoted himself to instilling in her a thorough understanding of affairs of state.

Eventually Victoria agreed to make some concessions; Albert was given his own key to her dispatch boxes and allowed to read and comment on state papers to assist his wife. Albert was very much a Renaissance man, with interests in architecture, agriculture, diplomacy, science, and industry. He was responsible for the abolition of dueling, helped pass legislation that finally outlawed slavery, established the Imperial College in London, and left a rich artistic legacy that included expansion of the National Gallery, the design of the new Palace of Westminster, and the museums of London's South Kensington.[37] In the end, Victoria and England were fortunate in her choice. His greatest personal triumph was the Great Exhibition in 1851. The prince had conceived such an exhibition as a means of demonstrating the progresses of the industrial age and the increasing reliance of countries on each other, at the same time highlighting British achievement. After much fuss and many arguments, the exhibition opened on May 1, 1851, in the new, enormous Crystal Palace, built by Joseph Paxton in Hyde Park for the event, and the royal family turned out in force. Victoria, clad in a pink satin gown, entered on her husband's arm as a fanfare of trumpets sounded and a band played Handel's *Athalia*. Six years later, after much maneuvering, the queen bestowed the title of prince consort upon her husband, in recognition for his numerous services to the crown and the country.

Victoria and Albert were a study in contrasts: she was impetuous, prone to outbursts, and loved gaiety, while he was measured, calm, and reflective. Before the wedding, in a rare moment of candor, she confided, "I have always had my own way. . . . Suppose he should endeavor to thwart me and oppose me in what I like, what a dreadful thing it would be."[38] Albert took Victoria in hand, urging her to act cautiously, to discipline herself to undertake the work that accompanied her position, and to be more conscientious of her duties. He helped smooth her rough edges, warning of her temper and the manner in which she could often unwittingly give offense. In many ways Victoria's relationship with her husband fit a pattern that she was to repeat throughout her life: the search for a trusted protector, a figure who might, in effect, fill the void left by the death of her father when she was just six months old. She, in fact, described Albert in precisely these terms, calling him "my father, my protector, my guide, and adviser in all and everything, my mother (I might also say) as well as my husband."[39]

Victoria was a deeply sensual woman, while Albert seemed moderate and less impulsive. Although first cousins, they were virtual strangers when they became engaged, and while Victoria was certainly the more passionately devoted of the two, in time both husband and wife developed a deep and abiding bond. Behind his prim exterior, Albert shared his wife's sensuality. The queen once wrote to her daughter that women were "born for Man's pleasure and amusement," noting that this was "a sin from which Dear papa even is not quite exempt, though he would not admit it."[40] Victoria loved her husband, but she was also passionately in love with him, and yearned for him; when, after the birth of the couple's ninth child, Victoria was advised to have no more, she is said to have asked her doctor, "Can I have no more fun in bed?"[41]

Yet the relationship was far from the passionate idyll that Victoria herself later described. The couple had a stormy relationship, and there were many battles fought, not only concerning Albert's lack of a proper role but also over Victoria's mercurial temperament. "There is often an irritability in me," Victoria confessed, "which . . . makes me say cross and odious things, which I don't myself believe and which I fear hurt Albert, but which he should not believe . . . like being miserable I ever married."[42] This gives some hint of the kind of scenes that often took place, but Albert was more forthright in his assessment. "Victoria," he once confided, "is too hasty and passionate for me to be able often to speak of my difficulties. She will not hear me out but flies into a rage and overwhelms me with reproaches and suspiciousness, want of trust, ambition, envy, etc."[43] At times it was a delicate balancing act and, often exasperated by her behavior, he simply avoided his wife: "I am trying to keep out of your way," he once wrote to Victoria, "until your better feelings have returned and you have gained control of yourself."[44]

To the end, Victoria remained deeply, passionately in love with her husband. "My dearly beloved Albert shows me not only as much affection and kindness as ever, but as much love and tenderness as on the first day of our marriage," she wrote after celebrating her twentieth wedding anniversary. "How can I ever repay him for it? How be sufficiently thankful to God for His goodness?"[45]

The death of Victoria's mother, the Duchess of Kent, in March 1861 coincided with a sharp decline in Albert's own health. With his years of constant work and worry and lack of exercise, he had lost the fine figure of his youth and prematurely aged. His face was worn and creased, his once-vibrant blue eyes clouded and tired, his hair thinning. Victoria, who disliked heated rooms, regularly kept the temperatures in all of her residences at an uncomfortable chill, and the prince increasingly suffered from colds, headaches, fits of shivering, insomnia, gastric trouble, and severe stomach pains.[46] Victoria, accustomed to his complaints, was less than sympathetic, writing that Albert "never allows he is any better, or will try to get over it, but makes such a miserable face that people always think he's very ill. . . . His nervous system is easily excited and irritated and he's completely overpowered by everything."[47]

Albert's decline was exacerbated in November 1861, when he inspected several new barracks at Sandhurst on a miserable, rainy day and quickly caught cold; as the days passed and his temperature rose, he complained of headaches, pains in his extremities, and insomnia.[48] Nevertheless, he insisted on traveling to Cambridge to speak directly to his eldest son, whose affair with a young Irish actress had recently been disclosed; by the time he returned to Windsor, Albert was exhausted.[49]

Victoria rejected suggestions that specialists examine him, and Albert became worse. At night, unable to sleep, he shuffled along the castle corridors in his quilted dressing gown; by day, he lay in bed as his fever rose. Typhoid was suspected; this was not altogether out of the question, nor was the matter of simple influenza, but the prince may have been suffering from stomach cancer.[50]

By the end of the first week of December, Albert asked to be moved to the Blue Room at Windsor, where he could enjoy the warmth of the winter sun from its tall windows. It was an ominous request: both George IV and William IV had died there.[51] One night, the couple's third child, Princess Alice, told her father that she had written to her elder sister, Vicky, saying that his illness was serious. "You did wrong," he told her. "You should have told her I am dying."[52] By this time the doctors had all but given up hope; the prince had eaten nothing for several days, and was provided only with a constant stream of brandy, given in the hope that it would ease his suffering.[53]

On Friday, December 13, the prince's condition worsened considerably, and his family gathered around him. That night, for the first time, Victoria was told that her husband was almost certainly dying. The queen, shocked, collapsed in sobs, unable and unwilling to believe the devastating news, but she managed to conceal her alarm when she returned to the Blue Room late that night, holding her husband's hand and kissing his forehead.[54] Albert was barely conscious, and he faded in and out of delirium, thinking that he was back at his childhood home, Schloss Rosenau.[55]

Saturday, December 14, was a clear, cold, sunny day; as Albert had wished, the winter sunshine spilled through the tall Gothic windows of his death chamber, though by now he was too weak to notice.[56] As night fell, Albert's breathing grew more shallow, and his painful gasps for breath filled the room; his brow covered with perspiration, he fell in and out of consciousness. "Oh, this is death!" Victoria screamed. "I know it! I have seen this before!"[57] With his wife at his side, Albert died at a quarter to eleven that night.

Victoria was plunged into a shattering grief from which she never fully emerged. She had lost her husband, lover, most trusted adviser, and most cherished friend. Her emotional instability came to the forefront, expressing itself in angry outbursts, headaches, and incessant weakness. Her grief was pervasive. To King Leopold, Victoria declared: "My life as a happy one is ended! The world is gone for me! If I must live on, it is henceforth for our poor fatherless children, for my unhappy country, which has lost all in losing him—and in only doing what I know and feel he would wish, for he is near me—his spirit will guide and inspire me. . . . His purity was too great, his aspiration too high, for this poor, miserable world."[58] "My only comfort," she confessed, "is the hope that I may soon be able to follow him and then be united with him forever!"[59]

"Day," Victoria wrote, "turned into night."[60] She decreed that "mourning for the Prince Consort shall be ordered for the longest term in modern times."[61] Windsor was immediately draped in black crepe; so much was used that the entire country's supply was depleted within a day.[62] In her determination to cherish her grief, Victoria created a cult devoted to the memory of her husband. The Blue Room at Windsor was to be kept "in its present state," she ordered, "and not be made use of in the future," although she herself added memorial wreaths and a bust of Prince Albert.[63] For forty years, to the end of her reign, Albert's rooms were the scene of an incredible ritual. Each morning, a servant delivered a fresh jug of hot water to the unused washstand, as if Albert's specter might appear and need a shave, and laid out a change of clothes amid the fresh flowers that covered the bed; even his unused chamber pot was scoured and replaced at night.[64] On Victoria's orders, everything remained as it had been on that fateful December day; nothing was to be changed. At Windsor, at Buckingham Palace, at Osborne, and at Balmoral, the prince's desks were preserved exactly as he had left them, his books in place and his papers ready.[65]

Mourning dominated every aspect of Victoria's life. Her writing paper was now edged in an inch-thick black border; a photograph of her husband on his deathbed was hung on the right side of every bed she occupied, and at night, Victoria fell asleep clutching her dead husband's nightshirt in her arms.[66] Gloom descended on the court. Victoria decreed an official year of mourning, though in practice she insisted on the observance from those in her service for decades to come. For three years, the ladies of the court were forbidden to appear in anything but black; after this, maids of honor were allowed to wear dresses in the colors of half mourning: white, pale gray, or mauve. Servants sported black armbands for the eight years following Albert's death.[67] Visitors calling on the queen were required not only to write their names in her register, but in Albert's as well, a macabre charade that Disraeli likened to "calling on a dead man."[68] When Disraeli himself was dying, he declined Victoria's offer to visit him, remarking, "She would only ask me to take a message to Albert."[69]

With Albert's body laid to rest, Victoria was determined that he would not be forgotten. Memorials to the prince consort were erected across the country, and cairns were built in his honor at Windsor and Balmoral. She personally approved the most magnificent and public display, the Albert Memorial at the edge of Hyde Park, depicting the prince, clad in Garter robes, beneath a 180-foot-high Gothic canopy adorned with allegorical representations of the continents and the arts and sciences; it faced Royal Albert Hall, which the queen opened in 1871.[70]

The queen inflicted her grief on every member of her family. She complained that she caught Bertie smoking two weeks after his father's death, a sure sign of his lack of respect.[71] Princess Victoria Melita, one of her granddaughters born long after Albert's death, later recalled that visits with the queen were often gloomy affairs, as Victoria talked incessantly of her dead husband, and fully expected even those too young to have known him to revere his memory as she did; even her youngest daughter, Beatrice, just four when Albert had died, was often made to feel guilty at enjoying any normal childhood fun.

Five days after her husband's death, Victoria retired to Osborne House on the Isle of Wight. This was not only a move to avoid the terrible ordeal of Albert's funeral, but also an attempt to immerse herself in the world her husband had created. For the next forty years, the queen spent as much of her time as possible at either Osborne or at Balmoral Castle in Scotland; it was no coincidence that Albert had designed and built these two residences. Osborne and Balmoral were the places most intimately connected with Albert, where at every turn Victoria was surrounded by memories of their life together, and where—if only temporarily—she could once again bask in his spectral presence.[72]

Victoria could not abandon altogether her duties as queen, but she insisted that she could no longer receive officials; even the prime minister was asked to conduct his official business through her daughter Princess Alice, who would then advise her mother. Government papers were still conveyed to her that required her assent, but she worked out a novel solution when the prime minister objected to having to make reports to a seventeen-year-old girl. Victoria would sit in one room, while several representatives of the Privy Council would stand in another; the door between the two rooms was opened slightly, and as the privy councilors read each item, the queen would nod her consent, her approval conveyed to them by a clerk stationed in the doorway.[73]

The queen refused to appear in public. At first she fell back on the period of mourning, but once this had ended, she turned to a series of constant complaints about her health. Few were convinced but, as Sir William Jenner, her physician, once candidly explained to an official, "Isn't it better to say the queen can't do so and so because of her health—which is to a certain extent true—than to say she won't?"[74] In reality, the only thing wrong with the queen was her emotional state. Jenner referred to her distress in these years as "a species of madness."[75] Victoria, whatever her fragile mental condition, was not mad, but she was so highly strung that nearly anything could cause sudden bursts of temper or tears, bouts of screams, or onslaughts of incessant headaches.

For the first few years, her subjects respected her privacy, but as month after month passed and she remained isolated at Windsor, Osborne, or Balmoral, the voices of complaint grew louder as Victoria indulged in unreasoned grief. "It is impossible," declared the *Times* of London, "for a recluse to occupy the British throne without a gradual weakening of that authority which the sovereign has been accustomed to exert."[76] Cartoons lampooning the incessant mourning began to appear in the press, and one wag was bold enough to affix a notice to the gates of Buckingham Palace, announcing: "These extensive premises to be let or sold, in consequence of the late occupant's declining business."[77]

"It is impossible to deny," wrote one official, "that Her Majesty is drawing too heavily on the credit of her former popularity, and that crowned heads as well as other people must do much that was not necessary in former days to meet the altered circumstances and altered tone of modern times. . . . The mass of the people expect a king or a queen to look and play the part. They want to see a crown and scepter and all that sort of thing. They want the gilding for the money. It is not wise to let them think . . . that they could do without a sovereign who lives at Osborne and Balmoral as any private lady might do."[78]

In time, Victoria's morbid isolation began to ease. Through his flattery and cautious exhortations, Disraeli managed to draw her out, but it was John Brown who did much to lead her back toward life. A former stable boy at Balmoral, Brown had become the queen's groom, and in 1865, he was appointed the queen's Highland servant. Brown was abrupt, uneducated, and frequently drunk. But Victoria saw him not only as the living embodiment of happy days with her husband at Balmoral but also as protector. She valued his presence, his strength, and his devotion, and in turn she drew from him the attention that nourished her vanity and satisfied—even if they did not replace—the emotional void left in her life after Albert's death.

While there was some grudging respect for Brown's ability to draw the queen out of her self-imposed isolation, it never extended to actual liking for the man himself, an attitude shared by her children. Her sons Bertie and Affie made no secret of the fact that they despised him, while her daughter Louise once called him "an absurd man in a kilt."[79] Some anonymous wag published a pamphlet titled *Mrs. John Brown*, leading to open speculation about the nature of the relationship.[80] Despite such controversies, Brown remained faithfully at the queen's side until his death in 1883.

Victoria's gradual return to public life was never complete, and she continued to resent the ceremonial obligations imposed on her, but the passing decades did much to lessen the pain of her loss. For the forty years following Albert's death, she was "the widow of Windsor," a misnomer, as she spent much of her time at Osborne and Balmoral. As her popularity returned, and her country and her realm flourished and expanded, the image of Victoria as head of a united royal family was gradually supplanted by a second vision, which sanctified her as a mystical symbol of empire. The Diamond Jubilee of 1897 was to be the final step in this sixty-year transformation, fashioning, as one historian noted, a "charismatic image of Victoria" that "overwhelmed and finally obliterated the old image of the melancholy, widowed queen."[81] The elderly Victoria, however, was somewhat less enthusiastic; she knew that her years were numbered, and as the summer of her Diamond Jubilee approached, she commented sadly, "Now comes my swan song."[82]

A FAMILY ON THE THRONE

BY THE TIME OF VICTORIA'S DIAMOND JUBILEE, the seventy-eight-year-old queen had lost not only her beloved husband, but also her daughter Alice and her son Leopold; her three favorite sons-in-law; and a number of grandchildren, including the Duke of Clarence, heir presumptive to the throne. The surviving children and grandchildren extended Victoria's influence not only across her vast empire but also to the courts of Germany, Greece, Norway, Spain, Romania, and Russia, to dominate a Europe destined to vanish within a generation.

The queen's nine pregnancies had filled the first seventeen years of her married life. Almost exactly nine months after her wedding, Victoria gave birth to the couple's first child, a daughter named Victoria, but called Vicky or Pussy; a year later came Albert Edward, the Prince of Wales and heir to the throne, called Bertie; he was followed by Alice in 1843, Alfred—called Affie—in 1844, Helena—called Lenchen—in 1846, Louise in 1848, Arthur in 1850, Leopold in 1853, and Beatrice in 1857. These births were celebrated with all the pomp and splendor the Court of St. James's could muster. Not only members of the royal family but also royal relatives from across Europe usually attended christenings, many of the latter being marked as godparents. Water brought from the Jordan River in Palestine filled the Lily Font, a monumental piece bedecked with extravagantly gilded cherubs and traditionally used in all royal christenings. Under Victoria's reign this ceremony would be repeated over and over again, first for her nine children, and then later for many of her grandchildren as well.

Victoria was at times a curiously diffident mother, with ambivalent feelings about her children. She despised pregnancy, accepting it only as a burden to be borne for enjoying married life. "I positively think those ladies who are always *enceinte* quite disgusting," she once complained to her daughter Victoria; "it is more like a rabbit or a guinea-pig than anything else."[1] To the end of her life, she remained far more devoted to Albert and to his memory than to any of her own children.

She resented the fact that she, as a woman, was saddled with the discomfort and pain of pregnancy, and in her position as queen, this resentment also extended to its intrusion on her role as sovereign. It was, she complained, like "being a cow or a dog."[2] Victoria thoroughly disapproved of mothers who incessantly fawned over their infants. In response to a letter from daughter Vicky on the subject, the queen wrote: "You know perfectly well that I do not hate babies (quite the contrary if they are pretty), but I do hate an inordinate worship of them and the disgusting details of their animal existence, which I try to ignore."[3]

While Victoria loved her children, she found it difficult to relate to them when they were young. Perhaps some of the problem lay in her own childhood, when she had largely been isolated from others her own age. She felt shy and awkward around her own children at times, impatient with their behavior, and resented that they intruded upon time she would much rather spend with Albert. Yet even when they matured, she often struggled to deepen the bonds. "I find no especial pleasure or compensation in the company of the elder children," she once confided, adding, "Only very exceptionally do I find the rather intimate intercourse with them either agreeable or easy."[4]

Albert himself was a far more devoted parent than his wife. He adored his children, and often played with them or visited them in the nursery, something his wife rarely did. He was capable of great warmth and indulgence, but his approach was often tempered—as with his eldest son—by his unbending quest for perfection. He was most harsh with the Prince of Wales, although his other sons also came in for their share of criticism. With his daughters, however—who had no future expectations other than to marry well—he was a doting father. "It is indeed a pity," Albert wrote to his wife, "that you find no consolation in the company of your children. The root of the trouble lies in the mistaken notion that the function of a mother is to be always correcting, scolding, ordering them about and organizing their activities. It is not possible to be on happy friendly terms with people you have just been scolding."[5]

The royal couple each had their own favorites among their children, and unwisely did little to mask their feelings. Albert preferred his eldest daughter, Vicky, and she was, in turn, far closer to him than to her mother—to the point that the queen was often jealous of the time and attention her husband gave to that daughter. Only later, after Albert's death, did the queen come to appreciate Vicky, and she became the closest thing her mother had to a confidante. Victoria was also particularly fond of her youngest daughter, Beatrice, who would remain at her side until the queen died. Of their sons, Alfred and Arthur were their father's favorites, while the latter was clearly the son Victoria loved best. The queen had a somewhat more difficult relationship with her daughter Alice; while she praised her thoughtfulness and devotion, she also frequently criticized her as too melancholy, too self-absorbed, and more unusually, too concerned with her own prestige. Prince Leopold was perhaps the most difficult of her sons after the Prince of Wales, and their relationship was often fraught with arguments and long periods of silence. Of the five daughters, Princess Louise most often clashed with her mother, both possessing extraordinarily strong characters.

These children grew up speaking English and German, and according to the queen's granddaughter Marie of Romania all of them save Leopold carried a Teutonic accent all of their lives.[6] Queen Victoria could be very blunt and rather harsh in her comments to her children. Always outspoken, she had little sense that her words, whether to the children or to others, could hurt. She was not always cold and distant, but she viewed her children not merely as children, but as royal children, and they were largely raised, according to the custom of the day, by a retinue of nannies, military governors, governesses, and tutors. While Victoria and Albert were quick to use their children to present an idealized family image, they saw far less of them than might be expected. There were teas, walks, picnics, and family gatherings that ensured that the children spent more time with their parents than most other aristocratic or royal offspring, but the carefully contrived image of a devoted family, as Stanley Weintraub has pointed out, "was largely legendary," noting, "when the royal children were small, they seldom appeared at the table, or anywhere else where their parents happened to be in the servant-saturated households. Except on holidays or ceremonial occasions, they were overseen rather than seen."[7]

Victoria, the princess royal and first child born to Victoria and Albert, arrived on November 21, 1840, within a year after the couple married, much to the queen's consternation. On being told that her first child was a girl, the queen is said to have replied, "Never mind, the next will be a prince."[8] Called Vicky or Pussy within the royal family, the princess was her father's daughter, precocious, intelligent, studious, and dutiful. When she was fifteen, her parents arranged her marriage to Prince Friedrich Wilhelm of Prussia, whom her father had selected as a potential groom when his daughter was just four years old. Although neither Victoria nor Albert ever forced their children into arranged marriages against their wills, they certainly encouraged and pushed, and, as the eldest girl, Vicky was the only one to make an important dynastic marriage. The princess, who had largely been isolated in her mother's palaces and castles, quickly convinced herself that she had fallen in love with the tall, handsome young man, known as Fritz, whom her parents had invited to spend a few weeks in the autumn of 1855 with them at Balmoral. Before the 1858 wedding took place, there was a tumultuous struggle over which country should hold the ceremony. The queen eventually won through sheer, stubborn persistence, writing: "The assumption of its being *too much* for a Prince Royal of Prussia to *come* over to marry the *Princess Royal of Great Britain* IN England is too *absurd*. . . . Whatever may be the usual practice of Prussian Princes, it is not *every day* that one marries the eldest daughter of the Queen of England. The question therefore must be considered as settled and closed."[9]

Albert hoped that by marrying Vicky off to the future King of Prussia, relations between that increasingly powerful country and Great Britain would dramatically improve. He envisioned a Europe where politicians took second place to the ruling families, and by marrying his sons and daughters into important royal houses, the prince sought to create a network of familial ties to guarantee the peace of Europe. Although the great Otto von Bismarck had already made his presence known, the unification of Germany under Prussia—a goal Albert fully supported—was still more than a decade away; but Fritz was known to harbor reformist tendencies, and under Vicky's democratic influence, Albert believed that the couple, when they ascended the throne of Prussia, might one day be able to put his dreams into practice.[10]

Despite the ambitions of her parents, Vicky found life in Berlin to be a difficult balancing act. She certainly believed that her prime mission in Prussia was to promote liberal reform and thus bring the country's policies more in line with those of her mother. Yet, being a mere future consort, her only means of enacting such change was in her roles as wife and mother. She was criticized as being too English; in fact, she was derided in Berlin as "Die Engländerin," and rumors even went around that she was having an affair with Count Theodor von Seckendorff, her court chamberlain.[11] Vicky found the sanitation and toilets in the palace in Berlin far cries from those at Buckingham Palace, and her suggested changes were inevitably taken for a hatred of Prussia. In her attempts to Anglicize the German court, she made little effort to understand or accept Prussian traditions.[12] "When she was in Berlin," recalled her niece Princess Marie Louise, "everything in England was perfect; when she was in England, everything German was equally perfect."[13]

Officials at the court in Berlin, accustomed to silent consorts, were at first confused and then angered at her frequent criticisms not only on questions of daily life but also on political issues. She failed to temper her views with tact, and made powerful enemies who suspected her of endless, pro-English intrigues. In these momentous years, as Prussia consolidated its power according to the machinations of Otto von Bismarck, Fritz was often away on military campaigns: first came the Schleswig-Holstein Crisis, then the Seven Weeks' War against Austria, and finally the Franco-Prussian War, which ended with a scene directly from Prince Albert's cherished dream: all of Germany unified under the authority of the powerful Hohenzollern Dynasty of Prussia. In March 1888, Fritz took the throne as Kaiser Friedrich Wilhelm III of a unified Germany on the death of his father, Wilhelm I, but his reign was to last a mere ninety-nine days. Already he was dying of throat cancer, the illness exacerbated by incompetent doctors called in to treat him.

Within a year of her marriage, Vicky was pregnant; her mother was angered that Fritz should have put her daughter in this predicament, believing—quite rightly, as it turned out—that the princess needed time to settle into married life and learn the ways of her new country. The first child, Wilhelm, was born in 1859, followed by Charlotte in 1860; Heinrich in 1862; Sigismund in 1864; Victoria in 1866; Waldemar in 1868; Sophie (who later became Queen of Greece) in 1870; and Margaret in 1872. Vicky, although she tried to act the part of devoted parent, ironically followed in the footsteps of her own mother, and often found her children troublesome enigmas. She was, by her own admission, not particularly close to her first three children, who spent much of their time with Fritz's parents, who spoiled them terribly and made Vicky's task even more difficult.

Princes Sigismund and Waldemar were particular favorites, which was ironic in that they would be Vicky's only children to die in childhood. Meningitis claimed Sigismund at age two in 1866: "I have to bear this awful trial alone," she wrote to her mother, "without my poor Fritz. My little darling graciously lent me for a short time, to be my pride, my joy, my hope, is gone, gone where my passionate devotion cannot follow, from where my love cannot recall him!"[14] The death of Waldemar in 1879 from diphtheria was an even more difficult blow, but sympathy was in short supply: a minister in Berlin publicly commented that the boy's death was a punishment sent by God to humble his haughty mother, while Queen Victoria added that while she understood her daughter's grief, nothing could match the profound pain she herself had suffered at losing her beloved Albert.

Vicky's relations with her children ranged from distant to loving. Princess Charlotte was an extremely difficult child, suffering from behavioral problems that may, in fact, have been linked to the genetic disease porphyria, while Heinrich grew into a rather bluff sailor with a violent temper. Victoria, who married Prince Adolphus of Schaumburg-Lippe, caused few problems, while Margaret, called Mossy in the royal family, was a plain, undistinguished young woman whose efforts to marry the morganatic Prince Alexander of Battenberg met with her parents' firm rejection.[15] Of all the children, it was Sophie who provided the most impressive legacy. She married King Constantine I of the Hellenes, and all three of her sons became, in turn, King of Greece.

The princess's most disastrous relationship was with her eldest son, Wilhelm. The birth was difficult, and the doctor who pulled the baby from the womb dislocated the infant's left arm. The damage was permanent, and Wilhelm's left arm would forever be shorter than the right, and withered in appearance.[16] The psychological impact of this damage affected both mother and son. Wilhelm had to learn how to ride, shoot, paint, write, and participate in military exercises using his one good arm; the memories of the painful attempts to correct the problem, as well as the constant pressure put on him to achieve more than any other prince of his station to show that he was not disabled, left him with severe feelings of inferiority. Vicky regarded her son's disability as a personal insult to her honor, a failure on her part, and she pushed him even harder to overcome the difficulties it posed. But her approach was schizophrenic in nature; at times she pretended that nothing at all was wrong with her son, and at others she could be unbelievably cruel, mocking his disability. In so doing, she ultimately alienated her eldest son with what one author has termed her "emotional unreliability," who was never certain of her feelings for him, and came instead to rely on a circle of pompous and disreputable friends for acceptance and affirmation.[17]

Such behavior ultimately left Wilhelm conflicted. He was aware that his mother regarded him as a disappointment, and must have suffered through the humiliation of rejection at his mother's hands. Vicky, too narcissistic to recognize the emotional damage she was inflicting, was in turn confused by her son's apparently unpredictable changes of mood, and his bursts of temper that threatened whatever harmony remained in the palace in Berlin. Whereas his mother took pride in her precocious brilliance, Wilhelm was not particularly intellectually gifted, and he soon realized that nothing at all he did would ultimately meet with her approval.

Wilhelm longed pathetically for acceptance, not only from his mother, but also from his grandmother Queen Victoria and from his relatives in England. One aristocratic woman complained, "The English royal family never treat the Emperor William as a sovereign, but like a little boy."[18] And a member of the queen's household recalled how, at one dinner, Prince George, the Duke of York, "spoke out loud and abused the German Emperor, not caring what he said."[19] It is scarcely surprising that Wilhelm felt himself disliked by his English relatives. Following Vicky's lead, they termed him abrasive and arrogant, and Wilhelm was left to founder between the two conflicting identities that forever pulled at his soul—German emperor and grandson of the English queen.

Princess Alice, Queen Victoria's second daughter and third child, was born on April 25, 1843. Although not as intelligent as her elder sister, she was perhaps the child most like her father in character and temperament. Filled with a sense of duty and responsibility, she helped look after her mother following her father's death. Alice's wedding to Prince Ludwig of Hesse und Bei Rhein, in July 1862, went ahead as scheduled, despite her father's death, for the queen refused to postpone any of his last remaining wishes, but it took place under rather more peculiar circumstances, in private, in the dining room at Osborne, surrounded by a family draped in black and openly weeping. Alice's wedding, her mother commented, was "more like a funeral."[20]

Alice's husband, Prince Ludwig, was a handsome young army officer, unimaginative though attractive, and the pair had little in common. One British aristocrat termed him a "dull boy," from "a dull family, in a dull country."[21] Alice and Ludwig had spent little time together before their engagement, and soon the princess realized that she possessed a more intellectual and inquiring nature than her husband. At first she was able to ignore what must have been occasional difficulties as she busied herself with both their children and her life in Hesse. The children came quickly: Victoria, born in 1863; Elisabeth, called Ella, born in 1864; Irene, born in 1866; Ernst Ludwig, called Ernie, born in 1868; Friedrich Wilhelm, called Frittie, born in 1870; Alix, called Alicky to distinguish her from her aunt the Princess of Wales, born in 1872; and Marie, called May, born in 1874.

Alice found life in Hesse difficult. With her strong liberal leanings and desire to help others, she soon set about launching a series of organizations.

Chief among these was the Women's Union for Nurses, founded in 1867 in the aftermath of the Seven Weeks' War. She also founded hospitals and institutions designed to help young mothers, and to train young women for careers. She maintained a lively correspondence with Florence Nightingale and put many of her ideas into practice. It was useful, important work that filled the increasing emotional void in her marriage, but it left Alice frequently exhausted and suffering from a number of complaints. She sought comfort in a deep friendship with controversial theologian David Strauss, who openly questioned the historical accuracy of the Bible. For a time he provided the intellectual companionship that Ludwig was unable to offer, though the friendship caused a great deal of malicious gossip.

Princess Alice's steadying influence in the lives of her children, however, changed forever in 1873, with the death of her youngest son. Frittie, who suffered from hemophilia, fell from a palace window while playing a game with his brother, Ernie, and died of a cerebral hemorrhage. Alice sank into a depression from which she was never to entirely emerge; always melancholy, she now gave vent to her feelings of grief, talking endlessly about death and joining her son in Heaven. A gloomy preoccupation with mourning and sorrow descended upon the Neues Palais in Darmstadt, one that she unwittingly inflicted on the youngest children, especially Ernie and Alix.

In November 1878, Alice's eldest daughter, Victoria, fell ill with diphtheria, and Ludwig and all the other children, except Ella, quickly came down with the disease. All the cases were severe, and Alice nursed the patients herself, a heroic effort that left her completely exhausted. Four-year-old May died from the disease, and, in an effort to comfort her heartbroken son Ernie, Alice kissed him in a fatal act of sympathy. By the beginning of December, Ludwig and the children were out of danger, but Alice had fallen victim to the disease. Weakened by her constant vigils, she did not have the strength to fight it, and on December 14— ironically the seventeenth anniversary of her father's death—Alice died, at age thirty-five.

Alice's death left five young children, on whom Queen Victoria constantly doted. Their widowed father, now Grand Duke Ludwig IV of Hesse und Bei Rhein, was a kind, genial man who enjoyed riding and shooting, but his powerful mother-in-law recognized that a stronger hand was needed in the lives of his children. She began a regular correspondence with fifteen-year-old Victoria, the eldest daughter, offering advice and plying her with endless queries about her family. Holidays to Osborne, Windsor, and Balmoral became annual events, allowing the queen to supervise their educational progress; Ernie and Alix particularly fell under her keenly observant eye, and she pampered them in ways she never did with their cousins or even with her own children.

In April 1884, Queen Victoria traveled to Darmstadt for the marriage of Alice's daughter Victoria to her father's cousin Prince Louis of Battenberg, only to find that her widowed son-in-law Grand Duke Ludwig of Hesse had taken up with a divorced Russian countess, whom he secretly married while his mother-in-law was under his roof. An enormous uproar followed, with a flurry of family letters and diplomatic pressure exerted on the grand duke. In the end, the queen prevailed, and the marriage was quickly annulled. Despite this ominous start, Victoria and Louis enjoyed a happy marriage, and throughout the princess maintained an extraordinary correspondence with her grandmother. Two months later, her sister Ella married Grand Duke Serge of Russia, son of Tsar Alexander II. The queen had opposed the Russian union, fearing that the country was unstable and that Ella would be unhappy. Serge, in fact, was among the most odious of Russian grand dukes, a narrow-minded, anti-Semitic reactionary who treated her like a prized possession and, according to rumor, satisfied his carnal desires elsewhere with young cadets and even his own priest. In 1888 Irene, the most unpretentious and unassuming of the Hessian children, married Prince Heinrich of Prussia, younger brother of future kaiser Wilhelm II. At the time of the engagement, there was much concern over the close family relationship between Irene and her fiancé. They were first cousins through their mothers, both daughters of Queen Victoria and Prince Albert, who were themselves cousins; the pair also shared the same great-grandfather, King Friedrich Wilhelm II of Prussia, through their fathers. Heinrich, an officer in the German Navy, had—like his elder brother—suffered under the hand of a stubborn, cold mother and brutal tutors who bullied and beat both boys into submission, and Irene and Heinrich's wedding, at Berlin's Charlottenburg Palace, marked the beginning of a difficult relationship.

Like her mother, Irene was a hemophilia carrier, and she passed the disease on to two of her three sons, who were to suffer all their lives from its horrific effects.

The death of Ludwig IV in 1892 left his effete, twenty-four-year-old son, Ernie, to take the Hessian throne. Queen Victoria was full of advice, telling him to always consult her and to ignore the kaiser. Deciding that he needed a wife to settle his character, Victoria pushed him toward a union with his cousin Victoria Melita, known as Ducky, daughter of the queen's second son, Alfred. At first, Ernie feigned ignorance, but as the queen accelerated her efforts, he protested that they were too closely related; when this failed, he was horrified. He was not in love with Ducky, and the idea of being forced into marriage terrified him. Couching his concerns in oblique terms, he confided to his sister Victoria that he worried he would prove a disappointment as a husband, incapable of fathering children.[22]

In the end, Ernie was unequal to his grandmother's machinations, and he reluctantly wed Ducky in 1894. She later complained that on their wedding night she discovered that she and her new husband were "sexually incompatible."[23] Not even the birth of a daughter could save the situation, and husband and wife lived uneasily together until, she later said, she found him in bed with another man.[24] "No boy was safe," Ducky complained to her niece Princess Ileana of Romania, "from the stable hands to the kitchen help. He slept quite openly with them all."[25] Victoria refused to consider divorce, but on learning the truth about the marriage, she broke down in tears, saying sadly, "I will never try to marry anyone again."[26] Although the marriage was a disaster, it was at his wedding that Ernie's sister Alix, the last of the queen's Hessian grandchildren, accepted the future tsar Nicholas II's proposal.

Ducky's father, Alfred, the Duke of Edinburgh, Victoria and Albert's fourth child, had been born in 1844. Known as Affie in the royal family, he was charming and astute if not intellectual, and widely considered to be the best-looking of the royal couple's sons. Albert, especially, doted on him, and considered him his favorite son. Victoria thought he certainly resembled his father in looks but added, "Oh, that he were as pure!"[27] She noted with dismay that the young prince seemed to delight in making fun of the servants and causing them endless difficulties.

From his birth Affie was destined to succeed his uncle as ruler of the German duchy of Saxe-Coburg-Gotha, but this did not stop his career in the Royal Navy. He did well at sea, but he also acquired from his comrades habits that horrified his mother, including a rude and brusque manner, a penchant for profanity, incessant smoking, and a seemingly unquenchable desire for alcohol. He fancied himself an accomplished musician, forcing members of his mother's household to sit through impromptu violin recitals. "Anything more execrable I never heard," recorded one courtier, adding that "the noise abominable," and "it was a relief when we got away from that appalling din."[28]

In 1873 he stunned his mother by declaring that he had fallen in love with Tsar Alexander II's daughter Grand Duchess Marie Alexandrovna. After their wedding in St. Petersburg the following year, he returned to England with his young wife, who brought with her a dozen trunks filled with furniture, paintings, carpets, icons, and gowns; a treasure trove of magnificent jewelry; a Russian priest, for she refused to change her religion; an enormous dowry; and the promise of a substantial annual stipend from the Russian government, impressive wealth that many suspected was the real reason Affie had married her.[29]

The new Duchess of Edinburgh was every inch a Romanov grand duchess, proud and refined. Accustomed to the splendor of imperial Russia, she found Queen Victoria's court dowdy and less sophisticated than that of St. Petersburg. Marie attempted to re-create a small slice of the Winter Palace in her new London home, Clarence House, filling its rooms with her exquisite furniture and creating an Orthodox chapel where she could worship in private. But she disliked life in England; she hated the weather, particularly the perpetual fog, and thought that the British Parliament was a dangerous and radical institution. She demanded that her imperial title should precede her newly acquired royal style, and that she be given precedence, as the daughter of an emperor, immediately after the queen.[30] Victoria would have none of this, but Marie knew how to retaliate. At state occasions she appeared covered in the splendid jewels she had brought from Russia, which far surpassed those worn by the queen herself. Seeing this display, Victoria fixed her with a stare "like an angry parrot," looking "like a bird whose plumage has been ruffled, her mouth drawn down at the corners in an expression which those who knew her had learned to dread."[31]

Affie and Marie had five children. There were four daughters: Marie (the future Queen of Romania), known as Missy, born in 1875; Victoria Melita, called Ducky, born in 1876; Alexandra, called Sandra, born in 1878; and Beatrice, called Baby Bee to distinguish her from her English aunt, born in 1884; and one son, Alfred, born in 1874. Aware of her husband's future role as Duke of Saxe-Coburg, and detesting England, Marie raised her children to share her prejudices, at the same time imbuing them with a love of all things German. As the only son, Prince Alfred was heir to his father's Dukedom of Saxe-Coburg-Gotha, but he proved a particularly vexing young man, falling in with a bad crowd and contracting syphilis. In 1899, during celebrations marking his parents' twenty-fifth wedding anniversary, he shot himself in a botched suicide attempt. Marie's response was cold: upset that her son caused an incident, she kept him hidden, refusing to heed the advice of doctors, and spirited him away from Coburg for treatment. The journey, however, proved too much for the severely injured young man, and he died alone except for a doctor and a valet.[32]

Princess Helena, Victoria and Albert's fifth child, was born in 1846. Called Lenchen, she was something of a rebel as a young girl. She adored science and nursing, and was a founding member of the British Red Cross.[33] Victoria termed her "most useful and active and clever and amiable," but noted that her daughter "does not improve in looks and has great difficulties with her figure and her want of calm, quiet, graceful manners."[34]

Helena's marriage to Prince Christian of Schleswig-Holstein caused an enormous row in the royal family. Princess Alice worried that her sister was being sacrificed to an older, less than satisfactory husband simply because he agreed to live in England and keep Helena close to her mother.[35] The queen frankly admitted: "In my terrible position, I required one of my daughters to always be in England."[36] Queen Victoria pushed the marriage despite her own misgivings about the prince's appearance. Fifteen years older than his intended bride, he smoked incessantly— something the queen despised—was balding, and had very poor teeth. In her letters, she spoke disparagingly of his appearance. "If only he looked a little younger!" she complained to Vicky.[37]

Despite these concerns, Helena and Christian seemed happy after their 1866 marriage, though in later years they presented an odd appearance. In 1891, Helena's brother Arthur accidentally shot his brother-in-law's eye out; thereafter, Christian wore an assortment of glass eyes. He had the disconcerting habit of calling for a selection while at the dinner table, explaining their uses and exchanging them in his socket, to the horror of the guests; he even had one replicated to simulate a bloodshot eye, which he wore when he had a cold.[38] Helena ignored such antics, as she was often lost in a haze of opium; when doctors forced her withdrawal, she retaliated by complaining of various ailments in an attempt to obtain laudanum.[39]

Helena and Christian had four children: Christian Victor, known as Christle, born in 1867; Albert, known as Abby, born in 1869; Helena Victoria, known as Thora, born in 1870; and Marie Louise, known as Louie, born in 1872. Christle became the first member of the royal family to attend a public (that is, in Britain, private) school; having entered the army, he fought in several campaigns, only to fall victim to malaria while fighting in the Boer War in 1900. He became Queen Victoria's third adult grandson to die in her lifetime.

Of these children, only Marie Louise married. In 1891 she wed Prince Aribert of Anhalt; the prince was homosexual, and the marriage was never consummated. When, after nine years, Aribert was apparently found in bed with another man, his father blamed Marie Louise, claiming that his son had been denied his conjugal rights, and accused her of indecency.[40] Marie Louise fled to Canada to avoid the scandal, but Queen Victoria dispatched a telegram to the governor-general: "Tell my grand-daughter to come home to me."[41] The queen fully supported her grand-daughter, although the marriage ended in a contentious divorce officially disguised as an annulment.[42] "Poor Marie Louise," her uncle the Prince of Wales commented, "she came back just as she went!"[43]

Princess Louise, Victoria and Albert's sixth child, was born in 1848. With her blond hair, deep blue eyes, and striking features, she was the most beautiful of the queen's daughters, but also the most difficult. She enjoyed her rank and position, yet chafed against the restrictions it imposed upon her. Capable of great warmth and kindness, she also possessed a cold, cruel streak, and her frustrations and jealousy often took the form of extended, exceptionally personal, battles with others, most notably her sister Beatrice.

In March 1871 Louise married John Campbell, Marquess of Lorne and heir to the Duke of Argyll. It was the first time a royal princess had married a subject since 1515.[44] The union did not seem destined to bring happiness to either party. The marquess was popularly believed to be homosexual, and the pair never had any children.[45] The princess and her husband went to Canada when the queen appointed the marquess governor-general in 1878, but Louise despised her time in Ottawa and, unable or unwilling to conceal the fact, left midway through his term to return to London.[46]

Louise became bitter and spiteful, engaging in dangerous romantic games that scandalized those around her. "Never have I come across a more dangerous woman," commented one of Victoria's courtiers. "To gain her end she would stop at nothing."[47] Her only refuge became her art, and she was a sculptor of immense talent. Her statue of her mother in her coronation robes still stands outside Kensington Palace in London.

Prince Arthur was born in 1850. A quiet, genial man, he was Queen Victoria's favorite son, and she considered him most like his late father; she once referred to him as "the flower of my sons, and my darling from his birth."[48] A career army officer, Arthur was created Duke of Connaught and Strathearn in recognition for his military achievements. In 1879 he married Princess Louise, daughter of Princess Louise and Prince Frederick of Prussia, somewhat against his mother's wishes, as the bride's parents had divorced in a scandal. He remained devoted to her, although he also maintained a decades-long liaison with Lady Leonie Leslie, sister of Lady Randolph Churchill.[49] Arthur was discreet and never caused a public scandal, although he was often absentminded and careless. He and Louise, who lived at Buckingham Palace, had three children: Margaret (future consort of King Gustav VI of Sweden), born in 1882; Arthur, born in 1883; and Patricia, born in 1886.

Prince Leopold, Victoria's youngest son, was born in 1853. His hemophilia came as a shock to the queen, who, finding his illness a difficulty, responded by attempting to seclude him from all harm. The vibrant prince was intelligent and vivacious, with an astute personality. "His mind and head are far the most like of any of the boys to his Dear Father," his mother recorded.[50] With his restless spirit, he constantly fought with his mother over his treatment. He was not allowed to play games with his brothers or sisters; he despised Balmoral; and he hated John Brown and his brother Archibald, in whose care he was placed. The queen, often intolerant of illness in those around her despite her own constant catalog of complaints, wrote after one of her son's attacks: "Leopold really is *a cause of sorrow and indignation* and has brought this bad leg upon himself; it made him quite ill for a week, purely through obstinacy and not following the advice of his doctor and attendant. . . . I am very indignant, I confess, and feel deeply the great ingratitude of this child of anxiety. One really cannot pity him."[51]

After much pleading, Leopold was finally allowed to go to Oxford, where he did quite well and proved himself a scholar in his own right, although, as he candidly noted, his relations with his mother were "never on such good terms as when we are absent from one another."[52] But in 1881 the queen created him Duke of Albany and let him act as a sort of unofficial adviser; she even gave him keys to her government dispatch boxes.[53]

In April 1882 Leopold married Princess Helen of Waldeck-Pyrmont, and their first child, Alice, was born a year later. But their happiness was not to last. Helen was pregnant with a son when, in March 1884, Leopold fell while visiting Cannes and suffered a fatal hemorrhage. He was only thirty years old when he died. In death, all was forgiven, as Victoria wrote in her journal: "My beloved Leopold, that bright clever son, who had so many times recovered from such fearful illnesses, and from various small accidents has been taken from us! To lose another dear child, far from me, and one who was so gifted, and such a help to me, is too dreadful. Am utterly crushed."[54]

Beatrice, the queen's youngest child, was born in 1857. Only four when her father died, she was doomed to endless mourning by her heartbroken mother. Victoria expected her youngest daughter to stifle all signs of happiness, and Beatrice became shy and introspective. Beatrice was expected to remain at her mother's side, serving as companion and trusted aide. "She had to be in perpetual attendance on her formidable mother," recalled her daughter. "Her devotion and submission were complete."[55] Victoria relied heavily on her daughter, and even gave her keys to the dispatch boxes containing government papers—a privilege not extended to the Prince of Wales, and which caused Bertie's wife, Alix, to treat Beatrice rather ungraciously.

Victoria was determined that Beatrice would not marry or, if she did, that she would reside with her. "A married daughter I must have living with me," she wrote, "and must not be left constantly to look about for help."[56] Eventually the queen began to relent on her position, pushing the idea that Beatrice should marry her widowed brother-in-law Grand Duke Ludwig of Hesse. To this end, the queen pushed her government to pass what was called the Deceased Wife's Sister Marriage Act, which would allow such a union under British law, but the proposal met with firm opposition in the House of Lords and from the clergy and failed.[57] Beatrice herself had taken a passionate interest in the exiled prince imperial, son of the deposed Emperor Napoleon III of France, but this ended when he was killed fighting the Zulus in 1879.[58]

Then, in April 1884, Beatrice accompanied her mother to Darmstadt for the wedding of Victoria of Hesse to Prince Louis of Battenberg, and quickly fell in love with the groom's dashing younger brother Prince Henry. Given the morganatic status of the Battenbergs, such a union was seen as unworthy of the queen's daughter, but Beatrice was determined. The queen's response was an icy, six-month silence during which mother and daughter communicated only by notes passed across the dining table.[59] When Victoria finally gave way, it was only on the understanding that Beatrice and her husband would agree to live with her, as it was "quite out of the question" that Beatrice would leave home.[60] To the end, Victoria feared that she would be abandoned.

Beatrice married Prince Henry, known as Liko, at Whippingham Church near Osborne House on the Isle of Wight in 1885; she was the only daughter to wear her mother's Honiton lace wedding veil.[61] The couple had four children: Alexander, born in 1886; Victoria Eugenie (future queen of Spain), born in 1887; Leopold, born in 1889; and Maurice, born in 1891. Beatrice proved to be a hemophilia carrier, and one of her sons, Leopold, inherited the disease, while her daughter, Victoria Eugenie, was to pass it to the royal family of Spain.

Henry suffered under his cloistered existence living with his mother-in-law, his life confined to a series of trips to Windsor, Osborne, and Balmoral, and surrounded only by his wife and his children. Victoria created him a royal highness and bestowed upon him the Order of the Garter, much to the displeasure of her sons, who believed that the Order of the Bath was sufficient for him.[62] The prince was charming, with pleasant manners, and was a favorite with the royal household; they particularly appreciated that he had managed to achieve what had seemed the impossible, and convinced the queen to not only relax her strict rules against smoking but also to provide comfortably furnished rooms to which the men could retire to do so. Aware of his favored position and lack of any real responsibilities, cartoonists and satirical papers of the day portrayed him as a man of no ambition, perpetually lounging about in a smoking jacket or playing billiards.[63] In 1896, after much pleading, he joined the Ashanti Expedition in Africa; he became ill, however, and died from malaria aboard his transport ship on January 20, 1896.

Beatrice was shattered by her husband's death, and the situation deteriorated when her sister Louise lashed out. Louise had never made any secret of her feelings for Henry, and claimed that she had refused his "attempted relations with her."[64] After this, Louise declared, Henry and her sister had spread ugly rumors that she had a number of secret lovers.[65] In the midst of mourning, Louise declared in front of the entire family and her grieving sister that "she was Liko's confidante," adding in an especially hurtful way that "Beatrice was nothing to him."[66] Not surprisingly, it took some time before the distance between Beatrice and her sister could be overcome.

Behind palace walls Victoria's children indulged in a multitude of disreputable behaviors, but from the moments of their birth, they had been held up to the nation as examples of the queen's new domesticated and moral monarchy. In an age of burgeoning popular press, George III and the two sons who succeeded him had been satirized and caricatured in papers and journals. If the message was one of contempt over their licentious behavior, it was tempered by undisguised glee at openly mocking members of the royal family and discussing their most intimate affairs for the enlightenment of their readers. The cartoons and editorials were scathing and, as most of what they claimed was generally true, the royal family dared not retaliate.

Victoria was accustomed to such a state of affairs; growing up, her mother had continually reminded her how low the royal family had sunk in the eyes of the public. At the beginning of her reign, the public associated the monarchy not with moral leadership but with mistresses, illegitimate children, and profligate spending. Albert found it all revolting, and with Victoria he launched upon an effort to improve the royal family's image, utilizing the modern media—newspapers, journals, prints, and photography. Morality was now seen to be a value central to the monarchy, and the couple used themselves as exhibits in this new campaign. "The bourgeois public," noted one historian, "saw in the royal pair the realization of their own ideal of married bliss: a household sullied by no breath of scandal, with a conscientious husband and a dutiful and adoring wife."[67]

In this campaign, the couple used their children to create a carefully contrived mythology that spoke of love and duty, familial devotion values that were clearly recognizable to the queen's most humble subjects. For the first time, the private life of the sovereign was willingly disclosed and sold to her subjects as a moral example. The public, invited to look upon the life of their sovereign and to see in the united happiness of her growing family an example for the nation, was gradually manipulated into a state of not only embrace but also expectation. "A family on the throne is an interesting idea," Walter Bagehot wrote in 1867. "It brings down the pride of sovereignty to the level of petty life." He warned, however, against too much exposure of the personal monarchy: "If you begin to poke about it, you cannot reverence it. . . . Its mystery is its life. We must not let in daylight upon magic."[68]

By 1896, this mythology had lifted Victoria from mere woman, mere sovereign, to a paragon of all moral virtues. Few of her subjects knew anything of the queen's personality; indeed, Victoria's character was largely fragmented, having been overwhelmed from age eighteen on coming to the throne. She had never enjoyed any real opportunity to simply be Victoria the woman, or Victoria the mother. She was, above all else, always queen; she came closest in her relationship with Prince Albert to discovering something of the personal happiness enjoyed by many of her countrymen, but to most people, she remained an enigma, a curious collection of conflicting ideas and emotions that could never fully be reconciled.

3

THE COURT OF ST. JAMES'S

A YEAR EARLIER, AS CARRIAGES AND HORSES jostled with trolleys and crowds along London's thoroughfares, work on the Diamond Jubilee was already under way. Beyond the summer foliage of Green Park and past the stately facades of private palaces along Piccadilly, tall, redbrick towers and crenellated roofs marked the picturesque sprawl of St. James's Palace. Begun by Henry VIII, its wings flowed around interior courts and contained imposing apartments that had housed three centuries of monarchs. After William IV's death, Victoria abandoned it in favor of Buckingham Palace; the warren of rooms was given over to officials in her household, although foreign ambassadors and envoys were still accredited to the Court of St. James's.

Here, down a crimson-carpeted corridor, was the paneled office of Lord Lathom, the lord chamberlain. Heavy, leather-bound albums filled bookshelves, each detailing ceremony and protocol; outlining official events; containing charts of precedence and guest lists; and carefully listing the queen's engagements and anticipated schedule for the coming year. As the chief official in the queen's court, the lord chamberlain—clad in his regulation black tailcoat with gold buttons—supervised the royal household, a complex and anachronistic structure that both coddled and catered to Victoria while surrounding her with the necessary trappings of royal tradition.[1]

The royal household encompassed hundreds of people with duties both ceremonial and real. The power of their positions derived from the continued survival of the British monarchy, ensuring loyalty to the crown and often breeding an odd mixture of entitlement coupled with fawning deference. In composition, the royal household was the province of the well-born, an "aristocratic monopoly," as David Cannadine observed.[2] Positions were often filled by the sons, daughters, nieces, and nephews of those already employed, who recommended them for their posts; such candidates, Elizabeth Longford noted, "would already have the right ideas about loyalty and discretion, besides knowing something of what they were in for, through family memoirs and legends."[3]

The extent to which the court relied on incestuous connections was particularly evident in Victoria's reign. In the first years, it was the Paget family that wielded power. The second Marquess of Conyngham, who served as the lord chamberlain in the first years of Victoria's reign, was married to a member of the Paget family, while Henry Paget, the Earl of Uxbridge, was lord steward. Both men installed their mistresses in official positions in the royal household to facilitate their liaisons.[4] Two of Uxbridge's daughters served as maids of honor, Paget cousins carried the queen's train on ceremonial occasions, and Lord Alfred Paget was the queen's equerry. So pervasive was this influence that the press mockingly referred to Buckingham Palace as "the Paget Clubhouse."[5]

The Ponsonby family dominated the last half of the queen's reign. General Charles Grey, Victoria's private secretary until his death in 1870, was succeeded by his nephew Sir Henry Ponsonby, whose wife was herself a woman of the bedchamber. Sir Henry's uncle Sir Spencer Ponsonby-Fane was comptroller to the lord chamberlain's department for nearly half a century, and Henry's son Lord Frederick joined the royal household in the 1890s as an equerry. General Grey's daughter Louisa, Countess of Antrim, was one of the queen's women of the bedchamber; a Ponsonby niece, Lady Susan Baring, served as maid of honor; and in 1899, Susan married the queen's senior personal physician, Sir James Reid.[6]

Such tangled connections and family ties made Lord Lathom's job as lord chamberlain something of a juggling act. Born in 1837, Edward Bootle-Wilbraham, the first Earl of Lathom, had joined the household as a lord-in-waiting, and served as captain of the yeomen of the guard before being appointed lord chamberlain.[7] Lathom was remembered as tall and "exceptionally handsome," proper and respectful, a man who not only met the queen's expectations but also befriended those who worked beneath him.[8]

Lathom was charged with arranging state visits, levees, investitures, the state opening of Parliament, royal artillery salutes, court mourning, and the weddings and funerals of members of the queen's family. The marshal of the diplomatic corps came under his department, as did the Central Chancery of Orders of Knighthood.[9] He also supervised the granting of royal warrants to companies whose goods were used by the court, and held titular responsibility for several of the queen's most famous protectors, including the gentlemen-at-arms and yeomen of the guard, who collectively formed part of the royal bodyguard.[10] Those seeking presentation formally applied to his office, and responsibility for deciding who received permission rested with his department. The lord chamberlain issued invitations to these and other ceremonies in the queen's name, and announced those being presented to the sovereign.[11] For these duties, Lathom received some £2,000 a year (approximately £151,188, or $107,343 in 2007 figures).[12]

Two men assisted Lathom in his task. The Honorable Ailwyn Fellowes acted as vice chamberlain, but real power lay with seventy-two-year-old Sir Spencer Ponsonby Fane who, as comptroller of the lord chamberlain's department, actually ran the office.[13] He had charge of most ceremonial and daily arrangements and stood at the head of the household, promoting men to their positions and controlling the operation of the court.

Sidney Herbert, the fourteenth Earl of Pembroke, served as lord steward in the royal household.[14] The lord steward was titular head of the master of the household's department at court; under his authority were gathered most of the domestic staff.[15] By Victoria's reign, the lord steward's chief duties were managerial: he presided over the Board of Green Cloth, the committee that regulated household expenses, salaries, and accounts. He also attended the queen on ceremonial occasions and, at state banquets, presented Victoria's guests to her.[16]

In August 1894 Sir John Cowell, who served as Victoria's master of the household, died; to replace him, the queen selected Lord Edward Pelham-Clinton. Fifty-eight at the time, Pelham-Clinton was the second son of the fifth Duke of Newcastle, and had previously served as a colonel in the military.[17] Pelham-Clinton first joined the royal household as a groom-in-waiting in 1881, but he was reluctant to assume the post of master of the household, with its onerous duties, and Victoria was reduced to asking him to undertake the position on a six months' trial basis. In the end, Pelham-Clinton found the responsibilities less burdensome than he had imagined, and remained in his post, much to the queen's delight. He was, she commented, "so amiable and gentlemanly and good," all qualities she highly prized.[18] In this role, Pelham-Clinton was assisted by Lord Arthur Hill, the comptroller of the royal household.[19]

The master of the household supervised the daily operation of the royal palaces and the domestic staff. This included not only cooks, maids, the linen staff, and pages, but also those employed for specific skills, such as painters; furniture craftsmen, repairers, and upholsterers; and florists. It fell to the master of the household to arrange all entertainments and dinners given by the queen, coordinating menus with the sovereign and with the *chef de cuisine*, drawing up seating plans, and selecting the services to be used.[20]

Pelham-Clinton was also responsible for issuing the daily court circular, which chronicled in detail how the queen and members of her family had spent their day. The court circular recorded not only official engagements but also daily walks, guests invited to dine with the queen, and any entertainments at court, all in excruciatingly stilted language dictated by the queen's wishes. Victoria never celebrated her birthday, according to the court circular, but instead had "an auspicious return of her natal day." She never walked, but "promenaded," nor were guests invited to dine, but instead "graciously invited to partake of a collation."[21] Only in the last decades of her reign were such labored descriptions finally abandoned in favor of simpler language. Victoria read and corrected the court circular every morning, ensuring it contained no inaccuracies.[22]

In ceremonial processions, the master of the horse—a position held by William Cavendish-Bentinck, the sixth Duke of Portland—rode behind the queen's carriage, attired in his scarlet tunic and cockaded hat dripping with white feathers.[23] Under his titular authority came all means and methods of royal transportation, including the royal mews, the queen's horses, the royal stables, and carriages. He also was responsible for the equerries, footmen, livery porters, and underbutlers.[24]

Actual responsibility for the royal mews rested with Major General Sir Henry Ewart, the crown equerry. The office was instituted by Prince Albert in 1854, when he promoted the secretary to the master of the horse as superintendent of the royal mews and charged him with general supervision of the male servants.[25] The crown equerry also accompanied the queen on all ceremonial occasions; planned processions; and organized Victoria's frequent railway journeys to Windsor, Osborne, and Balmoral.[26]

Beneath these men stretched hundreds of courtiers, disposed in various ranks and degrees of importance. Major General Sir John McNeill, Sir Henry Byng, and Lieutenant Colonel Arthur Davidson served as Victoria's personal equerries, and there were eight equerries in ordinary and another thirty extra equerries.[27] Equerries, the male equivalent to ladies-in-waiting, accompanied the queen on official events, looked after guests, and helped arrange any private engagements; most equerries were military men, seconded from the army to serve in rotation for several months at court.[28] When on duty at Windsor, Victoria insisted that her equerries wear the distinctive Windsor livery designed by Prince Albert: a dark blue tailcoat with crimson collars and cuffs.[29]

With her great dislike of change, Victoria tended to maintain these men in their positions for decades: when twenty-seven-year-old Frederick Ponsonby joined the royal household in 1894 as an equerry, he found that most of his senior counterparts were gentlemen of at least seventy. When on duty, he accompanied the queen on her drives if a second equerry was needed, but otherwise had little to do, and passed most of his days reading newspapers and writing letters.[30]

Ponsonby also discovered just how demanding Victoria could be when it came to the private lives of her courtiers. The queen accepted elderly married men into her household, but she was set against any younger male members marrying, suspecting that they would not only confide personal details of her life to their wives but also that family obligations would inevitably distract a courtier's attention from his duties of waiting on her. In 1896, when Frederick Ponsonby fell in love, Victoria refused him permission to marry, eventually relenting only after three years had passed.[31]

Eight lords-in-waiting attended the queen at court functions and acted as her official representatives throughout the country.[32] A number of aides-de-camp, drawn from the British army and navy and colonial forces, participated in ceremonial occasions, while the eight grooms-in-waiting likewise served in attendance at court functions as well as on a daily basis during postings that rotated every two weeks.[33]

Most of these courtiers were older and dignified, but one, the Honorable Alexander Yorke, who served as a groom-of-the-chamber, cut quite a startling figure in Victoria's usually sedate household.[34] Short and stout, with a dashing little mustache he carefully waxed, and always immaculately turned out, Alick Yorke was openly, proudly flamboyant in dress and manner, always trailing a thick aroma of perfume through the palaces.[35] He was a great favorite of the queen, though he took mild offense when she declared that he was "quite safe" to serve as an escort for her young granddaughters.[36] It was Yorke who supposedly was responsible for repeating a risqué story in the queen's presence, garnering her famous remark "We are not amused."[37]

The most powerful member of the royal household was undoubtedly the queen's private secretary, who advised her on all matters; liaised with her government; drafted her speeches; and answered her official correspondence. He also arranged the queen's annual schedule, from her private holidays to her rare public appearances, and worked with the queen's press secretary and the press office in responding to inquiries and questions from the late nineteenth century's growing mass media. With the inherent trust and dependence that inevitably developed with her private secretary, Victoria was loath to see changes in the office. In 1870 Sir Henry Ponsonby took over the post from his predecessor (and uncle by marriage) General Charles Grey, who had died in office; Ponsonby himself remained in the position until he suffered a stroke in 1895.[38]

To replace Ponsonby, Victoria selected Lieutenant General Sir Arthur

Bigge, a staunchly conservative, discreet, and loyal man. Born in 1849, Bigge was the son of a Northumberland rector, and had befriended the prince imperial, heir of the exiled emperor Napoleon III of France, during their time in the army; after the prince was killed in 1879, he served the prince's mother, Empress Eugenie, as a temporary equerry until his appointment to the royal household. For fifteen years Bigge worked under Ponsonby, learning the intricacies of the position and the necessary diplomacy before being called upon to himself assume the post.[39] At first Victoria refused to meet daily with her new private secretary, as she had regularly done with Ponsonby, insisting on a system of written communication; eventually, however, she relented.[40]

As Victoria entered the year leading to her Diamond Jubilee, Bigge unexpectedly found himself the object of Princess Louise's unwelcome attention. Bored and up to her usual mischief, she launched a campaign of unsubtle seduction, which left Bigge reeling and his wife scandalized. Soon her flirtations were the talk of the court, and although Louise attempted to blame her brother-in-law Prince Henry, claiming he had set out to create a scandal in revenge for her having spurned his advances, the princess convinced no one of her innocence. Soon Beatrice joined the fray, and drew the Princess of Wales and Princess Helena into her protests as well. Worried letters flew back and forth, warning that Lady Bigge knew Louise had ruined other relationships and was now determined to do the same to her marriage; Bigge, too, was said to have behaved indiscreetly, and was accused of having fallen under Louise's spell. The court was in an uproar, and soon enough, word reached Victoria, who acted swiftly and decisively. She asked Randall Davidson, the Bishop of Winchester, to warn Bigge of Louise's machinations, while Sir James Reid, Victoria's personal physician, was given the thankless task of confronting the princess with her behavior. Louise feigned ignorance, complaining of "the queen's unkindness" toward her, and laying the blame squarely on her sisters Beatrice and Helena who, she declared, "had laid their heads together to ruin her."[41]

Lieutenant Colonel Sir Fleetwood Edwards served as the keeper of the Privy Purse, a post that entailed responsibility for the queen's financial affairs and management of her personal fortune.[42] Edwards oversaw the queen's annual Civil List, a grant fixed at the beginning of each reign establishing how much the government would pay the sovereign to cover expenses. Victoria's Civil List was £385,000 a year (approximately £29,103,690, or $20,663,619 in 2007 currency).[43] She also received an annual income from the Duchy of Lancaster, ranging from £27,000 to some £60,000, throughout her reign (£2,041,038, or $1,449,136 in 2007 currency.[44] Of the Civil List, some £60,000 (£4,535,640, or $3,213,204 in 2007 figures) was set aside for the queen's Privy Purse for her personal use, with £131,250 (£9,921,712, or $7,044,415 in 2007 figures) dedicated to salaries of the royal household, £172,500 (£13,039,965, or $9,258,375 in 2007 currency) for expenses of the royal household, and £13,200 (£997,840, or $708,466 in 2007 figures) for royal bounty and alms.[45]

The queen was extraordinarily generous with her personal fortune; over the course of her reign, she gave away a staggering £650,000 (£49,136,101, or $34,886,631 in 2007 figures) to various charities.[46] But the death of the prince consort in 1861 marked a dramatic shift in the life of the court; all official entertainments virtually ceased, and, by the 1870s, there was a good deal of criticism over the amount of money Victoria continued to receive to meet her ceremonial obligations. In the ten years following Albert's death, she managed to save just over £500,000 (£37,797,001, or $26,835,870 in 2007 currency), which formed the basis of a private fortune that grew over the decades.[47] By the end of her reign, her private fortune was estimated to have reached approximately $25 million to $30 million.[48]

There were dozens of other high-ranking officials, with varying duties and interaction with the queen. Sir J. Charles Robinson, surveyor of the queen's pictures and works of art, was responsible for the immense wealth of the royal collection, including hundreds of priceless paintings by Leonardo da Vinci, Canaletto, Rembrandt, Raphael, Titian, and Michelangelo. Gentlemen ushers, usually drawn from the ranks of military and court retirees, opened and closed doors, introduced guests, and served during the larger official functions such as levees and garden parties.[49] The traveling yeoman and his deputy, the sergeant footman, supervised his staff of footmen on behalf of the master of the horse; in addition, the traveling yeoman was in charge of the queen's luggage when she traveled.[50] The page of the chambers supervised the pages of the presence and, in his capacity as a deputy palace steward, helped organize any of the queen's official engagements that took place within her residences.[51] Sir Walter Parratt, master of the queen's musick, was also in charge of the choristers at St. George's Chapel, Windsor, while Colonel the Honorable Sir William Colville, the master of ceremonies, dealt with members of the diplomatic corps and distinguished foreign guests at court.[52] By tradition, the queen maintained a royal bargemaster, although he had last performed his duties in 1849, when he conveyed Victoria and her husband down the Thames to open a coal exchange.[53]

The queen's medical household included three physicians-in-ordinary, responsible for treating her and members of her family, and three surgeons-in-ordinary, whose duties also encompassed care of Victoria's family. Under them were a number of physicians and surgeons extraordinary, who spent most of their time looking after members of the household. There were also ten honorary physicians, three honorary surgeons, two oculists, four honorary physicians-in-ordinary, a dentist, a pediatrician, and several apothecaries.[54]

At the head of the medical household was Sir Richard Douglas Powell, but it was Sir James Reid, who had worked at court since 1881, who held the preeminent place among the queen's medical staff. Originally from a middle-class family in Scotland, he attended Aberdeen University and practiced in both London and Vienna before taking up his post at court.[55] In 1887 he became physician extraordinary to the queen, and two years later was made senior physician-in-ordinary, equivalent to Victoria's personal physician.[56] With his straightforward manner coupled with the diplomacy necessary to a courtier, Reid was greatly liked by members of the household: "He gives excellent, sound opinions on questions," noted one official.[57] Victoria, according to customary etiquette, excluded him from her table when other courtiers dined with her, and the physician retaliated by giving his own dinner parties, which were livelier than those of his mistress. When Victoria got wind of this competition, she immediately broke with tradition and thereafter asked Reid to dine with her.[58]

As the queen's personal physician, Reid faced the unenviable task of not only ensuring her health as she aged but also humoring her numerous complaints, occasional bursts of temper, and fits of nervous exhaustion.

He learned very quickly how demanding she could be: when her famous Highland servant John Brown lay dying at Windsor, Reid—who was treating him—had a telegram informing him that his own father had died. Victoria refused to let him abandon his duties, and it was only after Brown died that he was finally able to join his mother in Scotland.[59]

Reid saw Victoria every morning, listening to her litany of complaints, and then again late at night before she went to bed.[60] Victoria also regularly dispatched notes to him throughout the day and even while he was on holiday, reporting her headaches and rheumatic pains.[61] Indigestion and flatulence were regular complaints, brought about by the queen's dining habits. She not only ate quickly, but also far too much, stuffing herself with her favorite sweets and desserts in addition to her regular fare.[62] "When she devours a huge chocolate cake followed by a couple of apricots washed down with ice water as she did last night," Marie Mallet, one of her ladies-in-waiting, noted, "she ought to expect a dig from the indigestion fiend."[63] But no amount of Reid's pleading convinced Victoria to alter her unhealthy dining habits.

By 1896, the queen's health had deteriorated to a sad state. A fall a decade earlier had brought on extended problems with her knees, and she now found walking a painful experience, often resorting to a wheelchair.[64] Insomnia was a constant problem: "Every time she wakes, even for a few minutes," Reid noted, "she rings for her maids, who of course don't like it, and naturally call the night a 'bad' one."[65] Reid sought to alleviate these restless nights with sedatives and narcotics, including chloral hydrate, morphine, and hemp.[66] She was also nearly blind, complaining that she had not been able to read a book for two years; in an attempt to improve her eyesight, Reid gave her belladonna, which mingled with a solution of cocaine dropped into her eyes every morning.[67]

Nothing, however, seemed to work, and Victoria was left dependent on her daughter Beatrice to read to her the contents of state papers and official communiqués. "The queen is not even au courant with the ordinary topics of the present day," recorded Frederick Ponsonby. "Imagine Beatrice trying to explain . . . our policy in the east. Bigge or I may write out long précis of things but they are often not read to Her Majesty as Beatrice is in a hurry to develop a photograph or wants to paint a flower for a bazaar. . . . Apart from the hideous mistakes that occur . . . there is the danger of the Queen's letting go almost entirely the control of things which should be kept under the immediate supervision of the sovereign. . . . The sad thing is that it is only her eyes, nothing else. Her memory is still wonderful, her shrewdness, her power of discrimination as strong as ever, her long experience of European politics alone makes her opinion valuable but when her sole means of reading dispatches, précis, etc., lie in Beatrice, it is simply hopeless."[68]

Reid also fell afoul of the aged queen when he fell in love with Susan Baring, one of Victoria's maids of honor. Victoria always disliked her unmarried courtiers finding spouses, and, as maids of honor were expected not to marry, Reid's romance was a double blow. When she first learned of the couple's intention, the queen was so angry that she refused to see her own physician for three days. When she finally relented, the charming Reid won her over by promising that he would do it only once.[69]

The clerk of the closet headed the queen's ecclesiastical household, composed of personal and domestic chaplains, deans of the chapels royal, and her choristers.[70] It also encompassed St. George's Chapel at Windsor; this was known as a royal peculiar, not subject to the ecclesiastical hierarchy of the Church of England but instead to the reigning sovereign, who appointed the Very Reverend Philip Eliot the Dean of Windsor to oversee its services.[71]

The queen's personal chaplains faced a thoroughly religious yet headstrong sovereign utterly convinced of her own opinions. Victoria, despite her position as defender of the faith and supreme governor of the Church of England, was always something of a religious enigma. "Never passionate about points of doctrine," wrote Stanley Weintraub, "she found her faith more and more limited, beyond ethical teachings, to the existence of a Hereafter in which her soul would be reunited with Albert."[72] Not that she took to the usual ministrations that followed her husband's death. When a cleric suggested to Victoria that "Henceforth you must remember that Christ Himself will be your husband," the queen declared, "This is what I call twaddle!"[73]

Victoria once expressed doubts about the reality of the Trinity; disliked equally evangelical and High Church proponents; and hated lengthy sermons. She once dismissed a list of proposed visiting chaplains with a number of complaints: one man's sermons, the queen declared, were "too long"; another's sermons were "like lectures"; while a third was an "excellent man, but tiresome preacher."[74] Victoria's beliefs were deeply held; she did "not altogether believe in the devil," once termed the idea of an eternal hell "unutterably horrible and revolting," and disliked the idea of having to kneel when praying.[75] She personally liked Catholics, but not their church, and when a cardinal once prayed for the pope before he did for her, Victoria angrily said, "It is a direct infringement of my prerogative!"[76] Yet Victoria also had a mystical side. She was fascinated with the growing interest in spiritualism, and tried several séances.[77] She remained superstitious of many things, particularly of the December 14 anniversary of Albert's (and later her second daughter Alice's) death, and even of the number fourteen.[78]

Members of the household attached to the office of the robes enjoyed the closest contact with the queen, and included her ladies-in-waiting and maids of honor. Louisa, Duchess of Buccleuch, served as Victoria's mistress of the robes. The daughter of the first Duke of Abercorn, Louisa was born in 1836; in 1859, she had married the sixth Duke of Buccleuch, a great aristocrat with a string of grand houses in England and Scotland, and she became one of the wealthiest women in the country.[79] The mistress of the robes attended the queen on all official and state functions but did not serve on a daily basis; she was, however, responsible for the female members of the queen's household, assisting in their selection and promotion and ensuring that they were thoroughly trained.[80] For her role, the mistress of the robes received a salary of £500 a year (£37,797, or $64,632 in 2007 figures).[81]

The mistress of the robes kept the roster of the queen's ladies-in-waiting, who fell into two ranks. Ladies of the bedchamber, the more senior position, were the female equivalent to lords-in-waiting.[82] Inevitably wives of British peers, they received £500 a year; they did not go into regular waiting, but instead attended the queen on public engagements and ceremonial occasions. Beneath them were eight women of the bedchamber, corresponding to the male rank of equerry.[83] Also of aristocratic background, they received £300 a year (£22,678, or $38,779 in 2007 currency), and regularly went into waiting, attending the queen on both public engagements and in the privacy of her own residences. There were also a number of honorary extra ladies and women of the bedchamber, a chiefly ceremonial position given to aged widows.[84]

The annual schedule for these ladies was announced at the beginning of each year; ladies-in-waiting served in rotations of two weeks three times a year.[85] The women were well trained: they never interrupted, always walked several steps behind the queen, and rarely spoke. Victoria, wrote on observer, "was always a little afraid of clever women; and a reputation for superior intelligence was no recommendation in her eyes. She liked the ladies about her to have extremely good manners and a pretty presence, but she shrank away from any woman who, she feared, was going to be clever. It had been very early instilled into her that it was the man's province to be clever, and that it was best for women not to intrude."[86]

One of the women of the bedchamber was always on duty. She accompanied the queen, even in the privacy of her own residences, acting as a companion and assistant. They were charged with attending her on public and ceremonial occasions; on her drives; reading to her; and answering much of the correspondence Victoria received. When there were guests, they entertained them, assisted them, and dined with them.[87] It could often be a dull and thankless existence: when on duty, they were denied the freedom to go out except when accompanying the queen, and when not needed had to occupy themselves in a sitting room, ready to answer a summons from their mistress. With Victoria's court settled into a boring routine, there was little opportunity for excitement: an invitation to dinner was often the highlight of the day, when they put the white ribbon of the Order of Victoria and Albert on their gowns and tried to chat amusingly with the queen's guests.[88]

Those who expected familiarity were quickly disappointed. Henry Ponsonby's wife, Mary, who had served as a woman of the bedchamber, rarely spoke to her mistress, but instead "became accustomed to see the door leading to the Queen's rooms shut silently behind the page who came backwards and forwards for orders."[89] Once appointed, they tended to remain in office until illness or death forced their retirement; most of Victoria's ladies and women of the bedchamber were well into their sixties in the last years of her reign.[90] Victoria almost always appointed widows to these posts, a move that ensured devoted attention, but also transformed her court, as one critic noted, into "a sacred college of vestal widows," condemned to "tend the flame of their sorrow (and of her convenience) forever."[91]

Undoubtedly the most powerful and influential of these women was Jane, Lady Churchill. Born in 1826, she was the daughter of the Marquess of Conyngham, and had married the second Baron Churchill. Appointed a lady of the bedchamber in 1854, she was the longest-serving member of the queen's personal household, becoming a trusted adviser and perhaps the closest thing Victoria had to a friend.[92] Mary Ponsonby, widow of Sir Henry Ponsonby, called the short, gray-haired Churchill "a lady in every way."[93] It often fell to Lady Churchill to convey the queen's messages to her household; more often than not, these were reprimands for some minor breach of etiquette. "There was no mistaking the meaning in her concise messages, which were often ill-appreciated," Victoria's physician, Sir James Reid, noted.[94] This made Lady Churchill less than popular, although everyone respected her and feared her influence.

The Honorable Harriet Phipps also enjoyed the queen's confidence. Born in 1841, she was the daughter of a former keeper of the Privy Purse and had first served as one of the queen's maids of honor before being appointed a woman of the bedchamber in 1889. Like Lady Churchill, she was exceptionally close to the queen, and Victoria frequently relied on her to answer correspondence and intercede with the household.[95] Trim, with golden hair and always adorned with a collection of bracelets and necklaces that rattled as she worked, Harriet Phipps was, as her fellow woman of the bedchamber Marie Mallet recalled, "the embodiment of early Victorian traditions, discreet almost to a fault, full of little mysteries and traditions, inspiring a certain amount of awe of the great queen and conveying Her Majesty's wishes, commands, and reprimands to the other ladies in a tactful but somewhat awe-inspiring manner. On the other hand she could be gay and excellent company and always warm hearted."[96]

Victoria expected service, but she also recognized that a court position could prove beneficial to an impoverished aristocrat, and she often filled vacancies with an eye to the financial needs of the candidates.[97] Thus, in the summer of 1895, Victoria called upon Edith, the Countess of Lytton, to fill a post in her personal household made vacant by the death of the Dowager Duchess of Roxburgh. Lady Lytton's husband—a former ambassador in Paris—had died in 1891 and left his wife with little income; she gratefully accepted the queen's offer and duly took up the post.[98] She found the queen full of solicitude: on first receiving her, Victoria asked, "May I be allowed to call you by your Christian name?"[99] It was a mark of the respect with which Victoria treated those in her household, despite her often-contrary behavior.

Another eight women, all unmarried daughters of aristocrats, hold the position of maid of honor. Two maids of honor were on duty at all times, alternating their rotation of serving a month at a time for four months spaced throughout the year.[100] If the young women did not have titles themselves, they were granted the courtesy rank of a baron's daughter, with the style of Honorable.[101]

Maids of honor were extensively questioned before being offered their post. They were expected not only to have impeccable morals, but also to speak, read, and write both German and French; play the piano; be good conversationalists; and be competent riders.[102] They were also grilled at length as to any existing romantic attachments—an affirmative reply guaranteed exclusion—or the possibility of any such future entanglements.[103] As one historian noted, Victoria "considered service to herself to be preferable to matrimony."[104]

Life for the maids of honor, who received some £300 a year, was full of restrictions: they were not allowed to receive any man—even their own brothers—in their rooms; could not go out unaccompanied or even leave whatever residence they found themselves in until given permission to do so by the queen; could not keep diaries; and had to be on call to attend to the queen around the clock. A framed set of these regulations hung on their bedroom doors, to remind them of the restrictions lest they forget.[105] Their chief functions were to hand the queen a bouquet of flowers each night when she left her private apartments to dine; to entertain the queen, reading to her; and to converse with her guests in the evening.[106]

Serving Queen Victoria as a member of the royal household often meant abandoning family obligations and following the court as it moved from

Windsor Castle to Osborne House and Balmoral Castle, a particularly thankless task during the holidays.[107] "The queen," noted one historian, "was notoriously inconsiderate of the families of her courtiers, refusing the latter permission to visit their relatives while they were in waiting, and resenting the demands made by their children and by childbirth."[108]

The position took its toll on many who served. One courtier, Lady Jane Ely, adored Victoria but was also terrified of her and the constant demands. She often complained that the queen's incessant orders were "killing her"; when the pressure became too much, she would feign illness and collapse into bed, where she could rest undisturbed and fortify her courage.[109] But these loyal courtiers remained the invisible framework upon which the monarchy rested, enabling its survival and, in the process, their own.

4

SPRING AT WINDSOR

PERCHED ATOP A STEEP MOUND overlooking the Berkshire countryside some twenty miles southwest of London, Windsor Castle rose against the English sky, its dramatic profile set against the green fringe of its surrounding park. Its towers and crenellations, as Victoria's grandson Edward VIII wrote, brooded "with an air of comfortable benevolence" over the town and surrounding park.[1] Windsor had the advantage of being close enough to the capital to make it convenient, but was surrounded by bucolic isolation that made it seem part of another world, far removed from the bustle and pollution of Victorian London.

By the time Victoria came to the throne, Windsor was the oldest continuously inhabited castle in the world, the most ancient of the queen's residences. It stood as a visible symbol of the country's military struggles and invasions, outwardly all brute force and power, capped with turrets and towers that lent it a martial atmosphere. And yet, behind the somewhat cold, stark statement of power, lay a succession of extravagantly gilded rooms adorned with a priceless collection of tapestries, paintings, sculpture, and porcelain, a majestic backdrop for Queen Victoria's court.

William the Conqueror built an outpost atop a chalk hill rising high above the Thames River, but the first monarch to actually live within its newly fortified castle was Henry II, in 1110. In the centuries that followed, the castle took shape, as masonry construction replaced wood, walls were ringed with towers, and the fortress spread in an arc along the crest. Three-foot-thick stone walls enclosed the Lower Ward, dominated by St. George's Chapel; dividing the public Lower Ward from the private Upper Ward was the Round Tower, a massive structure that dominated the castle's distant profile.[2]

Although various monarchs made minimal alterations to the structure, Charles II was the first sovereign to turn a knowingly artistic eye to the castle. In the aftermath of the civil war that had led to his father's execution and the monarchy's subsequent restoration, Charles was anxious to wrap himself and the throne in regal trappings that spoke of continuation. He therefore commissioned Hugh May to enlarge and renovate much of Windsor, including the state apartments, in the lavish, baroque style of the age, leaving a splendid palace in place of the austere hilltop fortress.[3]

One hundred fifty years later, King George IV became the second royal connoisseur to transform Windsor. The king had witnessed monarchies fall across Europe, and the loss of America to the whims of an increasingly vocal populace, and, like Charles II, he sought to invest the castle with the trappings of undisputed power and permanence. An indefatigable builder, he commissioned the brilliant Jeffrey Wyatt to "add to the magnificence of the castle."[4] Wyatt spent £1 million transforming Windsor, a quarter of which went toward furnishings and decorations.[5]

Wyatt shrouded the structure in a succession of neo-Gothic elements that gave the castle its picturesque, romantic appearance: walls were raised and topped with new crenellated battlements; new towers were built, with lancet windows looking over the countryside; and the Upper Ward was substantially transformed into a nineteenth-century Gothic fantasy, all looking back to an unambiguous past. But the stern facade sheltered a startling surprise: George IV transformed the state apartments into an opulent blaze of richly gilded woodwork, lavish ormolu and crystal chandeliers, and magnificent furniture, in an exercise designed to echo the splendors of the French monarchy.[6] Wyatt was so proud of this creation that he asked the king to be allowed to change his name to the more

Queen Victoria in her formal Diamond Jubilee portrait, 1897.

Queen Victoria and
Prince Albert, 1861.

Queen Victoria,
1885.

Queen Victoria,
1896.

Queen Victoria's first
grandchild, Kaiser Wilhelm II,
about 1900.

Empress Friedrich of Germany, about 1894.

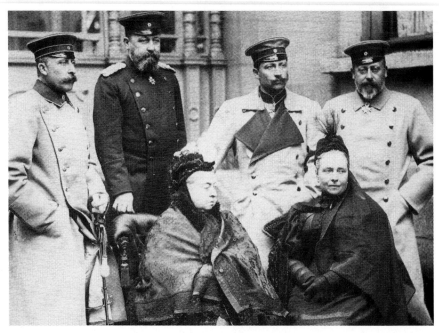

A family group taken at Coburg to mark the wedding of Queen Victoria's two grandchildren Grand Duke Ernst Ludwig of Hesse (Ernie) and Princess Victoria Melita (Ducky) in April 1894. Queen Victoria sits with her daughter Vicky at the front; behind them, left to right, are Prince Arthur, the Duke of Connaught; Prince Alfred (Affie), the Duke of Edinburgh and of Saxe-Coburg-Gotha; Kaiser Wilhelm II; and the Prince of Wales (Bertie).

Wedding photograph of
Queen Victoria's daughter
Princess Helena with
Prince Christian of
Schleswig-Holstein, 1866.

Queen Victoria's youngest
son, Prince Leopold, in
Highland costume, in
the late 1870s.

Queen Victoria with her Hessian grandchildren shortly after the death of their mother, Princess Alice, Victoria's second daughter. At the back, standing left to right, are Elisabeth (Ella, later Grand Duchess Serge), Ernst Ludwig (Ernie, later Grand Duke Ernst Ludwig of Hesse), and Victoria (later the Marchioness of Milford Haven, and grandmother to Prince Philip, the Duke of Edinburgh). At the front, left to right, are Irene (later Princess Heinrich of Prussia), Queen Victoria, and, sitting on the floor, Alix (later Empress Alexandra of Russia).

Wedding photograph of Queen Victoria's youngest daughter, Beatrice, to Prince Henry of Battenberg, Osborne, July 23, 1885. At front, from left to right, stand Princesses Victoria Melita (Ducky), Marie (Missy, later Queen of Romania), and Alexandra of Edinburgh, next to the bride and groom; in the second row, left to right, stand Princess Maud of Wales (later Queen Maud of Norway), Princess Alix of Hesse (later Empress Alexandra of Russia), and Princesses Marie Louise and (between the bride and groom) Helena Victoria of Schleswig-Holstein; at the back, left to right, stand the groom's brother Alexander, Prince of Bulgaria, Princess Louise of Wales (later Duchess of Fife), Princess Irene of Hesse (later Princess Heinrich of Prussia), Princess Victoria of Wales (Toria), and the groom's brother Prince Franz Josef of Battenberg.

Princess Louise, Queen Victoria's
fourth daughter, about 1870.

Windsor Castle in the late nineteenth century, viewed from the Thames.

aristocratic Wyatville. "Veal or mutton, call yourself what you like," came George IV's reply, though he did ennoble the architect.[7]

Windsor's magnificent situation, set proudly atop its natural pedestal, was best appreciated from the surrounding Berkshire countryside and across the placid waters of the Thames; the Gothic spires of Eton College offered a miniature, mirror silhouette of the hulking fortress dominating the southern sky. Beyond the river, at the base of the hill, Thames Street twisted up the slope, between a canyon of shops and hotels on the outer edge, and the immense walls and twelfth-century Curfew and medieval Garter and Salisbury towers of the castle on the left.[8]

The Henry VIII Gate, flanked by stationary sentries smartly attired in their regimental uniforms, opened in a wide arch to the Lower Ward. Small apartments and houses, including lodgings for the Military Knights of Windsor, ringed the outer walls, framing a slope of crisply manicured lawn stretching to the base of the Round Tower. Ahead, beyond the medieval brick and half-timbered arc of Edward III's Horseshoe Cloister, sprawled the flying buttresses and stone finials of the Lower Ward's dominant feature, St. George's Chapel.[9]

Completed in 1528 in the reign of Henry VIII, St. George's Chapel was a masterpiece of perpendicular Gothic. Within its walls of soft, golden stone and beneath an immense fan-vaulted ceiling, a Gothic wooden screen, topped with a multispired organ case, separated the nave from the choir. Carved oak stalls lined a choir hung with the banners of the Knights of the Garter, while the stained glass of the eastern window above the altar bathed the scene in a vibrant, shifting panoply of color. The chapel was the scene of numerous weddings, including that of Victoria's heir the Prince of Wales in 1863, which the queen watched from the seclusion of a carved wooden oriel called Catherine's Closet, high above the altar.[10]

To the east was Wolsey Chapel, where Prince Albert was temporarily laid to rest until a suitable mausoleum could be built in the park. Victoria ordered the building renamed Albert Memorial Chapel, and commissioned George Gilbert Scott to redecorate it in a curious mixture of High Gothic and Italian Renaissance. Medallions depicting members of the royal family topped colorful marble panels of biblical scenes inset into the walls; in a final flourish that removed any last vestige of the original medieval interior, the Gothic vaults were replaced with a new ceiling inlaid with Venetian glass mosaics. Here the queen erected a cenotaph to her husband, a second, spectral tomb complete with a recumbent white marble effigy of Albert by Henri de Triqueti clad in armor, ostensibly to provide the public with a funerary memorial at which they could pray for the prince's soul. The first person to actually be interred here was Prince Leopold, encased in a white marble sarcophagus; he was later joined by Victoria's grandson the Duke of Clarence, beneath an elaborate Gothic-style bronze tomb, in 1892.[11]

Wyatville had increased the height of the Round Tower to just over a hundred feet, providing a unifying focus between the Lower and Upper wards, and dominating the castle's silhouette for many miles.[12] Here, from a small turret, the queen's standard flew to signify that she was in residence. The Upper Ward beyond centered on a grassed quadrangle, ringed on three sides by Wyatville's enlarged state and private apartment blocks.

State visitors arrived through Wyatville's new, imposing George IV Gate flanked by tall crenellated towers, and swept around the quadrangle to his State Entrance Tower, its oak and glass doors shielded by a porte cochere created by extending the guard chamber above. The long, stone entrance corridor, with a handsome vaulted ceiling supported by banded columns, opened to the Grand Staircase. Wyatt had introduced a graceful, horseshoe-shaped staircase here, but in 1866 Victoria had it gutted and replaced it with a ponderous, modified imperial staircase by Anthony Salvin that was more in keeping with the castle's medieval character.[13] Its steps, cloaked in crimson runners, rose between walls of light gray stone adorned with armor, weaponry, and flags. At the landing, wide, open arches supported a ribbed and vaulted ceiling crowned with an oak lantern whose Gothic mullioned windows washed the staircase in light.[14]

From the landing, an arch opened to the Grand Vestibule, created at the beginning of the nineteenth century by Wyatville in the Gothic style, with a fan-vaulted ceiling reaching to a lantern that provided the room's only natural light. Here the martial effect of the queen's ponderous staircase was increased, as visitors entered an armory, with swords, guns, bayonets, suits of armor, and relics of the Battle of Waterloo all displayed in wooden cases and on the walls.[15]

Directly to the south, through a columned arcade, was the Guard Chamber, built over the porte cochere and dominated by immense arched windows overlooking the quadrangle. Like the Grand Vestibule, the Guard Chamber offered visitors a powerful visual reminder of the castle's tumultuous history, its walls adorned with a display of rifles, pistols, bayonets, and swords reaching to its ribbed and vaulted ceiling.[16] Inevitably, attention was drawn to a curious relic at the center of the room: a large memorial bust of Admiral Lord Horatio Nelson, mounted atop a piece of mast taken from his ship HMS *Victory*.[17]

Tall, impressively carved and gilded doors opened to Wyatville's state apartments, a series of impressive enfilades stretching west and east.[18] The suite to the west, created by Hugh May, had formed the apartments of Charles II and his consort, Catherine of Braganza; unfortunately, Wyatville's architectural intrusions largely destroyed their character, and only a few preserved their original seventeenth-century appearance. But these rooms, crowded with paintings, statuary, tapestries, and furniture, served as a magnificent gallery to display some of the most treasured and priceless pieces in Victoria's collection. The first, the Queen's Presence Chamber, offered a rich display of intricate garlands and swags carved by Grinling Gibbons against its paneled walls; above, Italian artist Antonio Verrio had covered the coved ceiling with an allegorical depiction of Queen Catherine surrounded by the virtues. The walls here, and in the adjoining Audience Chamber, were hung with eighteenth-century Gobelins tapestries based on the biblical story of Queen Esther. The fragrant woodwork, vibrant ceilings, colorful hangings, and astonishing carvings created an opulent effect redolent of the Restoration.[19]

Canvases by Anthony Van Dyck Room graced the silk moiré walls of the next room in the suite, named for the painter and adorned with three sparkling crystal chandeliers commissioned by George III.[20] Wyatville stripped the adjoining Queen's Drawing Room of Verrio's painted ceiling but kept the original cornice by Gibbons, elaborately carved with foliate designs and coats of arms adorned in gold.[21] Beyond the Queen's Bedchamber, stretching along the North Terrace, was Queen Elizabeth Gallery, a long room of alcoves and bays that housed the castle library.[22]

The King's Bedroom formed the center of Charles II's suite along the northern side of the state block; ironically, the king had never slept here, but used the room to receive his most important courtiers each morning in an elaborate pantomime. In 1855, Victoria commissioned the firm of Crace & Sons to redecorate the room for the visit of Emperor Napoleon III of France and his wife, Empress Eugenie, and the queen took the keenest interest in its extravagant transformation. Renamed the State Bedchamber, its walls were covered in a rich, red silk moiré, providing a dramatic backdrop to the luxurious eighteenth-century canopied French bed, hung in green and purple silk and topped with gathered white ostrich plumes at its corners. A crimson carpet adorned with gold medallions, and purple silk damask curtains fringed in gold bullion installed by Victoria, added to the unmistakably regal atmosphere. As a final, theatrical flourish, she had the footboard of the bed embellished with the intertwined initials of the emperor and the empress.[23]

While most of these rooms were merely ornamental, Victoria had often used the King's Drawing Room as a setting for amateur family theatricals and small concerts. Under George IV it had lost its last remaining vestiges of its original seventeenth-century decor, when the walls were hung with crimson silk moiré beneath a new, intricately stuccoed and gilded ceiling whose forms imitated Wyatville's Gothic additions to the castle.[24] Victoria called it the Rubens Room, after the works of the artist that hung on its walls though, as one lady noted, the paintings were "really too much crowded together."[25]

The King's Dining Room, at the end of the suite, was a riot of intricately carved garland- and festoon-bedecked walls by Gibbons, including—to emphasize its designation—fish, fowl, and fruit. Carved swags encased Flemish tapestries, while the ceiling, painted by Verrio in 1678, depicted a banquet of the gods. While much of the suite had suffered at the hands of Wyatville's "improvements," it was Victoria who had dealt the dining room its most devastating blow in 1866, when she installed her new Grand Staircase. As Salvin's ascent occupied more space than its predecessor, the architect extended its width into an adjoining court whose windows had provided the dining room with its light. Although Victoria directed that the room be preserved, the windows were bricked in; thereafter, the only natural light came from arched skylights set into the ceilings of the flanking alcoves.[26]

The principal state apartments stretched east of the Guard Chamber, occupying the northern side of the quadrangle. The largest of these, St. George's Hall, had originally served as the castle's banquet room before it was redesigned and dedicated to the Order of the Garter. In the seventeenth century, Hugh May had filled the space with both the hall and his magnificent Chapel of the Resurrection to the west. These were dazzling exercises in the high baroque, decorated with extraordinary tromp l'oeil paintings by Verrio and adorned with twisted columns, marble floors, and intricate carvings. Unfortunately, in 1828 George IV had the two rooms gutted to make way for a piece of pure architectural pastiche, Wyatville's new, imitation Gothic St. George's Hall.[27] Stretching 180 feet and lit by arched windows overlooking the quadrangle, St. George's Hall was an uninspiring addition dominated by a low-pitched, 60-foot-high ceiling of imitation wood, crossed and segmented by beams and dotted with hundreds of colorful carved shields of the previous Knights of the Garter.[28] On the rare evenings when the queen gave state banquets at Windsor, the hall was transformed into a cavernous dining room, with a long mahogany table that could be extended to accommodate 160 guests.

The Duke of Wellington's great victory over Napoleon was commemorated in the adjoining Waterloo Chamber. Created by Wyatville in a former courtyard, it rose two storeys to an imitation medieval ceiling whose hammer beams, carved and picked out in gold, supported a clerestory providing the room with its only natural light. Paintings of all the allied monarchs, diplomats, and commanders who fought in the war graced the oak-paneled walls, including large portraits of George IV and the Duke of Wellington; in 1855, during the state visit of Emperor Napoleon III, it had been discreetly renamed the Picture Gallery, to avoid offense during the ball held within its walls.[29] In 1861, Victoria had the room redecorated, adding a blue silk moiré patterned in gold to the upper walls and carved wooden garlands by Gibbons, rescued when the Chapel of the Resurrection was demolished, to surround the doors and frame the chimneypiece.[30] Beneath, the floor was covered with an extraordinary cream and crimson floral carpet, woven in Agra and presented to

Victoria; at eighty by forty feet, it was the largest seamless carpet in the world.[31]

Beyond the Waterloo Chamber was the Garter Throne Room. Created by joining Charles II's presence and audience chambers together with an open arch, the room was hung in panels of blue silk patterned in alternating golden stars and garters framed by carved and gilded fillets. Atop the deep blue carpet stood a long, polished council table ringed by gilded chairs covered in blue velvet sewn with the order's motto, *Honi soit qui mal y pense*, where Victoria presided over Garter investitures. But the room was dominated by a dais at its western end, shrouded by a red velvet canopy sewn with the royal arms: here stood the queen's fabled ivory throne. Exquisitely carved with foliage and animals, with a seat of alabaster hidden beneath a velvet cushion sewn in gold and silver thread, and adorned with diamonds, rubies, and emeralds, the throne had been presented to the queen by the Raja of Travancore in 1851, and served as a visible reminder of Victoria's extravagant and exotic empire.[32]

The Grand Reception Room, the most formal of all the state apartments, occupied the Cornwall Tower. Following George IV's instructions, Wyatville had created it in imitation of eighteenth-century French salons, using extravagantly carved boiseries from Paris to line its nearly hundred-foot-long walls. The room was a symphony of rich yet subtle colors, its sea-foam green walls adorned with white and gold rocailles, festoons, garlands, and cherubs, and hung with enormous, eighteenth-century Gobelins tapestries depicting the tale of Jason and the Golden Fleece encased in gilded fillets. Three immense bronze and crystal chandeliers hung above the Aubusson carpet and gilded chairs and sofas covered in eighteenth-century Beauvais tapestry, but the room was dominated by an enormous malachite urn, a gift from Tsar Nicholas I in 1844, that stood before the tall, mullioned window looking north to the spires of Eton across the Thames.[33]

Prince Albert had transformed the China Corridor to the north into a remarkable showcase. "On both sides," recalled one member of the queen's staff, were "handsomely decorated niches full of the most costly Indian arms and treasures." There were weapons "inlaid with the costliest gems," an Indian throne "entirely of gold inlaid with precious stones," cases "full of daggers and small carbines which all have golden handles inlaid with precious stones," and even a captured Indian tent of red silk, erected in the middle of the corridor so that visitors passed through its interior.[34]

Past the Stuart Room, and the octagonal Holbein Room—situated directly above the equerries' entrance at the northeastern corner of the quadrangle and hung with forty-one canvases by the great German court painter—was the private chapel.[35] Tucked in an oddly shaped octagonal space formerly used by George IV's band, unimaginative architect Edward Blore had created the chapel on Victoria's orders in 1843. This was an exercise in ponderous neo-Gothic style, its lower walls covered with dark oak panels carved with traceries, ogee arches, quatrefoils, and thin pilasters enriched with gilt; only the upper panels, painted white, helped to relieve the gloom. Rising two storeys to an ornate Gothic ceiling, the chapel was pierced with two alcoves: the one on the west held a choir loft and Father Willis pipe organ, while the one to the north—framed by an open arch held aloft by carved cherubs—was the sanctuary, complete with marble reredos set beneath a mullioned, two-tiered stained glass window. Above the carved and gated pews hung a Gothic-style brass gasolier, whose frosted globes were etched with the initials *VR*.[36]

Here, every Sunday morning when the queen was in residence, she diligently attended services; those members of the household in waiting were also expected to be present. Shortly before ten, the celebrants entered and took their places in the carved pews, followed by white-gowned choirboys from St. George's Chapel who crowded into the upper gallery around the organist. Victoria, as well as any members of her family present, was the last to arrive, escorted by a pair of brightly costumed and turbaned Indians and two Highland servants attired in kilts; as soon as she was seated, the service began, the selected minister—who always wore a black cassock at the queen's request—appearing rather suddenly through a jib door near the altar "like a jack-in-the-box," as one historian described it. Sermons, at the queen's request, were always short and rarely exceeded twenty minutes; she diligently followed the text, often nodding in approval. Often the several hymns included music composed by Prince Albert; Victoria would first fix the nervous choirboys with a direct gaze, then turn her attention to her own family to ensure that they were singing along before herself join-ing in. Within thirty minutes, it was all over; as the queen retreated to her private apartments, the choirboys usually beat a hasty retreat to the cavernous kitchens below, begging lavish pastries from an indulgent chef before they returned to their own lodgings.[37]

The Gothic-style Octagonal Dining Room, with arched windows and a ribbed ceiling, occupied the Brunswick Tower at the northeastern end of the China Corridor.[38] The State Dining Room beyond had been designed in a vaguely Elizabethan style, with a low-pitched ceiling segmented by decorative beams into coffers adorned with gilded pendants. The paneled walls, painted a light, rosy cream, were adorned with pilasters carved with gilded oak leaf garlands. A Gothic-style rosewood sideboard, designed by A. W. N. Pugin for George IV, held a collection of the queen's gold plate shimmering in light from the mullioned windows. With its crimson carpet and gold-fringed curtains, tall looking glasses, and crystal chandelier, it was an impressive room, although its gilt chairs could accommodate fewer than forty guests.[39]

By the time he rebuilt Windsor, George IV could no longer afford the expense of maintaining Carlton House, his lavish neoclassical palace in London. Designed by Henry Holland and altered by both Wyatville and John Nash, Carlton House was, as one historian noted, a place of "utmost splendor: columns of porphyry or yellow Sienna marble, with bronze or silver capitals; walls hung with crimson damask; a circular drawing room with the ceiling painted like the sky, from which crystal chandeliers cascaded down and were endlessly reflected in pier glasses," and rooms in Gothic and chinoiserie style.[40] Before its destruction in 1827, Carlton House was duly stripped of its elaborate fittings: twenty-three chimney-pieces, carved and gilded doors, stucco reliefs, paintings, carpets, curtains, furniture, and inlaid floors were all packed off to Windsor Castle, with the remainder sent down the Mall to adorn the rooms of Buckingham Palace.[41]

Using these fittings and furnishings, Wyatville created a series of exqui-site apartments. The Red Drawing Room, with a central bow of mullioned windows that flooded it with light, was a sumptuous, richly decorated space awash with crimson, white, and gold. Gilded fillets framed panels of patterned red silk against stark white walls, set below a deeply carved cornice picked out in gold. The doors, from Carlton House, were adorned with carved and gilded military trophies, their brilliant luster matched by the elaborate, tasseled pelmets and theatrical swags of gold bullion decorating the crimson curtains. Lavishly carved, gilded sofas and matching chairs, from Carlton House, nestled against ebony cabinets and consoles topped with bronze candelabra, Sèvres vases, and Meissen urns.[42]

Named for the gold-patterned silk panels on its walls, the adjoining Green Drawing Room occupied the castle's Chester Tower, where a deep bay of mullioned windows offered an expansive view over the east terrace. Decorated in much the same manner as the Red Drawing Room, its central feature was an immense Axminster carpet designed by Ludwig Grüner, the intertwined initials of Victoria and Albert flanked by floral garlands in red, cream, and beige.[43] The smaller White Drawing Room completed the suite, its gilded boiseries shimmering in the light of its crystal chandelier. All three rooms opened onto the East Terrace, where stairs descended to an exquisite, sunken garden rimmed by a crenellated parapet and planted by George IV with radiating beds of colorful flowers and topiary centered around a splashing fountain.[44]

Behind these rooms, its arched windows overlooking the quadrangle, lay the Grand Corridor, running in an impressive, 550-foot-long sweep along the length of the eastern and southern blocks.[45] This expansive passage, with its Gothic-style ceiling crossed by gilded ribs, was crowded with marble busts, paintings, ebony and Boulle cabinets, gilded stools covered in crimson silk, family portraits, Meissen and Sèvres porcelain displayed atop marble consoles, and shining candelabra and bronzes.[46] Most of these objects had been placed in the Grand Corridor by George IV. "When young," wrote John Cornforth, "the Queen had been staggered by the sheer quantity of her uncle's possessions and she probably respected the enormous care that he had expended on their arrangement."[47] The Grand Corridor offered "lovely corners and curtains behind which one could hide and leap out in the dark," one of the queen's granddaughters recalled. "Our wild romps . . . were often interrupted by one of the pages bringing a message from the queen that she would not have so much noise."[48]

The Grand Corridor gave access to the private apartments. An angular projection at the southeastern corner of the quadrangle shielded the ground-floor sovereign's entrance; beyond its carved oak doors set with glass panels, a short flight of steps led to a vestibule. One door opened to the queen's lift, its oak-paneled interior adorned with a crimson carpet, while, directly ahead, lay the Sovereign's Staircase, twin flights with exquisite white and gold balustrades carved with gothic designs and set into a triangular space.[49]

The octagonal Oak Dining Room lay just above the sovereign's entrance. Decorated in the Gothic style by Wyatville, its oak walls were carved with arches and quatrefoils, and hung with two large tapestries representing a boar hunt, given to the queen by King Louis Philippe of France. Four paintings of Victoria's daughters-in-law—Alexandra, Marie, Louise, and Helen—hung here, but the room was dominated by a large, ethereal portrait of the queen, painted by Heinrich von Angeli in 1877, above the chimneypiece. Here Victoria took most of her meals with her family.[50]

Queen Victoria's private apartments began just after the White Drawing Room, and included her audience room, where she received the prime minister. Hung in a silk subtly patterned with the insignia and motto of the Order of the Garter, the audience room held a number of glass cabinets displaying various military awards, orders, and decorations; in contrast to this military atmosphere were the purely domestic paintings: Winterhalter studies of all of the queen's nine children, and a grouping of fifteen portraits of the children of King George III and Queen Charlotte by Thomas Gainsborough.[51]

Just beyond the audience room was the heart and soul of Victoria's Windsor: the Blue Room, where Albert had died. After his death, the queen had declared that it "should remain in its present state and shall not be made use of in the future."[52] Thereafter, its blue silk walls sheltered nothing short of a shrine: the bed upon which Albert had perished, adorned with a miniature of his corpse; the table on which rested the glass from which he had drank his last gulp of medicine; and a large white marble bust, wreathed in mourning laurels, of a somber prince consort surveying the entire morbid scene.[53] It became, in the words of one writer, "not only a monument to Albert's memory but an altar to Albert's living presence."[54]

The queen's own rooms, recalled her granddaughter Marie of Romania, "always smelt deliciously of orange flowers, even when there were no orange flowers about the place."[55] Masses of furniture, pictures, books, bronze and marble busts, and sentimental ornaments, shielded by a profusion of potted palms and screens, presented an "extraordinary conglomeration of useful and useless, always decorative, but rarely aesthetically satisfying."[56]

The spectral presence of Albert dominated. Marie of Romania wrote of "Grandpapa in his full general's uniform. Grandpapa in his robes of the Order of the Garter, Grandpapa in kilt, in plain clothes, Grandpapa on horse back, at his writing table, Grandpapa with his dogs, with his children, in the garden, on the mountains. . . . Grandpapa with his loving wife gazing enraptured up into his face." And then, she recalled, there were "mysterious photographs of dead people, even of dead little children, which, although they made us feel creepy, we always furtively looked at again and again."[57]

Patterned red silk damask encased in gilded fillets hung upon the walls of the queen's sitting room in the Victoria Tower, the dark effect relieved by the white of the wainscoting, paneled doors, and delicate frieze adorned with gilded reliefs. It was a room of immense contrasts. A large ormolu chandelier hung from the center of the ceiling's shallow dome, above a table crowded with cheap souvenirs. The white marble chimneypiece, originally from Carlton House, was adorned with gilded caryatids, but the fender in the grate was of inexpensive brass; a basket of beech logs—the only fuel the queen allowed to be burned in her own fireplaces—stood nearby. Atop the chimneypiece, reflected in the tall looking glass, stood a large ormolu Empire clock set between ormolu candelabra, bronze statuettes, and a pair of exquisite antique Chinese vases hidden beneath cheap glass domes. The carved and gilded sofas and chairs, covered in crimson damask, were piled with velveteen pillows.[58] In no other room was Victoria's personal struggle between "the need for grandeur, and the desire for intimacy," as John Cornforth noted, quite so apparent.[59]

On the left side of the chimneypiece hung Landseer's *Windsor Castle in Modern Times*, a family group depicting Victoria, Albert, and Vicky in the deep bay window of the Green Drawing Room, balanced by Francis Grant's *Queen Victoria Riding with Lord Melbourne at Windsor* on the right. In one corner nestled a grand piano, draped in velvet and covered in serried rows of gilt-framed photographs. Victoria's desk was a tangle of ordered chaos, so cluttered with photographs and personal objects that there was scarcely room for the queen's silver inkwell, gold blotter, and golden tray filled with pens. Small bamboo tables next to the desk served as shelves for the queen's set of governmental reference volumes, bound in red leather and stamped with her cipher in gold, and held the red leather dispatch boxes that arrived each day from Whitehall, containing official papers.[60]

Family portraits and views of Albert's native Coburg covered the green and gold floral silk walls of Victoria's dressing room, a chaise longue, covered in green velvet, nestled in an alcove atop the carpet of cream arabesques strewn with green vines and red flowers. Here, each morning, one of the queen's maids laid out her clothes, and Victoria prepared for the day at her dressing table, with its looking glass festooned and draped in fine muslin, and top covered with a toilette service, assortment of carved crystal scent bottles, and little gold boxes.[61] Despite Albert's sanitary improvements to the castle, Windsor possessed only one bathroom, which opened from Victoria's dressing room; everyone else made do with portable copper tubs.[62] The queen slept in a lofty, comfortably furnished room hung in crimson and gold silk damask overlooking the East Terrace. The right side of her large mahogany bed, with its half canopy, featured—like all her beds—a painting of the prince consort on his deathbed.[63]

These rooms, hung with hundreds of photographs and some 250 paintings, contained a virtual illustrative record of Victoria's life.[64] Victoria, asserted one aristocratic critic, had "no more notion of what is right and pure in art than she had of the Chinese grammar."[65] She frankly admitted this herself, saying candidly that she "had no taste," but instead "only used to listen" to Albert's opinion.[66] "She loved the present," noted J. H. Plumb and Huw Wheldon, "and wanted it preserved; so every child was painted and sculpted at an early age—even their tiny feet and hands and ears carved in marble. The Queen's and Prince's dogs were painted by

Landseer, or even, as with Albert's favorite greyhound Eos, molded in zinc."[67]

What Victoria liked was a good picture, an excellent reproduction of a person or scene she could recognize. "She considered the likeness to be of paramount importance," recalled Frederick Ponsonby, "and the artistic merit of the picture itself to be quite a secondary matter."[68] The portraits by her favorite artists—Sir Edwin Landseer, Franz Xavier Winterhalter, and later Heinrich von Angeli—all offered idealized presentations of the royal family that appealed to the bourgeois instincts of the middle classes, as did the queen's penchant for immortalizing her favorite horses and pets in overtly sentimental canvases that dotted the walls. Albert's influence had brought the more refined works of early German and Italian schools to these rooms.[69] The royal couple also shared a passion for rather startling nudes—often birthday gifts to one another—that seemed somehow out of place amid the family groups and paintings of frolicking animals.[70]

These rooms largely remained the same for sixty years. Victoria disliked change, and great pains were taken to ensure that the private apartments in all of her residences looked exactly as she remembered them from her last visit. All of her rooms were periodically photographed from various angles, with special care taken to capture the positions of the immensely cluttered desks and tables. When they were worn out, carpets and curtains were replaced with newly made duplicates, and threadbare upholstery diligently copied and replaced.[71] But neglect gradually settled in as Victoria's eyesight and health faded; after her death, "a clatter of moths" scurried away when displays in the castle were investigated; faded tapestries were found rolled up in forgotten attics; cupboards were opened to reveal collections of jade objets d'art covered in dust; Oriental and French porcelain showed chips and hasty mending; and locked boxes piled in storerooms disclosed both the priceless and the mystifying, from Henry VIII's armor to hundreds of ivory elephant tusks.[72]

From the George IV Gate, the Long Walk, shaded by elms, stretched three miles to a distant equestrian statue of George III, called the Copper Horse, on a hill overlooking the castle.[73] Beyond this, roads cleaved through tranquil stretches of woodland and across meadows to a multitude of smaller royal residences, including Royal Lodge, Fort Belvedere, and Cumberland Lodge. But the heart of the park, Frogmore, lay a mile down the Long Walk, nestled in the castle's shadow and protected by a grove of trees.

Frogmore, a forty-five-acre plot originally used by Queen Charlotte, was, remembered Victoria's grandson Edward VIII, "a romantic garden, well laid out, with undulating lawns and a winding lake, lush with water lilies, shaded by spreading cedars and weeping willows."[74] The center-piece of the park was Frogmore House, a large white mansion originally built in the seventeenth century by architect James Wyatt and greatly altered through the succeeding years into a comfortable, Georgian-style residence with two projecting bow windows framing a glassed-in colon-nade.[75] It was here that the Duchess of Kent had lived when at Windsor and here, in 1861, that she had died. Victoria had her mother interred in these serene surroundings, in a magnificent new mausoleum, a small, circular structure ringed by pink granite columns and crowned by a low, copper-covered dome situated atop a mound.

A serpentine lake stretched languidly between lawns and artificial mounds that gave the garden its protected character.[76] Groves of beech, oak, and flowering cherry trees shaded fragrant rhododendrons and lush beds of flowers, providing the privacy that Victoria relished. She had a teahouse built here, with a steeply pitched roof and decorative Victorian details, where she often spent afternoons working in the shade of its porch, and a white marble kiosk, brought from India in 1858 after the capture of Lucknow.[77] But for Victoria, the most important building at Frogmore was one she herself commissioned, the royal mausoleum, built to contain her husband's body and eventually her own.

In February 1862 Victoria selected a plot of land for the structure, and the foundation stone was laid on March 15. In commissioning the mau-soleum, Victoria relied on the advice of Albert's artistic adviser, Professor Ludwig Grüner of Dresden, who suggested a Romanesque building that evoked the Italian Renaissance so beloved by the prince.[78] The royal mau-soleum, built of granite and Portland stone, was constructed in the shape of a Greek cross, with four transepts stretching out from the center. Above the octagonal rotunda was a seventy-foot-high dome faced in panels of Australian copper, and whose interior vaults were painted a deep blue and scattered with gilded stars. Above the tall bronze doors Victoria ordered this inscription: "*Vale desideratissime.* Farewell, Best Beloved. Here at last I shall rest with Thee. With Thee in Christ I shall rise again."[79] The interior was a stunning evocation of the Italian Renaissance, with a colorful mosaic floor, and mosaic- and fresco-covered walls; colored marbles were inlaid into the walls, surrounding niches and flanking stained glass windows that filled the space with diffused light; above, biblical quotations in German and English were lettered in gold.[80]

At the center of the mausoleum, beneath the dome, was the tomb. Winged bronze angels stood guard at the corners of the gray sarcophagus, carved from the largest single block of flawless granite in the world and set atop a base of Belgian black marble.[81] Atop, on the right side, rested the recumbent white marble effigy of the prince consort in his robes of the Order of the Garter, carved by Carlo Marochetti in 1867. Victoria also commissioned Marochetti to carve her own effigy at the same time; when finished, it was placed in storage, where it was to remain for more than thirty years, forgotten until her death in 1901.[82]

Queen Victoria became the first sovereign to open the state apartments of the castle to the public, in 1845, and it became a popular destination. Albert disliked the intrusive stares, and blocked public access to the terraces and the last mile of the Long Walk leading to the George IV Gate to preserve some sense of privacy.[83] Yet Victoria was curiously diffident about the castle. "I have no feeling for Windsor," she once declared. "I admire it, I think it a grand, splendid place, but without a particle of anything which causes me to love it."[84] She once complained that the castle "is so stiff, formal and full of etiquette, even somewhat like a prison, and the air there is very depressing."[85]

After 1861, Victoria found Windsor even more tainted. It was no longer a place of happy memories, and she preferred to spend her time at Osborne or Balmoral rather than at Windsor, which she once caustically referred to as "the Old State Prison."[86] To her daughter Vicky she described Windsor as "this dreary, gloomy old place," a sentiment due in no small part to the fact that it was at Windsor that her beloved husband had died.[87]

5

A DAY IN THE LIFE

As dawn broke over the battlements of Windsor Castle, Queen Victoria's life had settled into a predictable pattern. Her days, her weeks, her months, and her years were all mapped out for her, and she inevitably followed a rigid schedule whose very form gave her comfort. Her routine rarely deviated, whether at Windsor, Balmoral Castle, or Osborne House.

Each morning, at seven-thirty, one of the queen's wardrobe maids crept into her bedroom at Windsor, pulling back the heavy damask curtains and opening the shutters to reveal the sun shining over the East Terrace and the sunken garden beyond alive with colorful and fragrant flowers.[1] By the time Victoria entered her dressing room, her table had been set with lotions and perfumes, her silver hairbrush laid out next to a basin of hot water, and sponges and towels carefully folded and placed.[2] Working from books that listed all of the queen's clothes and a copy of her daily schedule, one of her dressers or wardrobe maids laid out a dress for the morning, and collected the nightclothes from the previous evening.

When she was younger, Victoria had used her clothing to convey her status. Her white silk and satin coronation gown, sewn with gold thread, had appeared regal yet virginal; the satin dress adorned with flounces of

Honiton lace she wore for her marriage helped establish the tradition of a white wedding gown.[3] But the queen's influence in fashion had never been great, and the styles of the period did nothing to enhance her appearance. The voluminous, wide, elaborate crinolines and lavish ball gowns created for her, with their profusion of embroidery, fringe, and flounces of lace, only had the unfortunate effect of emphasizing her short stature and ever-increasing girth, and rather than win her accolades, her wardrobe was frequently the object of ridicule. When Victoria tried to impress, as on her state visit to Paris, she paled in comparison to the beautiful and elegant Empress Eugenie and was ridiculed for her lack of taste.

The death of Prince Albert brought forty years of perpetual mourning; in many ways, the queen's mourning dresses suited her far better than had her attempts at haute couture. These mourning dresses, though of severely plain lines, were nevertheless of the finest work and materials, with panels of black silk, crepe, and satin adorned with delicate embroidery in silver thread and jet and complemented with inlays of delicate lace. Victoria favored the full, crinoline skirts of the 1860s, with square décolletage filled with a chemisette of white lisse and elbow-length sleeves finished with flounces of white tulle or lace.[4] In the years after Albert's death, the queen's annual clothing bills averaged some £3,376 (£215,219, or $368,024 in 2007 figures).[5] Victoria wore black silk stockings woven for her by John Meakin and embroidered with her initials by Anne Birkin.[6] Although her evening shoes were traditional satin slippers, for the daytime Victoria favored short black boots with elastic sides, which could be easily slipped on and off.[7] On her head she usually wore a widow's cap of white tulle, with a trailing cascade of veil and white lace streamers, occasionally ornamented with diamond stars or crescents, while around her neck she always wore a locket containing miniatures of her two deceased children, Princess Alice and Prince Leopold.[8]

Once she was dressed, the queen consulted her daily schedule, written out for her each morning to highlight any engagements or important events, before leaving her rooms for breakfast, which was always served at nine-thirty. Here at Windsor in early summer, if the weather was good, she preferred to take breakfast and luncheon outdoors, where she could enjoy the invigorating air. Sometimes a green, fringed tent was erected on the East Terrace and set with a table and chairs on a carpet; on other occasions, Victoria drove to nearby Frogmore, where similar arrangements had been made. Her breakfasts always began with hot porridge, and continued with a boiled egg set in a solid gold eggcup, and eaten with a gold spoon; there was also bacon, kedgeree, chicken, cutlets, game, and sweet rolls, although the queen herself rarely indulged in these heavier dishes.[9] She always took her coffee or tea in two identical cups, pouring the hot liquid from one to the other until it was cool enough to drink.[10]

Usually her recently widowed daughter Beatrice joined her for breakfast, served by her Indian and Highland servants; as they ate, the queen's pipe major marched up and down in the distance, the sound of his bagpipes filling the warm morning air. "A delicious fragrance of coffee, or of a certain brown biscuit which came in flat round tins from Germany, was characteristic of Grandmama's breakfasts," recalled Marie of Romania. "Our greedy little noses sniffed it in longingly, but it was not always that we were invited to have a taste."[11]

Shortly before eleven, Victoria was at her desk to begin the day's work. While she was away at breakfast, her rooms had been cleaned, and one of her maids had put away her journal from the previous evening.[12] Early each morning, no matter where she might be, one of the queen's messengers—his tunic adorned with a silver badge depicting a greyhound—had arrived from London, bringing with him three red leather dispatch boxes containing official government papers; a maid signed for them, and placed them on the queen's desk.[13] Victoria carried the keys on a chain she kept in the pocket of her dress throughout the day.[14]

As she sat at her desk, Victoria covered her lap with a little black silk apron to protect her dress from any stray ink. Once, when she was younger, Beatrice was playing in the sitting room as her mother worked and, bored, crept behind her, grabbed the loose strings, and tied them to the chair without her mother's knowledge before disappearing. When Victoria finished her work and tried to stand up, she found herself firmly lashed to the chair. Unable to reach the knots, she was forced to ring for a maid to untie her.[15]

Victoria worked on these papers—official communiqués, government bills, and various state papers—reading through them, initialing them, and occasionally adding her own comments at the bottom of the page. She took a keen interest in the problems of the day: during the infamous "Jack the Ripper" murders in London's East End in autumn 1888, she dispatched numerous notes on the victims—"unfortunate women of a bad class," she said—and suggestions on ways to catch the killer, including searching all boats and stationing extra police patrols.[16] There were also occasionally insights into her sheltered life: when reading a proposed bill outlawing homosexuality, she objected to the inclusion of lesbians, saying, "Women don't do such things!"[17]

Sir Arthur Bigge, the queen's private secretary, worked with her throughout the morning. His was a job requiring great diplomacy, as Victoria was often a difficult mistress. "When she insists that two and two make five, I say that I cannot help thinking they make four," Bigge's predecessor remarked. "She replies that there may be some truth in what I say, but she knows they make five. I drop the discussion."[18]

Bigge's work was made more difficult by the queen's insistence that all official business with her be conducted using handwritten memoranda. She abhorred typewriters, and he had to promptly write down every report he made, every encounter with her, and every piece of advice he offered, in long, third-person reports that inevitably began, "Sir Arthur Bigge humbly begs to submit to Your Majesty . . ."[19] The envelopes containing these communiqués had, by Victoria's order, to be sealed with wax, and not licked.[20] Victoria's comments and questions provided their own challenge: her failing eyesight, coupled with her cramped handwriting punctuated with abbreviations and frequent underlining, were often difficult to read, and to make matters worse, she often ran her sentences off the white of the page into the broad black mourning borders, making it impossible to see her words. Sometimes it took hours to completely decipher her comments, but no one dared to raise the issue with her.[21]

After Albert's death and the loss of his progressive influence, Victoria was reluctant to accept the scientific and industrial developments he had championed. She always preferred candles to gas. In 1888 she allowed technicians to install electric lights at Windsor, but only in certain rooms; when one of the electricians suffered a severe shock when wiring the chandeliers in the Red Drawing Room, Victoria ordered all work stopped; only in 1898 did it finally resume.[22] Even so, she remained deeply suspicious of electricity. When one official, told of her distrust, advised the queen that electric lights "were far the best," Victoria told him he was impertinent and uncharacteristically punched him on the shoulder.[23] Nor did she take to telephones. In 1878 a demonstration of the fledgling telephone was held at Osborne House; Victoria listened as several people spoke and sang at the other end of the line. She deemed it an interesting development but noted, "It is rather faint, and one must hold the tube rather close to one's ear."[24] In the summer of 1896, she finally relented and ordered lines installed at Windsor, although she herself refused to use them.[25]

Racing around her sitting room as she worked were the queen's constant companions, her pet dogs. Victoria had always had a soft spot for animals, and kept a string of collies, spaniels, and Skye and Scotch terriers.[26] In the last years of her life, her favorite was undoubtedly Turi, a fluffy white male Pomeranian.[27] Those favorites no longer alive were nevertheless present, staring down from paintings commissioned from Sir Edwin Landseer, or in marble or bronze effigies that dotted tables. Victoria decried cruelty to animals as "one of the worst signs of wickedness in human nature."[28] "Above all," remembered Marie of Romania, "there was Grandmama's bullfinch, such an angry little fellow, who became thin with rage, and screeched at you when you stuck your finger in between the bars of his cage; but when he liked someone he puffed himself up till he looked like a round ball of fluff and then he piped softly and enchantingly a gay little tune he had been taught."[29]

The sitting room, like all rooms in which Victoria lived, was frostily cold, with windows thrown open to maintain the chill. The queen, having been advised about the benefits of fresh air, abhorred heated rooms, and even in the dead of winter ordered the temperature in her palaces never to rise above sixty degrees.[30] Although many complained, Victoria refused to abandon the practice; indeed, her rooms inevitably sported small thermometers in ivory obelisks so she could check the temperature and satisfy herself.[31] This perpetual cold constantly antagonized the queen's rheumatism, and her youngest daughter, Princess Beatrice, also suffered from the disease from an early age, but no amount of pleading could induce Victoria to abandon her preferences.[32]

The queen's daughter-in-law Marie of Edinburgh found such regulations a nightmare. Coming from the Russian court, she was accustomed to swelteringly hot rooms even in the dead of winter. On being told that the queen allowed no fires lit by her family in bedrooms, she thought it must be a joke, and in her own room at Windsor ordered her maid to arrange one for her. The fire was crackling when Victoria appeared to ask if her daughter-in-law needed anything; spotting the fire, she chastised the maid and ordered her immediately to douse the embers. When Marie returned to the room, she found the watery remnants of her fire in the grate, and Victoria standing angrily before a window she herself had flung open.[33]

Luncheon was served promptly at one.[34] In good weather, this was usually served beneath a tent on the terrace or at Frogmore; in inclement weather, Victoria took luncheon in the Oak Dining Room.[35] Occasionally after luncheon was over, Victoria would call on a member of the household to join her at the piano; usually these were ladies of the bedchamber or maids of honor, although she also enjoyed the company of the lively Alick Yorke. The queen would prop up a piece of libretto and say, "Now, Mr. Yorke, you begin," and Yorke obediently followed her direction as they sang verses to each other. Once she stopped the music and said with a smile, "You know, Mr. Yorke, I was taught singing by Mendelssohn."[36]

There were also visits by the queen's grandchildren. "The hush round Grandmama's door was awe-inspiring," recalled Marie of Romania; "it was like approaching the mystery of some sanctuary. Silent, soft-carpeted corridors led to Grandmama's apartments, which were somehow always approached from afar off, and those that led the way towards them, were they servant, lady or maid, talked in hushed voices and trod softly as though with felt soles. One door after another opened noiselessly, it was like passing through the forecourts of a temple, before approaching the final mystery to which only the initiated had access." Once within, she remembered, they would find the queen, "not idol-like at all, not a bit frightening, smiling a kind little smile, almost as shy as us children, so that conversation was not very fluent on either side. Inquiry as to our morals and general behavior made up a great part of it, and I well remember Grandmama's shocked and yet amused little exclamations of horror when it was reported that one or the other of us had not been good. I have a sort of feeling that Grandmama as well as ourselves was secretly relieved when the audience was over."[37] In her old age, Victoria was far more indulgent of these numerous grandchildren than she had been with her own children. Once, when a grandchild was brought to her and told to kiss her hand, he approached, only to spit on the pudgy fingers; Victoria ignored the slight and merely called for a handkerchief.[38] "She was very kind," recalled one of her granddaughters, "but very strict with old fashioned ideas of how children must be brought up; the one she most insisted upon was that children must be seen and not heard."[39]

In the afternoon, Victoria usually went for a drive in the Home Park, accompanied by one of her daughters or granddaughters and a lady-in-waiting or a maid of honor. The queen occasionally used a carriage, pulled by a pair of Windsor grays with an outrider, though she preferred to drive in a cart pulled by Jacquot, her favorite white donkey, whom she had purchased in Nice.[40] By 1896 Victoria could no longer climb into a carriage unassisted; a baize-covered ramp allowed her to walk slowly, guided by one of her Indian orderlies, to the edge of the waiting vehicle, where she was eased into her seat and quickly covered with a lap rug.[41] The queen always wore a cape or a shawl, and either a bonnet or a broad straw hat to guard against the sun.[42] Occasionally, noted one lady-in-waiting, the aged queen fell asleep on these drives.[43] "On every change of temperature during a drive," recalled one relative, "the Queen has to have a thicker or lighter wrap, as the case may be, put round her."[44]

Members of the household took advantage of the queen's afternoon outing to temporarily escape from the confines of the castle, although their own walks in the park were always ruled by fear of accidentally encountering her. "It was a great crime to meet her in the grounds," recalled Frederick Ponsonby, who noted that if "by any unlucky chance we did come across her, we hid behind bushes."[45]

These afternoons at Frogmore usually passed in tranquillity, though on one occasion disaster nearly struck. Victoria sat at her desk beneath a tent, working on state papers, when a servant noticed several frogs hopping across the lawn; within minutes, hundreds of frogs had overrun the grounds, jumping onto the queen to escape the servants scurrying to catch them. At that moment, the Marquis d'Harcourt, the French ambassador, appeared for a previously scheduled meeting. Despite the absurdity of the situation, Victoria ignored the plethora of frogs and scampering servants and carried on a conversation as if nothing unusual was taking place.[46]

Tea was served promptly at five; in contrast to Victoria's regular meals, this was a simple affair, with tea, sandwiches, and pastries. A plate of freshly baked shortbread always accompanied tea; made by the royal pastry chef, it was stamped out in ovals or circles and marked with three rows of small indentations pressed into the dough before being baked.[47] After tea, the queen returned to her rooms to rest before dinner. Sometimes she played solitaire, using cards produced specially for her and stamped with her cipher in gold.[48]

Often a lady-in-waiting or a maid of honor would be called upon to read to the queen. Victoria tended to prefer British authors, although she admitted a fondness for the works of Washington Irving and Alexandre Dumas *père* as well.[49] She greatly admired Charles Dickens, but perhaps her favorite writers were two women, the romantic novelists Margaret Oliphant and Marie Corelli. The latter, in particular, was a source of consternation to her daughter Vicky. When the queen once assured her daughter that Corelli would "rank as one of the greatest writers of all time," Vicky dismissed the claim, saying that her "writings were trash." Frederick Ponsonby happened to be present; unaware of the queen's fondness for the sentimental Corelli, he answered Vicky's query as to his own opinion with a forthright declaration that "though she sold well," he believed her audience was composed of "the semi-educated." Vicky clapped her hands in delight, but the queen gave him a forceful stare.[50] Victoria also enjoyed poetry, particularly the works of Tennyson and Burns, though Sir Walter Scott remained her favorite.[51]

Victoria once admitted that she lacked any literary talent, but her journals belie this: some of her travel descriptions are remarkable for their detail and sense of liveliness. Her first foray into the world of publication came in 1868, when *Leaves from the Journal of Our Life in the Highlands*, a collection of her diary entries, was published. At first the edition was privately circulated among family and friends. Finally she was convinced to make it available to the general public, and it sold twenty thousand copies in the first week, with the royalties donated to charity. The public eagerly read these intimate accounts, but Victoria's children were appalled that their mother had thrown open her private life—with its frequent mentions of her Highland servant John Brown—in such a manner, and soon enough, some wag had produced an anonymous pamphlet titled *John Brown's Legs, or Leaves from a Journal in the Lowlands*.[52] Victoria, however, refused to listen to the criticism, and in 1884 issued a sequel, this one dedicated "to the memory of my devoted personal attendant and faithful friend John Brown."[53] She once gave a copy of *Leaves* to Dickens, inscribed "From the humblest of writers to one of the greatest."[54] Benjamin Disraeli, prime minister, amateur novelist, and inveterate flatterer, once famously greeted her by saying, "We authors, Ma'am."[55]

The queen often took a short nap in the late afternoon and early evening, being awakened by her maid just before eight so she could prepare for dinner. By this time her maids had seen to the usual arrangements: a ewer and bowl of warm water, perfumed with elderflower, waited on her dressing table side by side with a basin of lukewarm chamomile tea in which Victoria refreshed her eyes, and a silver tray with small round sponges scented with her favorite perfume, made in Grasse, that smelled of orange blossoms.[56]

A fresh pair of silk stockings waited along with the queen's evening dress, the latter inevitably of black silk or satin adorned with jet beading and lace appliqués. When the maid had assisted the queen into her clothing, she offered a velvet-lined tray or box containing a selection of jewels. Victoria had come to the throne with little jewelry of her own, and she lost many prized pieces that had belonged to George III's consort Charlotte when her uncle the Duke of Cumberland (reigning in Germany as King Ernst of Hanover) insisted that she honor bequests in the queen's will. For several decades Victoria had stubbornly resisted, and her uncle eventually threatened to take his crowned niece to court, demanding that she follow her grandmother's wishes. Only in 1857 did a special commission finally render a verdict in Ernst's favor, and Victoria reluctantly turned over the majority of the pieces to the Hanoverian royal family.[57]

Victoria was not exactly bereft of exquisite jewels. She inherited a large collection that, unlike the Hanover jewels, remained in England, and included diamond, pearl, and sapphire diadems, necklaces, bracelets, and earrings that had originally belonged to her crowned ancestors.[58] Over the years her private collection increased dramatically: in the course of her reign, she spent nearly £160,000 (£10,199,981, or $17,441,967 in 2007 currency) at one jeweler, Garrard, the majority on personal pieces; as Victoria also purchased and commissioned pieces from other jewelers, the actual amount spent on jewelry must have been significantly higher, but even so, the Garrard expenditures reflect an outlay of some $17 million in current figures.[59] There were exquisite diamond, ruby, emerald, sapphire, and pearl earrings; tiaras of rubies and diamonds, emeralds and diamonds, opals and diamonds, sapphires and diamonds, pearls and diamonds, and aquamarines and diamonds, in a variety of styles. Albert designed many of his wife's parures and demiparures, as well as brooches and bracelets, as anniversary and birthday gifts, lending the pieces a sentimental value that spoke to the queen.[60]

Some of her most magnificent and valuable pieces came from the far-flung corners of her empire, the richest source being India; to impress the queen—and win concessions as their own power slowly evaporated—many maharajas presented Victoria with a staggering stream of gems; more came when, in 1877, she was formally proclaimed Empress of India.[61] Chief among these jewels was the Koh-i-noor Diamond of 186 carats, looted from the treasury at Lahore by the East India Company and regarded as one of the most important symbols in India. Victoria had the diamond, whose name meant "Mountain of Light" in Persian, recut and set into a new tiara, of two thousand diamonds, in 1853; she often removed the central jewel and wore the diamond as a pendant on her bodice.[62] This Indian bounty was staggering, and included the Timur Necklace, featuring a 352-carat ruby presented to the queen in 1851; the Regal Indian Tiara, designed in 1853 to display a sweep of opals against a fretwork of diamonds; brooches set with large rubies and emeralds; and ropes of pearls with a ruby clasp.[63] After Albert's death, Victoria virtually abandoned her colored gems and took to wearing only pearls and diamonds. She also had a new crown made in 1870 that she could wear at the most important state occasions. Composed of some thirteen hundred diamonds, it was designed to sit atop her head rather than be worn over it.[64]

Most evenings, Victoria wore a diamond necklace and matching earrings. Stretching across the front of her bodice, the blue sash of the Order of the Garter was held in place by a diamond-encrusted order star she had bestowed upon Albert the night before their wedding. Several brooches might adorn the bodice: diamond bows and knots set with pearl pendants, or her Diamond Tassel Brooch with its glittering tendrils. Victoria's favorite brooch was the one given to her by Albert on their wedding, a large, oblong sapphire surrounded by twelve large diamonds.[65] Exquisite diamond and emerald bracelets mingled on her wrists with gold chains, from which hung sentimental charms and lockets containing portraits of her children. Inevitably, upon her right arm, was a pearl bracelet set with an enamel portrait of Albert, which he had given to her for their first Christmas together.[66] Her hands sported a profusion of rings, including an enamel band set with a small diamond given to her by Albert on their first meeting; her engagement ring, in the form of a serpent set with an emerald; and her gold wedding band.[67] Victoria once explained that her rings "improved an ugly hand."[68]

Although Victoria rarely presided over state banquets, dinners at Windsor were far from small affairs. Most evenings, Victoria took her meals in the Oak Dining Room, seated at an octagonal table in a gilded armchair covered in crimson brocade, with a little table nearby for her gloves, handkerchief, and fan.[69] Even these private dinners included family members and a few courtiers.[70]

The occasional guests invited to Windsor by the lord steward to join the queen for the night were usually from the aristocracy or the diplomatic corps. "One was barely given twenty-four-hours' notice," recalled Consuelo, Duchess of Marlborough.[71] Mary King Waddington, wife of a diplomat, vividly recalled the experience. On arriving from London by train at Windsor Station, she found herself met by a footman and led to a waiting carriage that quickly conveyed her to the castle. Two footmen greeted her at the castle and led her up to her rooms, "a pretty apartment furnished in yellow satin, with beautiful pictures, principally portraits: a small salon with a bedroom on each side, bright fires burning, and a quantity of candles. They brought us tea, beautifully served all on silver, with thin bread and butter (no muffins or toast)."[72]

Guests were carefully briefed on what to expect and how to behave. The master of the household or a lady-in-waiting would arrive once the guests were settled, informing them of the other members of the party that evening and instructing them to be ready for dinner at eight-thirty; guests were not to speak to the queen unless spoken to by her first, and then were to confine their replies to the questions she raised.[73] The male guests wore uniform or knee breeches, silk stockings, and frock coats, while the women wore elaborate evening gowns.[74] The women, in particular, suffered, one noting that the public rooms of the castle were "so cold for low dresses."[75]

Guests usually gathered in the Grand Corridor; if there were more than a dozen guests, they waited for the queen in the Red Drawing Room, but there were no drinks offered; the men could not smoke, and the women did not sit for fear of wrinkling their gowns.[76] Although dinner was officially scheduled for nine each evening, Victoria was rarely on time, and often did not arrive before nine-thirty.[77] At a signal, a footman loudly announced, "The Queen!" and Victoria left her private apartments and entered the Grand Corridor on the arm of the munshi. There was no small talk before she led her guests to the dining room.[78]

For larger dinners, a regimental band from the Life Guards or the Foot Guards was usually stationed beneath an awning on the East Terrace below the open windows of the State Dining Room.[79] When the queen entered, a discreet signal from above prompted them to play the national anthem.[80] Throughout the meal, they serenaded the diners with a selection of light music; Victoria had a preference for the works of Schubert, although one of her favorite tunes stood in stark contrast to her often expressed intolerance of racial prejudice. This was a rollicking song called "Happy Darkies Workin' in the Field," an 1882 tune from the American South that extolled the virtues of plantation life for black slaves.[81]

"The table," noted Mrs. Waddington, "was handsome, covered with gold and silver plate." She took in the "quantities of servants in red livery, plain black, and two Highlanders in costume behind the queen's chair."[82] According to etiquette, only Victoria could initiate a conversation.[83] Talk, recalled Frederick Ponsonby, "was supposed to be general, but the custom was to talk to one's neighbor in very low tones, and those on the right and left of Her Majesty were the only ones who spoke up. A great deal therefore depended on what mood the Queen was in; when she was rather preoccupied and silent the dinner was a dismal affair, but when she was inclined to talk and interpose with witty remarks it went with a swing."[84] During her visit, Mrs. Waddington remembered, "The conversation was not very animated. The queen herself spoke little and the English guests not at all— or so low that one couldn't understand them."[85] And Lady Randolph Churchill recorded that during these dinners, "conversation was carried on whispers, which I thought exceedingly oppressive and conducive to shyness. When the queen spoke, even the whispers ceased. If she addresses a remark to you, the answer was given while the company listened."[86]

Victoria reviewed suggested menus every morning, but she rarely interfered in the chef's choices.[87] Even the most informal dinners usually consisted of ten courses.[88] Dinners always began with consommé or other soup; Victoria was partial to turtle soup flavored with sherry, but the kitchens also produced thick, creamy soups garnished with wine and choice bits of game.[89] A fish course always followed, either baked, broiled, or fried, and doused in rich, creamy sauces: Victoria enjoyed salmon in a claret sauce, and trout simmered in Chablis, but there were also dishes of oysters or lobster that she particularly liked.[90]

An entrée of game or fowl followed. Victoria had several favorites, including quail stuffed with foie gras and garnished with oysters, truffles, prawns, mushrooms, tomatoes, and croquettes; and breast of chicken garnished with a white cream and butter sauce.[91] Sorbets to cleanse the palate came next, flavored with port, brandy, or Victoria's favorite, rum. The *relevé*, or main course, came next; this usually consisted of roast beef, lamb, or pork, followed by a course of roasted game, and finally salads and vegetables.[92]

There were always several dessert courses, including trifles, puddings, petits fours decorated with sugared flowers, cakes, pastries, tarts, and ice creams. Dinners always ended with fresh fruit from the orchards and conservatories at Windsor: little baskets of spun sugar held fresh strawberries doused in vanilla cream custard, and Victoria enjoyed fruit compote served in champagne.[93] The queen also liked sweet pears, and oranges with their tops removed so she could scoop out the juice with a small golden spoon.[94] Every Sunday she had roast beef and her favorite German vanilla custard.[95]

A selection of wines accompanied the meal: butlers poured champagne, while the claret and sherry were handed around by the queen's pipe major. Victoria disliked beer and champagne, preferring ale; she always drank Scotch whiskey with soda water, distilled especially for her by John Begg.[96]

Victoria, recalled the Aga Khan, "ate and drank heartily." Rather than select from the hot and cold entrées and dessert courses, she piled her plate with each one, enjoying them with great relish, only to later complain of indigestion.[97] As sovereign, she was always served first; Victoria ate rapidly as her guests struggled to maintain conversation and make their way through the courses. Although dinners usually lasted ninety minutes, few guests were able to fully enjoy the culinary offerings.[98] When the queen had finished her course, footmen quickly moved in and cleared away all the plates, even as guests attempted to seize one last bite. As a result, they frequently left these dinners hungry. Once, Lord Hartington was in the midst of eating when a footman took his plate. "Here, bring that back!" he loudly yelled, startling the other guests and the queen, who concealed her girlish giggles behind a handkerchief as she said, "His Lordship has not finished. Put back his plate."[99]

On informal occasions, Victoria often received her guests in the Grand Corridor after the meal had ended. "I wondered why, with all the rooms the Castle possessed," recalled the Duchess of Marlborough, "we should be confined to this small passage."[100] Victoria, remembered Mrs. Waddington, "stood a few minutes talking to the two princesses, while she had her coffee (which was brought for her alone on a small tray)." After she took a chair, Victoria greeted all the guests, questioning them at length about their lives. "She sat on rather a low chair, and I standing before her had to bend down always. She was dressed in black, with her usual little cap and veil, opal necklace, diamonds, and orders. While she was talking to the others the two princesses moved about and talked to us. It was pleasant—the whole cercle lasted about an hour." When the queen and the two princesses had retired, the guests retreated to the Red Drawing Room, where they took coffee with the members of the household. By eleven the evening was deemed to have ended, and the guests retired.[101]

On other occasions, she would ask her guests to join her in the Green or White Drawing rooms. "She had an odd accent, a mixture of Scotch and German," remarked the Aga Khan.[102] She was not quite the dour and prim woman of myth: Victoria laughed uncontrollably when a deaf admiral, not realizing that the conversation had switched from his ship to his sister, declared his intention to have "her turned over, to take a good look at her bottom, and have it scraped."[103]

There were occasional concerts in the castle's Waterloo Chamber: the queen preferred light Italian operas, Wagner, Rossini, and Mendelssohn, and the company of the Royal Opera House, Covent Garden, also occasionally came to Windsor to perform for Victoria and her guests.[104] Such productions were complicated affairs: whole companies—actors, choristers, an orchestra, and stagehands—had to be brought down to Windsor by special train, and fed before the evening's entertainment. The guests would assemble in the Waterloo Chamber to await Victoria's arrival; wheeled through the Grand Corridor and down the length of St. George's Hall by the munshi, she would rise from her chair at the room's entrance and, escorted by two equerries, walk to her chair in the front row.[105] The room was not particularly suited to such concerts—Frederick Ponsonby noted that "the acoustics were not really good"—and on occasion, attempting to compensate, several singers bellowed so loudly that the queen winced.[106]

Victoria enjoyed the popular operas and musicals of the day. Her granddaughter Marie of Romania recalled sitting beside her during a special performance at Windsor of Bizet's *Carmen*, which the queen had never before seen. After watching the story, the queen was "delightfully, pleasurably scandalized." Holding her fan up to her face, she leaned over to her granddaughter and whispered, "I am afraid she's really not very nice!"[107]

The queen also enjoyed the less artistic entertainments of the day: "She liked lion tamers and midgets," wrote Stanley Weintraub, "waxworks and French farces, melodramatic operas and paintings of animals, sentimental novels and moralistic sermons."[108] At other times, members of the household and some of the royal family would present *tableaux vivants*, re-creations of historic scenes, paintings, or allegorical depictions of mythology. Victoria took a keen interest in these productions, selecting the material, editing it to eliminate any scenes deemed offensive, and supervising the costumes and the scenery.[109] Victoria would sit "a little forward" of the audience, "in a low armchair. A footstool is placed before her, and a small table holds her fan, opera glasses, program, and book of the words. The applause is always led by the queen, who taps either her hand or table with her fan."[110] Although she enjoyed these evenings, Frederick Ponsonby recalled that they were "very wearying for the audience, who had to sit for two-and-a-half-hours with very long intervals between the tableaux."[111] After the death of Prince Henry of Battenberg in January 1896, however, most of these tableaux stopped altogether.[112]

On other evenings, the queen and her guests would remain in the Green Drawing Room; occasionally Princess Beatrice, at her mother's urging, would play the piano, sometimes accompanied by a singer or a violinist. The women broke off into groups, playing cards, but the men—according to etiquette—were forbidden to sit in the queen's presence, standing together in a corner "in a very stiff way," recalled a lady-in-waiting.[113] Despite her age, Victoria was something of a night owl, and she enjoyed chatting with her guests and listening to their humorous stories. "Sometimes," recalled a courtier, "even the beautiful smile broke across her face in the wonderful way it does."[114] It took some stringent though gentle persuasion to attract Victoria's attention. When eleven came and went, the ladies began to fidget, and looked to Princess Beatrice to intercede with her mother by gently reminding the queen that the hour was late and her guests must be tired.[115] Eventually Victoria reached for her cane and, "as if by magic," the doors opened and the munshi appeared, taking her left arm and guiding her to her feet. Sensing freedom, the guests circled the small figure, bowing and curtseying to her and kissing her hand before the munshi led Victoria out of the room, followed by members of her family.[116]

By the time Victoria returned to her rooms, a wardrobe maid had laid out the queen's nightclothes; after removing her widow's cap, a maid brushed the queen's silver hair before Victoria turned to her journal, which had been placed on her desk and opened to the correct page so she could make her nightly entry.[117] Even as an elderly lady in precarious health, Victoria rarely retired before one-thirty in the morning.[118]

With Victoria retired from the festivities, the remaining guests were left to their own devices. More often than not, the men hastily retreated to the smoking room for a much-needed cigarette or cigar. Victoria's horror of smoking, noted Frederick Ponsonby, was ironic, as "all her family smoked like chimneys."[119] Even her granddaughters smoked, sneaking cigarettes and blowing the smoke up chimneys and out windows.[120] At Windsor, framed notices warned guests not to smoke, and Victoria even once chastised Frederick Ponsonby for sending her a batch of official cables he had deciphered while smoking, complaining of the lingering smell.[121]

At Windsor, Victoria only reluctantly allowed men to smoke in the billiard room, which she regarded as "a sort of opium den."[122] This in itself could be an ordeal, recalled one courtier, if the Duke of Edinburgh happened to be present, as "he talks about himself by the hour. Those who go are quite exhausted."[123] Prince Henry of Battenberg even gave up smoking for a time rather than endure his brother-in-law's constant pontifications.

By midnight, when the queen ordered the lights turned off, most of the servants had retired; the male guests, leaving the billiard room, were often left to find their own way through the cavernous castle. One man got so confused that he spent the night on a sofa in the Grand Reception Room; on discovering him in the morning, a housemaid thought he was drunk and summoned the police.[124] Another guest, hopelessly lost after hours of trying to find his room, resorted to simply opening random doors, only to walk in on a startled Victoria in a nightgown, having her hair brushed by a maid before she retired.[125]

6

LIFE BELOW STAIRS

FROM VICTORIA'S EARLIEST DAYS, SERVANTS had formed a part of her life. A small army took care of her family, ensuring that the court was always perfectly maintained. Hundreds of servants scrambled through the queen's residences, from the impressively attired liveried footmen and discreet maids to the lowest chimney sweep. They groomed her horses and drove her carriages; cut her lawns and adorned her rooms with flowers; cleaned her clothing and washed her linens; and prepared her food and served her at table. From the page who ushered guests through the immense castle and the boy who unloaded wagons of vegetables from the Home Farm to the maids who scrubbed the floors and the rat catcher checking his numerous traps, all performed integral jobs on which the queen's court depended. Their names were often unknown, their faces unfamiliar, the grueling hours of their labor unsuspected, and their duties never fully appreciated, but without their contributions the court would have ground to a sudden halt.

Victoria was something of an anomaly when it came to members of her domestic staff. It was inevitable, given her sheltered style of life, that she should have been unaware of the enormous gulf that separated her from the members of her staff. She had little idea of their work schedules; of the onerous duties they performed; of the sacrifices they made; indeed, she disliked being bothered with matters concerning the staff, leaving them in the hands of the master of the household.[1] "She accepted their services in a dispassionate, professional way," declared one contemporary, "and she ever, by preserving a quiet tone of decorum, checked any exaggerated expression of personal affection the moment that it was threatened."[2] When she sat down to dinner, the long hours of work that made it possible were unsuspected; when she retired to her rooms, it is doubtful that she gave a thought to the men and women still laboring in the kitchens and pantries below, washing, scrubbing, drying, and polishing china, silver, and crystal into the early morning hours. The aura of sybaritic majesty their efforts created formed an unalienable part of royal tradition and splendor, unquestioned and enshrined as the prerogatives of the monarchy.

At the same time, Victoria was adamant that all those in her employ be treated with respect. While never forgetting that she was queen, Victoria hated snobbery, and once declared that the "division of classes is the *one thing* which is most dangerous & reprehensible."[3] Victoria might not be aware of the vast majority of her servants or their labors, but she took a great interest in the lives of those who attended to her personally. She once referred to her domestic servants as "belonging to her family," insisting that they be treated with kindness and consideration.[4] "Her idea," recalled her grandson Ernst Ludwig of Hesse, "was that when people were well-bred and well-educated, they should know better than to make mistakes. But she would always forgive humble people, whatever they did."[5]

Servants were thus frequently indulged, and, as one member of the staff noted, there was "a good deal of laziness" among them.[6] Many of the footmen, recalled a lady-in-waiting, "smell of whisky and are never prompt to answer to bell."[7] There were, said Lady Lytton, many "sad cases of drink among the servants," but the queen always ignored such complaints.[8] A Mrs. Chapman, in charge of the linen room at the castle, was usually so intoxicated that by night it often seemed that she was "bordering on delirium tremens."[9] Victoria held no class prejudices, and treated errant members of the domestic staff as naughty children. One lamplighter at Windsor proved particularly difficult. Always drunk, one day he fell down a flight of steps with a lamp and accidentally set fire to the landing; when she learned of this, Victoria refused to dismiss him, commenting only, "Poor man."[10]

Hours for domestics were long, and often conditions were less than ideal. Although they were provided with accommodations at Windsor Castle and Buckingham Palace, there was nothing regal about their utilitarian rooms, which were furnished simply with a bed, a chest of drawers, a chair, and a wardrobe.[11] There were, however, compensations. Salaries in the queen's domestic household were often better than those in aristocratic establishments. Mrs. Henderson, the housekeeper at Windsor, received £112 a year (£8,466, or $14,476 in 2007 currency); chimney sweeps got £111 a year (£8,390, or $14,346 in 2007 figures); the rat catcher had £80 a year (£6,047, or $10,340 in 2007 currency); linen women received some £60 a year (£4,535, or $7,754 in 2007 currency); and upper housemaids had £45 a year (£3,401, or $5,815 in 2007 currency).[12] By contrast, an upper housemaid in an aristocratic establishment received roughly £25 a year (£1,889, or $3,230 in 2007 figures).[13]

In addition to free if sparse accommodations, servants also received a daily allowance, meals, and free medical treatment.[14] There were gifts at Christmas, and many servants collected tips from visiting guests that ranged from money to cigarette cases, jewelry, and other trinkets. Service anniversaries of ten and twenty years were marked with additional gifts, and when they retired, the servants could expect comfortable pensions and often free accommodations for life in any of the number of grace and favor apartments and houses kept by the crown at Kensington Palace, Windsor, St. James's Palace, and Hampton Court Palace.[15]

The domestic staff encompassed not only senior servants such as the housekeeper, but also the culinary staff; the pantry staff, including stewards, maids, porters, and kitchen boys; a household staff of livery porters, butlers, underbutlers, body linen laundresses, linen women, washers, and room maids; two florists; a department dedicated to furniture restoration, repair, and upholstery; fire lighters and a fire brigade; a dozen chimney sweeps; and a rat catcher and his assistant. Some two hundred individuals were permanently posted to Windsor, and another hundred members of the domestic staff followed the queen from residence to residence. Some indication of this mass of servants is indicated by the fact that some two thousand footmen alone were employed to attend to the needs of the court.[16]

Victoria's court in the 1890s bore the firm imprint of Prince Albert's reforming hand. Four competing departments controlled royal life when

Victoria first came to the throne: the lord chamberlain's department had charge of housemaids and pages, and the general operation of life inside the palaces; the lord steward's department held sway over the royal kitchens and their staffs; the master of the horse regulated footmen, underbutlers, and porters; and the Office of Woods and Forests was charged with the upkeep of the grounds and exteriors.[17]

This division of responsibilities led to a myriad of petty difficulties and vexations. If a fire was wanted, servants attached to the lord steward's office arranged the logs in the grate, but when Victoria asked them to light it, she was told that this was the duty of the lord chamberlain's department, and neither division dared infringe on the prerogatives of the other. Victoria either had to light the fire herself, or summon an official from the lord chamberlain's department to do so.[18] Maids attached to the lord chamberlain's department cleaned the inside of the windows, but only the Office of Woods and Forests was authorized to wash the exterior panes; there was no set schedule, and more often than not, only one side of the window would be cleaned at the same time. If a pane of glass in the kitchen was broken, the court's ponderous bureaucracy dictated five signatures from three different departments to replace it.[19]

In a bureaucracy as large as the British court, waste was inevitable. Thousands of unnecessary free meals were cooked and served, the provisions disappearing into parcels that members of the staff took home to their families. Requisitions for courtiers' carriages were forged and the vehicles used for personal transport or even hired out by cagey staff members.[20] All candles were replaced daily, whether they had been used or not; the discards disappeared into the pockets of footmen, who sold them in London.[21] Orders for household supplies were staggering: in one three-month period, nearly two hundred brushes, brooms, and mops were delivered, despite the fact that hundreds were already in use.[22]

Albert reformed the entire archaic operation, with the master of the household placed in general charge of all domestic matters, in an effort to eliminate petty squabbles over jurisdiction. Hundreds of redundant positions were eliminated, as were many of the traditional perks of royal employment. Servants were no longer allowed to sell extra food from the kitchens or provisions from the household; Albert replaced the white silk stockings of the footmen with cheap ones of cotton.[23] In a final effort to save money, he even decreed that the servants' toilets no longer be stocked with paper, but instead with newsprint, cut into squares and neatly strung on a wire between two nails.[24] The ensuing reforms guaranteed that the household ran more smoothly, but also earned the parsimonious Albert much scorn.

In the late spring and early summer, the gardeners at Windsor were out early, cutting grass, rolling the lawns, tending to the flowers, cleaning the fountains, and watering the intricate, colorful beds that stretched below the East Terrace. As the first rays of morning slanted across the battlements of the ancient castle, workers were already busy within. Before five, coal porters had gone through the kitchen, laying and lighting fires and bringing stores of fuel to last through the day.[25]

The coming of the new day also witnessed the arrival of a procession of carts rattling across the cobblestones of the castle's courts, conveying the daily provisions to the immense kitchen. The clerk of the kitchen, ledger in hand, stood by as the items were unloaded. On any given day there might be 200 legs of mutton or 250 lamb shoulders, all brought, at Victoria's orders, from Wales; enormous sides of beef and pork from the Home Farm at Windsor; several hundred chickens, pheasants, partridges, and quails culled from the royal estates; deer and venison from Scotland; fresh salmon, turbot, and trout; boxes of rare truffles from Italy; prawns, scallops, and oysters from Cornwall and Devon; enormous loaves of sugar, each weighing fourteen pounds; and, from the royal dairy in the castle park, trays of newly laid eggs, several hundred pounds of butter and cheese, and cans of fresh milk and cream.[26]

The twenty-five-acre kitchen garden just beyond Frogmore had been created in 1841 "to provide adequate supply for the needs of Her Majesty's Household."[27] Each morning, Owen Thomas, in charge of the kitchen garden, read through the requisition orders from the clerk of the kitchen, selecting vegetables from the serried rows of plantings, and flats of fresh fruit from the hothouses and orchards, including apples, melons, strawberries, peaches, pears, cherries, grapes, oranges, and lemons.[28] Once unloaded at the castle, the fruit and vegetables were carried to the green room for preparation.[29] All of these provisions, carefully checked by the clerk of the kitchen, weighed, and ticked off his inventory lists, fed only the royal family, the household, and the staff; when a state banquet took place, the amounts nearly doubled.[30]

The domestic offices at Windsor were on the ground floor of the northeastern block. The kitchen, lacking any exterior walls, rose two storeys between white-tiled walls to a medieval wooden hammer-beam ceiling set with a glass lantern; in appearance, recalled one cook, it resembled a chapel.[31] Albert had introduced gas lighting and stoves and an improved system of steam heaters, which helped solve one of the perpetual problems in the royal residences: cold food at the dinner table. There were twelve ranges, along with cast iron charcoal grills and two enormous open spits, turned by a chain-driven mechanism, that could take several legs of mutton and six chickens at once.[32] Chefs worked on steel-topped tables heated by steam pipes to keep the food hot, squeezed side by side with long, marble-topped tables for pastry and breadmaking; above, and adorning the ends of the room, hung a vast array of copper pots and pans, all polished to a gleaming sheen by the kitchen maids.[33]

The kitchen, recalled a member of the culinary staff, "had some of the discipline of the barracks room. There was hardly a conversation apart from the giving of orders connected with the dishes on which each master cook was working, and I never saw anyone lounging round or sitting down during a spell from work." The latter would have been impossible, as the *chef de cuisine* had ordered all stools and chairs removed from the cavernous room, "to discourage idleness."[34]

An adjoining pastry kitchen, under the direction of M. Delorme, the queen's *chef patissier*, was beneath the Grand Reception Room; here, all of the castle's breads, cakes, rolls, and pastries were made daily.[35] Beyond were hot, cold, and dry storerooms; the green room, given over to vegetables; a confectionary kitchen; a larder kitchen, where meat and game were prepared; the sculleries, where dishes were cleaned and pots scoured; and a fish room, with large tanks in which the seafood could be kept alive until it was time to prepare it.[36] An ice room, buried deep within the bowels of the castle's ancient undercroft, was lined with shelves holding block after enormous block of ice. These were cut from the Thames River and the castle's ponds in winter, and hauled by horse and cart to the storerooms, allowing a fresh and ready supply of ice throughout the summer; one man was specially employed to convey several of these blocks up to the kitchen and to the cold storeroom twice each day.[37]

The rest of the northeastern ground floor was given over to remaining domestic offices, including the linen room in the Brunswick Tower, adjoining two sewing rooms; the gold pantry and gold storeroom, beneath the State Dining Room; the silver storerooms, beneath the Red Drawing Room; the plate rooms, china, and glass pantries; the hamper room; and the castle vaults.[38] There were several domestic rooms in the vaulted undercroft below St. George's Hall, including the steward's room, rooms for the castle superintendent's staff; the footmen; the traveling yeoman of the guard; the sergeant footman; and the servants' hall.[39] Vaulted passages led to lamp rooms and coal storage vaults. There was also the florist's room and offices; here, early each morning, the chief florist presided over a staff charged with arranging the thousands of fresh flowers brought daily from the castle's cutting garden and conservatories into lavish bouquets, which the flower girls then distributed throughout the building's rooms.[40] Formal dinners and state banquets called for additional helpers, as thousands of flowers were needed to frame doorways, cascade from golden epergnes set upon tables, and grace mantels.

The chef de cuisine had his offices below the China Corridor; here, shelves held blue leather ledgers in which the queen's menus were diligently entered each day.[41] From these offices, M. Menager, the queen's chef de cuisine, ruled the kitchens with a benevolent iron fist. A tall, dashing Frenchman with a bushy gray mustache, Menager was the senior member of the domestic staff, and the only member of the kitchen staff to have direct contact with the queen. With his annual salary of £400 (£30,237, or $51,705 in 2007 currency) and a special allowance of an additional £100, Menager was the highest-paid member of the domestic staff; he lived in a fashionable mansion in London with his own servants and, with his reputation, could easily have sought more lucrative employment at one of London's premier hotels, but he relished his powerful position and continually refused all offers.[42]

Menager, recalled one of his apprentices, was "extremely easy to work with," but "he would not tolerate any of the tricks or effects which so many cuisine experts use to disguise faulty workmanship."[43] He once explained his culinary philosophy: "A chef is an artist. And like an artist, he strives constantly for perfection. But he has as difficult a task as any man who creates beauty from wood or stone, and there are no memorials to his art. His triumph is a momentary one, between the serving of a dish and the minute when the last few mouthfuls are taken. To achieve that short triumph he must expend all his skill and experience."[44] Despite these high standards, he was "a very fair man to work for."[45]

The chef de cuisine supervised a large culinary staff. Under him were eighteen master chefs, each with his own specialization; two assistant chefs; two roasting cooks; two pastry chefs; two confectionary chefs; two larder cooks; assistant cooks; six bakers; two yeomen of the kitchen; eight kitchen maids; six scullery maids; ten kitchen boys; six pot scourers; and four young kitchen apprentices, as well as the staffs attached to the various pantries.[46] Wherever the queen was in residence, a majority of this large contingent followed her.

As the chefs began work, Mrs. Henderson, the housekeeper, also commenced her day, assisted by the housekeeper of the private apartments, who had charge of the queen's personal rooms. Under their direction, an army of domestic servants cared for the castle and its inhabitants. Their lives were controlled and defined according to their place in the hierarchy of the royal household, where they fell into two ranks. Upper servants constituted both the group of personal domestic servants who attended the queen, and those who held positions of responsibility; lower servants rarely met the queen, carrying out their duties often anonymously. The most junior members of the household woke their superiors, and from this moment until they retired, the lines separating one caste from the next were deep and persistent, dictating the order of morning baths and the time and location of meals. Courtiers and senior members of the household who waited on members of the royal family were, in turn, waited on by other upper servants, who themselves were waited on by lower servants. The most junior servants served themselves.

Even before the queen was awake, Windsor hummed with activity, as the lower servants put on their uniforms and left their cramped rooms to make their way through the labyrinth of the castle to begin their duties.

Housemaids, who fell into four classes, were up at six, attired in their black cotton dresses and white aprons and caps to begin the day.[47] Spreading throughout the building, they replaced lamps and candles, beat and swept carpets, brushed and polished furniture, and scrubbed and waxed floors. If by accident they encountered the queen, they were expected to avert their eyes and look at the floor, to save Victoria the embarrassment of the encounter.[48]

Every morning, the fireplaces were cleaned, the ashes raked out, the fenders polished, and the grates black-leaded. Above them, clambering across roofs, the chimney sweep and his assistants checked the 249 chimneys at the castle; most were swept using machines, although there were still instances when young boys were employed, despite the government's prohibition on such child labor. Below them, Sam Bostick, the rat catcher, roamed through the warren of ground-floor rooms, checking his traps.[49]

In her small room high in the Chester Tower, Mary Tuck, the queen's first dresser, had been up since seven, awakened by a housemaid.[50] On the death of Emily Ditweiler, who had served as the queen's first dresser from 1859 to 1892, Tuck was appointed to the post, having worked under her as a dresser for several years.[51] Mrs. Tuck was nearly on constant duty, subject to the queen's demands and whims as well as the vagaries of her health. The stress took its toll, and she had something of a short nervous breakdown in the last years of the queen's life.[52] She supervised a staff of two assistant dressers who acted as Victoria's personal maids, and two wardrobe maids, who cared for her clothing.[53] Each morning, Mrs. Tuck and her assistants follow an elaborate ritual whose details were strictly laid out by the queen, from when she expected to be awakened and how her baths were to be drawn to the times when tea, hot water, and towels were to be brought into her dressing room.[54]

Even before Mrs. Tuck woke the queen, Victoria's dressing table had been set with all her toilette articles and perfumes. The wardrobe maid on duty collected the previous evening's attire, left in the dressing room, and delivered the first of the queen's numerous changes of clothing for the day. When the queen was ready, her coiffeuse was summoned to attend to her hair, brushing it and smoothing it with pomade oil.[55]

Throughout the day, these dressers and maids attended to the queen's clothes. Tears in gowns were mended, loose buttons resewn, fragile lace appliqués strengthened, and dresses ironed.[56] Items that needed laundering were carefully logged into a ledger and sent to the royal laundries at Kew, outside London; when they were returned the following day, the maid on duty recorded their safe return.[57]

As soon as the queen had left her rooms, the housemaids attached to the private apartments moved in to clean.[58] Working from detailed photographs of the rooms, maids removed objects from tables and dusted, carefully replacing them according to the photographic record.[59] The linen women followed, stripping beds, replacing used linen with fresh stocks, each piece numbered and marked with a crown and the royal cipher VR sewn in red thread, brought up from the linen room in Brunswick Tower, and carrying the items to be laundered back to the ground floor in wicker hampers.[60]

Pages, clad in their black and gold coats and black knee breeches, also were at work, under the supervision of the page of the chambers.[61] Beneath him were Wagenrieder and Robertson, Victoria's two pages of the presence.[62] It was their job to greet those arriving at the castle to see the queen and attend to them, as well as waiting on any royal visitors.[63] Victoria had three pages of the backstairs: two brothers, A. Thompson and W. Thompson, and Weir, who served as her personal messengers within the household.[64] The queen also had two personal footmen, who also acted as messengers and attended her during most meals.

The sergeant footman also dispatched his contingent of household footmen throughout the castle. Footmen performed a number of duties, including conveying messages; escorting guests to the castle and attending to their needs; acting as valet to any male guests without their own; decanting wine; and assisting in the service of meals.[65] For ceremonial occasions and state banquets they wore scarlet waistcoats adorned with gold, scarlet knee breeches, white stockings, and, most uncomfortably, cornstarch and flour, combed through their hair when wet to simulate a powdered wig.[66]

Throughout the day, at carefully set, staggered intervals, the domestic staff took its meals. The kitchens produced four different sets of meals each day: one set for the queen and her family; one for the members of the household; and one each for the upper and the lower servants.[67] These meals followed the strict hierarchical order of the court: aristocratic members of the household dined in the household dining room; regular members of the household took their meals in the equerries' room; upper servants, including the housekeeper, the chef de cuisine, the queen's dressers, butlers, pages, messengers, and the housekeeper and the maids of the private apartments, took their meals in' the steward's room; and the lower servants dined in the cavernous servants' hall, crowded together on uncomfortable, narrow benches.[68]

The quality and quantity of the food served also offered a hierarchical culinary contrast. While lower servants dined on three-course meals composed of rather simple ingredients, menus for members of the household were affairs nearly as elaborate as the meals laid on the royal table. They often ran to seven courses and included such dishes as *consommé d'orge à la princesse, filets de truite à la reine, zéphirs de volaille à la Renaissance, asperges sauce pommes mousseline, parfaits glacés à la Victoria,* and *soufflés à la Sax Weimar.*[69]

As evening approached, lamps were lit, candles in chandeliers set ablaze, and curtains pulled across windows.[70] The master of the household carefully planned the evening meal. Whether an informal dinner with the queen and her family, a larger meal with a dozen invited guests, or a magnificent state banquet, Lord Edward Pelham-Clinton drew up all the details, from invitations issued and the seating plan and menu to the services used and the number of staff required to attend during the meal.

State banquets took the most organization. Those involving visiting royals and their suites inevitably brought issues of protocol, all of which had to be settled by the lord chamberlain's department. The question of invitations was a delicate one; on several occasions, those who had been presented at court assumed that they now had the right of entrée to all palace functions, but Victoria firmly rejected their claim, saying that she was the sole arbiter.[71]

Once plans had been approved, arrangements were made to accommodate the guests, selecting the rooms to be open to them and determining the number of servants needed to attend to them. Most state banquets called for a large serving staff of more than a hundred footmen, pages, and underbutlers, who not only waited at table but also ushered guests through the castle. Liveries were selected and brushed, and, as a final ritual, the footmen received orders to "powder," an official designation for the wearing of white powder in the hair to simulate a wig. Towels were draped around shoulders, and, in a terrible ordeal, the wet hair was covered with a thick white paste that, when dried to a flaky consistency, resembled a white wig.

On the day of the banquet itself, carts loaded with extra provisions had already begun to arrive at the kitchen court at dawn; they were unloaded by porters and their goods were taken inside, where the staff was already at work. State dinners at Windsor usually took place inside St. George's Hall, whose long, narrow length could accommodate the most guests. Workers carried in sections of the long mahogany table; once fitted together, the leaves extended its length to seat 140. Gilded chairs, covered in crimson silk damask, were set alongside the table, spaced at careful intervals down its polished length. Maids prepared the adjoining Waterloo Chamber and Grand Reception Room to receive the guests, drawing curtains and assisting the flower girls as they carried in enormous arrangements to frame doorways and decorate chimneypieces. Cascades of roses, hydrangeas, lilacs, lilies, and orchids from the greenhouses in the Home Park mingled with tendrils of ivy and misted greenery in artful and fragrant displays.

Below, deep in the bowels of the castle, the yeoman of the royal cellars worked with his staff, selecting bottle after bottle of wine from the extensive, brick-walled vaults. A typical banquet might call for ten dozen bottles of champagne, used for toasts and for the dessert courses; fifteen dozen bottles each of white wine and a Burgundy; fifteen dozen bottles of sherry; and ten dozen bottles of vintage port. Loaded onto trolleys, these hundreds of bottles were wheeled through the basement labyrinth and transported to service rooms adjacent to St. George's Hall, to be readied and decanted for the evening.

Also working in their offices below, the yeomen of the glass, gold, china, and silver pantries prepared for the evening. A state banquet called for an intricate assortment of crystal, china, and silver, carefully selected by the master of the household working with the palace steward. These rooms, protected by iron doors, held glass cupboards filled with the queen's priceless collection of table services and ornaments.[72] The gold pantry, recalled one member of the queen's household, was "most magnificent and interesting. I could scarcely have imagined such a display of gold plate."[73] Here shimmered George IV's gold dinner service for 140, with nearly 400 gold plates rimmed with decorative borders, salvers chased with intricate designs, goblets, centerpieces, flatware, saltcellars, and dozens of multibranched candelabra.[74] Many of the gold dishes, along with silver gilt candelabra, were selected to adorn the table, and to form an exquisite backdrop of shimmering ranks arranged in a golden cascade against a curtain of crimson velvet adorned with an embroidered crown at the eastern end of the hall.[75] The entire collection weighed some five tons, and it took a small army of men to polish the pieces, using chamois cloths, before loading them onto carts to be wheeled through the castle.[76]

Most dinners were served on silver gilt plates and a range of china; a state banquet often called for a mixture of services and pieces. The oldest was the Furstenburg Service, a gift from Prince Carl of Brunswick to King George III, whose plates were painted with scenes depicting the Brunswick countryside. The Etruscan Service, of black and white accented in red and gold, had been a gift to George III from King Ferdinand IV of Naples in 1787. A number of services were associated with George IV: the Orléans Service, originally ordered in 1787 by the Duke of Orléans and later partially purchased by the prince regent; the Royal Worcester Service, of deep blue; and George IV's Sèvres Service, made between 1764 and 1770 in a vibrant blue and white. The Rockingham Service had been added by William IV, a colorful panoply of exotic scenes adorned with dragons. Victoria herself commissioned several services, the most notable being the 1877 Minton Service, designed in imitation of Sèvres in blue and white and emblazoned with her cipher VRI in gold at the center. There also were hundreds of pieces belonging to partial services, including eighteenth-century Meissen tureens and wine coolers, which were used for magnificent floral arrangements. Desserts usually were served on William IV's Garter Service, made by Worcester in 1830, emblazoned with the royal arms, and painted with the insignia of the Order of the Garter.[77]

Once the master of the household made his selection, the yeomen of the gold and silver pantries, and of the china and glass pantries, assisted by pages of the pantry, carefully loaded the thousands of pieces of china, silver, and crystal onto carts, listing each in the outgoing logbook before they were wheeled through the castle to St. George's Hall, where Lord Pelham Clinton and the palace steward supervised as the table was set. Once the table was assembled, an enormous white damask cloth, so heavy it had to be loaded onto a cart and wheeled from the linen room to St. George's Hall, was carefully spread along its length. Young men known as table deckers, feet clad in cloth boots and hands cloaked in gloves to prevent fingerprints, struggled across the tabletop, straining to move the heavy gold epergnes and centerpieces into their appointed positions before their branches were bedecked with floral displays and trailing streams of ivy. The center of the table might be filled with George IV's mirrored *plateaux*, adorned with gilded scrolls, laurel wreaths, and bunches of grapes, and set with silver gilt vases to hold arrangements of flowers. Albert had designed one of Victoria's favorite centerpieces, a massive silver gilt tableaux made by Garrard in 1842, nearly three feet tall and depicting four of their favorite dogs chasing a number of rodents around the base, including several sculpted, dead rats. After this came silver gilt vases, silver gilt candelabra, and Meissen and Sèvres wine coolers and soup tureens filled with intricate floral arrangements.[78]

Only when these elements were in place could the table finally be set. Place settings were complex compositions, each one often consisting of more than a dozen pieces of silver, each stamped with the royal crest.[79] Plates went atop chargers, followed by smaller plates circled by half a dozen different glasses for several wine courses, champagne, water, and port. A variety of crystal was used, including a two-thousand-piece Waterford service made in the eighteenth century, and a newer crystal service ordered by Victoria and etched with her cipher, all the pieces carefully polished and set in place by gloved footmen.[80] Individual saltcellars, elaborately decorated menus, and illuminated place cards fought for room, each plate, glass, and utensil positioned and laid out using rulers and wands to ensure uniformity.[81]

By nightfall, everything had been prepared. The table, its gleaming length of mahogany covered in a succession of exquisite china and silver and adorned with golden ornaments and cascading sprays of flowers, shone in the light of hundreds of candles. Fires in the adjoining rooms were lit, wax candles burned in chandeliers, sconces, and candelabra, footmen donned their state liveries of crimson and gold and pages their black knee breeches, white silk stockings, and black and gold waistcoats and tailcoats, and carpets were hastily brushed one last time to vanquish any trace of footsteps.[82]

Before the guests arrived, equerries, footmen, and pages took up their assigned positions: they received the guests on arrival at the castle's grand entrance, guided them to the Grand Staircase, and escorted them, according to rank, to one of the state apartments, offering drinks as they waited for the banquet to begin. Any special royal guests, as well as members of the queen's family, waited separately for Victoria to make her appearance to them. When she had done so, the royal procession quickly formed, headed by several officials preceding the queen, members of her family, and any other royal guests, all lined up and partnered according to strict precedence. At a signal, the procession headed into the state apartments, its coming heralded by a loud announcement and the hushed silence that fell over the waiting guests.

Victoria walked straight to St. George's Hall, passing through the state apartments between the rows of her guests, who followed behind her; to avoid any unseemly scuffle or hesitation, the seating plan had been carefully inspected. As soon as the queen was seated in her armchair, positioned at the middle of the table, an orchestra, concealed in a high gallery at the room's eastern end, began to play, and the palace steward, who stood directly behind her, signaled for service to begin. Menus for state banquets were usually twelve courses, beginning with consommé and a cream-based soup, served with a pale sherry, followed by the fish course. Usually this consisted of two dishes, and often included oysters, salmon, trout, or lobster grilled and served in a cream sauce, accompanied by a Mosel wine. The entrée was often roasted chicken, duck, or lamb, followed by the relevé, or main course, usually a fillet of beef or grilled pork accompanied by rich sauces. After this came a sorbet, usually flavored with brandy, port, or rum and served in crystal dishes, to refresh the palate. The naive guest who mistook the sorbet for the final course was often stunned when the second round of courses began, commencing with the *rot,* roasted game accompanied by a variety of sauces, and a selection of vegetables roasted and in sauces served with a Burgundy. A salad and a final savory dish, often a mousse of ham or game in aspic, concluded the lengthy procession of dishes, but a range of desserts soon followed: ice creams, petits fours, cakes, artful pyramids of pears, raspberries, peaches, plums, apricots, and grapes, and individual baskets of spun sugar set with vanilla custard and filled with fresh strawberries, all washed down with champagne.[83]

Between the ranks of yeomen of the guard, clad in their scarlet uniforms, Tudor ruffled collars, and black hats, pages, footmen, underbutlers, and wine butlers moved in and out of the hall, conveying course after course and collecting plates.[84] Once the dinner had ended, they attended to the guests in the state apartments as they waited to greet the queen, serving coffee, tea, and liqueurs. Once the doors to St. George's Hall were closed, they began the intricate process of cleaning away the remains of the banquet. The services were taken to the sculleries, to be washed and polished by the scullery maids, and the room disassembled. After the china, silver, and crystal were washed, and the gold pieces polished, they were returned to their pantries, where their respective yeomen inspected each piece for any damage before logging it back into their ledgers. The napkins and tablecloths were laundered, the kitchen cleaned, the floors washed and swept, and the fires doused, all before the hundreds of servants could extinguish the lights and sleepily retire to bed, to prepare for another day.

7

THE WAYWARD HEIR

A PALE DAWN BROKE OVER LONDON on the morning of Wednesday, July 22, 1896, its faint light washing over the sprawling city. Along the Mall, beneath the sheltering green leaves of St. James's Park, a crowd began to gather; as the hours passed, their attention turned expectantly to Marlborough House, where windows had burned with light throughout the night. From here, in a few hours, Princess Maud, the youngest daughter of the Prince and Princess of Wales, would leave for her marriage.

Behind Marlborough House's dark brick facade, adorned with white casings, quoins, and cornices by Sir Christopher Wren, the exquisite rooms were alive with activity. Princess Maud sat in a room upstairs as attendants rushed around her dressing table, carefully avoiding the train of her gown cascading across the carpet. A looking glass reflected Maud's slender and graceful form, a face set with clear blue eyes framed by luxuriant hair. In a nearby room, Princess Alexandra, the bride's mother, formed the center of her own universe of attendants as she prepared for the coming ceremony. Far away from the hustle of activity, comfortably surrounded by paneled walls, the Prince of Wales waited impatiently, his corpulent frame settled into a blue leather chair in his study; oriental carpets spread beneath a multibranched ormolu chandelier, and two narrow windows diffused soft morning light that caught the wisps of smoke rising in a cloud from the prince's ever-present cigar.[1]

The fat, bearded man in his study had been born Albert Edward on November 9, 1841; when he was less than a month old, the infant was created Prince of Wales, the traditional title borne by a male heir to the throne. Called Bertie within the royal family, he was a good-natured boy who suffered greatly under the weight of his parents' unrealistic expectations. "Other children are not always good," he once complained. "Why should I always be good? Nobody is always good."[2] Attempts at vivacity and imagination were stifled in the name of intellectual discipline. He was educated in isolation from other young boys and was not allowed any friends in an effort to restrict contact with those whose morals might not quite be up to his father's stringent standards. Although Albert deeply loved his son, both he and Victoria, as Giles St. Aubyn noted, "were only too conscious they were nurturing a future king."[3]

Bertie suffered in comparison with his older sister, Vicky, well aware that she was his father's favorite and that he was constantly measured against her. He was not a stupid boy, but his father insisted on an educational regime that left Bertie physically and mentally exhausted, irritable and frustrated, and feelings of unworthiness led to bursts of temper that left his tutors bewildered. Both parents blamed such behavior on the queen's Hanoverian ancestors and worried that their eldest son would follow in the footsteps of her "wicked uncles," ignoring the fact that neither Albert's father nor Albert's brother had been examples of moral rectitude.

As future sovereign, Bertie was expected to excel in every subject; to demonstrate a complete understanding of all issues that faced the country; and to willingly submit himself to the will of his father. It was an impossible standard, and Albert, as one historian noted, "was too stubborn and dogmatic to consider that he might be wrong."[4] Believing that any sign of sympathy would only encourage further weakness, both Victoria and Albert took to openly mocking their eldest son in front of both family and guests, referring to him as stupid.[5] In his mother's eyes, he would never be seen as worthy of his father. "*None* of you can *ever* be proud enough of being the *child* of such a Father," Victoria wrote to her son, "who has not his *equal* in this world—so great, so good, so faultless. Try . . . to follow in his footsteps and don't be discouraged, for to be really in everything like him *none* of you, I am sure, will ever be."[6]

At the end of his secondary education, Bertie went up to Oxford and completed his time at university at Cambridge; he did surprisingly well, though he was forbidden to associate with other students. His father noted: "He is lively, quick and sharp when his mind his set on anything, which is seldom, but usually his intellect is of no more use than a pistol packed at the bottom of a trunk if one were attacked."[7] In 1860 he was sent to Canada and the United States, where he was received with wild acclaim and much praised for his demeanor; although Victoria congratulated him on his return, inevitably she took her son's triumph not as his own personal accomplishment, but rather as an expression of "the liking they have for my unworthy self."[8]

After much pleading, Bertie entered the army, and was sent to a military camp near Dublin. He enjoyed the conviviality of his fellow officers and made friends easily, but also fell in with their frequent drunken carousals; one night, his friends smuggled a pretty young actress, Nellie Clifden, into his bed, and the prince lost his virginity.[9] Bertie's parents were horrified. Having worked tirelessly to redefine the image of the royal family into that of unimpeachable moral respectability, Albert now imagined the worst possible scenario, including a pregnant Nellie Clifden lodging a paternity complaint against the Prince of Wales in a court of law. The strain, the queen believed, had killed her husband, and she forever blamed Bertie for his father's premature death. "I never can or shall look at him without a shudder!" she wrote of her son shortly after her husband's death.[10]

Even before the Clifden affair, both Victoria and Albert had believed that their eldest son must be quickly married to a suitable princess who would, it was hoped, calm his character. Several potential brides were considered before the choice fell on Princess Alexandra, whose father, Prince Christian of Schleswig-Holstein-Sonderburg-Glucksburg, had recently ascended the Danish throne as King Christian IX. Born in 1844, she was young and beautiful, Protestant, and amenable to the idea of marriage to the Prince of Wales. A meeting was arranged, and Bertie was quickly taken with her, though theirs was, to all purposes, an arranged marriage, a union contracted not for love but for duty. "I frankly avow to you," Bertie wrote to his mother, "that I did not think it possible to love a person as I do her. She is so kind and good and I feel sure will make my life a happy one."[11]

Victoria wanted a quiet, private wedding; she refused to acknowledge that it was an occasion for public interest and rejoicing, and continually interfered in its arrangements. Finally, in exasperation, *Punch* declared that as the ceremony appeared of so little importance, the *Times* of London should carry a simple announcement to mark the occasion, that "Albert Edward England" had married "Alexandra Denmark."[12] But the marriage of the future king and queen of Great Britain could not so easily be dismissed, and on March 10, 1863, Bertie married his princess in St. George's Chapel, Windsor. The day before the wedding, the queen had led him and his bride to the royal mausoleum at Frogmore and, standing before her husband's tomb, said somberly, "He gives you his blessing."[13] She refused to take part in the actual wedding ceremony, although she watched—draped in black—from Catherine of Aragon's closet above the chapel's high altar.

The new Princess of Wales soon eclipsed her husband in the affections of the British public. Tall and elegant, she rarely made a mistake, fulfilling her duties with good humor and a fragile grace. One diplomat called her "the most beautiful person I had ever seen."[14] With her zest for life and vivacious character, she stood apart from the rest of the royal family; while many saw her as simple and childlike, these very qualities endeared her to her adopted country.

The couple was installed in Marlborough House on the Mall in London, a magnificent mansion built in the eighteenth century by Sir Christopher Wren. The prince filled his rooms with Oriental carpets, leather sofas, tiger skins, horns, walking sticks, and a plethora of ashtrays for his endless stream of cigars, while Alexandra luxuriated in salons adorned with elaborate plaster reliefs and crammed with family paintings and photographs, small souvenirs, and a profusion of potted palms. They also had a new country residence, Sandringham, which Albert had selected before he died, in the hope that its remote situation at the edge of Norfolk would keep Bertie away from the licentious temptations of London.

Alexandra gave birth to two sons, Albert Victor in 1864 and George in 1865, but after the birth of her first daughter, Louise, in 1867, she developed rheumatic fever and thrombosis, which left her with a limp, and a latent deafness, inherited from her mother, Queen Louise, appeared.[15] She was still in her early twenties when she began to lose her hearing, and the effect was profound. Where once she had enjoyed the dinner parties and balls so beloved by her husband, Alexandra now found that she was unable to follow conversations, leading to a belief that the princess was rather dim. As the disease took hold, she began to withdraw from society, preferring the company of her children and a few trusted friends who, aware of her difficulties, ensured that they were understood.

Alexandra's illness marked a sharp downturn in her marriage. Bertie had embarked on the union with the best intentions, but his wedding vows fell victim to his impulsive nature and intrinsic selfishness. The contrast was vivid: he had a beautiful wife, worshipped and adored by all, but he turned to a series of affairs with society beauties to seek comfort. "Alexandra," noted one writer, "was too simple-minded, too inexperienced and young" to cope with her husband.[16] The queen, while not condoning her son's actions, ultimately laid the blame on her daughter-in-law. "He wants a cleverer and better informed wife to amuse and occupy him," she confided.[17]

The fact that the Prince of Wales took a series of mistresses was not unusual; his predecessors had certainly done so, and ultimately he only followed in their footsteps. As the interests of the couple diverged, he broke away from the last vestiges of propriety that kept him bound to his wife and sought entertainment elsewhere. Victoria and Albert had attempted to shroud the monarchy in a veneer of moral respectability, but their values and virtues were more recognizable to the middle and lower classes than to the aristocracy or members of the establishment, who had always indulged in affairs and sybaritic pleasures. Bertie was simply returning to form, which is one reason why his support among the last two groups never wavered.

Most of his ordinary future subjects, however, felt differently. The first real scandal came with the case of Lady Harriet Mordaunt, popularly believed to be among the Prince of Wales's mistresses. When she gave birth to a son in February 1869, her husband, Sir Charles, was certain that he was not the father, and she allegedly confessed her adultery with the Prince of Wales and several of his friends. When the pair divorced a year later, the Prince of Wales was forced to appear in a public court to deny an adulterous affair. Lady Mordaunt was conveniently declared insane and removed to an asylum, but the public was outraged, and Bertie was wildly hissed and booed.[18]

Alexandra's attitude toward her husband's mistresses was never consistent, and seemed to alter over time. She was tolerant of his affair with Lillie Langtry, who was discreet despite the fact that Bertie showered her with obvious gifts. "I've spent enough on you to buy a battleship," he once supposedly told her. "And you've spent enough in me to float one," came Lily's waggish reply.[19] But Alexandra was secure in the knowledge that no matter how many women her husband might bed, she would one day be crowned queen at his side. She consoled herself with the belief that the other women were merely temporary diversions and that there was no emotional bond between them and her husband. "He always loved me best," she once commented, and her words may, in fact, have reflected her husband's ultimate feelings for her.[20]

Things took a turn for the worse in 1891, at the height of Bertie's affair with the young and beautiful Daisy, Lady Brooke, the future Countess of Warwick. Bertie had treated previous affairs as temporary diversions, but Daisy captivated him, and he even gave her a "wedding ring." Known by the rather unflattering epithet of "the Babbling Brook," Daisy spoke openly of the liaison, and the scandal reached its height that summer, when Lady Brooke convinced Bertie to retrieve a compromising letter she had written to her former lover Lord Charles Beresford. It was found by Beresford's wife, whom the Prince of Wales cajoled and threatened; there were rumors that Lord Charles had stormed into Marlborough House and actually struck Bertie during an argument.[21] At the height of the sordid affair, some wag circulated an anonymous pamphlet titled *Lady River*, a thinly veiled reference to Lady Brooke, which soon became required reading among the aristocratic elite.[22]

The Princess of Wales retaliated in her own fashion. A holiday with her parents in Copenhagen grew longer as the weeks passed, and, near the end of October 1891, she unexpectedly left for Russia, to celebrate her sister Empress Marie Feodorovna's twenty-fifth wedding anniversary; in so doing, she blatantly absented herself from her husband's fiftieth-birthday celebrations.[23] "I was so angry about Lady Warwick," she commented later, noting that her husband "expostulated with me and said I should get him into the divorce court." Hearing this, she recalled, "I told him once and for all that he might have all the women he wished, and I would not say a word."[24]

By the time of his mother's Diamond Jubilee, Bertie had grown into a corpulent, graying man, whose 250 pounds and 48-inch waist sat uneasily on his 5-foot 7-inch frame. To combat boredom he threw himself into a hedonistic life of parties and indulgence. He ate five times a day, demolishing an inordinate amount of food; smoked several dozen cigarettes and a dozen cigars each day; and had a taste for fine alcohol.[25]

"Being one of the most human of men," recalled a member of his court, "he had his foibles and his failings. He was not gifted with a creative imagination, but had trained his mind and his memory to compensate what he knew himself to be a not naturally receptive brain."[26] He shared with his wife a rather absurd sense of humor: "Bertie's idea of a good joke," wrote one chronicler of his marriage, "was to tuck a dead seagull into the bed of a friend who had retired the worse for drink."[27] For all of his equanimity, Bertie possessed a terrible temper: he regularly berated his valet over minor incidents, more out of frustration at the enforced impotence of his role than any real anger.[28] But the smallest accident could set him off. Once, during dinner, the prince dropped a bit of spinach on the front of his starched white shirt. According to his nephew Prince Nicholas of Greece, he "got so cross with himself that he smeared it all over his shirt."[29]

Although Victoria complained about him, mother and son shared a number of qualities, including a shrewd if not bookish intellect, great personal charm, and lack of prejudice. "With a dignified presence, a fine profile and a courtly manner," recalled one courtier, "he never missed saying a word to the humblest visitor, attendant or obscure official. He would enter a room and, with the skill of an accomplished billiard player, look forward several strokes ahead, so that no one was left out. The appropriate remark, the telling serious phrase and the amusing joke accompanied by a gurgling laugh to a close friend made all delighted even to watch him."[30] With his homburg hats, capes, and walking sticks, he set a standard of personal style that influenced trends, and he took pride in his attire. At Sandringham, or visiting aristocratic friends at country houses, he indulged his love of shooting, killing hundreds of birds in a single day.

For Bertie, money and conviviality were enough to open society's doors, though his choice of companions occasionally led to scandal. In 1890, at the height of his affair with Lady Brooke, he joined a weekend party at Tranby Croft, the Yorkshire house of a friend, where a fellow guest was caught cheating at baccarat. The scandal soon leaked to the press, along with the identity of the guilty party, Sir William Gordon Cumming, who instituted a libel suit. For the second time in his life, the Prince of Wales was called to the witness box to give evidence in a British court case. This earned Bertie much scorn, and he was openly condemned in one paper as "a wastrel and whoremonger."[31]

To Victoria, it was all further evidence of her son's moral weakness. Even as a rather corpulent, middle-aged man, Bertie was constantly judged against his father's character and accomplishments, and to the queen he failed on every count. Ironically, for a woman who so adored everything that her husband had done, Victoria's treatment of her eldest son only undermined what Albert had intended. Whereas the prince consort had done everything to prepare his eldest son for a life of public and national service, the queen refused to allow her son any real responsibilities. She met suggestions that he assume a more public role on her behalf with horror; nevertheless, she recognized the inevitable, and in 1892 finally allowed him access to state papers. For his part, Bertie did everything in his power to please his mother, and he even dropped his high style of living to win her confidence. Ultimately Victoria realized that he possessed a talent for foreign affairs and a brain capable of offering reasoned advice. By the last decade of his mother's reign he had settled into a comfortable routine, where his public and private pursuits fell easily into carefully confined compartments.

This state of affairs—the self-indulgent, frequently absent husband, and the self-obsessed, attention-starved wife—played itself out as the couple raised their five children (a sixth, a son named Alexander, was born in 1871 but lived only a day). Like most royal children, the Waleses' princes and princesses were often left in the care of nannies and nurses; but mindful of his own tormented youth, Bertie made concerted efforts to befriend his children, although his concern rarely extended to interest in their upbringing or education. Alexandra was equally doting, but she fully encapsulated the very worst traits of the Victorian era. Rather than treat her children with benign neglect and leave them in the care of the nursery staff or tutors, she interjected herself into every aspect of their lives. Alexandra was the most possessive and jealous of mothers; while showering her children with unceasing attentions, she quite literally dominated them, attempting to confine them in a protective cocoon of innocence and immaturity. Having lost control of her husband, she became determined to maintain her hold on the only aspect of their shared life that remained to her, their children; she treated them in a parasitical manner that allowed her to draw strength and self-worth from her dominance. In a candid moment, her son George declared that his mother was "one of the most selfish people I know."[32]

Bertie's diffidence toward their overall education, when combined with his wife's indifference, ultimately led to a sad series of unnecessary failures. Bertie fatefully abandoned most of his say in his children's education to his wife, and Alexandra—following the rather carefree nature of her own education in Copenhagen—exerted a disastrous and meddling influence. Lessons were regularly interrupted for the most minor of excuses, from wishing to have the children at luncheon or tea, to having them accompany her on her afternoon drives, to providing her with companionship during her frequent visits to Denmark. The end result meant that none of the children of the Prince and Princess of Wales was left with a comprehensive education, and they even fell far behind the disappointing standards their father had managed to achieve. Their knowledge of history was spotty, and of languages—one skill required of their position—they had only cursory ability in French and German.

Prince Albert Victor, known as Eddy, was born prematurely, in January 1864. His premature birth may have contributed to the difficulties he later experienced, and he seems to have inherited a hint of his mother's deafness, which made him a diffident pupil. Alexandra herself charged her younger son with looking after his older brother, urging him not to quarrel but to help him. Together, the brothers entered the Royal Navy as cadets, sailing aboard *Britannia* and later the training ship *Bacchante*. To Queen Victoria, she explained that Eddy's disposition "is really an excellent one, and he is a very good boy at heart, though perhaps he is a little slow and dawdly."[33]

After his naval training, he completed his secondary education and went to Trinity College, Cambridge. He was popular, though the lessons apparently made little impact. James Pope-Hennessy famously described him as "backward and utterly listless. He was self-indulgent and not punctual. He had been given no proper education and as a result he was interested in nothing. He was as heedless and as aimless as a gleaming gold fish in a crystal bowl."[34] Eddy, according to one university friend, confessed to "being rather afraid of his father, and aware that he was not quite up to what his father expected of him."[35] Nor did a stint in the army prove beneficial. His commander was shocked that his new charge knew nothing of military theory or the Crimean War and was hopeless at drill. Although Eddy enjoyed his time mixing with his fellow officers and drinking late into the night, he did not manage to absorb any real skills.

Eddy was an enigmatic young man; those who knew him admired his thoughtfulness, his genial nature, and his sweet temperament. Handsome and thin, with an extremely long neck, he had a languid air about him that drew many admirers; but, like his mother, he remained naive and childish, and he seems to have fallen in with a disreputable crowd at Cambridge and in the military. He liked drinking, smoked constantly, and contracted gonorrhea, presumably from his wild nights.[36] He was rumored to keep a mistress in St. John's Wood whom he shared with his brother, George; more ominously, it was whispered that he frequented a certain club in Cleveland Street where gambling was succeeded by male prostitutes. When the police raided the establishment, Eddy's apparent connection with the club seeped out, and London gossips relished the irony of the virile Bertie's son having apparently given way to similar pursuits with young men.[37]

Queen Victoria tried to encourage Eddy to marry his first cousin Alix of Hesse, but the high-minded princess, in love with the future tsar Nicholas II, refused him. Eddy then turned his attention to the Catholic Princess Hélène, daughter of the Comte de Paris, pretender to the French throne; when her father refused to consider the necessary change of religion, and the pope threatened excommunication, the burgeoning romance came to a crashing halt. If Hélène was Eddy's grand passion, he quickly recovered, and he became obsessed with Lady Sybil St. Clair Erskine; when this potential romance failed, he allowed himself to be pushed into an engagement with a distant relative, Princess Mary of Teck.

Their relationship was short-lived. In early 1892, Eddy—now created Duke of Clarence by his grandmother—fell ill at Sandringham. Alexandra brushed it aside as nothing more than a normal cold, but his brother, George, himself recovering from typhoid, urgently summoned the physician Sir Francis Laking, who diagnosed influenza and incipient pneumonia. Eddy lingered in increasing agony for several days before dying on January 14, 1892, just five weeks before his wedding was to have taken place. When he was interred in the Albert Memorial Chapel at Windsor, his coffin carried Princess Mary's unused bridal wreath of orange blossoms.[38]

George became heir presumptive on his brother's death. With a surprising show of will, he rejected Queen Victoria's request to change his name to Albert.[39] George had fallen in love with his first cousin Princess Marie of Edinburgh, but she married the future King Ferdinand of Romania. Now he was essentially pushed into a union with his dead brother's fiancée. Queen Victoria pushed aside objections on romantic grounds, remarking candidly that Mary herself "was never in love with poor Eddy," and there was a family precedent, as Alix's sister Dagmar had married the brother of her fiancé Nicholas when the latter unexpectedly died.[40] Ever dutiful, George complied and proposed, and Mary—clearly recognizing this amazing second chance to one day become queen—accepted.

George, created Duke of York by his grandmother, wed Princess Mary at the Chapel Royal, St. James's Palace, in July 1893. The union, like the engagement between Eddy and Mary, was a dynastic match, without considerations of love or personal feeling; that the pair eventually came to love one another was fortunate, but it was certainly not the case in many arranged marriages. Until his marriage, George had been an unassuming, rather carefree young man, poorly educated but affable and a devoted son, but he gradually became noticeably stiff and brusque, qualities only exacerbated when he eventually took the throne as King George V. Somewhat cold, and plagued with inferiority from an impecunious childhood, Mary found her new role difficult. She lacked the social graces of her mother-in-law and, as one courtier recalled, found it an ordeal to engage in the usual conversation that followed royal evenings.[41]

Things began badly when, in the midst of their honeymoon, the new Duke and Duchess of York learned that his mother, Alexandra, and his sisters had come to stay with them.[42] Alexandra, deeply shocked at the loss of Eddy, was determined not to let her only surviving son escape, and George, caught between his oppressive mother and his stubborn wife, tried to please both proud women. "There is a bond of love between us," Alexandra admonished her son, "that of mother and child, which nobody can ever diminish or render less binding—and nobody can, or ever shall, come between me and my darling Georgie boy."[43] George and Mary's first child, Prince Edward (the future king Edward VIII and later the Duke of Windsor) was born in the summer of 1894, ensuring the succession to the throne. When a second son arrived on December 14, 1895, the parents were horrified that he had been born on the anniversary of the prince consort's death; in an effort to appease Queen Victoria, they named him Prince Albert (later King George VI).

The three daughters of the Prince and Princess of Wales also suffered from their mother's oppressive regime, "imprisoned in their mother's boudoir," wrote Anita Leslie, or the "horrific gilded cage of Sandringham."[44] The trio were known derisively as "the Hags," and Queen Victoria constantly worried that the Wales princesses were being stifled by their mother.[45] When she confronted her son on the issue, Bertie told her that "Alix found them such companions that she would not encourage their marrying," adding that he was "powerless" to intervene.[46] The real problem, as Theo Aronson noted, was that Alix "had become far too dependent on her daughters to bear the thought of them leaving her."[47]

Louise, the eldest, was treated as a child well into womanhood; her mother arranged her nineteenth birthday party to include childish games more appropriate for the nursery.[48] Like her sisters, she felt stifled in this rarefied atmosphere, and all of them suffered from constant complaints of headaches and exhaustion, as if illness became a companion to help them pass their days. Louise found most social occasions a terrible ordeal and hated greeting guests and making idle conversation. Her prime interest seems to have been fishing, and she was never happier than when in the country, standing along the bank of some river, casting her line.[49] A cousin remembered her as "extremely shy and retiring," adding, "Her one terror was to be spoken about, or to have people know what she did or said."[50]

In 1889, Louise became the first of the Wales children to escape from their mother's influence when she married Alexander Duff, the sixth Earl of Fife, whom Queen Victoria raised in the British peerage as the first Duke of Fife. At forty-nine, the new duke was twenty-seven years his bride's senior, prematurely balding, and scarcely a prize catch, but Louise seemed desperate to win any available freedom. The couple had two daughters: Alexandra, born in 1891, and Maud, born in 1893. After her marriage, Louise lived quietly; she refused to use the style of "Her Royal Highness," had no ladies-in-waiting, and spent her days at East Sheen Lodge in Richmond Park and at Mar Lodge, secluded in the Highlands near her grandmother's Balmoral Castle.[51]

Victoria, born in 1868, suffered most from her mother's determination to keep her children at her side. Called Toria in the royal family, the young princess became, as one cousin recalled, "a glorified maid to her mother. Many a time a talk or a game would be broken off by a message from my Aunt Alix, and Toria would run like lightning, often to discover that her mother could not remember why she had sent for her."[52] She had no life of her own, and Alexandra expected that she would remain with her as a constant, unmarried companion, a servant to her mother's selfishness. Although not as physically attractive as her sisters, Toria possessed a fine figure and a devastatingly black sense of humor.

She had the misfortune to fall in love with a Liberal MP, Lord Rosebery, a dignified, older widower. Their relationship was fraught with difficulties, not the least of which was that her father was vehemently opposed to it. But the story circulated widely in London, and newspapers even speculated on an engagement. In the end, despite Toria's feelings, nothing came of the flirtation. Toria later confided that Rosebery "would have been perfect" for her, but that the idea of marriage had been firmly vetoed. "We could have been so happy," she said through her tears.[53] Toria lacked the resolution to insist on her own happiness, but she became increasingly bitter over her situation as the years passed, and vented much of her frustration on her sister-in-law the Duchess of York, joining her mother in making snide, hurtful comments that stung Mary deeply.[54]

Only the youngest daughter, Maud, born in 1869, seems to have enjoyed a relatively happy childhood and youth. With her adventurous streak and somewhat wild manner, she was her father's favorite child, quick-witted, amusing, and without a hint of affectation or false sophistication, "always full of life and laughter," recalled one acquaintance.[55] Known as "Harry" in the royal family after a particularly brave admiral, she possessed a tomboyish love of riding and sporting pursuits. She was also the most beautiful of the sisters, and a great favorite within the royal family.[56]

Now, on the morning of July 22, 1896, Maud sat before her dressing table, robed in her magnificent gown, as she prepared for the journey to Buckingham Palace to marry her prince. For several years she had been hopelessly in love with Prince Francis of Teck, brother of her sister-in-law Mary. Dashing and sophisticated, the prince was known for his outspoken manner; he also was perpetually impoverished from gambling, and constantly begging loans from family members. Such a man might well have embraced the idea of marrying the daughter of the future king, but he ignored Maud's discreet overtures in favor of a liaison with a much older, married woman, to whom he was utterly devoted.[57]

Eventually Maud's thoughts turned to her cousin Prince Carl. At twenty-six, she was three years older than her prospective groom, but the prince was handsome and convivial, and the pair got along well together. Carl had known his cousin Maud since childhood; in marrying his bride, Carl's aunt the Princess of Wales also became his mother-in-law. As a younger son of Crown Prince Frederik of Denmark and his wife, Princess Louise, he had few prospects and even less money; most of his time was devoted to the Danish Royal Navy. "His charming manners, fine appearance, and amiable disposition, which predisposed everyone in his favor, had won him many friends," recalled his cousin Prince Nicholas of Greece.[58] The young couple had spent happy summer days together in Denmark, when the Princess of Wales took her family and returned to holiday with her parents. Maud found her cousin attractive but was uncertain of his feelings for her. Carl himself confided to a friend: "I am very much

The East Wing at Windsor Castle, viewed from the sunken garden in an early-twentieth-century view. At the extreme left is the Victoria Tower, on the first floor of which were the queen's sitting room and her bedroom. The Blue Room, where Prince Albert died in 1861, is on the first floor of the second tower to the left, followed by a suite including the White Drawing Room, the Green Drawing Room (in the third tower from the left), the Crimson Drawing Room, and the State Dining Room in the tower at the far right.

A late-nineteenth-century view of the Throne Room at Windsor, showing Queen Victoria's ivory throne.

A late-nineteenth-century view of the Waterloo Room at Windsor, with its table set for a state banquet.

A late-nineteenth-century view of the Grand Reception Room at Windsor.

Queen Victoria's sitting room at Windsor.

Queen Victoria at breakfast in the Oak Dining Room at Windsor, 1895. With her are her youngest daughter, Princess Beatrice; Prince Henry of Battenberg (Liko), Beatrice's husband; and three of the couple's children. Two of the queen's Indian servants stand behind her.

Queen Victoria's
Tea Cottage at
Frogmore.

The Prince and
Princess of Wales
(Bertie and Alix) on
their wedding day,
March 10, 1863.

The Prince of Wales,
about 1875.

The Princess of Wales,
about 1881.

Prince Albert Victor (Eddy), the Duke of Clarence, eldest son of the Prince of Wales, who died in 1892.

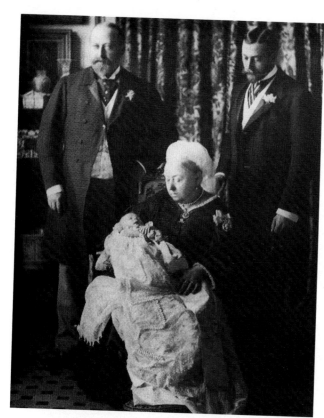

Queen Victoria at the christening of her great-grandson Prince Edward of York (the future king Edward VIII and later Duke of Windsor), with the Prince of Wales (the future Edward VII) and the Duke of York (the future George V), 1894.

Photograph commemorating the wedding of Princess Maud of Wales to Prince Carl of Denmark, July 22, 1896.

Balmoral.

The visit of Nicholas II of Russia to Balmoral, 1896. Queen Victoria sits next to her granddaughter Empress Alexandra, who is holding her daughter Grand Duchess Olga, while Nicholas II and the Prince of Wales stand at the rear.

in love; you know that I for many years have highly esteemed one of my English cousins, and now she is more charming than ever."[59]

Things changed in the autumn of 1895. During her holiday in Denmark, Maud spent a great deal of time with her cousin and, on October 22, Carl finally worked up the courage to propose. He was also agreeable to the idea of spending a considerable portion of each year in his wife's homeland, though in another decade he—with Maud at his side—would ascend the newly created Norwegian throne as King Haakon VII.[60] In a letter to a cousin, she wrote in surprise that Carl "really liked me for 3 years, but I never thought that it would last & that he would forget everything when he went to sea, but instead of that when he met me in the autumn again it became more so, & finally ended in this happy way!"[61] Others, however, were more cynical. A relative complained that Carl "looks *fully three years younger* than Maud, has *no* money," and speculated, "Maud does not care for him enough to leave England for his sake and live in Denmark, and I dread her finding this out when too late."[62]

The wedding took place in the private chapel of Buckingham Palace. It was, the *Times* of London noted, a fine day, with a "cool and pleasant breeze." At eleven-thirty, as the guns of the Royal Artillery fired in salute from nearby St. James's Park, the groom left Marlborough House and drove in a carriage, surrounded by an escort from Her Majesty's Life Guards Regiment, the short distance down the Mall to Buckingham Palace. The length of the route was lined by members of the Life Guards and the Coldstream Guards, who stood at intervals along the pavement between lines of police who held back the crowd of thousands who waved Union Jacks and Danish flags.[63]

The groom was followed by a procession of carriages that conveyed his brothers, followed by all of the bride's English relatives, with the exception of Princess Beatrice and her children, who were still in mourning for Prince Henry of Battenberg. The Princess of Wales, in a pale gray dress that accentuated the diamonds flashing in her collar *resille* and sunburst Russian fringe tiara, followed with her daughter Toria and her nephew Prince Nicholas of Greece. "The cheering and waving of hats and handkerchiefs was tumultuous," the *Times* reported.[64]

At twelve-ten, the gates of Marlborough House again swung open, and the bride appeared, riding in an open landau with her father, the Prince of Wales, who wore the crimson and gold uniform of an army field marshal, and her brother, the Duke of York, in a British naval uniform. As her escort of Life Guards rode out, a nearby band struck up "God Save the Queen," the guns in St. James's Park again fired salutes, and the crowd erupted in cheers.[65]

At Buckingham Palace, guests were ushered along the ribbons of crimson carpet and through the Marble Hall to the private chapel. Members of the royal family, including the bridal party, waited in the Bow Room, overlooking the garden.[66] When the guests had assembled, the queen arrived, wheeled into the Bow Room by an Indian servant. She wore a black satin gown embroidered with jet, with the blue sash of the Order of the Garter across the bodice and a lace veil trailing from her diamond diadem.[67] Escorted by two women of the bedchamber—the Honorable Harriet Phipps and Louisa, Lady Antrim—as well as the Duchess of Buccleuch as mistress of the robes and Lord Lathom, the lord chamberlain, the queen was pushed in her wheelchair through the semistate apartments to the chapel vestibule, where the great officers of state awaited her arrival. The lord great chamberlain, his stave of office in hand as he walked backward, preceded Victoria, who walked on the arm of her grandson Prince Christian of Schleswig-Holstein into the chapel, taking her place in an armchair near the altar.[68]

Although just over four hundred guests had been invited to the wedding, the private chapel could accommodate only a hundred people. To allow the majority of the guests views of the processions, a large white canvas tent was erected on the western terrace between the Bow Room and the entrance to the chapel; here, below awnings fringed in red and columns woven with white and red roses set amid potted palms ornamented with white ostrich plumes, four hundred gilded chairs were arranged along an aisle of crimson carpet, filled with those who could not fit into the chapel.[69]

At twelve-thirty, a band from the Coldstream Guards arranged on the terrace struck up the "Fest March" from Wagner's *Tannhäuser*, and the French doors from the Bow Room to the awning opened, signaling the

start of the processions. Two heralds, two gentlemen ushers, the comptroller of the lord chamberlain's department, and a group of officials led the
procession, followed by members of the royal family and foreign royal
guests. The groom's father, Crown Prince Frederick of Denmark, led his
sister the Princess of Wales into the chapel; finally, Prince Carl, clad in a
Danish naval uniform, appeared with his brothers, Christian and Harald,
and made his way down the aisle to the chapel.[70]

As the band struck up the wedding chorus from *Lohengrin*, the bride
finally appeared, walking on the arm of her father and followed by her
brother, George. "Never," declared the *Times*, "has a more charming and
graceful bride looked happier upon her wedding day than Princess Maud
of Wales." The princess wore an ivory satin gown whose skirt was edged
with a chiffon ruffle adorned with orange blossoms and myrtle. The low
bodice rose in pleats to chiffon bows adorned with myrtle, with short
puffed sleeves and a waist marked with a silver embroidered belt sewn with
diamonds. The twelve-foot train was sewn with chiffon bows and decorated with a lavish assemblage of white flowers arranged in trailing vines
between a border of orange blossoms, while from the diamond tiara and
wreath of orange blossoms atop her head cascaded her mother's wedding
veil of Honiton lace. As she passed down the aisle, "the perfume of the
orange blossom escaped from her dress and filled the air round her."[71]

With the princess came her eight bridesmaids: her sister Toria, and
Carl's sisters Ingeborg and Thyra; her cousins Princess Victoria of
Schleswig-Holstein, Princesses Patricia and Margaret of Connaught, and
Princess Alice of Albany; and her niece Lady Alexandra Duff. The
older bridesmaids wore white satin gowns adorned with clusters of red
geraniums and matching red aigrettes in their hair, while Maud's youngest
attendants wore white dresses with chaplets of red geraniums.[72]

The chapel had been bedecked with flowers: garlands of white and red
roses, echoing the colors of the Danish flag, adorned the columns down
the length of the nave. Tall sprays of white orchids and roses, framed by
palms, flanked the altar, above which hung a large floral cross of white
roses.[73] Prince Carl waited at the altar with his two supporters, his brothers Princes Christian and Harald, along with the Reverend Edward White
Benson, Archbishop of Canterbury, who officiated, and the bishops of

London and of Westminster. At the end of the ceremony, Carl led Maud first to her parents, and then to the queen, the prince bowing and the princess dropping a deep curtsy before Victoria embraced and kissed them both. The ceremony, recalled Prince Nicholas of Greece, "was very elegant, yet imposing in its simplicity."[74] To the strains of Mendelssohn's "Wedding March," the bride and groom left the chapel, passing onto the terrace and walking beneath the awning to the Bow Room, where the register was signed.[75] During the signing, the Archbishop of Canterbury recalled, Victoria "called me to her, and I knelt and kissed her hand, and she talked very spiritedly a few minutes. As soon as it was over an Indian servant wheeled in her chair to take her out; she instantly waved it back. 'Behind the door,' she said, and walked all across the room with her sticks most gallantly."[76]

Victoria retired to take lunch in her private apartments, leaving the bride and groom to preside over their wedding luncheon in the State Dining Room at Buckingham Palace.[77] Ten round tables, draped in white damask cloths and ringed with gilded chairs, crowded the room; atop each table, the queen's florists had arranged cascading bouquets of red and white roses, with trailing ivy tendrils framing the stiff menu cards, embossed with the queen's initials at the top and the bridal couple's monograms at the bottom in a red and white love knot.[78]

Footmen in crimson and scarlet liveries served the lavish, thirteen-course feast: *vermicelli à la Windsor, côtelettes d'agneau à l'Italienne, aiguilettes de canetons aux pois, filets de boeuf à la Napolitaine, poulets gras aux cressons, chaudfroids de volaille sur croûtes, salades d'homard, jambons decoupés à l'aspic, langues decoupées à l'aspic, mayonaises du volaille, roulades de veau à la gelée, haricots verts, épinards, gelées et crêmes*, and assorted pastries.[79] The luncheon culminated in the cutting of a twelve-hundred-pound, nine-foot-high cake whose three tiers were decorated with five thousand red and white rose petals.[80]

At the end of the luncheon, the bride and groom returned to Marlborough House, where they changed clothes and once again drove through the streets, along Piccadilly, to St. Pancras railway station; the entire length was lined with cheering crowds, and had been decorated with bunting and flags. "A demonstration of genuine and heartfelt congratulations met the eyes of bride and bridegroom at every turn," the

Times reported, "and was acknowledged by the smiles and bows of the Prince and Princess, who both appeared most gratified, nay delighted, with the cordial salutations of the loyal subjects of The Queen."[81] At the station, they boarded the royal train for Norfolk, where they were to spend their honeymoon at Appleton Hall, a country estate near Sandringham given to them by the Prince of Wales, leaving London to bask in the continued glow of a rare royal ceremony.[82]

8

AUTUMN AT BALMORAL

ONE DAY IN SEPTEMBER 1896, VICTORIA boarded her train and set off for Scotland. The puffing locomotive sped north, leaving England behind as it crossed through the low mountains of the border into Scotland. Far past Edinburgh and the clusters of little suburbs, it began its ascent into the Highlands, passing deep, emerald-colored lochs and hills cloaked in bright heather, climbing along the sides of desolate mountains brown with bracken and rumbling along narrow valleys split by violent ribbons of water.

Victoria traveled in comfort. The queen's household and servants, as well as cars for luggage, flanked her saloon carriage. Built for her in 1869 by the London and North Western Railway, it had originally been two separate cars linked by an enclosed bellows. Although the queen enjoyed rail travel, she found the rumbling, whistling bellows passage a test of her nerves, and after several journeys, she refused to use it; when she needed to change carriages, the entire train would halt. In 1895 the bellows was removed and the space enclosed to form a single carriage, sixty feet long and eight feet wide.[1]

The carriage was specially fitted to meet Victoria's needs.[2] The double floors were covered with oak over cork, and topped with carpet to deaden any noise; signal bells allowed Victoria to summon attendants, and a special pull soon stopped the train. The carriage was originally equipped with oil lamps; although it was electrified in 1895, Victoria still preferred the softer light of the oil lamps to the harsh, modern glow of electricity.[3]

A small compartment at the front of the carriage for the sergeant-footman included a small kitchen so that tea and light meals could be served, although the queen disliked dining while the train was in motion, and stopped at set intervals to take most of her meals.[4] The queen's day compartment followed. This was a large room, spanning the width of the carriage, and lit by windows on both sides. The walls, quilted to deaden any noise, were covered in buttoned, watered blue silk, while the ceiling was quilted and upholstered in white silk. Victoria had personally selected the bird's-eye maple, sycamore, yew, and satinwood that adorned the interior doors, windows, and fittings, along with the circular ceiling air vent, carved with *VR* around its perimeter, and the decorative white velvet hand grips sewn with the English rose, the Irish shamrock, and the Scottish thistle in blue thread. Beyond the overstuffed sofa and armchairs upholstered in blue silk, through the small passage, was the queen's night compartment. Finished in watered red and white silk, the compartment contained two small chests and twin brass bedsteads, one for Victoria and one for her daughter Beatrice.[5]

Although these railway journeys were regular occurrences several times a year, they involved intense regulations and preparations. At the queen's insistence, the train never traveled more than forty miles an hour, to avoid any excess rattling or shaking of the carriages.[6] Each mile of track was inspected, stops were scouted, and restaurants were investigated before the train ever left Windsor. Local police along the route were marshaled to guard crossings, bridges, and tunnels, and to provide additional security when the train stopped. An advance pilot locomotive always preceded the queen's train by ten minutes, to clear the track, and all trains running on parallel lines were forced to halt until Victoria had passed.[7] Each journey was detailed in a decorative timetable, bound into a small booklet so the queen could follow her progress across the country.[8] To keep the queen cool, pails filled with ice were placed beneath tables in the day compartment and the beds at night.[9]

The queen's granddaughter Princess Victoria of Prussia later recalled accompanying her grandmother on such a journey: "I was just dozing off when Grandmama came to bed. . . . She looked so clean and dear—all in white—and it took some time before she was settled—the shawls and cushions—then the lamps to be put out—then again, it felt too hot—then not warm enough, and in the night—Annie [McDonald, one of the queen's dressers] was called many a time—to bring her something to drink, etc.—Well finally we had some sleep."[10]

As the train approached its final destination, rugged hills and thick forests framed the line as it passed along the tumbling waters of the River Dee. Finally it reached Ballater, whose tiny station had been bedecked with flags and bunting in anticipation of Victoria's arrival. As the queen left her train and exchanged it for a carriage, porters and footmen busily unloaded the cases and trunks containing her wardrobe, her favorite paintings, and treasured photographs. Once safely settled beneath the carefully arranged folds of a lap rug, Victoria set off, her carriage ringed by outriders and followed by a procession of members of her household and staff; the drive took her along the banks of the Dee, twisting in a valley between the wooded Grampian Hills and amid stands of pine, fir, and birch framing the surrounding peaks of Cairngorm and Lochnagar before it swept past the granite piers and lodge that marked the entrance to Balmoral, the queen's Highland retreat. "Every year," Victoria wrote, "my heart becomes more fixed in this dear Paradise, and so much more so now, that *all* has become my dearest Albert's *own* creation."[11]

As queen, Victoria possessed an official residence, the Palace of Holyrood House, in Edinburgh, but the last monarchs to live comfortably within its walls had been Charles II and, before him, Mary, Queen of Scots. Holyrood, like Buckingham Palace and Windsor Castle, belonged to the Crown, and was administered by officials from the Office of Woods and Forests for the duration of her reign, and few things could be changed without permission. This chafed Victoria and especially Albert; seeking to escape this situation, the royal couple's chief desire became the purchase of a private residence that would truly be their own house, a place where they would be free to dictate the terms of their own lives.

Victoria and Albert had first visited Scotland in 1842, when they stayed as guests of the Duke of Buccleuch at Dalkeith Palace; a few years later, they were back, this time exploring the Highlands, when their attention was directed to Balmoral Castle, on the River Dee. Originally built in the fifteenth century, the castle had been enlarged by its previous owner, Sir Robert Gordon.[12] Victoria called it "a pretty little castle in the old Scotch style, a picturesque tower and a garden in front and a high wooded hill; at the back there is a wood down to the Dee; and the hills rise all around." In this secluded spot, she noted, "All seemed to breathe freedom and peace, and to make one forget the world and its sad turmoils."[13] After some discussion, Albert purchased the remaining lease on the castle, along with 17,400 adjacent acres, at a cost of £31,500 (£2,411,433, or $4,123,550 in 2007 figures). The money, it is often said, came from a bequest left to the queen by a wealthy eccentric, John Camden Nield; in fact, Balmoral was purchased two months before Nield died, with money the royal couple had saved from the Civil List.[14]

Balmoral was not a large castle, and Albert soon deemed it too small to suit the needs of the royal family and an accompanying household that numbered some sixty persons.[15] At first he considered enlarging the structure, but he eventually abandoned the idea in favor of erecting a new castle.[16] The old Balmoral was to be pulled down, and a site cleared a hundred yards northwest, nearer the banks of the Dee, on which the new structure would be built to provide better views of the surrounding forests and mountains.[17]

Albert saw the Highlands as a reflection of his native Coburg forests, and he was determined that the new castle would not only closely copy the baronial style of the building it replaced but also evoke memories of his childhood home, Schloss Rosenau. To help him accomplish his task, he commissioned Aberdeen architect John Smith; the architect, however, died soon into the project, and was replaced by his son William, who served as city architect and superintendent of works in Aberdeen. Preliminary work began in 1853, and in September 1854 the queen laid the cornerstone of the new castle; twelve months later it was finished, and on September 7, 1855, the royal family first took up residence.[18]

The Balmoral estate was some hundred miles northwest of Edinburgh, on the southern side of the thickly wooded River Dee valley, stretching between the villages of Ballater and Braemar deep in the Cairngorm Mountains. From the entrance gates, the driveway wound through groves of fir and birch, and along glades left wild to harebells, daisies, and heather, before a final curve revealed the castle itself, set at a bend of the Dee. To the north, across the churning river, rose the dramatic crag of Lochnagar, its jagged twin peaks surrounded by swirling mists and covered in fresh snow by early autumn; to the south, Balmoral nestled against the majestic Craig Gowan, its poplar-, ash-, and birch-clad slope providing a stunning green contrast to the light gray of the castle's walls.[19]

The new castle was built of locally quarried, light gray granite in the baronial style, with steep, stepped gables, arched and mullioned windows, and turrets topped with conical and pepper-pot roofs of Scottish slate. The principal block, containing the rooms for the royal family, their guests, and members of the household, sprawled around an internal courtyard; at its eastern end, a square tower connected it to the service block. Adorned with turrets at its corners and topped with crenellations, the hundred-foot-high tower marked the junction of the principal block, with the service block to the northeast. Like the larger, southwestern block, the service block was built around a central courtyard.[20]

Although Balmoral gave a deliberate impression of size, in fact it was quite small for a royal residence, containing only seventy rooms. "Within the Castle," noted one author, Albert "had wed his memories of German castles to his own taste, and his love for Scotland," in a highly detailed, slightly eccentric, and always colorful display of midcentury bourgeois comforts.[21] From the porte cochère at the southwestern end of the castle, doors opened to the entrance hall; on entering, recalled one of the queen's granddaughters, the distinctive smells of Balmoral—"wood fire, stags' heads, rugs, and leather"—filled the air.[22] The entrance hall was rather spare, with a white strapwork ceiling above stone walls adorned with an assortment of mounted stags' heads. It opened to a crimson-carpeted corridor whose walls, painted to imitate blocks of veined marble, were hung with a collection of antlers, trophies from Prince Albert's Highland excursions.[23]

The main rooms, opening off this corridor, were situated along the western side of the principal block. Tall wooden bookcases framed the library walls; a claret-colored tufted sofa and matching armchairs stood atop the tartan carpet, offering the only hint of color in the otherwise dark room.[24] Victoria preferred to take her meals here in privacy, unless guests demanded her presence.[25]

The drawing room occupied the center of the western wing, its mullioned bay window overlooking the formal garden beyond. Etchings and watercolors of the surrounding countryside hung upon walls covered in a cornflower blue paper stenciled with golden thistles, while overstuffed sofas and chairs upholstered in the white, gray, and red dress Stuart tartan flanked a white marble chimneypiece topped with a gilt-framed looking glass. The Scottish theme continued in the royal Stuart tartan carpet, its crimson ground crossed with lines of white and blue, and in the cashmere curtains of Stuart tartan; in contrast, the doors, wainscoting, window embrasures, and tables were finished in light, honey-colored satinwood, birch, and maple. The room—like the castle itself—evinced Albert's attention to detail, from the silvered hinges engraved with the royal couple's entwined initials and the sconces designed to resemble antlers, to the Minton candelabra sculpted as Highland figures.[26]

It was a comfortable room of domestic intent and scale, though critics were divided as to the end result. Marie of Romania called the decoration "more patriotic than artistic."[27] Lady Augusta Bruce thought "The effect is very good," but noted "a certain absence of harmony" in the decoration, while Lord Clarendon complained, "The thistles are in such abundance that they would rejoice the heart of a donkey if they happened to *look like* his favorite repast, which they don't."[28] Lord Rosebery offered the most devastating critique, commenting that he had always believed the drawing room at Osborne House to be the ugliest room in the world—until he saw the one at Balmoral.[29]

The dining room, beyond the billiards room at the castle's northwestern corner, contained the most classical decoration, with a dentilated frieze and cornice, and an eastern alcove framed by white Corinthian pilasters that contrasted with the deep green walls and the crimson and green Turkish carpet.[30] A large bay window pierced the northern wall, opposite a gray granite chimneypiece adorned with blue and white Minton tiles. The long, oval table ringed by chairs covered in red morocco leather could be extended to accommodate the queen's extended family and guests.[31] The rest of the principal block's ground floor was given over to rooms for visitors and members of the household, while service rooms stretched east to the main tower at the corner of the kitchen block.[32] Here, at the very end of the castle—where it could be reached only by crossing the open kitchen courtyard—Victoria reluctantly installed a smoking room to accommodate her son-in-law Prince Christian. Cold and sparsely furnished, it was a deliberately inconvenient, uncomfortable retreat whose lights, at Victoria's orders, were extinguished at midnight to prevent idle lingering.[33]

The largest of the interiors was the ballroom, constructed in 1856 in an annex on the northern side of the castle. Twenty-five feet wide and nearly seventy feet long, it rose one and a half storeys to an arched ceiling of wooden beams atop decorative brackets. Lower walls covered in a light blue-green paper patterned in gold contrasted with the upper part of the room, which was whitewashed and adorned with an assortment of traditional Scottish weaponry and clan insignia. Five tall arched windows opened to a sunken garden, while four bronze gasoliers provided the necessary light. Opposite the windows, an alcove lined with carved, Gothic-style panels and looking glasses offered a dais from which the queen and her family could watch the festivities. Because the ballroom was built at a slightly lower level than the ground floor, a double flight of wooden stairs at the southern end allowed direct access from the castle's principal block and provided a dramatic point of entrance for the queen.[34]

A life-size, white marble statue of Prince Albert by William Theed guarded the foot of the staircase, which ascended between a decorative iron balustrade in three flights to the upper floor. The queen's rooms occupied the entire western side. The largest, her sitting room, was directly above the drawing room and duplicated its tartan carpet and curtains. Victoria's bedroom was a symphony of rich colors designed to echo the landscape beyond the windows: the walls were hung with a green paper woven with silver fleurs-de-lis, while the blue Brussels carpet was patterned with a design copied from the Stuart hunting tartan. The half canopy of the large maple bed was hung with Balmoral chintz, white patterned with blue thistles, and the same fabric was used for the curtains and the upholstery on the chaise longue and on the overstuffed chairs. In addition to the usual portrait of her dead husband that hung on the headboard of all of Victoria's beds, Albert was memorialized in a large, framed photograph of his tomb, flanked by marble casts of his hands, which decorated a round table draped with a cloth of the mauve and gray Balmoral tartan designed by Prince Albert, in the center of the room.[35]

A large, three-part maple wardrobe on the southern side of the bedroom concealed a door that opened to the queen's bathroom and dressing room beyond.[36] The inside of the queen's copper bath, encased in a wooden frame, was painted and lacquered to resemble veined marble and, in addition to the lavatory and sinks, there was a large shower.[37] Victoria's dressing room, directly above the entrance hall, had soft blue walls, a hunting Stuart tartan carpet, maple wardrobes, and furniture upholstered in the same white Balmoral chintz used in her bedroom.[38]

Smaller rooms for the royal children and members of the household were scattered over this floor and the third floor above. Despite the fact that Albert had specifically demolished the old castle in favor of one with more accommodation, bedrooms at Balmoral—aside from that of the royal couple—were small, and often in short supply. Lady Lytton recorded that she found her ground floor room "not very large," and added, "one could hardly move when the two boxes were brought in."[39]

The queen was delighted with the castle. Victoria wrote: "The new house looks beautiful. An old shoe was thrown after us into the house for good luck, when we entered the hall. The house is charming; the rooms delightful; the furniture, papers, everything—perfection."[40] Albert had also laid out the surrounding gardens, called "policies" in the Scottish manner, with terraces framed by carefully manicured hedges, and a sunken garden crossed by colorful beds of flowers. Graveled walks led past dense plantings of rhododendrons through groves of spruce, fir, and poplars brought from Coburg, to the edge of the Dee, fringed with wildflowers. A new stable block, also in granite, lay hidden behind the kitchen wing.[41]

Surrounding the castle were a number of smaller royal estates. Albert had purchased the sixty-five-hundred-acre estate of Birkhall, which included an eighteenth-century manor house with stuccoed bays set on terraced gardens several miles from Balmoral.[42] He also took an extended lease on the small sixteenth-century castle of Abergeldie, on the western bank of the River Dee some three miles from Balmoral; the castle was given to the Prince of Wales as a home.[43] Victoria's great-grandson the future Edward VIII recalled that Abergeldie's "most conspicuous architectural feature was a tall stone tower surmounted by a wooden cupola infested with bats."[44] In 1895 Victoria's granddaughter Louise, Duchess of Fife, built a large, Tudor-inspired house, Mar Lodge, twelve miles from Balmoral, for herself and her family.[45]

Victoria came to Balmoral twice a year, once in the spring, and then again at the end of summer, when she remained in residence until the beginning of November. It was, she wrote, the closest she could be to Albert, "the place where everything, even down to the smallest detail, is somehow associated with Him and His memory."[46] Balmoral offered the queen freedom; although she was never anonymous, here she could drive out in the countryside accompanied by a few guards, stopping in villages and chatting to those she encountered.

Although the queen adored Balmoral, others were less enthusiastic: her son Leopold once described it as "that *most vile* and *most abominable* of places."[47] Members of the queen's household, too, dreaded serving at the remote castle. No one was allowed to leave the castle and walk in the grounds until the queen did so; once, when her private secretary dared to go out without her permission, he received a handwritten, four-page letter of reprimand.[48] The lack of any life outside the court led to boredom. "We see nothing of the queen except at dinner, on alternate nights," noted one lady, "we have no duties to perform to occupy our minds and the weather is horribly cold and wet. . . . We just exist from meal to meal and do our best to kill time."[49]

The prevailing impression left with most visitors to Balmoral was one of severe cold. "I can safely say I never remember a warm, congenial day in the Highlands," one member of the household recalled.[50] It was particularly trying for most of the ministers-in-attendance, a government official dispatched—usually with great reluctance—to remain at Balmoral while the queen was in residence so he could advise on any complicated political issues she might encounter in reading through her daily state papers.[51]

Disraeli once famously complained of "carrying on the government of the country six hundred miles from the metropolis," but no one could escape the obligation.[52] One man likened the experience to that of a monastery: "We meet at meals and when we are finished each is off to his cell."[53] Lord Clarendon spoke for many in recalling a visit in August 1856: "It is very cold here, and I believe my feet were frostbitten at dinner, for there was no fire at all there, and in the drawing room there were two little sticks which hissed at the man who attempted to light them."[54]

Mary Ponsonby recalled that while at Balmoral Victoria became a different person, "so easy to satisfy . . . so warmly genial . . . so completely charming."[55] According to her dictates, she attempted to impose a Scottish regime on her court. Food was plain and simple, and included fresh salmon and trout from the Dee; grouse and venison from the estate; and oatmeal porridge and smoked haddock for breakfast.[56] She often took breakfast beneath the sheltering porch of the nearby wooden garden cottage as the queen's piper marched up and down, playing the bagpipes.[57]

Every afternoon, Victoria went for a carriage drive, even when, as in early October, the first snows began to cover the surrounding hills.[58] During Albert's life, she had often accompanied him as he roamed the estate, watching as he trekked across the hills, shooting and stalking while she painted and sketched. As infirmity overtook her, however, she abandoned her horse rides in favor of the comforts of a carriage or pony cart. During her drives she was always accompanied by a lady-in-waiting and usually by one of her daughters or granddaughters. These excursions, in the fog, cold, rain, and even snow, were agony to the queen's ladies. "I could only occupy myself in gathering up all my hottest clothes," one lady-in-waiting wrote. "I put on endless others and toasted myself at the fire till the fatal moment."[59] And Marie Mallet recorded: "The wind was so cold my face turned first blue and them crimson, and by dinner time I looked as if I had been drinking hard for a week—and this was in *June*."[60]

Most evenings at Balmoral passed quietly, with dinners of pheasant, salmon, trout, or deer, followed by an occasional musician invited to perform for the guests.[61] There were few exceptions to what most people considered to be these unendurably boring weeks. One was the annual Braemar Gathering, sponsored by the Braemar Highland Society. Victoria liked to attend the festivities, watching the traditional Highland games, including hammer throwing, races, and the tossing of the caber.

The other annual event was the queen's ghillies' ball, held for the estate staff each autumn in the ballroom. Frederick Ponsonby recalled it as a "bacchanalian" event that frequently resulted in "hard drinking" among the staff. Servants were "in rather a hilarious mood," dropping glasses whose crashes punctuated the evening. "The Queen," he noted, "had been brought up to think that everything was excusable on the night of a Ghillies' Ball."[62] Despite her age and infirmity, Victoria still occasionally joined in the intricate jigs and reels, a sash of Balmoral tartan slung across the bodice of her black satin gown as the pipers played. She had, according to one observer, "light airy steps in the old courtly fashion; no limp or stick, but every figure carefully and prettily danced."[63]

Every Sunday, when in residence at Balmoral, the queen attended services at Crathie Church, a few miles from the castle. In 1893 the old, whitewashed church was pulled down and replaced with a larger building that Victoria had helped fund.[64] With its bare, granite walls and arched, beamed ceiling, it was a deliberately sparse house of worship, its simplicity suited to the rugged Highlands.[65] Dr. Cameron Lee, minister of St. Giles Cathedral in Edinburgh, served as dean of the chapels royal of Scotland, while Professor Robert Story served as chaplain-in-ordinary to Victoria in Scotland, and the two usually alternated religious duties with Crathie's own minister.[66]

In 1844 Victoria was widely condemned in the British press for attending Presbyterian services held by the Church of Scotland.[67] Both the Archbishop of Canterbury and the Dean of Westminster advised Victoria that she, as supreme governor of the Church of England, should on no account partake of communion in a Scottish church, but she did so in 1871, and would continue to do so every fall during her visits to Balmoral.[68] "It would indeed be impossible to say how deeply we were impressed by the grand simplicity of the service," Victoria wrote. "It was all so truly earnest."[69]

Victoria cherished her time in the Highlands, and Balmoral was always a place of refuge for her. She once wrote to her daughter Vicky of the trauma of "leaving this beloved place which, with its wonderful beauty of scenery, and its great solitude and peace, its purest of airs and its simple, dear, devoted inhabitants, is more and more congenial to my broken and bleeding heart."[70]

9

"THE RUSSIAN
OCCUPATION"

IN THE FALL OF 1896, VICTORIA WELCOMED her granddaughter Alix of Hesse, newly crowned Empress of Russia, with her husband, Nicholas II, on a private visit to Balmoral. From the moment of her mother's death in 1878, Princess Alix of Hesse had been carefully guided and groomed by her powerful grandmother. Queen Victoria had been determined to marry the beautiful princess to her grandson Eddy, the Duke of Clarence and heir presumptive to the British throne.

Alix, serious and shy, was horrified at the idea. Although she was possessed of only average intelligence, she quickly dismissed her cousin as "too stupid."[1] When Queen Victoria heard of this, she protested, "Eddy is not stupid," but her granddaughter was adamant.[2] To Alix's sister Victoria the queen wrote: "Is there no hope about Eddy? She is *not* nineteen—and she should be made to reflect seriously on the folly of throwing away the chance of a very good husband, kind, affectionate and steady and of entering a united happy family and a very good position which is second to *none in the world*. Dear Uncle and Aunt wish it so much and poor Eddy is so unhappy at the thought of losing her also. Can you and Ernie not do any good? What fancy has she got in her head?"[3]

That fancy was Tsesarevich Nicholas, the eldest son of Tsar Alexander III and heir to the Russian throne. A childish flirtation at the 1884 wedding of her sister Ella to his uncle Serge Alexandrovich had evolved into a burgeoning romance five years later, when Alix spent the winter in St. Petersburg. Although Alix's feelings for the handsome tsesarevich were strong, there was one obstacle: she resolutely clung to her Lutheran faith, refusing to consider the conversion to Orthodoxy necessary to the wife of the heir to the Russian throne.

Queen Victoria was firmly opposed to this match. "Russia I could not wish for any of you," she wrote to Alix's sister Victoria, "and dear Mama [Princess Alice] always said she would never hear of it."[4] The queen's prejudices were strong, and rooted in decades of experience, from the Crimean War to the assassination of Nicholas's grandfather Alexander II by a group of nihilists in 1881, Russian intervention in eastern Europe, and her personal dislike of the tsesarevich's father, Alexander III. Ella was determined to break down her sister's religious reservations, leading the queen to warn, "No marriage for *Alicky in Russia* would be *allowed*."[5] Russia, Queen Victoria presciently warned, was "*so bad*, so rotten, that at any moment something dreadful might happen."[6]

Ella, as her grandmother suspected, was indeed doing all she could to promote the union. To her brother Ernie she warned: "Be yourself very careful what you say in your conversation with Grandmama." She advised him to "give an idea of the happy family life so that Grandmama's prejudices may be lessened. That will be a great step and help when the deciding moment arrives. Through all the idiotic trash in the newspapers she gets impossible untrue views and founds all her arguments on facts which probably never existed."[7]

Then, in April 1894, Alix and Nicholas were thrown together at the wedding of her brother Ernie to his cousin Victoria Melita in Coburg. More than a hundred royal relatives flooded into the quaint German town: Tsesarevich Nicholas arrived at the head of a Russian delegation; Kaiser Wilhelm II and his mother, Empress Friedrich, came from Berlin; Victoria Melita's sister Marie of Romania arrived from Bucharest accompanied by her husband, Crown Prince Ferdinand; and the Prince of Wales, joined by the Duke and Duchess of Connaught, made the journey from London. It was one of the largest royal gatherings in history. "I never saw so many in one place," noted Queen Victoria's private secretary.[8]

On Tuesday, April 17, a triumphant Queen Victoria, who had arranged the marriage between her two grandchildren Ernie and Victoria Melita, arrived in her beloved Albert's native Coburg. A squadron of the Queen of Great Britain and Ireland's Own First Prussian Dragoons heralded her arrival in the sleepy little town, the strains of "God Save the Queen" following her open carriage as she drove through the flower-bedecked streets hung with flags and bunting. She settled into rooms at the Ehrenburg Palais, where her son Affie, the bride's father, lived as the reigning Duke of Saxe-Coburg-Gotha with his family.

The tension surrounding the romance of Alix of Hesse and Nicholas of Russia overshadowed the festivities. On his first day in Coburg, the tsesarevich had proposed, only to be rejected by a tearful Alix, who refused to change her religion. "No, I cannot," she cried, pleading for Nicholas to leave her in peace.[9] Ella, who had converted to Orthodoxy a few years after her marriage to Serge, tried to reassure her sister that the differences in the two religions were minimal; she was followed by the kaiser, who told Alix that it was "her bounden duty" to marry the tsesarevich; the peace of Europe, he declared, was worth the sacrifice of her religious doubts.[10]

The next day, the tsesarevich succeeded in his task, and Alix finally accepted his proposal. "I was sitting in my room," recalled Princess Marie Louise of Schleswig-Holstein, "quietly waiting to get ready for a luncheon party when Alix stormed into the room, threw her arms round my neck, and said, 'I'm going to marry Nicky!'"[11] Yet one person was unaware of the decision: Queen Victoria. Knowing how opposed her grandmother had been to the idea, Alix took Nicholas and went to break the news to the queen in person. "I was quite thunderstruck," Queen Victoria wrote, "as though I knew Nicky much wished it, I thought Alicky was not sure of her mind. Saw them both. Alicky had tears in her eyes but she looked very bright and I kissed them both."[12]

The deed was done, and the queen was forced to accept her granddaughter's fait accompli. But the queen's doubts continued. "The more I think of sweet Alicky's marriage the more unhappy I am," she confided to her granddaughter Victoria of Hesse. "*Not* as to the personality, for I like him *very much*, but on account of the country, the policy, and the differences with us, and the awful insecurity to which that sweet Child will be exposed. . . . But I will *try* and bear it and make the best of it. Still, the feeling that I had labored so hard to *prevent it* and that I felt there was *no longer* any danger and all in one night—*everything* was changed. . . . My blood runs cold when I think of her *so* young most likely placed on that very unstable throne, her dear life and above all her Husband's constantly threatened and unable to see her but rarely; it is a great additional anxiety in my declining years."[13]

Alix's transformation into the stern, aloof, and stubborn Empress Alexandra began just six months after her engagement, when Alexander III died and his son prematurely acceded to the Russian throne as Tsar Nicholas II. A week after the funeral came Alix and Nicholas's wedding, a vibrant panoply of white and gold in the midst of the incessant black of mourning. Alix duly converted to Orthodoxy, embracing her new faith with the fiery passion of a convert, and was abruptly thrust into the Byzantine ritual of the opulent Russian court. With few social skills and no practical experience, she was quickly condemned as a failure in her ceremonial role as empress. Marie Feodorovna, Nicholas's mother and sister of the Princess of Wales, disliked her new daughter-in-law and did nothing to assist her in the enormous transition. From the tragedy of Alexander III's death and the hasty wedding that followed to a stampede at Nicholas II's coronation in May 1896 in which more than a thousand people were crushed to death, misfortune and disaster seemed to attach themselves to Alix and her unlucky husband, and she looked forward with undisguised pleasure to the reunion with her beloved grandmother in Scotland.

The queen's first inclination was to treat the visit purely as a family affair. The Prince of Wales, however, set about the difficult task of persuading his mother to at least surround the comings and goings with a modicum of ceremony. "Though I know the Queen expects the visit to Balmoral to be a private one," he wrote to Sir Arthur Bigge, the queen's private secretary, the prince hoped, "as it is the first time that the Emperor and Empress visit our shores in the high position they occupy," that his mother would "wish all honor to be done to them in the eyes of the world, especially in those of Russia. I am so anxious that the arrival should be marked with every possible compliment for the Emperor."[14]

It took some doing, but eventually the queen came around to her son's position. "The more I think over the question," she wrote to him, "the stronger is my conviction that in order to do as much honor as possible to the Emperor on his landing for the first time in this country as such you should receive him on my behalf."[15] The Prince of Wales agreed that they should be met at Leith, the port of disembarkation for Edinburgh, with a guard of honor, and a guard of honor mounted at Ferryhill Junction in Aberdeen and at Ballater Station. He himself should meet his niece and nephew, and escort them to Balmoral; he also convinced his mother that a guard of honor drawn from the Royal Scots Grays Regiment of the Second Dragoons Regiment be mounted along the route from Leith to Ballater, as well as joining in the carriage procession to Balmoral.[16]

A small public ceremony, set to take place on the quay at Leith, as well as stops at various rail stations along the route, caused much security concern. The queen, who had always believed Russia an unsafe country crawling with anarchists, was terrified lest an attempt be made on the imperial couple while in Scotland. Okhrana agents, working with the security services at Scotland Yard, had recently uncovered a plot to assassinate the emperor during his visit, finding a large cache of dynamite in an anarchist's basement in Antwerp.[17] To the queen's repeated queries, however, Sir Edward Bradford, commissioner of the Metropolitan Police, replied, "The Emperor is safer in England than anywhere else in the world."[18] Nevertheless, security was tightened. For the train journey from Leith to Ballater, a pilot engine would run ahead on the tracks in case an anarchist had managed to plant a bomb along them. Additionally, the entire line was to be patrolled by agents of the railway line and local police, while the imperial party would travel with a contingent of not only their own bodyguards—stationed behind bushes and armed with spyglasses—but also some two dozen detectives detailed from Scotland Yard.[19] "Every precaution," the *Times* of London assured its readers, "has been and will be taken which human foresight can compass to ensure a safe and speedy arrival," noting: "On no previous occasions have such elaborate preparations been made for the reception of royalty as on present, while the precautions taken to secure the safety of the Imperial visitors were extremely thorough and minute."[20]

The trip to Balmoral quickly assumed the proportions and problems of a state visit. For some time, Russia—pushed by its European ally France—had been protesting the Anglo-Egyptian campaign to recapture the Sudan, and the queen hoped to win the emperor's support for a new British expedition; there also was the delicate question of the eroding Ottoman Empire, which Russia coveted. Such colonial expansionary concerns led Victoria to summon Lord Salisbury, the prime minister, to Balmoral for the duration of the visit. The prime minister was none too keen on the idea; the only thing he disliked more than Russia was the dreadful chill at the remote Scottish castle, and Salisbury's secretary entered into cautious negotiations to guarantee that his master's rooms would be properly heated; when he received the necessary assurances, Salisbury reluctantly agreed to come to Balmoral.

Shortly before ten on the morning of Tuesday, September 22, the Russian imperial yacht *Standart* slowly steamed into the harbor at Leith, having sailed through the North Sea accompanied by an escort of six battleships, two cruisers, and two gunboats from the Channel Squadron. As a salute of twenty-one guns echoed across the sky, a flotilla of steamers, tugs, and small boats rushed into the harbor, their decks lined with cheering crowds bobbing and weaving on the choppy waters of the Firth of Forth. It was, the *Times* noted, a miserable day: "An easterly wind was accompanied by a drenching rain, and for several hours there was a ceaseless downpour. Nevertheless, every part of the route and every obtainable point in the docks were crowded with sightseers, who waited throughout dreary hours with exemplary patience."[21]

On the quayside, wrapped in the heavy gray rain, a hastily erected pavilion offered shelter from the storm. The red, white, and blue British bunting and flags had been intertwined with the imperial standard and ribbons of the Romanov black and yellow to decorate Victoria Jetty, but they limply flapped in the strong wind. Here, the Prince of Wales, dressed in the uniform of a colonel in chief of the Twenty-seventh Kiev Imperial Dragoons, waited with his brother Prince Arthur, Duke of Connaught; the prime minister, Lord Salisbury; Baron George de Staal, the newly appointed Russian ambassador to Great Britain; and a party composed of members of the royal household. This included the Duchess of Buccleuch, the queen's mistress of the robes, as well as Edith, Lady Lytton, one of the queen's ladies-in-waiting who had been appointed to attend to the empress during her visit.[22]

As soon as *Standart* dropped anchor, the two princes, joined by the prime minister, Baron de Staal, and the rest of the official party, boarded a tender and fought the uneven bay to reach the imperial yacht.[23] The Prince of Wales's thick red and gray coat and Astrakhan cap offered little protection against the driving rain, and he stood bent with the rest of the little group beneath the temporary shelter of umbrellas.[24]

The emperor and the empress waited on the deck of *Standart*. Nicholas wore the uniform of honorary colonel in chief of the Royal Scots Grays Regiment, with bearskin busby. "You will understand," he wrote to his mother, "how unpleasant it was to have to say goodbye to our officers and crew in a foreign uniform!"[25] Alix, as the *Times* duly reported to its readers, appeared in a white dress, with a large hat and a white ostrich feather boa.[26] Indeed, with the imperial couple secluded at Balmoral and left with little of substance to report, her choice of clothing seemed to preoccupy the British press; even the rather staid *Times* felt moved to brief its readers on her "pink silk dress with a train, heliotrope colored traveling cloak and cape with white lace, trimmed with white fur at the throat," and her "small bonnet to match the cape, decorated with heliotrope, white, and light blue colored flowers."[27] And the correspondent for the *Graphic* commented: "Charming and graceful as the Russian Empress is, it is to be hoped that she is not going to set the fashion for us— that of traveling in such fine clothes as Her Imperial Majesty affects."[28]

The British guests joined the emperor and the empress for a light lunch in *Standart*'s dining saloon. "I longed to taste all," wrote Lady Lytton, "but was rather too giddy to run risks. The Emperor sat at the head of the table, with the Empress on his left and the Duchess of Buccleuch on his right. . . . There was no whispering, and the Emperor and Empress being so young makes them so little alarming compared to old Royalties. The conversation was exactly what you might suppose, but the Duke of Connaught was the most cheerful. . . . One longed for *haute politique* to be discussed, and when one looked at the very young Tsar it seemed more than ever ridiculous of the papers to say that all depended on him for decisions in the Eastern Question."[29]

Just before two, the party boarded the waiting tender and steamed to Victoria Jetty, where a band played "God Save the Tsar" and "God Save the Queen," and a guard of honor composed of members of the Argyll and Sutherland Highlanders and the Royal Scots Grays regiments stood crisply at attention in the pouring rain. Andrew MacDonald, lord provost of Edinburgh, greeted the imperial couple with an engraved golden box, while the wife of John Bennet, the provost of Leith, presented the empress with a large bouquet of orchids.[30] "The Emperor very shyly whispered a few words of thanks," declared Lady Lytton, "but he ought to learn to do this sort of thing better. She smiles, but neither of them take trouble enough to bow to all assembled as our Queen did *so* well."[31]

It was still raining when the imperial couple and their hosts climbed into a string of open carriages and drove, escorted by the Scots Grays, through the town to the railway station, the cannon of Leith Castle thundering in salute.[32] A four-and-a-half-hour train ride across the Scottish Highlands followed, with ceremonial stops along the route so local officials could present the emperor and the empress with welcome addresses and floral bouquets. "The train," the emperor later wrote, "was rather rocky, so that Alix was very nearly ill."[33]

George, Duke of York, along with his wife, Mary, and the Duke of Cambridge, waited at Ballater Station to greet their cousins. The entire siding had been hung with bunting and flags, and strung with electric lights that shimmered in the darkness; the decorations, noted Sir James Reid, "looked sadly lashed" by the inclement weather.[34] Along the platform, beneath the ghostly halos of light, stood a guard of honor composed of members of the Black Watch and the Queen's Own Highlanders, attired in regimental kilts.[35]

From Ballater there was another, hour-long drive through the wild and wet night. The emperor and the empress rode in an open landau pulled by eight white horses through Deeside to Balmoral itself. Members of the Scots Grays Regiment, the Balmoral Highlanders, and the men of the Crathie and Ballater Volunteers carried flaming torches to light the way;

on the hills above, massive bonfires burned their welcoming lights into the dark night.[36] Just before eight, as the procession neared the castle, a contingent of pipers blared their music through the mist and fog, and the bells of the nearby Crathie Church rang out, announcing their approach.[37]

Queen Victoria, dressed in black silk and with a white lace cap and veil atop her head, waited on the steps of the castle's porte cochere to welcome the imperial couple. She embraced the emperor and the empress, introducing them to the gathered members of her household before leading them out of the chill night air into the tartan-bedecked drawing room, where a fire blazed and drinks waited. As soon as Nicholas and Alix had changed, they joined the queen and her family for dinner.[38] Thus began what Sir Arthur Bigge later termed "the Russian occupation" of Balmoral.[39]

"I didn't think her much changed," Nicholas wrote of the queen to his mother, "except that she seemed a little smaller—just as you found her. Again she is marvelously kind and amiable to us, and so delighted to see our little daughter!"[40] The ten-month-old grand duchess Olga, in fact, quickly became the center of all attention at Balmoral. She was, Queen Victoria wrote to her daughter Vicky, "magnificent, bigger than she and Ella ever were, and a lovely, lively [great] grandchild."[41] The little grand duchess found an attentive playmate in her second cousin Prince Edward (later King Edward VIII and Duke of Windsor), who, just a year older, was full of solicitude. When the pair was romping and Olga tumbled over, Edward rushed to her side and, full of courtly manners, helped her to her feet and kissed her.[42]

Her parents, however, made a less admirable impression. Queen Victoria wrote: "Dear Nicky and Alicky are quite unspoilt and unchanged and as dear and simple and as kind as ever. He is looking rather thin and pale and careworn, but sweet Alicky is in great beauty and very blooming."[43] But after observing the imperial couple for the duration of their stay, Marie Mallet described Nicholas as "a weakling," and his wife as "a rabid, pathetic hausfrau."[44]

Alix spent her days with her grandmother, telling her of her married life in Russia and her position as empress; the Prince of Wales, much to the emperor's consternation, quickly swept up his nephew and thrust him onto the wild, windy, rain-soaked hills and into the forests to hunt. "They seem to consider it necessary to take me out shooting all day long with the gentlemen," he complained to his mother. "The weather is awful, rain and wind every day and on top of it no luck at all—I haven't killed a stag yet."[45] Worse still, he had to don a kilt. "I never before exposed my knees," he later commented to a friend.[46] Despite the inclement weather, the imperial couple were forced to drive out with the hardy queen, who took them to neighboring lochs; isolated, roaring waterfalls; and rustic, sparsely furnished forest shiels for tea.[47]

For the empress, who had spent many childhood holidays with her grandmother, it was a chance to relive happy memories, far away from the incessant protocol and censorious looks of St. Petersburg. She showed Nicholas where she had fished; where she and her siblings had hiked; and even took him to a small shop in nearby Crathie Village, run by an elderly woman named Mrs. Symonds, who had once taught her how to bake scones.[48] Now, visiting the old woman as empress of Russia, she proceeded to fill a basket with candies, pastries, tartans, and other local wares, her spree undoubtedly a boon to the local economy.[49]

There were no official duties; one afternoon, however, the queen took Nicholas aside and warned him of the dangers of Russia's growing ties to France. "Tell France," she said, "not to be so hostile to England."[50] But Nicholas was noncommittal; Lord Salisbury attempted to press for an answer, only to be politely rebuffed. "The Queen wanted to know whether his sentiment towards England was really friendly, and whether he was likely to be influenced by political conversations in Paris," noted E. F. Benson. "She was uneasy about it and, conscious that she had got nothing definite out of him, in spite of all these private talks after tea, wrote to him, almost as soon as he left, to say that she hoped he would firmly impress on the French his disapproval of all their unfriendliness towards England. But it was in vain that she waited for any assurance. He merely did not answer her letter, and neither she nor England, nor Lord Salisbury knew any more about his real sentiment towards England than if he had never been to Balmoral at all."[51]

On Sunday, September 27, the emperor and the empress accompanied the queen to services at Crathie. "It was very interesting seeing the two pews full of the royalties," noted Lady Lytton, "and the Emperor and

Empress standing by the Queen even in the Scotch Kirk, where all is simple and reverend, and the prayer for Their Majesties was good, but the sermon so dull I could not say what it was." Bertie's horse Persimmon was due to run in the Jockey Club Stakes at Newmarket on October 1, and the Prince of Wales left Balmoral midway through the visit.[52] This, at least for Nicholas, was a relief, as he wrote to his mother: "I had an easier time, because I could at least do what I wanted to, and was not obliged to go out shooting every day in the cold and rain."[53]

Nicholas was also ill-tempered from a tremendous toothache. Despite the fact that he was emperor of Russia, with the best medical care at his call, he had a horror of dentists, and his teeth began to rot early. When, at Balmoral, he complained of a swollen gum, Sir James Reid stepped in to see what he could do, and found an infection at the root of his decayed, lower left molar. He managed to alleviate the emperor's toothache and, for his troubles, received a gold cigarette case emblazoned with the imperial arms and adorned with diamonds.[54]

On the day after the imperial couple arrived at Balmoral, September 23, the seventy-seven-year-old Queen celebrated a momentous occasion, becoming the longest-reigning British monarch. "Today is the day on which I have reigned longer, by a day, than any English sovereign," Victoria wrote in her journal.[55] The queen preferred not to mark the occasion with any special celebration, however, waiting for her Diamond Jubilee the following summer.

During the Balmoral visit, members of the imperial suite were housed at the castle, while those in the queen's household were scattered across Deeside, lodged at the neighboring estates of Birkhall and Abergeldie. The ordinary servants at the castle were forced to vacate their own regular apartments for the Russians. Many were lodged in temporary Humphrey huts, constructed near the stables; the overcrowding was so intense that, for the duration of the visit, four laundry maids had to share a single bed.[56] The emperor, however, made certain that such discomfort was duly compensated; before he and his wife left Balmoral, they gave the master of the household £1,000 (£77,105, or $131,849 in 2007 figures), to be distributed among the regular servants who had been forced to endure the week.[57]

At the end of eleven days, Nicholas and Alix prepared to bid farewell to the queen. On October 3, the last day of the visit, the emperor and the empress planted two commemorative trees in the castle park.[58] John Michie, the head forester at Balmoral, selected two Cumbrian pine saplings for the event, but Nicholas seemed confused by the ritual, asking what he was supposed to do. Michie handed him a shovel and told him to fill in the base around one of the trees with soil; Nicholas duly complied, followed by his wife.[59]

After this, the emperor and the empress joined the queen and her family on the castle terrace where, Victoria wrote, "we were all photographed by Downey by the new cinematograph process, which makes moving pictures by winding off a reel of film. We were walking up and down, and the children jumping about."[60] Seven weeks later, Victoria watched the film at Windsor: "After tea went to the Red Drawing Room, where so-called 'animated pictures' were shown, including the group taken in September at Balmoral. It is a very wonderful process, representing people, their movements and actions, as if they were alive."[61] For Victoria, it was a powerful reminder of the tumultuous and revolutionary century her reign had spanned: these shaky reels were the first time the image of a British monarch was captured on motion pictures, an echo of the dramatic technological changes over which the queen presided in her sixty years.

10

CHRISTMAS AT OSBORNE

IN THE THIRD WEEK OF DECEMBER 1896, Victoria traveled south aboard the royal train to Portsmouth, where she boarded *Alberta*, a 160-foot-long, 370-ton paddle-wheel steamer built as a tender to her larger yacht *Victoria and Albert II*.[1] The little steamer carried the queen across the silent, gray waters of the Solent to the Isle of Wight. Landing at East Cowes, Victoria entered a carriage and set off through the small town, following York Avenue as it wound its way up the hillside, past the prosperous brick houses of her courtiers and between a pair of granite piers adorned with bronze stags. The passage of her carriage down a gently curved drive flanked by the bare-leafed trees of winter sent a flagman scurrying up a twisting staircase to the top of a tall tower. In the bitterly cold wind he raised the royal standard, a signal that the queen had taken up residence in Osborne House, her Italianate seaside palace.

Victoria had fled to Osborne less than a week after Albert's death on December 14, 1861, to spend her first Christmas as a widow in the safety of its seclusion, and with the passing years she regularly returned to the Isle of Wight to celebrate the holiday. Her schedule rarely varied: she visited the mausoleum at Frogmore on the anniversary of Albert's death and soon thereafter departed for Osborne, arriving a few days before

Christmas and remaining until the middle of February. Although several of the queen's children, including Beatrice, her constant companion, regularly joined her, the Prince of Wales preferred to celebrate the holiday with his own family at Sandringham; he found Osborne, he once declared, "utterly unattractive."[2]

Victoria had first visited the Isle of Wight in 1831. Situated in the Solent off Portsmouth and Southampton, it was a place of peace and tranquillity, rural in feel and far removed from the hustle of London or the stiff etiquette of Windsor. From Cowes, the small town that ringed its northern harbor, roads twisted around the island, past hundreds of acres of verdant farmland, open meadows, and lush forests, offering both seclusion and stunning views over the English Channel.

Sir Robert Peel, the queen's second prime minister, had first recommended the island as a possible retreat for Victoria and Albert, noting that Lady Isabella Blatchford owned a fine Georgian mansion with views over the Solent that she wished to sell.[3] The couple initially leased the eight-hundred-acre Osborne estate rather than purchase it outright; Lady Isabella was asking £30,000 (£1,805,123, or $3,086,760 in 2007 figures) for the house and grounds, and Albert, thinking this was too much, feigned disinterest.[4] The prince, noted Phillip Hall, "was not shy about using the royal status in his bargaining, which gave him a distinct edge." With Victoria and Albert in residence, Lady Isabella "could not really sell it to anyone else, and had to settle for rather less" than she originally wished. There was also the intimidation factor, as Hall pointed out: "Albert could also involve senior government ministers in the negotiations, which must have been daunting."[5] After much discussion, Lady Isabella agreed to sell Osborne for £26,000 (£1,564,440, or $2,675,192 in 2007 figures) in 1844; eventually some £200,000 (£12,617,532, or $21,575,979 in 2007 currency) would be spent on the estate.[6]

At first, Victoria was pleased with the house. "It is impossible," she wrote to Lord Melbourne, "to see a prettier place, with woods and valleys and *points de vue*, which would be beautiful anywhere, but all this near the sea . . . is quite perfection. We have a charming beach quite to ourselves. The sea is so blue and calm that the Prince said it was like Naples. And then we can walk about anywhere by ourselves without fear of being followed and mobbed."[7] The estate had the benefit of bucolic isolation, yet it was within a few hours of London by train, ensuring that government business could be conducted without any undue hardship on the ministers.

With sixteen bedrooms, Osborne was not small, but it was also not large enough to serve as a royal residence, even a holiday house, where the queen would, of necessity, be attended by a domestic staff and household suite of more than a hundred.[8] To enlarge the structure, Albert turned to Thomas Cubitt, who had grown wealthy transforming much of Belgravia in London. Cubitt was a builder rather than a trained architect, but he had an inspired eye and a sure hand.[9] Cubitt offered another benefit that appealed to the money-conscious prince: he came with his own workforce, provided his own building materials, and worked according to a fixed rate, ensuring that there would be no unexpected expenses.[10]

After examining the existing Georgian house, however, Cubitt advised that it would be cheaper to pull it down and replace it with a new, enlarged structure rather than add on to the older building.[11] Cubitt may have exaggerated the estimated expenses, hoping to parlay his selection as builder into the more prestigious—and financially advantageous—role of royal architect, but Albert, at least, welcomed the news, and immediately seized on the opportunity to plan and build a new residence. The situation, high on a bluff above the Solent, had reminded the prince of Italy, and his thoughts naturally turned to the Italianate style, which would suit and complement the surrounding landscape. The queen wrote: "It does my heart good to see how my beloved Albert enjoys it all, and is so full of admiration of the place, and of all the plans and improvements he means to carry out."[12]

The new Osborne House was almost certainly influenced by British architect Sir Charles Barry, and in particular drew on his work at Trentham, an Italianate palace constructed in the English countryside for the Duke of Sutherland.[13] The queen laid the cornerstone on June 23, 1845, and construction continued for the next six years.[14] The resulting building was, as Robert Rhodes James has pointed out, the work of the "inspired trio" of Albert, Cubitt, and German art professor Ludwig Grüner. The prince was responsible for the style of the design and its situation, with Grüner adding historically accurate artistic touches to the interior decoration, and Cubitt providing the necessary technical skill to bring their ideas to fruition.[15]

Visitors accustomed to the ponderous gloom of Buckingham Palace or the manipulated Gothic dominance of Windsor inevitably found Osborne a startling and pleasant surprise. Beyond the estate's wrought-iron gates, the graveled drive snaked past open meadows to an avenue of lofty cedars whose foliage framed the arcaded loggias and campaniles of the new house. At the center lay the royal pavilion with its tall flag tower; colonnades topped with open loggias linked the pavilion to the eastern main wing, with its ninety-foot-high clock tower, and to the southern household wing. Osborne utilized the latest technology: large plate glass windows took advantage of views to the Solent; iron girders rather than wooden beams protected against fire; a forced-air heating system warmed its rooms; and walls were insulated with crushed seashells.[16] To save money, it was constructed of brick, plastered and stuccoed over, and then carefully etched to give the appearance of stone.[17]

The domestic offices, under the rigid control of the housekeeper, Mrs. Mitchie, occupied the southeastern end of the building, far from the royal pavilion.[18] The kitchen was a model of midcentury technology, with roasting spits, cold storage rooms, and ten gas ranges, installed by Prince Albert a year before his death.[19] A labyrinth of storage and service rooms filled the basement, including the silver pantry, beer and wine cellars, linen rooms, an upholstery shop, the servants' hall, a telegraph office, and a furnace room with nearby coal stores.[20] There was also a room specially given over to the three lamplighters, charged with cleaning and stocking the house's eighty-seven oil lamps. Despite cleanliness and convenience of gas, Victoria disliked it and refused to have it installed in the building's main rooms.[21]

Osborne's design carefully shielded the rooms of the royal family in the pavilion from those dedicated to the queen's ceremonial duties in the main wing, where a light blue audience room overlooked the sloping lawn. Used by Victoria to receive visiting dignitaries, its crimson carpet, gilded furniture, and green and pink German glass chandelier added a suitably regal touch.[22] It offered a hint of the splendor of the adjoining Council Room, designed by Grüner as Osborne's most impressive interior. Here, a carved and gilded frieze circled sky blue walls, adorned with portraits of Victoria and Albert framed by hanging ormolu sconces, but the room was dominated by Sir Edwin Landseer's gigantic canvas *The Deer Drive*, depicting an expedition in the Scottish Highlands.[23]

Also in this wing was a private chapel. For most of Osborne's life, Victoria—when in residence—attended services at the nearby church of St. Mildred's, Whippingham, but in the 1880s she commissioned a private chapel, selecting a long room whose crimson-curtained windows overlooked the terraces. A wainscot of polished walnut circled the room, contrasting with the pine pulpit and an altar dominated by several religious paintings.[24] The cost, as one member of the household recalled, for the "ugly decoration" of the new chapel had run to more than £5,000 (£335,414, or $573,557 in 2007 currency).[25]

Slicing through the main wing and linking it to the pavilion was the impressive Marble Corridor. Designed by Grüner to evoke the Italian Renaissance, it was a passage of dramatic colors, from the floor of blue, red, brown, and black encaustic Minton tiles set within marble borders to the light blue walls ornamented with arabesques and Florentine motifs in orange, yellow, crimson, white, and green. Pilasters and paired columns of light gray scagliola supported the vaulted ceiling and framed niches displaying contrasting white marble statuary.[26] The numerous neoclassical sculptures proved irresistible to the queen's grandchildren and the more restless members of her household. After an equerry accidentally chipped one while examining it, Victoria ordered that the household "must not touch the statues and certainly not play with them."[27]

At the heart of Osborne was the royal pavilion, a square, three-storey structure with bow and bay windows on its northern and eastern sides, and a hundred-foot-high flag tower at its corner.[28] Because the pavilion was intended only for the royal family, Albert and Cubitt eliminated any grand approaches or grand corridors. The drawing room spanned the width of the pavilion, with a central bow and tall windows overlooking the Solent; at night, mirrored panels concealed in the walls could be drawn over the windows, enhancing the light from the cut-crystal chandeliers and eight-foot-tall candelabra hung with shimmering prisms. Light blue scagliola panels encased in gilded borders adorned the walls, set between yellow scagliola pilasters matching the open screens of Corinthian columns at the eastern and western ends; the ceiling was ornamented with gilded carving and painted with classical details, creating a subtle symphony of pastels. The drawing room was elegant yet above all, comfortable, crowded with furniture and mementos: a suite of carved and gilded sofas and chairs upholstered in amber-colored silk to match the curtains stood atop an Aubusson carpet, with consoles and cabinets crowded with miniature bronzes of the royal couple's long-dead pets, family busts, and even the tiny hands and feet of their young children, modeled in marble and displayed on crimson velvet cushions like macabre anatomical specimens.[29]

The southwestern end of the room gave way, through another screen of Corinthian columns, to the billiard room. Albert had been responsible for this unusual arrangement, which combined the two rooms into one larger, L-shaped space that allowed men to technically remain in the queen's presence while retreating around the corner to play billiards on a slate table adorned with Renaissance-style decorations.[30] Victoria had occasionally tried her hand at the game under her husband's tutelage, and deemed it entertaining.[31]

Double doors, which could be thrown open to form a U-shaped suite with the drawing room and the billiard room, led to the dining room, on the pavilion's eastern side. This was a light, airy room of soft salmon-colored walls dominated by a large bay window overlooking the terrace and sunken garden. An oval mahogany table surrounded by chairs upholstered in red morocco leather stood atop the crimson carpet, while the frieze and ceiling above were decorated with colorful geometric designs. Large family portraits hung upon the walls: Vicky and Fritz, with Wilhelm and Charlotte, painted by Winterhalter in 1862; the Prince and Princess of Wales, with Eddy and Maud, after Heinrich von Angeli; and another von Angeli canvas, depicting Alice and Ludwig, with several of their children. But the room was dominated by a large, idealized painting of Victoria and Albert with their children on the southern wall, painted in 1849 by Winterhalter and hung above an elaborately carved sideboard. The portrait and sideboard had acted as a makeshift altar when, in 1862, Princess Alice was married to Prince Ludwig of Hesse here; nearly forty years later, the queen's body would first lie in state in this room following her death.[32]

The impression left by these rooms was often one of subdued disdain. Frederick Ponsonby described them as "startling in their ugliness."[33] And his mother, Mary Ponsonby, declared: "You cannot think . . . how some of the atrocities here strike me. It certainly is the oddest combination of upholstery; hideous presents they have received, and as ill-arranged rooms as I ever saw, yet sprinkled also with beautiful things—pictures by Landseer, De la Roche, Scheffer, in this very room, and a certain kind of *luxe* which exists nowhere else."[34]

At the center of the pavilion, a U-shaped staircase rose between walls covered in imitation sienna marble, and beneath a massive fresco by Scottish artist William Dyce called *Neptune Entrusting the Command of the Seas to Britannia*. It was a flamboyant, theatrical work whose cavorting, bare-breasted nymphs scandalized the more prim ladies of the court.[35]

As in all of Victoria's residences, Albert's rooms remained exactly as he had left them, their walls hung with an impressive collection of Italian Renaissance art.[36] Victoria's sitting room, directly above the drawing room, was light and airy, with bright yellow silk walls and a floor covered in a vibrant floral carpet. Overstuffed sofas and armchairs, upholstered in bright floral chintz, emphasized the informality of the room, but two mahogany writing desks, pushed together and crammed with framed photographs, miniatures, bronzes, marble busts, and souvenirs, emphasized Victoria's role as working monarch. Above the ivory-veneered piano was a large canvas by Winterhalter, *Florinda*, depicting a group of female nudes frolicking in the forest, a gift from Victoria to Albert for his birthday in 1852.[37] In the evening, Victoria liked to sit on the small balcony that ringed the room's bow window, enjoying the views down the yew walk to the Solent; here, too, beneath the shade of a striped awning, she often took her morning coffee when the weather was warm.[38]

On the other side of the sitting room, occupying the pavilion's northeastern corner, was Victoria's combination dressing room and bathroom. The walls, painted a light peach color to contrast with the crimson floral carpet, were hung with family portraits, etchings, Italian landscapes, and pictures of the queen's favorite horses and pets. The furnishings were comfortable rather than luxurious, with a mahogany dresser and table, and an overstuffed armchair upholstered in chintz, but the dressing table was crowded with an elaborate looking glass and blue and white Minton toilette service, Christmas gifts from Albert in 1853. Hidden behind mirrored cupboard doors was a deep copper tub encased in mahogany with rope handles along the sides, and a separate, concealed shower lined in sienna scagliola. Such plumbing innovations were almost unknown in the 1840s, when Osborne was built, and were certainly more modern and luxurious than anything at Buckingham Palace or Windsor Castle. The lavatory was concealed in a part of the wardrobe that gave access to the bedroom beyond.[39]

A deep, three-sided bay flooded Victoria's aqua-colored bedroom, directly above the dining room, with light. Against the opposite wall stood an immense mahogany bed, its half canopy draped in white, red, and green chintz that covered the furniture and was hung on the windows. Family portraits and mementos cluttered the room, but the centerpiece was a large canvas, *The Entombment of Christ*, that hung over the chimneypiece; it was the last thing a dying Victoria would see.[40]

Osborne's situation made it among the most pleasant of all the queen's residences. Along the northern side, balustraded terraces adorned with urns filled with flowers in the summer offered views across the sloping lawns to the distant Solent, framed by tall cedars, elms, oaks, and chestnut trees selected and carefully placed by Albert.[41] Staircases descended to a sunken garden, laid out in the Italian manner with graveled paths, a splashing fountain with a figure of Venus, and ornamental statuary; in summer, the topiary-framed beds of geraniums, camellias, and azaleas mingled with the bright rhododendrons and the smell of magnolia and jasmine planted along the walls.[42]

Northeast of the house, the tree-framed High Walk stretched half a mile across lawns and past open meadows bordered by honeysuckle in the summer to a compound ringed by a fringe of trees.[43] Here Albert had laid out a garden for his children. There was a miniature fortress, built under the direction of an officer from the Royal Engineers and complete with earthen redoubts, a brick building christened the Albert Barracks, a moat crossed by a working drawbridge, and a miniature cannon. There also was a working garden, where each of the children had planted, tended, and harvested vegetables and cut flowers, using spades, shovels, and wheel-barrows monogrammed with their initials. This work was supervised by an agricultural expert, and the children were paid for their efforts, in an attempt to imbue them with a sense of the value of money.[44]

The centerpiece of the compound, however, was the Swiss Cottage, "a place of supreme enchantment," as Marie of Romania described the picturesque building, with its low, pitched roof adorned with stones, leaded windows dotted with boxes of colorful flowers, and second-floor balcony.[45] Purchased in Switzerland in 1853, it had been disassembled, shipped to the Isle of Wight, and then erected, making it the first prefab-ricated house of its size to be erected in Great Britain. The lower floor contained a child-size kitchen, where the princesses were taught to cook and bake; the results of their endeavors were served in the dining room upstairs, furnished with rustic, alpine-style furniture and reached by an exterior staircase.[46] "The location," wrote Stanley Weintraub, "a half-mile from Osborne House, suggests that the royal brood was to amuse itself (under household supervision) remote from parental eyes and ears."[47]

Osborne included a number of farms and cottages, where a thriving community soon developed. The queen had purchased the adjacent Barton Manor, a fifty-seven-room, Tudor-inspired building said to be haunted, to accommodate members of the household and staff, supple-mented with model workers' cottages, new stables, and a coach house.[48] There also were a number of houses built along the approach from York Road, including Albert Cottage, where Princess Beatrice lived for several years, and Kent House, used by the queen's physician, Sir James Reid, and later by her granddaughter Princess Victoria of Battenberg and her husband. To meet the queen's religious needs, Albert designed the Church of St. Mildred's at Whippingham, just down the hillside from Osborne, in 1860. It was here that the royal couple's youngest child, Princess Beatrice, married Prince Henry of Battenberg in 1885.

Victoria's fascination with India took visible form at Osborne. "Since age and frailty and distance had prevented her from going to India," wrote Stanley Weintraub, "she would have her own India."[49] She commissioned Austrian court painter Rudolf Swaboda to commemorate her Indian servants in canvases to adorn the lilac walls of a new corridor, along with a number of paintings and sketches of Indian dignitaries, members of the army, and schoolchildren.[50] The passage led to the most extraordinary manifestation of this obsession for, in 1890, Victoria did the unthinkable and, altering Albert's design, ordered the Durbar Wing to be added to the western end of the pavilion.

The Durbar Room, conceived as an evocation of colonial India, was designed by John Kipling, curator of the Lahore Museum and father of the famous Rudyard Kipling. The elaborate plaster reliefs on the walls and ceiling, as well as the carved teak fretwork and the jalti screens, were designed by Bhaj Ram Singh, from the Mayo School of Art in Lahore. Slender teak columns ornamented the white walls, along with traditional Mughal and Hindu motifs in sculpted plaster and in gold, including arabesques, peacocks, and representations of Ganesha. Despite her dislike of electricity, Victoria took advantage of it here, and the Durbar Room's stylized lamps, designed according to Indian motifs, made it the first room in a British royal residence designed specifically to showcase the new technology.[51]

After Albert's death, the queen preferred to reside at Osborne or at Balmoral, the two houses designed and created by her husband, in whose secluded surroundings she felt closest to his spirit. She came to Osborne twice each year, once in summer, from the middle of July to the end of August, and then again for Christmas, when she remained until the end of February.[52] Osborne was at its best in summer, when the gardens were in bloom, the emerald lawns stretching to the sparkling blue waters of the Solent and the sun washing over the building's mellow facade. Winter brought desolation, with rows of bare, leafless trees beneath a leaden gray sky, but Victoria preferred to spend Christmas here, surrounded by memories of happier times and far away from Windsor, with its associations of Albert's death. During the queen's absence, the house operated with a skeleton staff under the direction of Mrs. Mitchie, but the week before her arrival witnessed a flurry of activity. Extra maids were sent from Windsor to put the house in order: sheets were removed from furniture, chandeliers divested of their protective shrouds, windows and mirrors polished, floors scrubbed and swept, and desks and tables cleaned of dust.[53]

Although not as far removed from the capital as Balmoral, Osborne still presented strategic difficulties for the government. At ten every morning when the queen was in residence at Osborne, the royal tender *Elfin* sailed from Portsmouth, carrying the day's latest dispatches and government papers, brought by a messenger from London by early train. On landing at Trinity Pier at East Cowes, the dispatch boxes were handed to a second messenger for delivery to Osborne, while the previous day's communiqués were returned to Portsmouth and carried by train back to London.[54]

At Osborne, Victoria followed the same unvarying routine that regulated her life at Windsor. Although the weather was generally too inclement for her to take breakfast and luncheon outside, she still insisted on her regular afternoon drives, setting out in her pony cart or in a carriage under skies often gray and even wet with sleet. A favorite stop was the nearby Barton Manor. Here, when the small lake froze over, members of the household, together with Victoria's grandchildren, would gather to skate, and the queen would sit in her carriage, protected by a lap rug, and applaud their turns on the ice before returning to the comfort of Osborne House.[55]

Christmas at Osborne was celebrated with all the festive touches of previous royal holidays at Windsor, although, after Albert's December death in 1861, Victoria always regarded the celebrations somewhat wistfully. Conscious of the queen's sensitivity about the issue, Bishop William Boyd-Carpenter, one of her regular correspondents and a man frequently invited to deliver royal sermons, wrote to her that December of 1896: "I am thinking of the many memories, so rich in sorrowfulness, which the day must bring. I can but pray that over them all God will reach out His light to give comfort and sustain hope. . . . Time cannot heal the wounds of the heart. Light minds might think it can, but there are [depths] which the years cannot fill, there are vacant places which can never be occupied . . . though the heart aches as it views the empty place, it would not have it filled by any save the one who owns it."[56] In response to this sympathetic message, Victoria dispatched a Dutch Testament as a Christmas gift to the minister.[57]

Footmen and housemaids spent hours decorating the house: chimney-pieces were draped with boughs of holly, yew, and ferns, woven with cloves and set with candles to provide a sparkle; garlands of evergreen, dotted with holly and ivy, framed doorways; and poinsettias glowed red against the pastel walls. The florist provided miniature topiaries adorned with shimmering ropes of imitation jewels to grace tables, and large, festive bouquets of forced flowers to add scent and color. Even the kitchen and the white marble bust of Prince Albert in the foyer were jauntily adorned with garlands of holly and ivy.[58]

The celebrations called for a dozen trees. Although Albert had popularized the German custom of erecting a Christmas tree, it had actually been introduced to England by Victoria's grandmother Queen Charlotte.[59] The largest tree was placed in a tub at the foot of the grand staircase; another went into the drawing room, with trees for the queen's sitting room, the dining room, Princess Beatrice's suite, and rooms for the royal household. The household tree was erected in the Durbar Room. Several of these smaller trees, like that in the queen's sitting room, stood on tables covered in white cloth. All were carefully decorated by servants, their branches hung with blown glass and tin ornaments, bundles of cloves and cinnamon sticks, toffees and other small candies, silver tinsel, and red bows. Hundreds of candles, their holders clipped to branches, provided illumination, but the trees were not lit until Christmas Eve.[60]

On the afternoon of Christmas Eve, Victoria usually appeared at the staff party in the servants' hall at Osborne. Members of the domestic staff, along with employees on the estate, and their wives and children, crowded the room, awaiting the queen's arrival. Tables were filled with pastries, cookies, tea, and ale as the children raced around in anticipation. Presents for the servants, piled high on several tables, were always practical: clothing, bolts of cloth, meat pies, game, joints of meat, shoulders of lamb, and crocks containing plum pudding.[61] A footman handed each package to the queen, who presented it to its recipient as they passed by her in a receiving line. She took particular delight in meeting young children, handing each a gingerbread man and their own gifts of toys, clothing, or books. Carols were sung, followed by the national anthem, before the queen retired from the festivities.[62]

After tea, the queen distributed gifts to members of the household in the Durbar Room. The trees throughout the house had been lit, and

Osborne glowed with candlelight as night fell. Long tables, draped in white cloth, filled the length of the Durbar Room, crowded with presents and adorned with miniature trees of sugar crafted by the confectionery chef.[63] The queen repeated the ritual of handing out gifts, this time assisted by members of her family, who also gave presents to the household. Invariably these gifts were more lavish than those given to the domestic staff: men received silver or gold cigarette cases, dressing gowns, jeweled cufflinks, and watches, while women were given dresses, furs, and jewelry. There was also an assortment of expensive though useful household items, including silver salvers, tea services, silver coffeepots, paintings, and books, along with signed photographs of members of the royal family encased in gilded or leather presentation frames.[64]

Only after these two events were over did the queen and her family exchange their own presents, in private.[65] These were usually paintings, vases, busts, expensive porcelain toilette and dressing services, and jewelry. Once they had been given, they were all displayed on the tables in the Durbar Room; each member of the royal family had his or her own table, with all the gifts each had received artistically arranged on top so the queen could be wheeled up and down the room to inspect them.[66]

Christmas morning began with a religious service, followed by luncheon at one, and tea at five in the queen's sitting room, but the traditional Christmas meal was a late dinner that began at nine. The pink and crimson dining room glowed in the light of the candles set within garlands of evergreens and holly, while bright red poinsettias and tendrils of ivy adorned the white damask tablecloth. Preparations for Christmas took a month. Not only did the queen and her family have to be fed, but the day also called for elaborate meals for members of the household and domestic staff. To meet the holiday's culinary needs, the *chef de cuisine* ordered up to 50 turkeys, a 140-pound baron of beef that took 10 hours to roast over a spit, hundreds of pounds of lamb, dozens of geese, and crate after crate of vegetables, all shipped by train from Windsor.[67] The confectionery chef and his staff spent days crafting 82 pounds of raisins, 60 pounds of orange and lemon peel, 2 pounds of cinnamon, 330 pounds of sugar, 24 bottles of brandy, and cup after cup of sugar into the Christmas mincemeat.[68]

Footmen and underbutlers handed around the courses to the queen and her family. A stiff white vellum card, bordered with golden garlands and topped with a painting of Osborne set beneath the royal coat of arms, listed the queen's Christmas dinner for 1896: *la tête de veau en tortue, aux trois racines; le turbot bouilli sauce hollandaise; les filets de soles frits; les Kromeskys à la Toulouse; les dindes rôties à la Chipolata*; chine of pork; roast sirloin of beef; plum pudding; *les asperges sauce mousseline*; mince pies; and *le pain de riz à la cintra*. A side table offered even more selections: a baron of beef, woodcock pie, brawn, a wild boar's head, and game pie.[69] Inevitably the meal ended with plum pudding, crafted from 150 eggs, 30 pounds of sugar, and 4 gallons of ale, generously soaked with rum and brandy and topped with a butter custard sauce.[70] This stupor-inducing feast was usually followed by Christmas entertainment: a specially invited musician or singer who performed for the queen and her family before midnight brought the holiday to an end.

Even in its desolate winter isolation, Victoria found comfort at Osborne. In the Italianate palazzo on the Isle of Wight, as at Balmoral, she felt herself embraced by the legacy of her departed husband. To the end of her life, as she wrote to her daughter Vicky, she regarded Osborne as "a dear paradise, which I always deeply grieve to leave."[71]

11

EASTER IN FRANCE

ON MARCH 10, 1897, QUEEN VICTORIA climbed into a closed carriage and drove from Windsor to her private railway siding at the station below the castle's walls. Safely ensconced in a luxurious railway carriage with her daughter Beatrice and Beatrice's children in tow, she set off for Folkestone.[1] In a few hours she would escape the gray, rainy English spring for her annual holiday in the south of France.

Victoria had been in the habit of going abroad each spring since 1890, staying at Biarritz, Aix-les-Bains, and Florence. In 1895 she visited Cimiez, a small village above Nice, and fell in love with the lush surroundings and tropical gardens; she returned to Cimiez for the next five years.[2] With the approach of each year's holiday, Marie Mallet recalled, Victoria displayed a girlish excitement, "as if she were seventeen instead of seventy-two."[3]

Such visits took months of planning. Victoria always stayed in a hotel, which reserved several floors or a wing for her exclusive use; staff had to be interviewed and screened by security officials; menu preferences discussed so that the required provisions were always ready; routes for proposed excursions were walked and inspected to avoid any unforeseen hazards; schedules for receptions and officials welcomes worked out; and railway timetables reviewed and selected.

These holidays did not lack royal trappings, and Victoria traveled with a massive entourage whose size was matched only by the mountain of possessions that always accompanied her. Among those joining the queen to attend to her needs were upward of a hundred courtiers and servants.[4] When Colonel Sir William Carington, one of her equerries, reviewed the list, he gently suggested that she might not require such a large body at her disposal while staying in a hotel. But after going over the names, Victoria dismissed his concerns, saying that she could not do without a single person who was scheduled to accompany her.[5] And so the queen was joined by a lady-in-waiting and two maids of honor; a dresser and five wardrobe maids; her private secretary; four equerries and four grooms; a French chef, Monsieur Ferry, with several assistant chefs; kitchen and scullery maids; housemaids and butlers; footmen; coachmen and a dozen grooms and stable boys; several doctors, along with a dentist and a nurse; detectives; her Highland and Indian servants; her chaplain; and an assortment of domestic servants.[6]

And then there were the possessions: suitcases and trunks of clothes; familiar sofas, chairs, and desks from Windsor, as well as Victoria's own bed, packed into crates and cases and loaded aboard the train; the queen's own linens; her favorite paintings, busts, and objets d'art; family photographs and Oriental carpets; books, china, silver, and crystal; several carriages and her pony chaise; two dozen horses; and Jacquot, Victoria's favorite white donkey.[7] On one journey this amounted to seventy-six crates of possessions, all stamped "H. M. The Queen of England."[8] Despite such flamboyance, Victoria insisted on anonymity, and traveled as the Countess of Balmoral or the Countess of Lancaster, though no one was fooled.[9]

The 1897 holiday was the queen's seventh visit to the Riviera.[10] After the train journey from Windsor to Folkestone, the queen left her compartment and drove to the dock, where the royal yacht *Victoria and Albert II* lay at anchor. As she appeared, the guard of honor saluted, and a regimental band struck up the national anthem. The queen was now too frail to board *Victoria and Albert II* by herself, and her Highland servants carried her, sitting in her wheelchair, up the steep gangway, which had been covered with a protective awning to shield her from curious eyes.[11]

Victoria and Albert II had been commissioned in 1854 to replace the slightly smaller, twelve-year-old *Victoria and Albert*. The original vessel had been the first royal yacht powered by steam, propelled through the water by port and starboard paddle wheels driven by steam engines below. It was, however, cramped, particularly when the royal family traveled with the voluminous household and domestic staff. The new yacht, built at Pembroke Dockyard in Wales, was designed not only to impress, but also to offer more space for the queen and her family. Like its predecessor, it featured twin paddle wheels on either side of its black wooden hull, capable of propelling it through the water at fifteen knots, but at 360 feet and 2,400 tons it was much larger than its namesake. It also featured cleaner lines, modeled after a schooner, with a gold-encrusted sprit jutting from its black bow, a white superstructure of day cabins, two buff-colored funnels, and three tall masts towering above the teak deck.[12]

Victoria and Albert II featured three decks. The main rooms were on the upper deck, where the large, square windows of the dining saloon allowed views out over the water; the walls were hung with pleated green silk and circled with fitted mahogany sofas covered in green leather. At the center, atop the crimson Brussels carpet, stood the dining table, ringed by delicate gilded chairs upholstered in green leather.[13] The drawing room, similarly decorated in green, white, and red, was finished in bird's-eye maple and included tables fringed with gilded iron railings to prevent their contents from sliding off in rough seas, bookcases, sofas and armchairs, and even an upright piano.[14]

Victoria's bedroom was hung in green pleated silk, the half canopy of its mahogany bed draped in bright white chintz patterned with rosebuds.[15] Immediately below were further cabins for members of the royal family, the household, and members of the queen's personal domestic staff, each equipped with sofas that transformed into beds at night. The lowest deck, lacking any portholes, housed the galleys, crowded ratings for the members of the crew, and holds for the luggage.[16]

The complement of 240 sailors and officers, clad in their white and blue uniforms, fell under the direction of Rear Admiral Fullerton, commander of the yacht.[17] It was Fullerton's job to ensure that the queen's nighttime voyage to the Continent was a pleasant one; the yacht was always accompanied by a contingent of torpedo boats to maintain security and to be on hand in the event of any unforeseen emergency.[18]

The voyage to Cherbourg was generally uneventful, though occasionally the vessel encountered heavy seas. Victoria enjoyed sea travel, though rough weather often brought seasickness, which her doctor attempted to quell through doses of chloroform.[19] There were also lighter moments. Once, she was seated on deck when an officer asked her if she would move. "Move my seat?" said the queen. "Why should I? What possible harm can I be doing here?"

"The fact is," he replied, "Your Majesty is unwittingly closing the door of the place where the grog tubs are kept, and so the men cannot have their grog."

"Oh, very well," replied Victoria. "I will move on one condition: that you bring me a glass of grog." This was done, but after tasting it, she replied, "I think it would be very good if it were stronger."[20]

Despite the pretense of anonymity, Victoria's arrival in France witnessed a full display of pageantry. A red tent fringed with gold stood along the quay, sheltering the mayor and local officials; a guard of honor presented arms as Victoria descended the gangway, her progress announced by the shrill salutes of buglers. As soon as she set foot on the dock, a regimental band struck up "God Save the Queen" followed by "Le Marseilles." "What with the band playing and the crowd continually cheering vociferously," recalled Frederick Ponsonby, "it was difficult to hear anything."[21]

On the Continent, Victoria kept several private railways cars for her use. The two carriages had been built and outfitted in Belgium, according to instructions from the queen and from British railway officials.[22] The first contained a small compartment reserved for the queen's Highland servant Rankin and opened to Victoria's drawing room. The lower walls of the drawing room were quilted with blue silk, with a brocaded gray and yellow silk woven with the English rose, the Scottish thistle, and the Irish shamrock, above. An overstuffed sofa and armchairs in the Louis XVI style, covered in blue silk edged with yellow fringe, offered seating during the day. At night the queen retreated to the second carriage, containing a small dressing room adorned with Oriental motifs; a bedroom, with two beds, one for Victoria, and one for her daughter Beatrice; and a small compartment for the queen's dresser.[23] Xavier Paoli, the French official charged with arranging security for the queen, noted that "its somewhat antiquated splendor" gave the train "the exact appearance of an old fashioned apartment in a provincial town. Everything about it was heavy, large and comfortable. I used to feel as if I was traveling in a steam bath chair; and I must confess that in this rolling palace, the journey never appeared either very long or very tiring."[24]

For these journeys, Paoli worked with the courier Ernest Dossé, who had served as Director of Her Majesty's Continental Journeys since his appointment in May 1890.[25] The queen's own railway carriages had no brakes, so that the noise of stopping would not wake her. The locomotive that pulled the train on the Continent was instructed not to exceed thirty-five miles per hour during the day and twenty-five miles per hour at night.[26] Although the Wagon-Lits Company had introduced restaurant cars a decade earlier, Victoria ordered regular stops so she could take meals at station restaurants carefully selected in advance.[27] The one exception was tea, for which the queen brought her own copper kettle and which was prepared and served to her during the journey.[28] The train halted between eight and nine each morning so Victoria could dress, and again for breakfast, luncheon, and dinner.[29] These frequent stops, coupled with the deliberately slow speed demanded by the queen, meant that the railway journey to the Riviera, which normally took eight hours, was more than doubled, lasting some twenty hours.[30]

Although the visit was a private one, and Victoria traveled using an assumed name, diplomatic niceties still dictated an official welcome. For her arrival in Nice on Friday, March 12, 1897, the railway siding was decorated with potted palms and covered with a length of crimson carpet bordered in gold. The queen, assisted by the munshi, stepped from her carriage and, leaning heavily on her cane, was greeted by the mayor with a short welcoming speech before she climbed into an open landau to drive to her hotel. Four infantry regiments and an artillery battery ringed the station and lined the route, holding back an immense crowd that cheered and waved miniature Union Jacks as the queen's carriage passed through the city.[31]

Located in the hills just over a mile above Nice, the town of Cimiez and its surrounding districts had long been a destination for members of Europe's royal families seeking cures and relaxation in the restorative climate. In addition to the English, it was a favorite holiday resort among members of the Russian imperial family: Tsesarevich Nicholas, son of Alexander II and onetime fiancé to the sister of the Princess of Wales, had died in a villa here in 1865, and by the 1890s the assassinated tsar's second, morganatic wife, Princess Catherine Yourievskaya, lived in an ornate little palace high above the sea. Cypress, palm, and olive trees cloaked the hillsides, offering shade, while in the distance the crystal blue waters of the Mediterranean sparkled and shimmered in the southern sunshine.

On her previous visits to Nice, Victoria had stayed at the Grand Hotel at Cimiez, on a slope above the city center. It was, however, somewhat small and suffered from a pervasive damp.[32] In March 1897 she was installed in the new Beaux Arts Hotel Excelsior Regina, a long, six-storeyed building erected on the hillside at Cimiez by a wealthy perfume merchant from Grasse and named in her honor.[33] Although one of the queen's household called it "an insult to dear old Cimiez," the new hotel, gleaming white and dotted with blue balconies, boasted ample space for Victoria and her entourage.[34] Parisian architect Sebastien-Marcel Biasini had designed an entire wing, facing west to the sea and topped with a cupola adorned with a crown, for the queen's use. The royal household took over some seventy rooms in the hotel, at a cost of 80,000 francs or £3,200 (£241,900, or $413,649 in 2007 currency) for the eight weeks of the queen's stay.[35]

Victoria's suite of rooms was on the first floor, reached by an elevator in an elaborate ironwork cage. There was a small chapel just off the lobby, where the queen could worship in private, with members of the household forming a choir.[36] Her drawing room, hung in red brocaded silk, was filled with her own furniture brought from England, potted palms, and a grand piano.[37] The dining room sported a "vulgar, glaring paper," hung with copies of the coronation portraits of George III and Queen Charlotte that looked down on the square mahogany table ringed with leather-covered chairs.[38] Victoria's bedroom, hung in rose-colored silk, was dominated by her own mahogany and chintz-hung bed, sent from Windsor.[39] These rooms, decorated with the queen's own possessions, formed the seat of the British monarchy that spring. Every detail duplicated her life in England: flowers were sent from Osborne and Windsor, and even the writing paper was identical, with "Hotel Regina Excelsior, Cimiez" engraved beneath her embossed royal cipher.[40]

Victoria's days on the Riviera passed leisurely. She generally rose late, dressed, and took her breakfast beneath an open tent in the garden at nine-thirty.[41] Her breakfasts consisted of an assortment of dishes: eggs, fried fish, sweet rolls, grilled bacon, and sausages, taken with coffee, tea, or hot chocolate. Usually, just as Victoria finished breakfast and returned to her rooms, street musicians and singers would gather. "Morning serenades were provided by the Neapolitan strollers," recalled Xavier Paoli, "those wandering singers and guitar players who so picturesquely bring home to one the sun of Italy and who in many cases are gifted with admirable voices. The queen liked their songs and was amused by their animated gestures. The whole brotherhood of strummers and garden Carusos knew her partiality and of the generous fee that awaited them; and every morning at the stroke of ten, some of them would be seen entering the grounds. They crept stealthily to a spot just under the royal balcony when for an hour at a time they spun out their songs," watched by the queen above. At the end, Victoria always rewarded them with generous gifts.[42]

After this, Victoria settled down to the official business that, regardless of her location, never ceased. Several times a week, the queen's messengers brought her red leather dispatch boxes from the British government, containing official correspondence and state papers; there were also regular telegrams, in cipher, that her private secretary read, advising on their contents. There were also, despite the queen's pretense of anonymity, hundreds of unsolicited letters outlining injustices or pleading for gifts of money or intervention. Xavier Paoli reviewed all of these letters, charged with not only sorting out the obvious crank letters from the genuine pleas, but also investigating what could be done in certain cases. The majority, as he admitted, "eventually found their way into the waste paper basket."[43]

The queen's private garden at the hotel was a tropical paradise, with lush flower beds, carefully graded graveled walks to allow Victoria's wheelchair to be pushed along them, and larger paths beneath the shade of tall palm and cypress trees for her donkey cart. Fountains splashed in sunken lawns rimmed with statuary, providing a tranquil oasis in which the queen could sit and answer correspondence and listen as books were read aloud.[44] After luncheon at one, which the queen frequently took in the shade of a tent in the garden, she often drove in her pony cart, drawn by her favorite white donkey brought specially from Windsor, in the adjoining gardens of the Cazalet Villa Liserb, which had been lent to her by the owners during her tenure.[45]

On these drives, Victoria met and befriended a young Dutch girl named Annie, who also was staying at the hotel, with her family. Completely at ease with the queen, Annie introduced the queen to her dog, Johnnie, and Victoria responded by inviting the pair on her rides through the gardens, and even to join her for tea.[46] It was but one example of the change in the queen during her holiday; members of the household noted that she became more lighthearted and seemed to enjoy herself.[47]

In the afternoon Victoria usually left the protective confines of the hotel and the gardens of Villa Liserb to drive along the Corniche; there were calls to visiting European royal friends and relatives, including the widowed empress Eugenie, who holidayed in her Villa Cyrnos at nearby Cap Martin. There were also less pleasant destinations. In 1884 the queen's son Leopold had fallen and suffered a fatal hemorrhage at Cannes, and Victoria often visited the Villa Nevada, where he had died, and the Church of St. George, erected in his memory.[48] Most afternoons, however, the queen played tourist, traveling to the small, picturesque towns along the rugged coastline, though her progresses were scarcely quiet excursions: the guards on duty signaled her departure with a bugle announcement, and once more than a hundred carriages filled with curious onlookers crowded the hotel driveway, hoping to catch a glimpse of Victoria as she left the confines of its protective gardens.[49] Local children, recognizing her, chased her carriage, shouting, "Madame la Reine!" Victoria did not mind such attention and appeared moved at the reception, saying that she liked what she termed "the foreign easy manner."[50] "I was given a purse full of copper coins," recalled a relative who accompanied her, "which I had to give to all the children who threw flowers into the carriage."[51]

Victoria found the countryside entrancing. To her granddaughter Victoria of Hesse she rhapsodized about the "masses of olives," "orchards laden with lemons, and also orange trees growing half up the fine, high mountains," and "eucalyptus as high as elms" that made "the vegetation quite wonderful to see. Over all this a deep blue sky and the calm sea from which you have delicious breezes and you can well imagine the enchantment of the whole country, though the sun is too hot to walk in except quite early in the morning."[52]

The queen, Paoli recalled, "liked to go to the local festivals, particularly those which recalled the ancient customs of the country," including religious services and street markets, where she often purchased gifts for her family and household.[53] Beggars, hungry children, and the homeless lined the queen's route, and she was regularly shadowed by Charles Alberque, a one-legged man from Marseilles, driving wildly in a cart pulled by two large dogs in an effort to attract her attention.[54] After she bestowed some coins on him, he took to driving about the town with a placard on his cart that read: "By appointment to Her Majesty the Queen."

Alberque was not the only recipient of this royal largesse. Victoria always carried a small purse, from which she distributed various amounts to those she encountered.[55] There were also visits to local churches and museums, where she examined the paintings, frescoes, and works of art keenly; during one foreign holiday, she startled those around her by pulling out a locket with her dead husband's portrait and waving it around in the air, explaining that she thought Albert would enjoy it as well.[56]

Dinners were almost always informal, though occasionally a favored local official or a royal guest on holiday joined the queen. Victoria's French chef, Monsieur Ferry, worked with the hotel kitchens to produce suitable dishes; a member of the household recalled that the results were "really excellent."[57] Dinners began with a soup course, usually the queen's favorite, *crème de volaille*, followed by a fish course; a main course of beef, pork, or lamb; vegetables; salad; and a selection of desserts. Occasionally the queen liked to sample more exotic dishes, including curries from India.[58]

In the evening, musicians, singers, and actors often came to entertain the queen. On April 22, famed actress Sarah Bernhardt, who was giving a performance in Nice, came to the hotel to recite for the queen. Victoria had never seen her perform and had requested a special presentation. Shortly after six that evening the queen, accompanied by several dozen members of her household, crowded into the private drawing room at the

Hotel Excelsior Regina to watch the actress perform a short selection from *Jean Marie* by André Theuriet.[59] "It was extremely touching," Victoria wrote, "and Sarah Bernhardt's acting was quite marvelous, so pathetic and full of feeling. She appeared much affected herself, tears rolling down her cheeks. She has a most beautiful voice, and is very graceful in all her movements." At the end of the recital Bernhardt curtsied to the elderly queen, saying that "it had been such a pleasure and honor to act" for the queen.[60]

Before the actress returned to her hotel, she signed the queen's birthday book, a large, leather-bound album whose appropriate page she filled by writing, "*Le plus beau jour de ma vie*," followed by a florid signature. When Victoria learned of this, however, she expressed dismay: Bernhardt, she told her equerry Frederick Ponsonby, should not have signed the birthday book, but the similar artists' book. She ordered Ponsonby to correct the error, and obtain the actress's signature in the appropriate volume. This task proved somewhat more difficult than the equerry had imagined. The actress was due to leave the Riviera in a day, and Ponsonby had to rush to the theater for her last performance. He explained his mission to the manager, who believed him to be simply another ardent admirer and dismissed him. After several hours Ponsonby managed to reach Bernhardt's secretary, explaining the error and asking that she sign the appropriate volume. Ponsonby duly presented the correct book, and Bernhardt, with characteristic wit, inscribed a new entry: "*Je l'ai déjà écrit*," With the signature secured in the proper volume, Ponsonby was able to report to his mistress that her request had been satisfied.[61]

The queen's reception of Bernhardt caused a good deal of comment, particularly among members of the royal family. Her daughter Vicky was horrified that her mother had stooped so low. She had warned her own daughter Sophie against meeting the actress, as "no *lady* can, she is so very bad, and has an awful reputation."[62] A good deal of this reputation, Vicky might have noted, derived from Bernhardt's well-known affair with her own brother Bertie, the Prince of Wales. The queen, however, was delighted.

To the queen's consternation and despair, much of her spring 1897 visit to Cimiez was consumed with one distasteful question: the behavior of her greatly trusted munshi, Abdul Karim. He had first appeared at court in 1887, at age twenty-four, along with several other newly imported Indian servants, including his brother-in-law Hourmet Ali and the rather plump Mahomet Buksh. Tall and dark, with a black beard and piercing eyes, Abdul Karim at first served as little more than a glorified footman, waiting on the queen and handing around dishes during meals.[63] In their blue or white robes, adorned with turbans and colored sashes, these attendants served breakfast and tea; at night, attired in richly embroidered scarlet and gold robes, they assisted at the dinner table, lending a festive touch to the proceedings.[64]

"At first," noted one observer, "the queen was merely excited about them as a child would be with a new toy. Their attendance in their picturesque costumes gave a ceremonial reminder that she was Empress of India."[65] Then, in 1889, Victoria elevated Abdul Karim to the position of her personal Indian servant, with the title of Munshi Hafiz Abdul Karim. He was relieved of any ordinary domestic duties. Although he was barely literate, he began to teach the queen Hindustani, and he was richly rewarded in a way that no one had seen at court since the death of John Brown in 1883. Among his gifts were fully furnished houses at Osborne and Balmoral as well as a cottage at Frogmore.[66] Victoria favored the munshi and his compatriots, she once explained, because they were "so clever when they help me out of my chair or into a carriage," adding that "they never pinch me."[67]

The queen had elevated Abdul Karim partially in response to his constant complaints that the menial work he was routinely given was beneath his class. He was, he maintained, the son of the surgeon-general to the Indian army at Agra. Victoria accepted this, though no one else was convinced, and most of the rest of her household despised him. When the munshi was granted the right to eat with the household and to join the male members in the billiard room in the evenings, there was a near revolt, which Henry Ponsonby, Bigge's predecessor as private secretary, barely managed to quell. It was all he could do, he complained, to prompt the rest of the household into offering the munshi a polite greeting each morning.[68] Many members of the household, wrote James Pope-Hennessy, "loathed the Munshi." One member of the household later recalled: "The Indian servants behind her chair looked rather splendid, we could take them, but the Munshi was so personally repulsive and disagreeable that he was impossible. He made endless troubles, too."[69]

"Though one can understand that the Munshi was disliked, as favorites nearly always are," wrote one author, "it is difficult to believe that he was 'so personally repulsive,' for Queen Victoria was as sensitive as any woman to male attraction. One cannot help feeling that the repugnance with which he was regarded by the Household was based mostly on snobbery and color prejudice."[70] This took the form of vicious gossip, which hinted that the munshi was a spy who acted to influence the queen in governmental affairs related to India. But there were also rather more concrete reasons for the antipathy the munshi engendered. In 1889 Victoria lost a jeweled brooch that had been given to her by her son-in-law Grand Duke Ludwig IV of Hesse; it was later found for sale in a jeweler's store, where it had been brought by Abdul Karim's brother-in-law Hourmet Ali. Mary Tuck, the queen's dresser, managed to get it back, along with a letter stating that it had been sold by Hourmet Ali; the clear inference was that Ali had stolen the brooch, but Victoria was furious at the suggestion that he had done anything wrong. She insisted that, like his brother, Ali was "a model of honesty and uprightness and would never dream of stealing anything."[71]

The munshi was far from the model of moral rectitude Victoria believed him to be; by 1897 he was suffering from venereal disease, and one of his chief delights was to find ways in which to enforce the royal favor that had fallen onto him, in increasingly unsubtle displays of what he took as his unassailable position.[72] Insistence on what he took as his rights and precedence, coupled with a barely disguised air of haughtiness, made Abdul Karim the most hated man at court.

The situation erupted into a crisis when, in spring 1897, the queen declared that she wished to take the munshi with her to France. His inclusion meant that the gentlemen of the household would, by virtue of etiquette, be forced to not only associate with him but also to share meals with him. This idea was simply too much for most to contemplate, and the male household threatened to resign en masse if the queen forced the situation. Hoping to avert disaster, the men delegated the Honorable Harriet

Phipps to present their ultimatum to the queen, but Victoria was never receptive to threats. Told that she must choose between her household and the munshi, Victoria responded in an uncharacteristic burst of temper, furiously sweeping the contents of her desk onto the floor and declaring that she would not be told what to do.[73]

The 1897 journey to Cimiez was fraught with difficulties; the munshi insisted on his own sleeping compartment and refused to associate with the other Indian servants, considering himself their social superior.[74] The litany of complaints continued as he ran up bills and made indiscreet remarks about his treatment, all somewhat gleefully chronicled by Sir James Reid in anticipation of a future confrontation.

The storm was not long in coming. The Prince of Wales had given Reid his assurance that he would fully support any stand the household took against the munshi. On March 27 the queen, who had no idea what was taking place, sent Prince Louis of Battenberg—husband of her granddaughter Princess Victoria of Hesse—to the gentlemen of the household in attendance, demanding that they associate more with the hated Abdul Karim. This once again forced the issue, and the gentlemen all agreed to resign if she insisted. There the matter rested for forty-eight hours, as strategies were discussed and options weighed.[75]

Then there was the question of the munshi's supposed background. Frederick Ponsonby, who had been aide-de-camp to the viceroy of India, had investigated the munshi's father at Victoria's request. He discovered that, contrary to Abdul Karim's claim, his father was not surgeon-general to the Indian Army at Agra but rather a regular apothecary at a local jail. When Ponsonby had delivered this news a few years earlier, the queen refused to believe him, protesting that he must have interviewed the wrong man; when Ponsonby insisted on the matter, Victoria refused to speak to him for a month; in retaliation, she also refused him the customary invitations to dine with her for a year.[76]

Victoria had been angry, writing that the attacks on "the poor, good Munshi" were baseless, and "really *outrageous* and in a country like England." For good measure, she added that she had known "two archbishops who were the sons respectively of a Butcher and a Grocer, a Chancellor whose father was a poor sort of Scotch Minister, Sir D.

Stewart and Lord Mount Stephen both who ran about barefoot as children and whose parents were very humble. . . . Abdul's father saw good honorable service as a Dr. . . . It probably comes from some low jealous Indians or Anglo-Indians. . . . The Queen is so sorry for the poor Munshi's sensitive feelings."[77]

On April 2, 1897, the government warned that the munshi was suspected of associating with members of the radical Muslim Patriotic League, an organization determined to undermine British colonial rule in India; it was even said, largely on the basis of rumor, that the munshi had passed on the contents of confidential state papers to its members. Reid also had new cables from the viceroy of India, supporting Frederick Ponsonby's account of Karim's family history. In an extraordinary conversation with the queen on April 4, he laid out his litany of rather petty complaints; to reinforce his position, he bluntly added—and with a fair amount of hyperbole—that many highly placed people "say to me that the only charitable explanation that can be given is that Your Majesty is not sane." Confronted with this accumulation of evidence mingled with gossip, Victoria broke down, believing that she had allowed herself to be used by the munshi.[78]

Armed with this royal repentance, Reid challenged Abdul Karim, laying out the list of facts uncovered, abuses indulged in, and rumors eagerly accepted. Calling him "a scoundrel," Reid informed the munshi that his actions would now be carefully watched and warned that any infraction would result in dismissal. By this time, however, the queen had thought better of her earlier contrition; perhaps she recognized something of the class and racial prejudice that may have underlain much of the collective antipathy toward the munshi. In any case, she now refused to part with the chastised Abdul Karim. Indeed, she issued instructions to the gentlemen of the household that they "should not go on talking about this painful subject either amongst themselves, or with outsiders, and not combine with the household against the person."[79] The munshi remained at her court for the rest of her reign.

After this fracas, the rest of the queen's holiday was something of a skillful dance, with everyone avoiding the subject uppermost on all minds. Victoria continued to undertake her excursions and, on Easter, celebrated the holiday with a religious service and by enjoying the illuminated gardens and the fireworks that burst over the Mediterranean. But the household fireworks had soured the holiday, and on April 29 the queen left Cimiez to return to England.[80] Less than four years later, as an increasingly ill Victoria entered the last few weeks of her life, her journal entry said simply, "If I were only at Nice I should recover."[81]

12

SUMMER AT BUCKINGHAM PALACE

AT THE WESTERN END OF THE MALL, framed by leafy trees and reflected in the languid lake of St. James's Park, stands Buckingham Palace, the ceremonial seat of the British monarchy. Behind its dour facade stretched an enfilade of twenty richly appointed rooms that had provided an exquisite background to the balls, banquets, and investitures over which Victoria had presided in the years before Albert's death. With her retreat into solitude, windows were shuttered, furniture covered in cloth, and chandeliers shrouded against the pernicious London air, and Victoria rarely returned to its gilded splendors. Now, as the Diamond Jubilee approached and the queen reluctantly returned to her principal residence to embark on its ceremonies and celebrations, the hulking building slowly came to life, once again witness to the parade of society and the pageantry of the British court.

In her later years, Victoria disliked London, and she particularly hated Buckingham Palace, a "curiously built house," she once declared.[1] It had begun life two centuries earlier as Goring House, an aristocratic residence in what was then an isolated and tranquil mulberry garden. Rebuilt by the Earl of Arlington after a disastrous fire in 1674, it passed through a succession of owners before the Duke of Buckingham, one of the wealthi- est and most powerful aristocrats in the country, purchased it at the beginning of the eighteenth century. His Buckingham House, enlarged and decorated in a lavish style, was not only the envy of all London but also of the royal family, who possessed nothing as luxurious in their capital.[2] Indeed, George III had once famously declared on visiting the Duke of Marlborough's splendid Blenheim Palace in Oxfordshire, "We have nothing to equal this."[3]

It was another sixty years, however, before it came into the possession of the royal family. In 1761, the Buckingham heirs sold the structure to King George III, who presented it to his wife, Queen Charlotte, on their wedding.[4] Although their official residences in London remained St. James's Palace and Kensington Palace; the building at the end of the Mall was rechristened the Queen's House, and George and Charlotte were the first monarchs to live within its walls. But it was their eldest son, George IV, who, inheriting the house on his mother's death, transformed the structure into a grand palace.

George IV was an inveterate builder, lavishing millions of pounds on his fantastic Indian and Oriental Royal Pavilion at Brighton and the equally luxurious Carlton House, just down the Mall. The Queen's House, with its simple brick facade and lack of space, possessed none of the grandeur George IV deemed necessary to his reign; what it did have, however, was a fine situation, overlooking St. James's Park and the broad length of the Mall to the east, and a large, secluded garden to the west, benefits not possessed by Carlton House. Armed with a parliamentary grant of some £200,000 (£12,967,770, or $22,174,886 in 2007 figures), George IV embarked on a program that completely transformed the building into a suitably regal residence.[5]

To undertake the transformation, George called upon his favorite architect, John Nash. Nash, the man responsible not only for the Royal Pavilion in Brighton and Carlton House but also for London's famous Regent Street, turned his refined eye to the structure at the end of the Mall. Although he kept the basic shell of the old house intact, he extended the central block, adding a suite of rooms to the west, marked at intervals with projecting columns and small pavilions to enhance the regal effect.[6] A balustraded terrace, flanked by conservatories ringed with Ionic columns, stretched below a projecting bow topped with a low dome that one wag condemned as a "common slop pail turned upside down."[7] On the eastern side, Nash constructed a new, two-storeyed portico supported by paired Corinthian columns, flanked by long wings ending in matching porticoes to frame the courtyard.[8] To further increase the impression of size, the architect built colonnaded screens stretching north and south and, in a final flourish, he erected the Marble Arch—commemorating the British victories at Trafalgar and Waterloo—at the center of the forecourt.[9]

By 1829, Nash's work at the palace had cost nearly four times the amount allotted by Parliament, and the structure was still incomplete when George IV died in 1830. The new king, William IV, hated the unfinished palace and even offered it to Parliament for their use, but too much money had been poured into the project to simply abandon it. Parliament fired the extravagant Nash and commissioned Edward Blore to complete the building.[10] Blore was a dependable if unimaginative architect, his style somewhat staid and uninspired, but he had one asset above all others that commended him to the government: a reputation for thrift.[11]

Blore raised the palace's central block and removed Nash's ridiculed dome, leaving a building stripped of its original Regency delicacy but more monumental in appearance.[12] He had nearly completed his work when, in June 1837, William IV died, and Victoria became the first sovereign to take up permanent residence in the new Buckingham Palace. For several years she was happy enough, but Albert did not disguise his opinion that the palace was unworthy of the monarchy. Although George III had housed his fifteen children and his court here in a much smaller house, Victoria—under her husband's influence—gradually found much to criticize, complaining of the "total want of accommodation for our own little family, which is fast growing up." In addition, she wrote, "Most parts of the Palace are in a sad state, and will ere long require a further outlay to render them *decent* for the occupation of the Royal Family or any visitors the Queen may have to receive."[13]

In truth, there were genuine problems: windowless servants' rooms were tucked away in damp attics, and the sanitation was abysmal, with sewage pipes emptying into courtyards and onto roofs, creating an overwhelming stench. Waste pooled on the cobblestones of the kitchen court, and rats overran the structure.[14] Most of the fireplaces did not work, doors would not close, and windows could not be opened.[15] The influential architecture magazine *The Builder* spoke of the "amusing report of the distressing position of our illustrious Queen and accomplished Consort," and their "domestic discomforts and miserable home," scathingly noting: "So melancholy a picture, so touchingly set forth, deprived the House of Commons of anything but thought for immediate improvement and, with tears in their eyes, they at once voted £20,000 in part of the sum of £150,000 for the enlargement of Buckingham Palace."[16]

With this new grant, Victoria called on Blore; in addition to the necessary structural and sanitary changes, Blore suggested a new, eastern wing, which would provide more space. This work closed off the forecourt and necessitated the removal of the Marble Arch to its present position in Hyde Park; unfortunately, it also concealed Nash's magnificent grand portico, depriving the palace of its central feature. Nor did his new wing attempt to replicate the stylistic elements of Nash's existing building; Blore adorned its Caen stone façade with rusticated quoins, decorative reliefs, urns, and statuary in an attempted display of splendor, but the results were less than impressive. *The Builder* declared: "It will be seen that the design does not pretend to grandeur or magnificence, scarcely to dignity," and noted: "The architect was probably right in attempting, in the present instance, little more than an ordinary piece of street architecture in stone instead of stucco."[17] These renovations brought the number of rooms at Buckingham Palace to just over six hundred.[18]

The bulk of the completed palace concealed its gardens, some thirty-nine acres enclosed behind a high brick wall. After 1840, when seventeen-year-old Edmund Jones broke into the palace, Prince Albert had the top of the wall set with revolving iron spikes to prevent further incursions.[19] Unlike most European palaces, the gardens were deliberately informal; here, the elaborate parterres, splashing fountains, careful allées, and ornamental sculptures were replaced with an idyllic scene that echoed the work of the great eighteenth-century landscape architect Lancelot "Capability" Brown. An artificial, serpentine lake, rimmed by wild reeds and set with a small island planted with weeping willows, provided an expansive mirror to the golden Bath stone of the palace's western facade. Sweeping, rolled lawns, crossed by winding graveled paths leading to hidden pavilions, were planted with oak, elm, and chestnut trees, and framed in the spring by colorful herbaceous borders.[20] Marie of Romania, who often played in the garden as a child, remembered it as a place of "delightful, mysterious corners," though the incessant soot cloaked the trees and bushes in a dirty black smut.[21]

Victoria's Buckingham Palace was a cold, rather stark building of three principal storeys, its new eastern facade facing a forecourt ringed by an ornamental iron fence and impressive gates, and dominated by a triple archway opening into the quadrangle beyond. Above the arch, at the center of his new wing, Blore placed a balcony, looking down the length of the Mall, which Victoria used for the first time in 1854 when she watched troops leave for the Crimean War.[22]

Passing through the archway, visitors arrived in the quadrangle, a large, graveled space at the center of the building's hollow square. Only here was something of the building's magnificence apparent in Nash's grand portico, held aloft on paired Corinthian columns and crowned by a pediment topped with sculptures depicting Britannia and Neptune.[23] Doors opened directly to the Grand Hall, a classical space of colored scagliola walls adorned with paired Carrara marble columns topped with gilded Corinthian capitals; by the end of Victoria's reign, the polluted air of London, remembered one man, had turned the once-colorful panels a dingy gray.[24] The ceiling, painted with Renaissance motifs, was too low for the size of the hall; in an effort to compensate for this, Blore had lowered the white marble floor bordered with scrolls and rosettes of contrasting yellow and black marble, but despite the gilded trappings, the effect was still claustrophobic.[25]

Eight crimson-carpeted steps ascended to the Marble Hall, whose two-hundred-foot length opened to a suite of semistate apartments largely decorated by Nash in the Regency style.[26] At the southern end, beyond a small vestibule, lay the palace chapel, created by Blore in 1843 in the southwestern conservatory. With the windows walled in, the architect raised the roof and added a clerestory to provide natural light.[27] Sixteen slender columns formed the nave, holding aloft a coffered ceiling ornamented in gold; dark-paneled wainscoting and heavy crimson and gold cut velvet further darkened the space, which was dominated by an alabaster pulpit.[28]

The household dining room and household breakfast room stretched north, ending in the 1855 Room, named for the year it was occupied by the visiting Emperor Napoleon III and Empress Eugenie.[29] A semicircular projection, pierced by five French doors opening to the terrace, gave the Bow Room at the center of the wing its name. Originally intended as George IV's library, it still bore the open shelves in alcoves formed on either side of the bow by screens of Corinthian columns. Guests invited to attend one of the queen's garden parties at the palace passed through the room, between rows of potted palms and gilded sofas covered in crimson damask, to reach the lawns beyond the terrace.[30]

The 1844 Room, named for the year it was remodeled to house a visiting Tsar Nicholas I, mirrored the 1855 Room on the opposite side of the bow. Victoria had been at first rather startled and then bemused at the tsar's peculiar demands: he refused to sleep in the magnificent bed she provided and instead retreated to his own, small camp bed, which he had brought with him from St. Petersburg. The mattress, of straw, had somehow suffered during the trip from Russia to England, however, and his first request of his hostess was that his valet be allowed to visit the nearby royal mews and collect clean straw with which to stuff his narrow bedding. Victoria thought it all most peculiar. Still, it was nothing compared to the temporary residence in 1873 of the visiting shah of Persia who, it was said, had not only largely destroyed the fittings of his private suite but also had actually sacrificed a sheep on one of the queen's expensive carpets.[31]

In 1838 Victoria commissioned Blore to add the Ministers' Staircase at the northern end of the Marble Hall, which gave officials direct access to her audience room on the floor above. Rising in three flights between an ornamental gilded metal balustrade of stylized acanthus leaves, it was lighted by a stained glass window and a leaded skylight hung with a gilded chandelier.[32] Tucked behind it was an apartment known as the Belgian Suite, in honor of Victoria's uncle King Leopold I. Consisting of a small dining room, a sitting room, a bedroom, and several dressing rooms, it was used to house visiting monarchs, who could enjoy the views from the French windows over the balustraded terrace to the garden and the lake beyond.[33]

On the northern side of the palace, hidden from public view by one of Nash's colonnaded screens, a smaller bow contained the queen's private entrance, with a floor of black and gray Belgian marble and a stylized and gilded frieze of acanthus leaves supported by a screen of Corinthian columns.[34] It led to the queen's staircase; later in her reign, when the infirmity of age made climbing the stairs difficult, Victoria had an electric elevator installed to transport her to her rooms above. This technical innovation had not come easily, and there were months of arguments about its safety before the queen finally consented to its introduction.[35]

The main ascent at the palace, however, lay just off the Grand Hall. This was Nash's Grand Staircase, which provided a suitably regal approach to the state apartments above. Broad marble steps, covered in crimson runners bordered in gold, rose to a half landing before branching left and right in a gentle curve between a balustrade of gilded bronze rosettes, scrolls, and acanthus, and oak leafs topped by a mahogany handrail. A third flight, flanked by paired Corinthian columns supporting a barrel-vaulted ceiling whose coffers were picked out in gold, opened from the center of the landing, ascending directly to the East Gallery. Under Prince Albert's direction, his friend and artistic adviser Ludwig Grüner had transformed the Grand Staircase from Nash's stark yet imposing white, crimson, and gold into a riotous symphony of color: pale blue walls adorned with Renaissance-style bas-reliefs depicting the four seasons in white against pink pastel backgrounds rose to sculpted panels set within dark blue borders; above the carved and gilded frieze, lunettes embellished with classical bas-reliefs arched toward a domed ceiling pierced by a skylight.[36]

At the top of the main landing, twelve-foot-high doors of Spanish mahogany, mirrored and encased in ornate frames of chased ormolu, opened to the Guard Room.[37] This small anteroom, hung with tapestries and ornamented by Corinthian columns holding aloft the coffered and gilded domes of its apsidal ends, served no purpose other than to dazzle, offering an introduction to the splendors of the state apartments beyond.[38]

The effect was all the more brilliant when visitors passed from its white scagliola walls into the rich saturation of the adjoining Green Drawing Room.

Lavish silk brocade hangings, framed by white pilasters adorned with a lattice design in gold and encased in gilded fillets, lent the Green Drawing Room its name. Here, all was magnificence: a sculpted frieze of swags and laurel wreaths, picked out in gold, supported a ceiling hung with five sparkling cut-crystal and ormolu chandeliers above a crimson Axminster carpet woven with a pattern of Tudor roses and scrolls of golden acanthus leafs.[39] The carpets throughout the state apartments—many designed by Blore to echo the decoration of the ceilings above—were a necessity, as lack of sufficient funds had led the architect to impose unwanted economies. In place of the magnificent inlaid parquetry floors of many European palaces, Buckingham Palace's floors were of simple oak and, in a convenient trick, only the visible borders were adorned with intricate geometrical designs in walnut, holly, pear, and satinwood.[40]

The Throne Room followed, a sixty-foot-long symphony of crimson silk moiré-hung walls and elaborate carved and gilded reliefs in an atmosphere of undoubted magnificence. Pilasters adorned with carved oak leafs and acorns picked out in gilt supported a sculpted frieze depicting the War of the Roses; above stretched a coved cornice embellished with heraldic shields in a blaze of gold. Carved and gilded ceiling beams framed a shallow dome ribbed in gold, from which hung an enormous cut-crystal and ormolu chandelier, eight feet in diameter and complemented by four smaller fixtures of matching design suspended from the corners of the room. At the northern end was the royal alcove, framed by winged genii representing victory; from the carved and gilded garland in their out-stretched hands they held a central wreath adorned with the cipher of George IV.[41] A dais beneath a canopy hung with red velvet fringed in gold bullion and flanked by gilded trophies from Carlton House held the queen's throne, an elaborately carved chair adorned with festoons of scrolls, oak, and acanthus leafs, upholstered in crimson velvet ornamented with gold thread, and surmounted by a sculpted crown.[42]

The Picture Gallery, 155 feet long, lay at the center of the principal floor, separating the rooms on the eastern side overlooking the quadrangle from those to the west facing the garden. Five immense doors, framed by white scagliola cases adorned with sculpted caryatids, opened to the major state apartments, with screens of columns at the northern and southern ends. Lacking any windows, the Picture Gallery was crowned with an elaborate series of oval and square domes, initially designed by Nash after the work of Sir John Soane and installed by Blore, their long rows separated by hanging pendants and adorned with alternating lilac and pink lunettes; from this spatially complex cove hung four immense ormolu gasoliers. Until 1854, when Victoria and Albert commissioned a new ballroom, the Picture Gallery was often used for state dinners.[43]

Upon the soft lilac-colored walls of the Picture Gallery hung a small portion of the queen's immense collection of paintings, from works by Rembrandt and Reubens to Prince Albert's favorite Italian and German Renaissance works, all crammed together from floor to ceiling. When Sir J. C. Robinson, surveyor of the queen's pictures, dared to suggest that the paintings should be rearranged, Victoria's reply was adamant: "The pictures at Windsor and Buckingham Palace were settled by the Prince Consort, and the Queen desires that there shall be no change."[44] Unfortunately, in his desire to crowd as many works of art upon the walls as space allowed, Albert had most of them taken from their immense, antique carved frames and reset into new, rather cheap, mass-produced gilded imitations. Victoria's infrequent habitation of the palace, coupled with her refusal to allow any changes and the polluted London air, meant that the priceless canvases were nearly all covered with thick layers of dust and grime, so thick in some cases that the paintings had turned black.[45]

Immediately off the Picture Gallery, the Royal Closet overlooked the palace gardens. Furnished as a small drawing room and adorned with a marble chimneypiece decorated with ormolu caryatids that had originally been in the Throne Room at Carlton House, the Royal Closet served as a gathering place for the royal family on ceremonial occasions, where they waited to appear before their guests.[46] Beyond it, stretching the length of the western facade, were four large state apartments. Added by Nash when he enlarged the Queen's House, their layout—a great enfilade stretching 225 feet—created a sense of dramatic splendor. The most luxurious rooms in the palace, they were adorned with scagliola columns replicating sienna marble, lapis lazuli, and onyx; hung with colored silk damasks; and topped with elaborately molded ceilings embellished with plaster reliefs and shallow domes ornamented in gilt.[47]

A tall looking glass and ebony console magically swung open to the adjoining White Drawing Room. Victoria was never quite happy with the room's decoration, and in her reign its forty-eight-foot-length underwent a number of changes; originally known as the North Drawing Room and then the Music Room, it was, for most of her reign, called the Yellow Drawing Room, after the sienna scagliola columns that adorned it.[48] In 1873, despite her virtual withdrawal from society and rare occupation of the palace, Victoria transformed it into a frothy concoction of white and gold, flooded with light from three tall windows overlooking the gardens. Pilasters, a carved and gilded frieze, and a white ceiling crossed with molded ribs detailed in gold added to the luxurious effect; three shallow, gold-ribbed domes echoed the circular floral motifs of the Axminster carpet below. Carved and gilded Regency sofas and armchairs from Carlton House, upholstered in gold damask, sensuous bronze nude candelabra, and glittering crystal and ormolu chandeliers all combined to make it a distinctly feminine room.[49] In 1856 Victoria added an elaborate piano in a gold case; both Richard Strauss and Felix Mendelssohn had played upon the piano.[50]

The Bow State Drawing Room occupied the center of the enfilade.[51] Walls covered in yellow damask provided a dramatic backdrop for the eighteen scagliola lapis lazuli columns with gilded Corinthian capitals that circled the room and supported the gilded plasterwork relief frieze and sculpted lunettes. Two ribbed golden domes, hung with immense ormolu chandeliers from Carlton House, rose above a floor inlaid with satinwood and holly in a pattern of fleur-de-lis alternating with ciphers of George IV in contrasting tulipwood. After Victoria installed a magnificent grand piano of walnut adorned with ormolu that had originally been in the Royal Pavilion at Brighton in the bow, she took to calling it the Music Room, a designation that remains today.[52]

The Blue Drawing Room that followed was one of Nash's most lavish interiors. Walls hung with patterned blue silk moiré complemented the paired scagliola columns of honey-colored onyx crowned with gilded

Corinthian capitals. At nearly seventy feet long, it had been the largest of the original state apartments, and for the first fifteen years of her reign, Victoria used it as a ballroom. For dances, the suite of carved and gilded sofas and chairs upholstered in blue silk damask was removed and the crimson and gold carpet rolled up, allowing guests to waltz beneath the shimmering light of its large cut-crystal and ormolu chandeliers.[53]

Blore had finished the decoration of the State Dining Room beyond, resulting in one of the palace's most unfortunate interiors. The architect employed a subdued scheme of light peach-colored walls and a crimson patterned carpet and curtains, whose delicate effect might have succeeded had he not crowned it with an "extraordinarily restless bracketed ceiling" in white and gold set with three shallow domes atop a clumsy frieze of molded papier-mâché medallions.[54] An eight-foot-wide Spanish mahogany table occupied the center of the room; it could be extended, with twenty-seven leaves, to accommodate sixty guests, seated on gilded, crimson-covered chairs.[55]

In 1853 Victoria and Albert commissioned Sir James Pennethorne to add a ballroom and a larger dining room at the southwestern corner of the palace.[56] From the State Dining Room, his West Gallery, lined with Gobelins tapestries and topped with an arched skylight, led to the Ballroom, built in a new extension over newly expanded domestic offices and the relocated palace kitchens.[57]

At 60 feet wide, 123 feet long, and 45 feet high, the Ballroom was not only the largest room in the palace but also, at the time of its construction, the largest ballroom in all of London. At the western end, Pennethorne built a dais, where a second throne sat in an alcove framed by an arch and flanked by red scagliola Corinthian columns surmounted with allegorical figures representing history and fame. At the opposite end, above the tiered rows of built-in benches upholstered in striped red silk, was a musicians' gallery, dominated by a pipe organ that had previously been in the Royal Pavilion at Brighton. Albert supervised the decoration of the room according to Renaissance schemes by Ludwig Grüner; like his work on the Grand Staircase, this was a rather ponderous exercise in imitation Italianate designs. The lower walls were hung in a very Victorian crimson silk brocade woven with a lattice pattern in gold, topped by a gilded, sculpted cornice that separated them from the upper walls. Here the treatment was entirely different, with brightly colored panels painted by Nicola Consoni representing the Twelve Hours alternating with double windows fitted with gas jets to provide illumination at night. A colorful frieze of red and blue panels set with white sculpted reliefs rose to a cove, painted blue and adorned with golden figures framing shields that bore the queen's cipher. From the ceiling, segmented by painted beams into coffered squares, hung twenty-one small pendant crystal chandeliers, quite out of scale to the enormity of the room.[58] This elaborate decoration had added to the cost of construction, said to have reached some £250,000 (£15,152,792, or $25,911,274 in 2007 figures) for this single room.[59]

The polychrome theme continued in the new, adjoining State Supper Room, a square, two-storeyed space designed by Pennethorne in 1855 to act as a buffet during balls. The lower walls were lined with colored scagliola; above them, panels painted with Florentine designs alternated with mirrors and decorative pilasters, rising to a bracketed cornice ringing the gilded stucco reliefs around the ceiling. From the four corners hung small crystal pendant lamps, while above, a shallow dome of blue sprinkled with gold stars reflected the light from the hundreds of candles.[60]

These decorations reflected Albert's taste rather than Victoria's, and he injected further, exotic notes into the private apartments, including the palace's most extravagant interior, the Chinese Luncheon Room, created using fittings salvaged from the Royal Pavilion at Brighton. Its pictorial panels, encased in lacquered and gilded fretwork frames, were set beneath a ceiling painted with a fierce dragon from whose mouth hung a chandelier of painted glass in the shape of a water lily; gilded dragons stretched across the pelmets of the curtains, while Ludwig Grüner had provided a new carpet to harmonize with this fantastic concoction of gold leaf, silk, vibrant colors, and fanciful scenes.[61]

The Chinese Luncheon Room marked the beginning of the private apartments, in the northern wing overlooking Constitution Hill. The Indian Room, west of the Chinese Luncheon Room, served as a link to Victoria's colonial empire, its walls adorned with traditional Indian weapons, tiger skins, and elephant tusks, and lined with dark wooden cases displaying the spoils of empire.[62] Beyond this, Prince Albert's dressing room and sitting room had, by the queen's orders, been left untouched since his death in 1861, his walking sticks in place, pens casually left on his desk, and books stacked in readiness.

Victoria's own rooms, rarely occupied, also remained largely unaltered, frozen in a haze of dust and treasured memories. In her first taste of freedom from her forceful mother, the young queen had rejoiced at taking up residence in the new palace; the rooms, she declared, were all "so high, pleasant, and cheerful."[63] Yet she soon found that, despite her position, being queen did not automatically bring with it either comforts or even a response to her requests. Buckingham Palace, like Windsor, was considered Crown property, administered by the Office of Woods and Forests. Nothing could be done—from redecoration to structural repair—without the authority of the Crown officials, whose stated goal was to operate as "a check upon any extravagant act." If they approved an expenditure, the necessary funds were granted to the queen; if they did not, she had to seek the intervention of Parliament for a grant.[64] This situation meant that the Queen of England was, in effect, the Crown's tenant, and not mistress of her own house.

Inevitably this resulted in difficulties. A few months after first moving in to Buckingham Palace, Victoria requested that several alterations be made to her private apartments: among other things, she asked that a staircase be closed off, that new doors be made into adjoining rooms. The question was put before the Office of Woods and Forests, which did nothing; two years later, the lord chamberlain was forced to again take up the issue, complaining that no response had been given and no work undertaken as the queen had asked.[65]

Once the requested remodeling was finally finished and the rooms redecorated, Victoria's suite offered a glimpse at her bourgeois sensibilities and tastes. As at Windsor, the refined and the expensive mingled with the sentimental and the cheap. There was nothing extraordinary about their decoration: light-colored striped silk hung on the walls of her dressing room, furnished with a chaise longue and overstuffed sofa and chairs covered in a vibrant chintz to complement the floral carpet, in a scene that could have been found in the houses of any of her well-to-do subjects.[66] Her bedroom was a sea of tranquil green, from the floral silk on the walls and floral carpet to the dark, richly fringed curtains and the floral hangings of the mahogany bed's half canopy. Yet even in this subdued atmosphere the regal raged against the ordinary: a molded plasterwork frieze adorned with gilt supported a fantastic neo-Gothic ceiling of gilded quatrefoils, circles, and squares, yet common chintz covered the overstuffed sofa and chairs, while the white marble chimney-piece embellished with ormolu cherubs was crowded with inexpensive souvenirs.[67]

The war continued in the queen's sitting room, situated in the bow above her private entrance. Delicate boiseries in white and gold orna-mented the pale, mauve-colored walls, while the white and gold cornice and ceiling echoed the Gothic forms in the queen's bedroom. The white marble chimneypiece opposite the bow, originally from Carlton House, was adorned with an ormolu clock encased in a protective glass dome, while gilded candelabra and pieces of porcelain fought for supremacy atop bamboo tables crowded with photographs, albums, and souvenirs. At the center of the room, atop the plum-colored carpet, with its vibrant swirls of green foliage and red and white flowers, stood the queen's writing desk, facing furniture that was comfortable rather than luxurious: a tête-à-tête chair, an overstuffed sofa and chaise longue, and armchairs, all uphol-stered in mass-produced chintz scattered with red roses and green foliage.[68]

During her husband's life, Victoria had occupied Buckingham Palace regularly, and socially approved elements could even purchase tickets from the lord chamberlain to stand in the grand hall and watch her leave when she was on her way to open Parliament.[69] After Albert's death, how-ever, Victoria all but abandoned Buckingham Palace, preferring Osborne and Balmoral, or, if she had to be near the capital, Windsor. In the hush that settled over the palace, servants still carried on as if their mistress might return. "There are naturally many things lying about on tables, chairs, and on the floor," noted the Earl of Crawford, "books, for instance, shawls, and old envelopes. These are carefully picked up; numbered, catalogued, inventoried; chalk marks are made upon the carpets, pins stuck on to chairs."[70] Visiting grandchildren found dusty rooms filled with decades of cast-off toys, including a stuffed lion that, when wound by its tail, could swallow up a model Russian solder.[71] Not surprisingly, the Prince of Wales caustically referred to the palace as "a sepulcher."[72] For forty years, Buckingham Palace slumbered in this state, windows shuttered and cloths draped over furniture; only rarely did its glorious and gilded rooms awaken to the witness the court ceremonies reluctantly presided over by the widowed queen.

13

A DAY AT BUCKINGHAM PALACE

IN THE LONG YEARS OF HER LONELY WIDOWHOOD, Queen Victoria
virtually abandoned her ceremonial role as sovereign. She loathed the
dinners, drawing rooms, and balls that had once so amused her. After the
death of the prince consort, she had attempted to ignore these obligations
altogether, relenting only occasionally and usually under intense pressure.
But the approach of her Diamond Jubilee meant a new round of entertainments and duties that could not so easily be swept aside. Although she still
looked upon them as unwelcome and tiring intrusions, in the late spring of
1897 Victoria reluctantly again embraced her ceremonial role, and
embarked on a round of presentations, drawing rooms, and investitures
whose reflected glory added luster to the prestige of the monarchy.

Victoria and Albert had carefully cultivated the aura of majesty surrounding the British monarchy after years of disrepute. Servants and
courtiers added to the image of power, providing a regal backdrop against
which the aristocracy basked in the queen's favor and reveled in the exclu-
sivity of their world. Thus the ceremonial of the court offered both a
theatrical stage for their enjoyment and a mantle of prestige that cloaked
its dinners, receptions, and investitures in an unquestioned language of

order and authority designed to increase Victoria's own position at the center of this glittering firmament.

This regal idea found visible expression each season as thousands of stiff vellum cards, embossed in gold with a crown and the queen's cipher, invited recipients to functions at Buckingham Palace or Windsor Castle. Drawn up and issued by the lord chamberlain's office, invitations to dinners, drawing rooms, levees, receptions, and investitures offered entrée to this privileged milieu; although dispatched on behalf of the queen, they came in the lord chamberlain's name, for an invitation from the queen carried the strength of a royal command and could not be refused.[1]

As the Diamond Jubilee approached and the London social season erupted in a vivid celebration of privileged pleasures, Queen Victoria returned to her capital to preside over her court. Shortly after eleven on the morning of Monday, May 10, 1897, her Indian servants assisted her into an open carriage that took her from the protective battlements of Windsor to the town's train station. Accompanied by Helena and Beatrice, she boarded a special saloon compartment and traveled to Paddington Station in London, where a dozen officials, including the director and the manager of the Great Western Railway, waited to greet her on a crimson-carpeted platform. An escort from Her Majesty's Second Life Guards Regiment accompanied the queen's open carriage through a densely packed, cheering crowd that lined the route to Buckingham Palace; as soon as her carriage passed through the forecourt gates, her flagman, high atop the structure, hastily hoisted the royal standard, signifying that Victoria had taken up residence in London.[2]

Victoria had come to Buckingham Palace to preside over a drawing room the following day. Presentation at court was deemed a social necessity. When aristocratic daughters reached eighteen, they were considered of marriageable age and were prepared for their entrance to society. A seemingly endless round of parties, dinners, and balls would follow, all in the hope of attracting the attention of a suitable young man. Only those who had formally been presented to the queen could receive invitations to court functions, and there were strict rules governing eligibility. Aristocratic ladies had automatic entrée, as did the wives and daughters of military and naval officers, physicians, clergy, and barristers. Application was made to the lord chamberlain's department, but a lady hoping to be presented could not inquire for herself; instead, candidates had to be recommended by a lady who had already been presented at court. Often this was a mother or senior female family member; in cases where an untitled lady married into the aristocracy, it fell to her mother-in-law to request presentation. Foreign ladies could apply to their respective embassies, and their diplomats and envoys sorted through the lists and made selections. Not all of the women presented were young debutantes: they could also be distinguished visitors, or older women. Presentation not only allowed access to future functions, but also paved the way for introductions at foreign courts; at a time when aristocrats and the wealthy regularly traveled across Europe, this was an important extra incentive, for no one wished to be precluded from any extravagant balls if visiting Berlin, Vienna, or St. Petersburg.[3]

It was left to the various sponsors to vouch for the respectability of their candidates. The lord chamberlain's department ultimately examined the various candidates and approved or rejected their requests; rejection usually came only if there was some moral impropriety attached to the candidate's name. Although Victoria personally read through the approved lists, she rarely interfered, though on one occasion she insisted on revoking an invitation to a lady that had already been sent, presumably on moral grounds.[4]

Drawing rooms always took place at Buckingham Palace and always were held at three in the afternoon.[5] Usually the queen held four to five drawing rooms each season, each of which could involve as many as three thousand guests.[6] An intricate series of instructions dictated nearly every aspect of the occasion, from the clothes the guests wore to the entrance they were to use in gaining access to the palace.

For Victoria's drawing room on Tuesday, May 11, the gates at Buckingham Palace were opened at two in the afternoon. The entire length of the Mall was jammed with carriages and landaus conveying nervous debutantes toward the dour gray stone facade; by this time, anticipation had often given way to restless discomfort. It took several hours for a debutante to dress, and generally those attending left their houses by noon; often they sat in their carriages for several hours, waiting to reach their destination.[7] In warm weather, they sweltered in their voluminous gowns; in cold weather, they froze.

Through their open carriage windows as they neared the palace gates, these debutantes could hear the bands of the Second Battalion of Her Majesty's Life Guards in the forecourt and the Second Battalion of the Scots Guards hidden in the quadrangle beyond, playing rousing tunes to enliven the mood.[8] Coachmen approached the police constables on duty at the three entrances. Shortly after two, the Prince and Princess of Wales, accompanied by their daughter Toria; Helena, Princess Christian of Schleswig-Holstein; Arthur, the Duke of Connaught; and Helen, the widowed Duchess of Albany, all arrived at the northern gate, disappearing across the forecourt through Nash's colonnaded screen to the queen's entrance; here they were met by equerries-in-waiting and the groom of the chamber, and taken to the Royal Closet to await Victoria's arrival.[9]

Members of the diplomatic corps and those attached to embassies used the Entrée on the southern side of the palace and were escorted to the Green Drawing Room, where they assembled.[10] The vast majority of those arriving for a drawing room, however, used the grand entrance. As they slowly passed through the gates, the coachmen displayed invitations to the constables on duty, leaving cards printed with the names of their occupants and received tickets that allowed them to return and collect the guests after the drawing room had ended.[11] The carriages swept across the forecourt and passed beneath Blore's archway to enter the quadrangle.

The Duchess of Buccleuch, the queen's mistress of the robes, waited in the Grand Hall; at her side stood Lord Edward Pelham Clinton, master of the household; Baroness Southampton, lady of the bedchamber; the Honorable Mrs. Ferguson, woman of the bedchamber; the Honorable Judith Harbord and the Honorable Frances Drummond, as maids of honor; and the Honorable Josslyn Seymour Egerton and the Honorable J. E. de G. Henniker Major, the queen's pages of honor. The women all wore elaborate court gowns, the young pages scarlet and gold coats, crimson breeches, and white stockings. As the line of colorfully costumed guests entered the hall, Lord Pelham Clinton collected their invitations, and the mistress of the robes, assisted by the other gathered courtiers, directed them toward their destination.[12] Pages, butlers, and gentlemen ushers motioned guests to cloakrooms before the debutantes ascended the crimson-carpeted Grand Staircase, crowded with flowing trains and voluminous skirts alive with shimmering embroidery.

The state apartments were crowded; on this day, Victoria received just over sixteen hundred guests; despite the crush, many of the ladies in their low-cut gowns found the cavernous rooms of Buckingham Palace frightfully cold, and they shivered and huddled awaiting the queen's entrance.[13] At intervals stood yeomen of the guard, the oldest of the royal bodyguard units originally founded by Henry VII, distinctive in their Tudor-inspired uniforms consisting of scarlet coats embroidered in gold, white Elizabethan ruffled collars, and black velvet hats banded in blue, red, and white.[14] Matching them in picturesque appearance were the Honorable Corps of Gentlemen at Arms, the queen's ceremonial bodyguard drawn from retired military officers and attired in scarlet coats with gold facings and epaulettes, blue trousers, and brass helmets plumed with a cascade of white feathers.[15]

When all was ready, the Earl of Lathom, as lord chamberlain, met the queen in the private apartments and escorted her to the Royal Closet, where the royal family waited. Victoria wore a gown of black moiré trimmed with arabesque lace, and a train of striped black satin and moiré also adorned with lace. Across the front of her bodice stretched the blue ribbon of the Order of the Garter, held in place by Prince Albert's diamond order star; the Victoria and Albert Order; the Imperial Order of the Crown of India; and the family order of Coburg and Gotha. From her diamond diadem cascaded a veil of Brussels lace. At her side was the Princess of Wales, in a gown of ivory stain embroidered in pearls and sequins, with an ivory velvet train and diamond tiara and lace veil, while Princess Victoria of Wales appeared in a vibrant green gown sewn with silver thread and embellished with panels of silver chiffon.[16]

At a few minutes before three, Victoria and her courtiers enacted an intricate ritual that defined the pageantry of the Crown. The queen entered the Picture Gallery, attended by the lord chamberlain and the fourteenth Earl of Pembroke as lord steward, who preceded her, walking backward and carrying their wands of office, and by two military officials, Viscount Wolseley and Colonel Neeld, the gold stick and the silver stick-in-waiting, respectively, drawn from the household cavalry and named after their respective symbols of office.[17] Behind her, holding her train, were the two young pages of honor, followed by the Duchess of Buccleuch, the mistress of the robes; the Prince and Princess of Wales, with their daughter; Princess Helen; the Duke of Connaught; and a dozen other courtiers. When Victoria had taken her place in the Throne Room, the presentations began, following a strict precedence.[18]

The lord steward took up his place in the Throne Room, standing to the right of the throne, with the Duke of Portland as master of the horse; the Earl of Coventry as master of the queen's buckhounds; and the Honorable Ailwyn Fellowes, vice chamberlain of the household; on the left side of the throne stood Lord Pelham Clinton, master of the household; Sir Arthur Bigge, the queen's private secretary; Sir Fleetwood Edwards, the keeper of the Privy Purse; Viscount Curzon, treasurer to the royal household; Lord Arthur Hill, comptroller of the royal household; Lord Bagot as lord-in-waiting; Lord William Cecil as groom-in-waiting; and the Honorable Henry Legge and Lieutenant Colonel Sir Arthur Davidson as equerries-in-waiting. The men all wore official court dress: dark blue swallowtail coats adorned with gold embroidery, white knee breeches, and white silk stockings. Closer to the throne, the mistress of the robes, Baroness Southampton as lady of the bedchamber; the Honorable Mrs. Ferguson as woman of the bedchamber; and the Honorable Frances Drummond and Judith Harbord as maids of honor, stood in a semicircle.[19]

The band of the Scots Guards Regiment stationed in the quadrangle beneath the open windows of the Throne Room provided a suitable selection of music that drowned out all but the booming voice of the lord chamberlain as he announced the names of those being presented.[20] First came the members of the diplomatic corps, led by Baron George de Staal, the Russian ambassador, accompanied by his wife, and followed by the ministers and envoys from Germany, Austria-Hungary, France, Italy, Spain, Turkey, the United States, Persia, Brazil, the Netherlands, Belgium, Japan, Serbia, Sweden and Norway, China, and Switzerland.[21]

Full court dress was required of all of the ladies being presented. Their dresses were intricate affairs. Young, unmarried debutantes wore gowns of white silk and satin, with full skirts; tight, boned bodices with low décolletages; and separate, regulation trains of twelve feet hung from the shoulder. Married women were allowed to wear pale colors or, for those in mourning, black; married women also wore lappets. Atop their carefully coiffed hair were three white ostrich feathers, arranged to duplicate the crest of the Prince of Wales; unmarried women wore long, flowing veils of white tulle, often held in place by a discreet diamond tiara. Regulations also dictated long white gloves, white satin shoes, and a white fan, carried in addition to a carefully arranged floral bouquet with streamers that offered hints of color.

Navigating in these ensembles was often difficult, and it was made more so by the complicated rules the women had to follow. Trains were carried folded over the left arm until reaching the door of the Throne Room, when gentlemen-in-waiting spread them out with long, ivory wands as the ladies entered. Ladies made three curtsies: the first on entering the room, one midway down the length of the room, and then, on reaching the queen, a full court curtsy, dropping completely to the floor and bowing forward; this was a perilous move, as ladies attempted to hold their fans and bouquets, keep their low décolletage in place, and not lose the three feathers atop their heads. The queen's subjects also kissed her hand, but foreign ladies only curtsied. If the lady being presented was the wife of a peer, the wife of the eldest son of a peer, or the daughter of a duke, marquess, or earl, Victoria kissed their cheeks.[22]

After making her obeisance, the lady was required to rise and walk backward, trying to avoid tripping on her train, extending her arm to receive its bulk as an attendant bundled it and placed it back on her left arm, before turning and exiting the Throne Room into the Picture Gallery.[23] "They were generally timid and nervous when they passed," recalled one lady, "some bracing themselves as if they were facing a terrible ordeal, some racing past very quickly, forgetting to take their trains in their arms, and pursued down the room by an impatient chamberlain."[24] Drawing rooms were often uncomfortable, arduous affairs for those being presented, and there were no refreshments: Victoria, when asked, refused, saying that even the serving of a cup of tea would turn the affair into a party.[25] As sought after as presentation was, there were often complaints: "Many left their homes at 12 o'clock, and were not home again till after 7 o'clock," the *Times* of London reported after one drawing room, noting, "During three hours of it they were fighting their way through an anxious crowd."[26]

A levee was the male equivalent of a drawing room, where gentlemen were presented at court, and was the only court function from which ladies were excluded.[27] The rules for presentation at a levee were as stringent as those for a drawing room: gentlemen hoping for presentation had to be sponsored and had to fall within certain accepted categories: aristocrats had automatic admission, but members of the gentry, officers in the army and navy, members of the clergy, physicians, barristers, bankers, wealthy merchants of good social standing, and artists such as writers and painters could all apply for presentations. Those employed in positions of trade had to first become mayors, justices of the peace, or members of a volunteer service before seeking a presentation. Distinguished foreign gentlemen could apply to their respective diplomatic representatives for admission.[28]

Like drawing rooms, levees had their own dress codes. Gentlemen not entitled to wear official or military uniforms were directed to wear full court dress: a long, maroon-colored swallowtail coat over a white shirt adorned with lace and ruffles and a waistcoat, knee breeches, and white silk stockings.[29] Levees usually took place in the afternoon at St. James's Palace and, like drawing rooms, were held several times a year; occasionally they were presided over by the Prince of Wales on his mother's behalf.[30] All of the major officials in the royal household attended, as did members of the diplomatic corps. The lord chamberlain announced each gentleman as he approached the throne. On being presented, gentlemen bowed and bent down on one knee, holding out their right hand; Victoria would lay her hand upon theirs, and they would kiss her hand. On rising, they again bowed, and backed away, usually without having exchanged a word with the queen.[31]

Less formal presentations took place throughout the year, often when the queen was in residence at Windsor. Stripped of the elaborate trappings of court ceremonial and the gilded surroundings of Buckingham Palace, Victoria often appeared as a rather common figure to those who expected a bejeweled figure enthroned in splendor. "I shall never forget my bitter disappointment the first time I was taken, at a very early age, to see Queen Victoria," recalled one diplomat. "I had pictured to myself a dazzling apparition arrayed in sumptuous robes, seated on a golden throne; a glittering crown on her head, a scepter in one hand, an orb in the other. I had fancied Her Majesty seated thus, motionless during the greater part of the twenty-four hours, simply 'reigning.' I could have cried with disappointment when a middle-aged lady, simply dressed in widow's weeds and wearing a widow's cap, rose from an ordinary armchair to receive us."[32]

On arriving at Windsor Station, those invited to meet the queen found a carriage and a scarlet-coated footman awaiting them. After sweeping up the hillside and through the castle gates, they were escorted, as one woman recalled, by "a Highlander and butler in black, who ushered us into a large drawing room with an enormous bow window looking on the park." Soon a lady-in-waiting and a maid of honor appeared, along with a lord-in-waiting, who invited the guests to partake of luncheon or tea. The private secretary and the lady-in-waiting advised the caller on issues of protocol before finally saying, "Will you come to see the Queen?" After passing down the Grand Corridor, they entered a room, announced by the lady-in-waiting who formally presented the visitor. "I made a first low curtsey," recalled Mary King Waddington of her first meeting with Victoria at Windsor, "but before I had time to make another the queen, who was standing in the middle of the room with Princess Beatrice, advanced a step, shook hands, and said with a very pretty smile and manner, 'I am very glad to see you.' She asked me to sit down and talked a great deal, was most gracious." Victoria, she noted, "was very simply dressed in black, with her white widow's cap and veil, no ornaments, but a gold chain and pearls around her neck, and a medallion with a portrait of a man in uniform, whom I supposed to be Prince Albert. . . . She is short, stout, and her face rather red, but there is a great air of dignity and self-possession, and a beautiful smile which lights up her whole face."[33]

As sovereign, Victoria was the "Fountain of Honors." She not only headed society, but also conferred its titles, honors, and awards. These included peerages, baronetcies, knighthoods, decorations, and military awards. Honors were first given out en masse in 1887 to mark her Golden Jubilee, and each year after that, announced biannually, once at New

Year's and then again on the queen's birthday. Victoria became the first British sovereign to knight an actor, Sir Henry Irving, and the first to bestow a knighthood on a Jewish subject, Sir Moses Montefiore, sheriff of the city of London. Victoria, noted one author, "was lavish in bestowing orders and awards to relatives, but not to those who served her; she disliked to see those who were her servants wearing the decorations of foreign royalty, and kept to an absolute minimum her consent to the wearing of foreign orders by British subjects."[34]

Victoria instituted several medals and awards during her reign. There were two new Indian orders, commemorating the queen's love of her distant empire, that were primarily awarded in recognition of service to the state. The Most Exalted Order of the Star of India and the Most Eminent Order of the Indian Empire were awarded to those who had served with distinction overseas on her behalf.[35] In 1877 Victoria also created the Imperial Order of the Crown of India, awarded to distinguished women in both Britain and India, including the wives of Indian princes, viceroys, and the wives of provincial governors.[36]

These awards were presented during formal investiture ceremonies and also during informal presentations. Lady Randolph Churchill, who received the Imperial Order of the Crown of India in 1885 from the queen at Windsor, recalled how the event nearly ended in disaster. Victoria greeted her, and pinned the order to her left shoulder. "I remember that my black velvet dress was thickly embroidered with jet," Lady Churchill wrote, "so much so that the pin could find no hold, and unwittingly the Queen stuck it straight into me. Although like the Spartan boy I tried to hide what I felt, I suppose I gave a start, and the Queen—realizing what she had done—was much concerned. Eventually the pin was put right, and I curtseyed myself out of the door."[37]

The queen's most lasting additions to the empire's honors were two awards, one military and one for personal service. The first, the Victoria Cross, had been designed by Prince Albert to mark acts of bravery during battle. At the time it was conceived, England was in the midst of the Crimean War against Russia, and, uniquely, the Victoria Cross was to be awarded to all distinguished men, regardless of their rank. By the time the award had been approved, the war had ended in a hollow British victory, and the new medals, emblazoned with the words "For Valor," were cast using the bronze from melted Russian cannons seized at Sevastopol.[38] The second award, the Royal Victorian Order, was founded in April 1896. From the first, it was to be the personal gift of the sovereign, given as a reward for distinguished service to the monarch. It went most often to the queen's senior courtiers and to her most trusted friends and advisers.[39] In addition to these honors and awards, the queen presided over the various orders of chivalry. These included the Order of the Thistle, the highest honor in Scotland; the Order of St. Patrick, the principal Irish order; the Order of St. Michael and St. George; and the Order of the Bath.

In the spring and summer of 1897, large numbers of honors were awarded in commemoration of the coming Diamond Jubilee. Most were bestowed during investiture ceremonies at Windsor, when a group of varied recipients would gather to receive their decorations; only rarely did Victoria hold investitures at Buckingham Palace. On Monday, May 17, at Windsor, the queen held a ceremony during which she bestowed honors on some twenty recipients. On this occasion the queen was attended by two orderly officers from the Gurkha Rifle Regiment, a tradition she began in 1876.[40]

The lord chamberlain announced the name of each recipient and the reason for the award as the candidate came forward. An equerry stood next to the queen, holding a tray on which the awards had been placed. When the candidate reached her, he bowed, and Victoria pinned the decoration on his coat. Those receiving a knighthood bowed and knelt on a low stool before the dais; the gold stick-in-waiting handed the queen a sword, and as the candidate knelt, she touched him on each shoulder with its tip, at the same time naming him with the knighthood selected. The new knight kissed her hand, bowed again, and backed away from her presence.[41] On this particular Monday, Victoria created Major General Sir Owen Tudor Burne a knight grand commander in the Order of the Indian Empire; three men were installed as knight commanders in the Order of the Bath; and just over a dozen men were created knight companions in the Order of the Bath.[42]

There were often mishaps and fits of nerves. Princess Marie of Erbach-Schönberg, a German relative, recalled one investiture by Victoria: "The

Queen, seated, struck on the shoulder with a sword several gentlemen who, in knee breeches and silk stockings, had been led in the highest state of embarrassment, and had to kneel before her. On standing up again, before they retired backwards—in which proceeding they had the assistance of two gentlemen, who took them by the waist and guided them—they had to kiss the queen's hands, which many of them forgot, or performed very awkwardly."[43]

The most distinguished of all chivalric orders, however, was that of the Garter. The Most Noble Order of the Knights of the Garter was said to have originated in a mishap. During a dance, or so the legend went, the Countess of Salisbury lost her garter, and King Edward III stooped to pick it up from the floor; noticing the eyes of his courtiers boring into him as he did so, the king placed the garter on his own leg, exclaiming, *"Honi soit qui mal y pense"* (Shame to him who thinks evil of it). It made for a charming story, although its veracity is open to question.[44] What is certain is that, in 1348, Edward III did indeed found the Order of the Garter, and it became the kingdom's premier order of chivalry thereafter.[45]

The Chapel of St. George at Windsor Castle served as the seat for the order; originally intended as a mark of royal favor, by Queen Victoria's reign the order had largely fallen victim to the influence of government interference, and the prime minister of the day most often suggested new candidates to the queen. The Order of the Garter, however, was among the smallest and most exclusive orders of chivalry. At any given time, no more than twenty-four knights could hold membership in its ranks; the reigning sovereign was always the twenty-fifth knight. This severely curtailed the sovereign's ability to bestow membership in the order upon members of the royal family and foreign monarchs. To solve this problem, beginning in the late eighteenth century it became possible to create "royal" knights, who would not count toward the limit of twenty-four. This allowed Victoria to reward her closest relatives and most important fellow European sovereigns. During her reign, except for the queen herself, the order was exclusively a male domain.[46]

In Victoria's reign, the honor was much sought after, though there were few ceremonial duties involved. The queen always invested the new knights of the order, usually at Windsor, though the ceremony itself played out only for the privileged members of the elite. Summoned to Windsor, the knights would arrive at the castle on the appointed day and hour, changing into the distinctive chivalric garb: long, midnight blue velvet mantles lined with white taffeta, black velvet caps plumed with white ostrich feathers, and the order's blue sash and diamond star shimmering beneath the jeweled collar worn around the neck. Investitures were held in the Garter Throne Room, its blue carpet and silk wall panels sewn with the order's diamond stars alternating with garters emblazoned with its motto, Edward III's famous utterance, "*Honi soit qui mal y pense.*"[47]

Victoria herself always wore a court gown beneath her mantle; she forsook the jaunty black velvet cap with its distinctive ostrich plumes in favor of a diadem or crown. The front of her gown was adorned with the order's blue riband, stretching to the left shoulder and held in place with a diamond order star; after Albert's death she always wore his Garter star as a sentimental remembrance. The order's actual garter, a blue band sewn, in the queen's case, with a blaze of diamonds flanking the motto in the gold thread, was worn discreetly on her upper left arm; indeed, a large painting of Victoria, clad in a white silk décolleté gown, the Garter mantle falling loosely around her shoulders and the shimmering George IV diadem atop her head—painted in earlier, happier times—hung upon the wall of the Throne Room, providing a vivid contrast to the black-draped figure who followed in the wake of Albert's death.[48] Investitures were followed by luncheons, although the current, colorful processions through the precincts of Windsor Castle to attend annual services in St. George's Chapel came into existence only decades after Victoria's death.

The most informal of all court ceremonies were the queen's garden parties, most often held at Buckingham Palace. It was Victoria who first began the tradition of inviting several thousand guests to invade the privacy of her gardens several times a year, as a means of dispensing with several of her hated formal obligations. This was no free-for-all at the palace; specially selected organizations received a certain number of invitations, and a guest list—drawn up in consultation with the lord chamberlain's department—ensured, at least in theory, a varied cross section of distinguished society.

At any one garden party, several thousand guests—the men in uniforms or morning suits, and the women in formal afternoon dresses with gloves and parasols—formed undulating lines across the great sweep of lawn along the palace's western facade, their rows carefully arranged and orchestrated by prim ranks of the Honorable Corps of Gentlemen-at-Arms, equerries, and gentlemen ushers. At the appointed time, a band stationed on the western terrace struck up the national anthem, and the queen appeared; to save herself the hardship of having to cover the acres of lawn, Victoria usually rode along the undulating avenues of guests in a pony cart, the lord chamberlain walking at her side and occasionally pausing to speak to one of the guests; other members of the royal family, including the Prince and Princess of Wales, followed her. Eventually the queen's route took her to the royal tent, where she would rest briefly and take tea.

The queen's watermen, attired in scarlet uniforms, rowed guests in gondolas on the garden lake as a band played a concert of light musical selections. White tents, shipped from Windsor Castle, sheltered buffet tables, where guests could select from an array of ham, chicken, tongue, and beef sandwiches; fruits in champagne; vanilla custards; pastries; ice creams; and tea, coffee, wine, and lemonade. For many years, guests used the solid royal silver, stamped with the queen's cipher. One year, however, a group of American guests apparently managed to make off with more than a thousand pieces; after this the queen ordered that ordinary silver be used, to avoid the future indignity of pieces of her crested silver appearing for sale in shop windows in New York.[49]

14

A NIGHT AT DEVONSHIRE HOUSE

AS SPRING TURNED TO SUMMER in 1897, and thoughts turned to the queen's approaching Diamond Jubilee, her aristocratic subjects plunged headlong into a London social season destined to radiate its fantastic privileges for decades to come. The windows of private palaces, long shuttered against the cold winter, were flung open to welcome the warming spring air from the tree-lined squares they overlooked. Dustcovers and sheets disappeared, crystal chandeliers were divested of their protective shrouds, French and Turkish carpets were unrolled across stretches of gleaming parquet floor, and maids filled silent halls, polishing, brushing, and cleaning.

The London season was the province of the country's wealthiest and most privileged inhabitants, who moved through its gilded entertainments as if "a race of gods and goddesses descended from Olympus upon England," in the words of one observer, living "upon a golden cloud, spending their riches as indolently and naturally as the leaves grow green."[1] The Diamond Jubilee added to the anticipation, inspiring a frenzied round of parties, receptions, and balls that dazzled in their splendid opulence.

The aristocracy formed the core of this community. Often related over the centuries through marriages, they formed a tightly knit group with shared backgrounds, aspirations, prejudices, and secrets. Their participation in the season, recalled Lady Randolph Churchill, was "looked upon as a very serious matter," and "no self-respecting persons who considered themselves 'in society' would forego" its pleasures.[2]

Britain's nineteenth-century aristocracy consisted of roughly three hundred families.[3] They fell into five ranks. At the very top of the peerage were the dukedoms, made more exclusive by the fact that fewer than thirty existed. The ranking dukedom in Great Britain, by tradition, was that of the Duke of Norfolk, held by the Fitzalan-Howard family. Although they were Roman Catholics, the dukes of Norfolk also held the most important of the ceremonial great offices of state, that of earl marshal. In this capacity, the Catholic Fitzalan-Howard family was responsible, ironically, for planning the most solemn ceremonies of the Church of England related to the Crown, including the coronation and the funeral of the sovereign.

Dukedoms were rarely created, and passed through a handful of families from father to son. In their hands, Great Britain's dukes held a majority of aristocratic power and possessions. To them belonged the country's most splendid estates, set on thousands of acres of parkland; houses filled with priceless treasures; centuries of exquisite jewelry; and fortunes that far outshone that of the queen. Below the dukes stretched the vast sea of Great Britain's aristocracy: those who held the rank of marquess, then a hundred earls, followed by an ever-expanding pool of viscounts and barons.

Aristocrats began life blessed with the coupled privileges of position and birth, but there were disadvantages as well, including many not endured by the lowest of Victoria's subjects. There was little social interaction between the gilded drawing rooms of aristocratic houses and mansions and the inevitably distant nursery wing, carefully confined to upper floors and concealed behind green baize-covered doors. Aristocratic fathers, consumed with their own endeavors and interests, often saw their children only at tea or before dinner, when a nanny might bring her young charges to say good night. Nor were many aristocratic mothers more comforting, devoted as they were to social obligations. While relations between children and servants were usually warm and loving, they also set the tone for aristocratic life, and inflections of social hierarchy infused these childhood influences.

Education began at an early age, with sons separated from daughters. For the latter group, there were few expectations: girls needed languages, classes in the arts, lessons on the piano and in dancing, and perhaps a few rudimentary lectures in history and literature, coupled with an emphasis on etiquette and decorum. Aristocratic girls were viewed not as contributors to society, but instead as social adornments and future wives, spheres that did not call for astute intellect or highly developed thought. Everything was geared toward a girl's eighteenth birthday, when she could make her debut and formally enter the aristocratic marriage market. "Girls," noted one historian, "were not expected to *know*, they were expected to *amuse*."[4]

"We acknowledged," recalled the Countess of Warwick, summing up this lethargic attitude, "that it was necessary that pictures should be painted, books written, the law administered; we even acknowledged that there was a certain class whose job it might be to do these things. But we did not see why their achievements entitled them to recognition from us, whom they might disturb, over-stimulate, or even bore. On rare occasions, if a book made a sufficient stir, we might read it, or better still, get somebody to tell us about it, and so save us the trouble."[5]

Boys were subjected to a more rigorous system, often at the hands of strict and severe tutors who quickly passed over the niceties of literature and the humanities in favor of more practical pursuits designed to pave the way for military and political careers. When they reached an acceptable age, they were packed off to public (that is, private, in Britain) schools: the Catholics to Ampleforth, the less well-to-do to Charterhouse, the traditionalists to Harrow and Winchester, and the elite to Eton, where headmasters shaped them into subservience.[6] At the end of their tenure, they might go to a university, or enter the military academy at Sandhurst; the goal was to turn out patriotic young men of unquestioning loyalty, inspired to do their parts in the country and across the empire.

As late as 1897, the aristocratic hold on power seemed inviolable. They largely governed the country, filling the House of Lords and a majority of seats in the House of Commons. The great families provided the country with its prime ministers; comprised its diplomatic representatives; dominated society; and, as the nineteenth century faded, began to control its banking institutions. Women were sheltered, cosseted, and raised to respect convention, but their husbands, sons, and brothers took advantage of the changing mores of the fin de siècle, gambling away family fortunes at country house parties and private clubs, and lavishing expensive jewels on discreet mistresses.

The Prince of Wales set the tone. Attendance at his parties at Marlborough House and Sandringham marked social acceptance in a vibrant court that rivaled that of his mother, the queen. The Countess of Warwick, former mistress of the Prince of Wales and an intimate member of his circle, was later scornful of his "useless, but glamorous, circle that was so much discussed, so much envied, and so sadly overrated," who "fluttered in the sunlight of pomp and circumstance" in search of adventure.[7] Bertie's circle of friends, known as the Marlborough House Set, broke with convention. Money, an amusing personality, and, for the women, beauty opened previously closed social doors. He welcomed not only dignified members of the aristocracy, but also diverse groups entirely unknown to respectable society, including, uniquely for a man of his time and rank, many Jewish friends, including the Rothschilds, the Sassoons, and Ernest Cassel.[8] "We resented the introduction of the Jews into the social set of the Prince of Wales," remembered the Countess of Warwick, "not because we disliked them individually, for some of them were charming as well as brilliant, but because they had brains and understood finance. As a class, we did not like brains. As for money, our only understanding of it lay in the spending, not in the making of it."[9] The same stigmas applied to the nouveau riche gentlemen, gamblers, stockbrokers, and industrialists who waved expensive cigars with an air of defiance as they discussed fortunes won and lost like exotic animals thrust into the midst of a curious and politely condescending assemblage.

American heiresses also found favor with the Marlborough House Set. Often pressured into loveless marriages at the hands of their social-climbing, Gilded Age mothers, these young women were derisively known as "dollar princesses," their impoverished aristocratic husbands wedding them in exchange for enormous dowries to settle family debts and reno-vate crumbling ancestral houses. "As a rule," recalled American heiress Jennie Jerome, who married Lord Randolph Churchill in 1874, "people looked upon [a dollar princess] as a disagreeable and even dangerous per-son, to be viewed with suspicion, if not avoided altogether. Her dollars were her only recommendation, and each was credited with the possession of them, otherwise what was her *raison d'être*?"[10]

The beautiful Lady Randolph, mother of the future Sir Winston Churchill, at first found favor in the Prince of Wales's Marlborough House Set, but her husband's unstable behavior and threats to expose Bertie's affairs led to a decade of social exile. Others quickly filled her place: Minnie Stevens, who married Lord Alfred Paget, grandson of the Marquess of Anglesey; Consuelo Yznaga, wife of the future Duke of Manchester; and Mary Leiter, married to George Curzon, future Viceroy of India. The most famous, and beautiful, of these women was undoubt-edly Consuelo Vanderbilt. In 1895 she was pushed by her forceful mother—very much against her wishes—into a marriage to the ninth Duke of Marlborough, who desperately needed her money. The new Duchess of Marlborough became one of society's shining stars, but her marriage was a disaster, doomed to end in a scandalous divorce.

That summer of 1897, London society glowed with life. Unlike society in other European capitals, where the court dictated the season, London's society revolved around the sitting of Parliament, when the country's peers and the aristocratic members of the House of Commons reluctantly abandoned shooting at their country estates to return to the capital. Even so, most of the important receptions and balls did not begin until late spring, when the annual exhibition at the Royal Academy of Art signaled a start to the round of entertainments. "Dinners, balls, and parties suc-ceeded one another without intermission till the end of July," recalled Lady Randolph Churchill.[11]

Houses shuttered for eight months of the year came alive. Gathered along broad avenues and around tree-lined squares named after their families, these houses rose in splendid ranks, their facades adorned with Italianate loggias, ornamental pilasters, and lines of sculpture that danced across their roofs. Conceived as opulent stages upon which the theater of the aristocratic season could be celebrated, they contained enormous halls and sweeping staircases, lined with marble columns supporting gilded and painted ceilings, and offered fantastic settings where a richly clad chatelaine could receive her guests in splendor and preside over elegant balls. Dining rooms, hung in silk damask and set with tables sparkling with gold, silver, and crystal, played host to twelve-course midnight suppers served by liveried footmen. Everything was meant to dazzle and to cement social reputations as the season progressed.

In this restricted world, gentlemen played little part. They were mere ceremonial adornments to the wives, mothers, sisters, and parade of fresh debutantes, who planned the great parties, gave the exquisite balls, presided over the long banquets, and gently flirted in the hope of attracting a suitable husband. In the mornings, most gentlemen went off to Parliament; those not in the House of Lords or the House of Commons disappeared to government offices in Whitehall, or to their oak-paneled offices from which they presided over their fortunes. By early afternoon, they retreated to the privacy of exclusive clubs along Pall Mall where, like the aristocracy itself, class and pursuit divided these bastions of male power and prestige. White's was the oldest of all London's private clubs and also its smartest, the province of the country's dukes and senior politicians. The Turf Club attracted distinguished members, with its concentration on traditional country sporting pursuits. The Athenaeum drew the most accomplished, while the Carlton and the Reform offered respite for, respectively, Parliament's conservatives and liberals.[12]

From these clubs, with their paneled rooms and clouds of cigar smoke, the more adventurous men sallied forth to keep discreet rendezvous with their mistresses. In the swirl of London's season, affairs offered forbidden excitement, although they were conducted according to strict rules of etiquette. Many aristocratic husbands and wives indulged in liaisons, with the tacit understanding that none would lead to the scandal of divorce or shatter the illusion of marital harmony. Gentlemen often turned to the wives of their friends and acquaintances. Married women offered safety; an unplanned pregnancy would cause comment only from their husbands. "It did not matter terribly if one or two rather different looking children arrived at the *tail end* of the family," wrote Anita Leslie.[13] If a man reached

Osborne House from the garden. The main wing is to the left, and the royal pavilion is to the right.

An early-twentieth-century view of the council chamber at Osborne.

The Swiss Cottage at Osborne.

Christmas trees erected in the Durbar Room at Osborne.

The Hotel Excelsior
Regina in Cimiez.

Queen Victoria at work; the
munshi, Abdul Karim, stands at
her side.

A late-nineteenth-century view of the eastern facade of Buckingham Palace.

The Prince of Wales in the
costume he wore to the
Devonshire House Ball in
July 1897.

Queen Victoria is greeted by the Lord Mayor of London at the boundary of the City on her way to St. Paul's Cathedral for the Diamond Jubilee service, Tuesday, June 22, 1897.

Queen Victoria arriving at St. Paul's Cathedral for the Diamond Jubilee service.

A view of the Diamond Jubilee service at St. Paul's Cathedral, Tuesday, June 22, 1897.

The royal pavilion at Osborne. The bow window on the second floor is that of Queen Victoria's bedroom, where she died in 1901.

Queen Victoria's coffin is borne through the streets of London on a gun carriage during her funeral procession, Saturday, February 2, 1901.

King Edward VII, flanked by Kaiser Wilhelm II on his right and the Duke of Connaught on his left, riding behind Queen Victoria's cortege through the streets of London, Saturday, February 2, 1901.

Queen Victoria's coffin being taken up the stairs of St. George's Chapel, Windsor, for her funeral service, Sunday, February 3, 1901.

The Royal Mausoleum at Frogmore, Windsor.

beyond his aristocratic circles, his choice often fell on popular actresses of the day, following in the wake of the Prince of Wales's liaison with Lillie Langtry, but a subtle code alerted the initiated to the affair. If a man appeared in public with his mistress, he always placed her on his left; gentlemen who ignored such etiquette would swiftly and unceremoniously face condemnation from their peers.

Women displayed their power late each morning when they ventured out to Hyde Park to ride or drive. Dowagers sat beneath wide lace parasols as their smart equipages conveyed them beneath the canopy of early summer foliage. Younger women, attired in tight, dark habits, veils, and gloves, rode splendid mounts along the park's famous Rotten Row. "Between the hours of twelve and two," recalled Lady Randolph Churchill, "the park was still the most frequented place in London, the fashionable world congregating there to ride, drive, or walk."[14]

Afternoons were spent on the social obligation of calling. Ladies paid brief social visits to each other; calls were made on friends and acquaintances, but also on strangers, with an eye to improving social position. The ritual of calling followed a series of intricate rules. Butlers ushered visitors into a drawing room, announcing that they would inquire if the lady of the house was at home; even when home, she rarely appeared except to greet personal friends or social superiors. An actual meeting between caller and lady was not necessarily the objective; the attempt by the visitor fulfilled expected social obligation. The caller would then leave her card with the butler; differing folds made at the corners indicated the reason for the call, whether social, condolence, welcome, or leave-taking. Calls were always, according to etiquette, to be returned within two weeks, either by a personal visit or by a similar exchange of cards. In this way, two ladies might call on each other yet never meet face to face, but social obligations had been satisfied.[15]

This absurd and time-consuming pantomime was but one of many such intricacies in the rigid society of the day. Aristocratic etiquette not only emphasized good manners, but also allowed society to distinguish between their equals and those whose aspirations exceeded their breeding or status, a convenient tool for immediately recognizing and excluding the unwelcome interloper. To this end, the rules of etiquette dictated nearly every aspect of an aristocrat's day. No proper woman ever left her house alone, and she never received gentlemen callers in the absence of her husband. When walking, gentlemen always passed to the right of a lady; a gentleman offered his right arm to a lady, assisted her from her carriage by taking her left hand, and never left her alone at the theater or the opera. If stepping from the pavement or crossing a muddy path, a lady raised her dress or skirt to the level of her ankle; to do this, she always used her right hand. A woman seen lifting her dress with both hands was instantly condemned as vulgar.

Evenings found society in a frenzy of elaborate dinners, attending the opera at Covent Garden, where the season opened on May 10 with a production of *Faust*, followed by *Carmen*, *Lohengrin*, and *Tannhauser*. There were visits to the theater and dancing at glittering balls. This round of entertainments could be exhausting: during the season, members of society could expect to attend perhaps twenty-five dinner parties, fifty receptions, and another fifty balls. "One had to exercise discretion in one's acceptance in order to survive the three months' season," recalled Consuelo, Duchess of Marlborough.[16] For the newly presented debutante, the season offered not only the excitement of spectacular diversions but also, more importantly, the chance to meet eligible young suitors.

"Entertainment among the elite was undoubtedly an art," recalled the Countess of Warwick. "The enchantment lay in setting us at ease in a luxury that was exquisite, without thought of the cost."[17] Preparations for a ball were intense. A dazzling success would win the hostess admiring accolades from her friends and impress her social superiors; a failure could easily result in social death. Thus weeks were lavished on the smallest details. Guest lists were composed, checked, and double-checked; engraved invitations were ordered, addressed, and sent. "Every invitation was personal," remembered the Countess of Warwick; "no hostess asked strangers to her house, or suffered their intrusion. There were no gate-crashers because there was more self-restraint. In spite of invitations being restricted to friends and acquaintances, five hundred was no large figure for a reception."[18] Orchestras were engaged, the program of dances selected, and menus discussed. Most dinners at a ball were served as a buffet supper; this was the practical solution to feeding guests, for only the wealthiest of aristocratic families could marshal the resources necessary to accommodate hundreds at the dinner table.

Most balls did not begin until ten, and they often lasted until three in the morning. With the exception of young officers, gentlemen invariably appeared in white tie and tails, providing a dark canvas against which the women shone. Months of planning went into ladies' wardrobes each season, with special attention given to their exquisite gowns. Orders went out early to the great couture houses, with the most attention lavished on the designs of the famous Charles Frederick Worth. From his salon on the Rue de la Paix in Paris, society women set out to conquer, wrapped in exquisite gowns of intricate design that cost thousands of pounds. Whether by Worth or another couturier, these gowns were models of opulence: full skirts of silk or satin, adorned with panels of velvet and lace and sewn with floral designs in gold and silver thread. Rich brocades, laced with layers of chiffon and sprinkled with shimmering jewels, were trimmed with fringe, tassels, braiding, and fur. Necklines were low, revealing shapely décolletages. Skirts swept back in folds, mingling with trains embroidered with floral garlands and edged with gold lace or fur. Long white mousquetaires, so tight that they could be buttoned only with assistance, encased hands and lower arms.

And then there was the jewelry, worn to dazzling effect: platinum and gold rings set with diamonds, pearls, sapphires, rubies, or emeralds flashed on gloved fingers; diamond bracelets jangled and spat fire on wrists; earrings set off faces aglow with excitement. Parures and demiparures adorned the ladies: tiaras, set with diamond spikes and hanging pearls, heavy necklaces cascading over necks, and stomachers falling in jeweled waves down bodices. The diamond *collar resille*, made famous by the Princess of Wales, graced many aristocratic necks, while luxuriant coils of hair were set with diamond crescents, stars, and moons that sparkled with every movement.

At the appointed hour, lines of carriages snaked along Park Lane and Piccadilly, carrying their privileged occupants to the festivities. Within the elegant houses, footmen in white silk stockings, velvet knee breeches, and shirts with lace jabots peeking through coats sewn with gold braid, collected cloaks, hats, and gloves as guests made their way inside, following ribbons of crimson carpet across marble floors to drawing rooms shimmering in the glow of a thousand candles. Each carried a tiny vellum card with a tiny gold pencil attached by a colored ribbon. One side listed the evening's dance program, while the other was used to record the names of partners selected for a particular dance. Young ladies were advised to consider offers carefully and not hastily fill in their dance cards, lest an acquaintance or more desirable partner arrive after their schedule had been set.

Balls usually opened with a quadrille; as the ladies moved through the doors, footmen quickly scooped up and handed them the loops of their trains before they took to the floor. The quadrille gave way to waltzes, lively polkas, and energetic gallops. Dancing was often a difficult operation, given the push of the crowds and the lack of space, as couples swirled across the floor, skirts and trains sweeping over gleaming parquet, diamonds flashing in shifting prisms of color and motion.

Shortly after midnight, supper was served, the guests passing down a buffet line of tables piled with chafing dishes and salvers of delicate and rich food before retreating to the corners of the rooms, the men standing behind the ladies in their gilded chairs. "There were no sterner critics," declared the Countess of Warwick, "of champagne, foie gras, quail, and the rest of the familiar luxuries than the people who attended receptions."[19] Footmen in sumptuous liveries handed around wines and spirits in crystal glasses balanced on silver trays. No one smoked, lest they give offense.[20] After supper, the dancing resumed, though the heavy gowns, the earlier exertions, and the lavish food began to take their effect. "No ball or entertainment was considered a success unless there were far more guests present than the ball and supper rooms could accommodate with comfort," recalled Victoria's granddaughter Marie Louise.[21] One guest at a ball recalled "400 or 500 people packed close in a house which holds about 150," the rooms "so warm that you almost stifle—and so cold on the staircase and halls where the door is always open wide."[22]

Of all the parties and balls that marked Queen Victoria's Diamond Jubilee that summer, none was as fabled as that given by Spencer Compton Cavendish, the eighth Duke of Devonshire. Sixty-four years old, tall and bearded, with a long face and sleepy eyes, he was heir to one of the country's greatest aristocratic legacies. Through the centuries, the dukes of Devonshire had served at the pleasure of England's sovereigns, accumulating treasures and houses to become among the wealthiest members of the peerage. They owned enormous estates: the fabled Chatsworth House in Derbyshire was the most magnificent, situated in an immense landscaped park and housing works of art rivaling those of the crown. The duke also owned the Elizabethan Hardwick Hall in Derbyshire, Holker Hall in Lancashire, Bolton Abbey in Yorkshire, Lismore Castle in Ireland, Compton Place in the south of England, and the magnificent Chiswick and Devonshire houses in London. The duke himself owned more than 180,000 acres, from which he derived an income of £180,000 (£13,195,973, or $22,565,113 in 2007 currency), and further funds came from investments.[23]

The eighth Duke of Devonshire succeeded to the title in 1891. He fully embraced the idea of aristocratic noblesse oblige and had held more government posts than any other man of his day; three times Queen Victoria asked him to form a government, but he always refused.[24] In 1882, his brother Lord Frederick Cavendish, then serving as chief secretary in Ireland, had been assassinated in Dublin's Phoenix Park; thereafter, Spencer kept his houses filled with loaded guns. Unfortunately, he was also forgetful, and rarely could remember where he had put them, terrifying both family and servants. His nephew later estimated that he had "no less than twenty of them knocking about Devonshire House."[25]

The Duke of Devonshire's sleepy appearance was often matched by undisguised boredom, and he was known to fall asleep sitting in Parliament. When startled awake by a particularly fiery speech, he would yawn, look around, and declare, "This is damned dull."[26] His two greatest interests were his racing stud and sleeping. One afternoon, the Duke of Portland remembered, he found his friend asleep on a bench in the House of Lords. He woke up, looked at his watch, and said sleepily, "Good heavens, what a bore, I shan't be in bed for another seven hours."[27] His dry humor was well known. He once met a greeting of "Pleased to meet you" with a huffed "So you damn well ought to be!"[28] After Lady Randolph Churchill told him she had enjoyed her tour of Chatsworth, the duke's only reply was a droll "Did you break anything?"[29] After listening to a peer declaim on the greatest moment of his life, the duke leaned over to his neighbor and said, "My greatest moment was when my pig won first prize at Skipton fair."[30] Nor was he impressed with the trappings of his privileged position. When he was created a grand commander of the Victorian Order, his only response was to ask what he was supposed to do with "the thing." Frederick Ponsonby recalled: "Anyone less anxious to receive an order I have never seen. He seemed to think it would only complicate his dressing."[31]

In 1892, the Duke of Devonshire married his mistress of some thirty years. Born the daughter of the German count Charles von Alten of Hanover in 1832, the stately and proud Louisa had married the future seventh Duke of Manchester in 1852 and borne him five children.[32] The marriage was far from successful, however, and his profligacy quickly ruined the family fortune. Disappointed, Louisa took up with the future, and much wealthier, Duke of Devonshire; their affair was no secret, but the Duke of Manchester was content to turn a blind eye to his wife's liaison. The situation continued for thirty years, until the Duke of Manchester's death freed his wife. Not surprisingly, Queen Victoria was duly scandalized, asserting that the duchess had "done more harm to Society from her tone . . . than almost anyone."[33]

"To all outward appearances," wrote the Countess of Warwick, "both the Duke and Duchess of Devonshire were devoid of the normal human sympathies, but there was no other man in the world for her, and there was no other woman for him."[34] Louisa, known to society as "the double duchess," had been, recalled an acquaintance, "one of the handsomest women in Europe."[35] "Rumor had her beautiful," declared the Duchess of Marlborough, "but when I knew her she was a raddled old woman."[36] She was also ambitious. "The Duchess," wrote a contemporary, "was a political intriguer to be reckoned with, and she exercised great influence over the Duke."[37] She made little secret of her political machinations as she tried to maneuver her husband closer to the post of prime minister. The duke, however, was uninterested and, much to his wife's chagrin, made no effort to help her achieve her dream.

Frustrated in her efforts to propel her husband to the center of power, the Duchess of Devonshire threw herself into her role as society's leading hostess. The Duchess of Marlborough remembered her as "virtually dictator of what was known as the fast set."[38] Her parties were the most splendid, her balls incredibly lavish, her rooms always filled with the smartest people. Society clamored for her invitations, although behind the duchess's back many spoke of her in less than glowing terms. She was too outspoken, her behavior too scandalous, and her manner too free. She openly gambled, keeping stacks of cards and betting chips piled on tables incongruously set next to lecterns displaying Bibles; wore tartan underwear; and covered her face with a thick layer of makeup at a time when only prostitutes and actresses used the new cosmetics, her mouth "a red gash," recalled the Duchess of Marlborough, and her thinning hair hidden beneath a furry brown wig.[39]

The center of the duchess's London world was the lavish Devonshire House, situated on Piccadilly overlooking Green Park. A rather plain, severe redbrick building, Devonshire House sat at the end of a forecourt surrounded by high brick walls, lending it a "fortresslike appearance." The interior, however, stood in complete contrast to the house's forbidding appearance. In the eighteenth century, architect and designer William Kent had adorned its rooms with carved boiseries framing walls hung with silk damask; inlaid parquet floors of rare and contrasting woods; gilded doors; coved ceilings with painted lunettes; and enormous chandeliers of ormolu and crystal. The house's most famous feature was also the first that visitors encountered: a magnificent curved staircase with a balustrade of sparkling crystal.[40]

Devonshire House formed the background for arguably the most lavish ball ever given in London society. To mark the celebration of the queen's reign, the duchess devised a unique evening, a costume ball that evoked centuries long past. In noting that summer of parades, reviews, banquets, and receptions, the *Times* of London rhapsodized that "none is comparable with the magnificent fancy dress ball" given by the Duke and the Duchess of Devonshire.[41]

Seven hundred invitations, eagerly awaited, went out from Devonshire House, inviting the recipients to join the duke and the duchess at Devonshire House at ten-thirty on the evening of Friday, July 2, 1897. Guests were advised that the ball would take the form of a series of historical or allegorical courts, and costumes must be drawn from previous centuries. These invitations sent a wave of panic through London society; ladies might possess extravagant gowns from Worth in Paris, but no one had recourse to the sort of clothing deemed necessary. Immediately, designers, dressmakers, costume shops, and theatrical costumers found themselves besieged for advice and assistance. "For weeks, not to say months, beforehand," recalled Lady Randolph Churchill, "it seemed the principal topic of conversation." She remembered: "Historical books were ransacked for inspirations, old pictures and engravings were studied, and people became quite learned in respect to past celebrities of whom they had never before heard."[42]

As the day approached, hundreds of workers transformed Devonshire House. A dais for the royal guests was built at the end of the drawing room and covered with crimson carpet.[43] Devonshire House, large as it was, lacked the necessary space to accommodate all of the duchess's guests at the formal, seated midnight supper she deemed necessary to impress; the problem was solved by clearing the garden and erecting an enormous marquee. To link it to the rooms on the floor above, carpenters constructed a new staircase that flowed from the windows of the saloon to the terrace.[44]

Such an enormous ball called for hundreds of servants; although the duchess had footmen and maids brought to London from Chatsworth, their numbers were still not sufficient, and she engaged a number of temporary servants for the week. To maintain the illusion of a bygone age, the duchess decreed that these servants also be attired in suitable costumes. Those in the regular employ of the duke had specially designed wardrobes, the footmen in new blue and buff-colored liveries copied from those worn by the family's male retainers a century earlier, and the women in Elizabethan dresses and caps. For the servants engaged temporarily, the duchess hired Egyptian and Elizabethan dress from a theatrical supply company in London.[45]

On the day of the ball, all of London society was in a whirl of activity. At Devonshire House, florists arranged luxuriant cascades of roses, lilies, and orchids shipped by train from the great conservatory at Chatsworth for the evening.[46] In the boudoirs and dressing rooms of London's private palaces and houses of privilege, excited guests readied for the evening.

Society ladies accustomed to leisurely afternoons promenading and taking tea with friends devoted themselves to the impending ball. "Every coiffeur in London and Pairs," wrote Lady Randolph Churchill, "was requisitioned, and so busy were they that some of the poor victims actually had their locks tortured early in the morning, sitting all day in a rigid attitude."[47] Ladies' maids fussed and fretted, dressing their mistresses in velvet, brocade, or satin gowns. The men, too, were busy. Valets cleaned ceremonial swords and polished boots to a gleam as bright as patent leather. The elaborate costumes were brushed and laid out, beards trimmed, and mustaches waxed as darkness fell across the capital.

"Whatever may have been the anxieties and the difficulties of the preparation," the *Times* declared, "there can be no doubt as to the splendor and beauty of the result."[48] Long before the appointed hour, smart carriages jammed the length of Piccadilly, conveying guests past the curious throngs who stood in the street and crowded the courtyard gates of Devonshire House to watch in anticipation. Stepping from their equipages, the guests entered Devonshire House, to be met by elaborately costumed footmen and maids, who collected coats and ushered them into the entrance hall. Here, in a corner framed by potted palms, the Blue Hungarian Band played a selection of tunes as the guests formed into a line that moved slowly through the hall.[49] At the end, at the top of the crystal staircase, stood the Duke and the Duchess of Devonshire. The duke had dressed as Emperor Charles V of Austria, his costume copied from a portrait by Titian. He wore a coat of dark blue silk woven with alternating panels of black satin, sewn with black jet and edged in gold braid and black fur; a cloak of blue Genoese velvet, also edged in fur, hung loosely over the large, puffed sleeves of his white silk shirt. His blue silk pantaloons, incised with inset panels of white satin edged in gold embroidery, ended above the knee, with black silk stockings and black velvet shoes completing the ensemble. Atop his head perched a blue Elizabethan velvet cap, adorned with a feather, and around his neck he wore the jeweled collar of the Austrian Order of the Golden Fleece, lent to him for the event by the Prince of Wales.[50]

At his side stood the duchess, attired as Zenobia, Queen of Palmyra. Her gown, created by Worth, was of ivory satin, ornamented with foliate

designs in gold thread. The skirt, overlaid with gold tissue, was embroidered with emeralds, diamonds, pearls, and sapphires; stylized peacock
feathers, sewn in gold thread and adorned with further jewels, framed the
split of the overskirt to reveal a cream, crepe de chine underskirt sewn
with diamonds and pearls against a design of gold thread beneath. The
bodice, of gold tissue, was sewn with panels of crepe de chine. A high
Elizabethan collar of gold lace framed her neck and shoulders; matching
gold lace adorned the cuffs of her sleeves. A train of green velvet, lined
with turquoise satin and sewn with lotus flowers composed of rubies,
emeralds, and diamonds, hung from her shoulders. A stomacher of emeralds, rubies, and diamonds rippled across her bodice, its glow matched by
the golden crown studded with jewels and swags of pearl festoons and
drops below two tall, white ostrich feathers.[51]

As guests ascended the staircase, there were gasps of admiration and a
few unwelcome surprises. Many of the guests had come costumed as the
same historical figures. In the hall stood two Napoleons, openly glaring at
each other. "It was indeed another Waterloo for both of them," wrote
Lady Randolph Churchill.[52] Three queens of Sheba faced each other, as
did two ladies who had come costumed as Cleopatra. Lady de Grey, the
first Cleopatra and a member of one of the courts, had taken great pains
with her costume, only to be upstaged by the American Minnie Paget, who
appeared in a dress of white and gold by Worth, so completely covered in
emeralds, rubies, and diamonds that even the jaded aristocrats were
stunned at the display.[53]

Shortly after eleven, the band struck up the national anthem, announc-
ing the arrival of the royal party.[54] All came costumed for the event. The
Prince of Wales appeared as grand master of the knights of the Order of
St. John of Malta, with a tunic of black velvet embroidered with jet,
matching pantaloons, and a cloak of black Sicilian silk sewn with the
Maltese cross in contrasting white. The Princess of Wales appeared as
Marguerite de Valois, in a cream satin gown richly embroidered with gold
thread, with gold-brocaded panels sewn with floral designs. Below the
high, Elizabethan lace collar stretched ropes of pearls, cascading in layers
down the bodice to mingle with clusters of diamond brooches in a shimmering display.[55]

The Duke of York came costumed as the Elizabethan George Clifford, Earl of Cumberland. He wore a tunic of silver and crimson Genoese velvet, embroidered in gold and piped in silver, with pantaloons of crimson velvet inset with panels of gray satin. A mantle of matching Genoese velvet, embroidered in gold thread and studded with jewels, and a high felt hat adorned with three ostrich feathers completed his outfit.[56] His wife, the Duchess of York, wore a gown of pale blue satin sewn with foliate designs in silver thread and adorned with pearls. The bodice was nearly hidden by an abundance of diamond brooches, a stomacher, and ropes of pearls, and the front of the gown was ornamented with seven large diamond clusters shaped like stars.[57] The Duke of Connaught appeared as a military commander of the Elizabethan period, in a tunic of gray velvet sewn with steel beads, matching pantaloons, and a mantle of gray velvet sewn with geometric designs in gold thread, while his wife, Louise, wore a gown of rose-colored velvet embroidered in silver thread and adorned with inlays of white satin and flounces of lace sprinkled with pearls.

Pages in medieval dress escorted the royal guests to a dais in the saloon, from which they would watch the proceedings, and, at a signal, the orchestra struck up, announcing the beginning of the processions.[58] The first of the courts was that of Queen Elizabeth, portrayed by Lady Tweedmouth, "a striking figure," recalled a guest, surrounded by "eight gigantic guardsmen" dressed as yeomen of the guard, and followed by a range of historical figures of the period.[59] The other courts followed, led by the Austrian court of Empress Maria Theresa. Portraying the empress was Theresa, Marchioness of Londonderry, in a gown of cream satin embroidered with golden thread and pearls; from her shoulders hung a long train of cream satin, sewn with acanthus leaves and foliage designs in gold thread. Festoons of pearls framed her diamond stomacher, complemented by two necklaces, one of pearl drops, the other of diamond clusters to match the tiara atop her powdered hair. She was followed by the Russian court, with Lady Raincliffe as Catherine the Great in a gown of white satin and a mantle of gold velvet sewn with the Romanov double-headed eagles in block.[60]

The Oriental court came next, headed by the Duchess of Devonshire as Queen of Palmyra, precariously perched atop a palanquin borne by her slaves. Not surprisingly, the duchess's court was composed of some of the most beautiful women in society, all in elaborate costumes: Lady Randolph Churchill as Empress Theodora, in a gown by Worth and a crown adorned with diamond and emerald pendants; Lady de Grey as Cleopatra; and the Countess of Dudley as Queen Esther, in a gown of white crepe embroidered in gold and sewn with pearls, amethysts, and turquoises.[61]

More processions followed: the Italians, led by Lady Plymouth as Caterina Cornaro; the Venetians, with the Earl of Lathom as Doge Giovanno de Medici; the court of Savoia, led by the Duke and Duchess of Portland; and the courts of Louis XV and XVI, with Bertie's former mistress, the difficult and beautiful Countess of Warwick, in full splendor as Marie Antoinette. The court of King Arthur and Queen Guinevere gave way to the allegorical court, the processions ending with Lady Wolverton attired as Britannia, who dropped a final curtsy before the royal dais as the dancing began.[62]

A quadrille opened the ball as the various courts moved through the glittering rooms in a slow, stately procession. "Nothing more harmonious could well be imagined than these slow dances," declared the *Times*, "walked through by magnificently dressed men and by women whose beauty and jeweled costumes set off one another with all the charm of something strange, exceptional, and unique."[63] But the heaviness of the costumes and the heat of the packed rooms soon took their toll. "Few people danced," recalled Lady Randolph Churchill, being "much occupied in gazing at each other or in struggling to play up to their assumed parts."[64]

Guests wandered down the specially constructed staircase and out into the garden, hung with twelve thousand colored lights and Japanese lanterns, before entering the marquee for supper.[65] The walls of the tent, hung with Louis XIV tapestries, were lit with festoons of flowers woven with thousands of tiny electric bulbs.[66] Each round table had been built around a potted palm tree, which sprung up magically from its center amid a bed of ivy and flowers laced with flickering electric lights.[67]

"The ball lasted till the early hours of the morning," recalled Consuelo, Duchess of Marlborough, "and the sun was rising as I walked through Green Park to Spencer House, where we then lived. On the grass lay the dregs of humanity. Human beings too dispirited or sunk to find work or favor, they sprawled in sodden stupor, pitiful representatives of the submerged tenth. In my billowing period dress, I must have seemed to them a vision of wealth and youth, and I thought soberly that they must hate me. But they only looked, and some even had a compliment to enliven my progress."[68] For the privileged guests, the *Times* rhapsodized, the world must indeed "seem commonplace in comparison with the jeweled page of romance upon which, for a moment, they gazed last night."[69]

15

TRIUMPH

WHEN, ON SEPTEMBER 23, 1896, Victoria succeeded her grandfather
George III as the longest-reigning British monarch, the occasion was celebrated quietly. Hundreds of congratulatory cables arrived at Balmoral,
but the queen passed the day quietly with her visiting granddaughter Alix
and her husband, Tsar Nicholas II. "People wished to make all sorts of
demonstrations, which I asked them not to do until I had completed the
sixty years next June," the queen wrote in her journal.[1] These private
words set in motion the plans for a celebration to mark the sixtieth
anniversary of the queen's ascension to the throne.

That summer of 1897, more than three million visitors poured into London to witness the celebrations. They had to be housed, fed, and entertained,
and the city's hotels were strained to capacity. Several days before the Diamond Jubilee, nearly a million anxious spectators staked out places along the
length of the processional route, sleeping on the sidewalks. Others rented
spaces on rooftops of buildings, in windows, and on balconies along the
route; the majority of the seats in the hundreds of grandstands erected along
the route were reserved for groups of dignitaries, but many were also
available for purchase, through the lord chamberlain's department, by the

wealthy, with the proceeds given to various charities.[2] The majority of the visiting twenty-five thousand colonial troops made do with tents erected in Hyde Park.[3]

After months of preparations, the jubilee celebrations finally began on Sunday, June 20. "I pray God to help and protect me as He has hitherto done during these sixty long, eventful years," the queen wrote in her journal, adding: "How well I remember this day sixty years ago, when I was called from my bed by Dear Mama to receive the news of my accession!"[4] At eleven that morning, Victoria, who had returned to Windsor from Balmoral a few days earlier, attended a service at St. George's Chapel to inaugurate the ceremonies. Escorted into the chapel on the arm of the munshi, she took her place near the altar. Surrounded by her children and grandchildren as well as members of her household, she listened as the choir intoned the new jubilee hymn, composed by Sir Arthur Sullivan of Gilbert and Sullivan fame, followed by a "Te Deum" arranged by Prince Albert forty years earlier, and Mendelssohn's "Hymn of Praise."[5] At the conclusion of the service, lost in a wave of memories, the queen retreated to the royal mausoleum at Frogmore, to pray before her husband's tomb.

The following day, Victoria boarded a train, pulled by a locomotive bedecked with flags, bunting, and the royal coat of arms, which took her to Paddington Station in London.[6] Here the queen, a tiny figure dressed in black, with a black crepe bonnet adorned with a white egret feather, was discreetly wheeled toward an open state landau, whose door had been widened so her chair could be pushed into the vehicle—a measure of just how painful and limited her mobility actually was.[7] Victoria sat beneath the shade of a black parasol trimmed with white lace, watched over by her daughter Helena, sitting forward in her seat. A contingent from the First Life Guards Regiment accompanied her carriage as it passed beneath a magnificent triumphal arch erected just outside the station, adorned with flags and emblazoned with "Our Hearts, Thy Throne" in large white letters, on her way past a cheering throng.[8] "It was," Victoria wrote, "like a triumphal entry," noting that the "heartfelt, loyal and affectionate welcome" left her "deeply touched and gratified."[9]

Shortly after one, Victoria's carriage passed through the ornamental gates and across the forecourt at Buckingham Palace, disappearing from view as, high above Blore's fussy, overly ornamented eastern facade, her flagman raised the queen's standard, signifying that the monarch had taken up residence. That afternoon, Victoria presided over a reception in the palace's Bow Room—"seated in my chair," she noted, "as I cannot stand long"—at which she received nearly a hundred visiting foreign royals.[10] In the evening, the usually silent palace came alive, windows blazing with light as Victoria gave a state banquet for a hundred guests, including family members, foreign royals, and diplomats and dignitaries. The vibrant scagliola columns, silk-brocaded walls, and crystal chandeliers of the state apartments shimmered as they awaited the queen's arrival, and her appearance that evening was magical: Victoria wore a magnificent gown embroidered in India, with panels of golden thread and lace woven with tiny jewels that sparkled and flashed as she moved.[11]

Victoria led her guests to the State Supper Room, where the Italian Renaissance reliefs and pastel decorations blazed in the light of thousands of candles. Footmen clad in white stockings and scarlet and gold liveries moved through the room, past screens of potted palms framing a display of the royal plate, the gold salvers, saltcellars, and candelabra gleaming against a crimson velvet background. The hundred guests took their places at eight white damask-draped round tables, each adorned with silver gilt candelabra and lavish floral arrangements: Archduke Franz Ferdinand of Austria-Hungary and the Prince of Naples flanked the queen; Victoria's three surviving sons—the Prince of Wales, the Duke of Saxe-Coburg-Gotha, and the Duke of Connaught—presided over their own tables, as did her grandson the Duke of York and sons-in-law Prince Christian of Schleswig-Holstein and the Marquess of Lorne. In addition to her own children, she was joined by the Grand Duke and Grand Duchess of Hesse; Grand Duke Serge Alexandrovich of Russia and his wife, Elizabeth; Prince Albert of Prussia, Regent of Brunswick; the Grand Duke and Duchess of Mecklenburg-Strelitz; the Crown Prince of Siam; Princess Fredericka of Hanover; the Prince of Japan; Prince and Princess Heinrich of Prussia; Prince Waldemar of Denmark; Prince Ruprecht of Bavaria; Grand Duke Kirill Vladimirovich of Russia; Duke Albert of Wurttemberg; the Crown Prince of Montenegro; the Hereditary Grand Duke of Luxembourg; Prince Eugene of Sweden and Norway; the Prince and

Princess of Bulgaria; Prince Mohammed Ali of Egypt; and Prince Amir Khan of Persia.[12]

The Prince of Wales escorted his mother into the Ballroom after dinner. As the queen's orchestra played in the gallery, she took her place on her throne; at her side stood the lord chamberlain, who introduced her guests as they passed. Parading across the length of polished parquet were the invited colonial premiers and their wives, the special envoys and attachés appointed to represent their respective countries for the Diamond Jubilee, the three Indian princes attending the celebrations, the officers of the queen's Indian escorts, and the members of the foreign royal suites.[13] "The Ballroom was very full and dreadfully hot, and the light very inefficient," Victoria noted.[14]

Tuesday, June 22, 1897, had been declared a bank holiday, and the streets of London were thronged with a curious, enthusiastic crowd. All traffic along the processional route had been banned for the previous three days, allowing the public to pour through the streets.[15] The early morning was slightly overcast and cool as privileged spectators allotted tickets to wooden stands along the route gradually took up their places. In the pale, encroaching light of dawn, the ribbons and flowers wrapped around cast iron street lamps; red, blue, and white bunting shrouding building facades; and lithographs of the queen draped with Union Jacks gradually revealed their prisms of color.[16]

By six, crews had finished sanding down the roadways, and members of the police began to line the route, standing side by side with troops whose scarlet tunics and tall bearskins added a traditional touch alongside the drab khaki of the colonial deputations. One stand had been reserved for the pensioners of the Chelsea Royal Hospital, resplendent in their crimson uniforms and rows of carefully polished medals; another tribune housed elderly veterans of the charge of the Light Brigade at Balaklava during the Crimean War.[17]

At Buckingham Palace, Queen Victoria had been up early. Although her family had begged her to abandon mourning on this momentous occasion, she was steadfast in her refusal to do so. Instead, the queen wore her customary black dress, although it was, by any measure, an extraordinarily ornamental ensemble. Panels of pale gray satin draped with black net adorned the full black silk moiré skirt and bodice, alternating with foliate designs sewn in silver thread, deep flounces of black lace, and embroidery of shimmering black steel and jet. A shoulder cape of black chiffon, embroidered with silver thread and ornamented with expanses of white lace, protected Victoria from any breezes. Her black bonnet, embellished with jet and silver thread, was trimmed with a wreath of white acacia flowers, held in place by a diamond aigrette and a plume of white ostrich feathers at the rear.[18] In her hands she carried an ornate, long-handled parasol of black lace lined with white satin, a gift from Lady Lytton's uncle.[19]

The processions began shortly after nine that morning. The eleven colonial premiers came first, led by the newly ennobled Sir Wilfrid Laurier of Canada, each accompanied by troops from his own country.[20] They drew wild applause as they passed in a shifting kaleidoscope of races and colors: hussars in dress tunics, members of the Royal Canadian Mounted Police in red serge from Canada, zaptiahs from Cyprus in fezzes, lancers from New South Wales with plumed helmets, regiments from North Borneo atop their camels, mounted rifles from the cape, police from Hong Kong in long robes and conical hats, the British Guiana police in white uniforms, Bengal lancers atop sleek mounts, and turbaned Sikhs.[21] "Up they came," reported the London Daily Mail, "more and more, new types, new realms at every couple of yards, an anthropological museum—a living gazetter of the British Empire." The correspondent could not resist a bit of colonial condescension: "With them came their English officers, whom they obey and follow like children. And you begin to understand, as never before, what the Empire amounts to."[22] From the crimson-draped balcony at Buckingham Palace, the young children of the Duke and Duchess of York, including the future kings Edward VIII and George VI, peered out at this passing spectacle, carefully watched by a white-clad nurse.[23]

As the last of the colonial processions turned up the Mall and headed toward the distant, embracing dome of St. Paul's Cathedral, the quadrangle and forecourt at Buckingham Palace rapidly filled with foot guards, cavalry regiments on horseback, and a string of landaus that rounded the corner from the royal mews to await their passengers. As the last of the colonial representatives disappeared from the jumbled crowds that packed

Trafalgar Square, Queen Victoria pressed an electric button linked from Buckingham Palace to the Central Telegraph Office in London, dispatching for the first time a simultaneous message around the world to all of her dominions: "From my heart I thank my beloved people. May God bless them!"[24]

Shortly after eleven, troops from the Royal Artillery Brigade began to fire their cannon salutes in Hyde Park, announcing the start of the royal processions. As thousands of eager eyes turned expectantly toward Buckingham Palace, its monumental gates parted, disgorging a colorful sea of uniforms. First came the Queen's Life Guards, followed by the Royal Dragoons, the Royal Hussars and Lancers, and the Royal Horse Artillery Regiment, horses clattering across the roadway and forming a seemingly unending string beneath the struggling sun.[25] More horses followed, conveying members of the queen's household: aides-de-camp, equerries, gentlemen-in-waiting, and military attachés in black, crimson, and gold dress uniforms.[26]

The appearance of the Queen of Great Britain and Ireland's Own First Prussian Dragoons heralded the approach of the royal family. Officers of the Indian Imperial Service Troops, in exotic *kirtas* with gold sashes, preceded the sovereign's escort of the Second Life Guards Regiment, led by Lord Wolseley, the much-decorated commander in chief of the armed forces.[27] Against the thunderous ovations, the ringing church bells, and the measured salvos that split the summer sky, the rattle of carriage wheels announced the departure of members of the royal family. Crowded into the open landaus were obscure foreign princes and princesses, Victoria's grandchildren, cousins, and crowned relatives from across Europe, followed by a mounted contingent of thirty-six princes in sleek uniforms hidden beneath glittering decorations.[28] One observer recalled: "We did not pay any attention to the first seven carriages. But we woke up very wide when those containing the little Battenberg, Connaught, and Albany children came by, the children bowing their little best."[29]

The strains of the national anthem echoing from the palace forecourt signaled Victoria's appearance. She had been adamant in her refusal to use the State Coach, an elaborately carved and gilded rococo concoction adorned with festoons and cherubs that had borne her to her coronation sixty years earlier.[30] Instead, she rode in an open state landau, its dark maroon sides emblazoned with the royal coat of arms, drawn by eight cream-colored horses caparisoned with scarlet and gold to match the liveries of the postilions.[31] Opposite Victoria sat the Princess of Wales and Princess Helena; two Highland servants in kilts rode on the rear of the vehicle. The Prince of Wales and Victoria's seventy-eight-year-old cousin the Duke of Cambridge—both in the scarlet uniforms and plumed hats of an army field marshal—rode alongside the landau, followed by the Duke of Connaught and a mounted escort of officers drawn from the queen's Indian Imperial Service Troops and from the Second Life Guards Regiment.[32]

As the queen appeared, the gray clouds above parted as if on cue, and a stream of summer sunshine bathed the procession in its golden rays—"Queen's Weather," it was said.[33] "What a cheer they gave her," recalled one spectator, "it made the tears come to my eyes. She was sitting quite upright and brisk in the carriage not looking flushed or overcome, but smiling and bowing."[34] Directly behind Victoria came her daughter the widowed empress Friedrich of Germany, in a landau pulled by four black horses caparisoned in red; she would have accompanied her mother, but as a crowned empress protocol prevented her from sitting with her back to the horses.

"No one ever, I believe, has met with such an ovation as was given to me," Victoria wrote, "passing through those six miles of streets, including Constitution Hill. The crowds were quite indescribable, and their enthusiasm truly marvelous and deeply touching. The cheering was quite deafening and every face seemed to be filled with real joy. I was much moved and gratified."[35] At times the response overwhelmed her, and keen observers noted that she frequently wiped away tears as she received this thunderous ovation.

At Temple Bar in the Strand, the procession halted when the Right Honorable Sir George Faudel-Phillips, the lord mayor of the city of London, greeted the queen and welcomed her to the city, according to protocol. Attired in his ceremonial robe, he approached the state landau, bowed, and lowered his jeweled sword in homage to the queen.[36] According to ritual, Victoria touched the sword and thanked the lord mayor, who then retreated to mount his white horse and join the procession. Burdened by the heavy crimson robes, however, he had barely mounted his horse when the animal bolted. Trying to keep control, the lord mayor lost his hat as his mount charged ahead.[37]

The royal procession continued as if nothing had happened, proceeding up Ludgate Hill toward St. Paul's Cathedral. Before the carriages reached their destination, they halted once again, so that the survivors of the Charge of the Light Brigade could offer their tributes from their wooden stand along the roadway; when the vehicles stopped, the crowd spontaneously erupted into "God Save the Queen." "Through an avenue of eager faces," wrote the *Daily Mail*, "through a storm of white-waving handkerchiefs, through roaring volleys of cheers, there was approaching a carriage drawn by eight cream colored horses. The roar surged up, the street keeping pace with the eight horses. The carriage passed the barrier; it entered the churchyard; it wheeled left and then right; it drew up at the very steps of the cathedral; cheers broke into screams and enthusiasm swelled to delirium."[38]

The procession moved around the monument to Queen Anne, the queen's landau stopping before the cathedral steps. Thousands of troops, including the colonial armies, had gathered in front of the cathedral, standing in ranks as a guard of honor while, behind them, crowding the sidewalks, above them, peering from windows and balconies, and perched precariously on every inch of rooftop, stretched the cheering crowd. To the left of the cathedral, an entire warehouse had been demolished to make way for rows of stands, packed with some fifteen thousand spectators.[39]

A crimson carpet covered the steps of St. Paul's, converting them into impromptu stands on which stood specially invited guests: members of the cabinet and the government, the diplomatic corps, and the clergy, along with five hundred white-robed choristers and two massed bands.[40] At the bottom of the steps clustered the members of the clergy who would celebrate the service: the archbishops of Canterbury and of York, in purple robes embroidered in gold; the Bishop of London, attired in a brilliant yellow cope; the Bishop of Winchester, in dark blue robes; and the Dean of St. Paul's, in a robe of green richly adorned with gold, all shimmering in the now brilliant sunlight.[41]

The Diamond Jubilee service opened with a prayer, followed by a "Te Deum." The choir, gathered on the cathedral steps, chanted the Lord's Prayer, after which a special prayer was offered: "O Lord our Heavenly Father, we give Thee hearty thanks for the many blessing which Thou hast bestowed upon us during the sixty years of the happy reign of our gracious sovereign lady, Queen Victoria. We thank Thee for progress made in knowledge of thy marvelous works, for increase of comfort given to human life, for kindlier feelings between rich and poor, for wonderful preaching of the Gospel to many nations, and we pray Thee that these and all Thy other gifts may be long continued in us and to our Queen to the glory of Thy Holy Name."[42]

The special jubilee hymn, with the words of the Bishop of Wakefield set to music by Arthur Sullivan, followed, sung with passionate fervor by the assembled throng:

> O Royal heart, with wide embrace
> For all her children yearning!
> O happy Realm, such mother grace
> With loyal love returning!
> Where England's flag flies wide unfurled,
> All tyrants' wrongs repelling.[43]

There were more prayers before the choir and the gathered crowd sang the hymn "Old Hundredth," followed by "God Save the Queen." The service ended with a benediction, during which the queen openly wept.[44] As her carriage slowly drove away, the Archbishop of Canterbury shouted, "Three cheers for the Queen!" and the crowd again erupted into a deafening, jubilant acclamation.[45]

The crowds were just as thick along the procession into the City and the imposing Mansion House, where the lord mayor and his wife waited to receive the queen. As Victoria's landau stopped, the wife of the lord mayor presented her with a silver basket filled with masses of colorful and fragrant orchids, before the parade continued.[46] The procession turned south, proceeding over London Bridge and into the poorer sections of London. Here the crowds were even more dense, the cheers louder, and the welcome somehow more heartfelt. The queen found the reception there "just as enthusiastic and orderly as elsewhere."[47] The last part of the route took the queen along the Thames, across Westminster Bridge, through Parliament Square, up Whitehall, into Trafalgar Square, and once again into the Mall, to return to Buckingham Palace, the whole of the length filled with a sea of smart uniforms, waving handkerchiefs, white summer parasols, and lavish toilettes adorned with lace.[48]

The queen arrived at Buckingham Palace at one-forty-five in the afternoon; the ceremonies had gone well, but the six-mile procession through the streets beneath the hot sunshine and in the stifling air had greatly tired Victoria. Journalist T. A. Cook, watching in the palace quadrangle, recorded her return: "The Royal Princes rode in and took up their line all along one wall to greet the returning queen, and servants in livery stood before their horses to keep a space clear for her carriage. The tears were pouring down the queen's face, as she first came in sight. She remained sitting upright in the sunlight, with the Princess of Wales holding her hand."[49]

Another ordeal followed that night, as Victoria presided over a state banquet in the Ballroom. Attired in a gown of black and silver silk, with a diamond necklace adorned with a trefoil and a pearl and diamond brooch given to her by members of her household, Victoria learned heavily on the arm of her eldest son as he escorted her into the room.[50] A signal to the footmen began service of the fourteen-course dinner, prepared by twenty-four chefs brought specially from Paris for the occasion: *bernoise à l'Impératrice*, parmentier, whitebait, *filets de saumon à la Norvégienne*, *timbales à la Demidoff*, roast beef, *poulardes farcies*, *pois sautés au beurre*, *pouding Cambacères*, *pain d'oranges à la Cintra*, and *canapés à la princesse*.[51] The Ballroom was a mass of bowers and cascades of flowers, culminating in a nine-foot-high bouquet of some sixty thousand orchids, topped with a floral crown and emblazoned with the letters *VRI* in contrasting colors.[52] The Prince of Wales, recognizing his mother's weariness, acted as host, proposing a toast to the health of his sister Empress Friedrich and to all of the queen's distinguished guests. By the end of the meal, although she was "very tired," Victoria moved through the crowd "to speak to most of the princes and princesses" before retiring to her rooms at eleven.[53]

The following day, June 23, the queen presided over a reception at Buckingham Palace. Accompanied by the mistress of the robes, a lady of the bedchamber, a woman of the bedchamber, and a maid of honor, the queen left her apartments for the East Gallery, where a lord-in-waiting, a groom-in-waiting, and two equerries waited. Here she was joined by Sidney Herbert, the fourteenth Earl of Pembroke, in his capacity as lord steward, and Edward Hyde Villiers, the fifth Earl of Clarendon, serving as lord chamberlain, who ushered her into the Ballroom. When Victoria had taken her place on a throne atop the dais, the doors at the other end of the room were opened and the invited guests entered. It was all so badly organized, recalled Frederick Ponsonby, that the guests seemed "like a crowd being let onto the grounds after a football match."[54]

Victoria received addresses and expressions of congratulation from four separate delegations. Members of the House of Lords came first, followed by members of the House of Commons, chairmen of county councils, and more than four hundred English and Welsh mayors and Scottish provosts. The heat, she noted, "was dreadful," and the crush of people pressing forward to see her shocking.[55] Lord Halsbury, the lord chancellor, presented the address from the House of Lords, declaring that it "proudly shares the great joy with which her people celebrate the longest, the most prosperous, and most illustrious reign in their history, joining with them in praying earnestly for the continuance during many years of Her Majesty's life and health."[56] While this was taking place, the Speaker of the House—worried that he would be denied his moment in the spotlight—pushed his way through the crowded halls toward the dais, delivering his address before most members of the House of Commons had even made it into the Ballroom; the mismanagement underlined just how long it had been since such ceremonies had regularly occurred at court.[57] Surveying this melee, Victoria, remembered Frederick Ponsonby, was "thoroughly put out at the mismanagement of the function and did not hesitate to let the two great officers of state know what she thought."[58]

As soon as the muddled reception had ended, Victoria hastily abandoned the hated Buckingham Palace, leaving early that evening in an open landau, accompanied by Vicky, Beatrice, and Arthur, to drive to Paddington Station, from which she would take the royal train to Windsor. The streets were still thick with cheering crowds, and Victoria repeatedly acknowledged her appreciation to them. At Hyde Park Corner, her landau halted as a guard of honor came forward and yet another ceremony took place. Lord Londonderry presented a congratulatory address on behalf of the British School Board, followed by the Bishop of London, who offered the good wishes of the Church of England schools; Cardinal Vaughan spoke on behalf of Roman Catholic schools, while Lord Rothschild proclaimed the congratulations of the country's Jewish schools.[59] Some ten thousand schoolchildren filled a nearby grandstand, enthusiastically singing the national anthem as the queen bowed to them in recognition.[60]

From Paddington, the queen's train traveled southwest, stopping at Slough for yet another congratulatory address, before continuing toward Windsor. At Eton, her landau rolled beneath a triumphal arch "on which stood three boys dressed as heralds," she noted. "Inside the arch stood four young Indian boys, in their native dress, sons of the Maharajahs of Kuch, Behar, the Minister of Hydrebad, and the Prince of Gondal. The Eton volunteers formed a guard of honor."[61] By twilight, when she reached the foot of Castle Hill, the Mayor of Windsor offered another speech; a choir, formed of thousands of schoolchildren, lined the roadway to the gates, singing "God Save the Queen" as Victoria finally passed into the precincts of her castle.[62]

A few quiet days of rest alternated with even more ceremonies. On Friday, June 25, the schoolboys from nearby Eton College came to Windsor to present their congratulations; at ten that night, as Victoria watched from the windows of the Oak Dining Room, they gathered in the quadrangle of the Upper Ward. They carried lanterns and flaming torches, and, for thirty minutes, this flickering sea serenaded the queen with hymns and patriotic songs.[63]

On June 28, Victoria reluctantly returned to London to host a garden party at Buckingham Palace attended by members of the royal family, visiting royal guests, important officials, members of the diplomatic corps, and a number of leading artists, including the actors Henry Irving and Ellen Terry. It was a beautiful, warm afternoon as the guests began arriving, passing through the grand entrance and the Bow Room to descend the terrace steps to the green lawns. A military band played selections from several operas and popular music as the guests gathered in weaving columns that snaked around the cool garden. The strains of the national anthem announced Victoria's arrival; she was followed by members of her family to the edge of the terrace, where, too infirm to stroll across the lawns, she climbed into an open carriage drawn by two Windsor grays and traveled down the carefully arranged rows of guests. Lord Lathom walked at her side, presenting various dignitaries to her as they passed on their way to the queen's tent. Here, attended by the munshi and a Highland servant, Victoria took a cup of tea and a bowl of strawberries, a white apron spread over her black dress, while beyond her, guests consumed trays of pastries and creams between long, inquisitive glimpses toward her distant, canopied black figure.[64]

The celebrations continued into July. On July 1, the queen attended a review at Aldershot, sleepily watching from her landau as colonial and British troops participated in a march past punctuated by artillery salutes.[65] The following day, Victoria's spirits noticeably perked up when she presided over a review at Windsor of the colonial troops who had come to London for the Diamond Jubilee. She sat in an open carriage, watching the colorful march past and receiving their salutes; an officer and a noncommissioned officer from each regiment personally conveyed their congratulations. The master of the household had already prepared the court circular for the following day, including a statement that the queen had spoken to her Indian troops in Hindustani; when Frederick Ponsonby presented the text to her, Victoria pointed out that this was incorrect, but let the false statement be published, as, she declared, "I could have done so had I wished."[66]

In the aftermath of the disastrous reception for members of the House of Commons at Buckingham Palace, Victoria held a special garden party for them on Saturday, July 3, at Windsor Castle, asking their wives and daughters as well.[67] In an unusual and thoughtful gesture, Victoria opened the castle's state apartments, and the members were allowed to roam through them at will before making their way to the East Terrace, where the garden party was held. To keep them happy, the champagne flowed freely, and the queen, in a carriage, drove among her guests, stopping at intervals to speak to various members and greet their families.[68]

The following day, Victoria received forty members of her Indian escort at Windsor before visiting the Roman Catholic Boys' School at Old Windsor. Accompanied by her granddaughter Princess Victoria of Battenberg, the queen received a congratulatory address and a bouquet of orchids on behalf of the pupils.[69] There were more ceremonies on July 6, when Victoria received U.S. special diplomatic envoy Whitelaw Reid, who had been appointed to convey the congratulations of the U.S. government; that night she presided over a family dinner at Windsor, where her guests included her grandchildren the Grand Duke and Grand Duchess of Hesse.[70]

On July 7, Victoria entertained the colonial premiers and their wives and suites, followed by an elaborate luncheon in St. George's Hall at Windsor before they bade her farewell to return to their countries.[71] The next day, at three in the afternoon, members of the Anglican clergy, led by Frederick Temple, the Archbishop of Canterbury, and followed by more than a hundred bishops, paraded before the queen in the castle's glittering Grand Reception Room, each bowing before her, kissing her hand, and offering his congratulations.[72]

At the end of the reception, the queen, accompanied by her grand-daughter Princess Marie Louise and by Lady Lytton, escaped the crowd and went for a drive in Windsor Home Park. Two long weeks of ceremonies had begun to wear upon the elderly queen, and she had found the religious reception a particularly trying ordeal. "A very ugly party," Victoria commented as they drove, then added, "I do not like bishops." According to Marie Louise, "Edith Lytton nearly fell out of the carriage in surprise and horror." Turning to the queen, she said, "Oh, but Your Majesty likes *some* bishops?" Victoria replied: "Yes, I like the man, but *not* the bishop."[73]

The series of services, receptions, reviews, dinners, and parades had finally ended. Victoria had been deeply moved by the enthusiasm of the crowds and the incessant cheers that greeted her every appearance. At the conclusion of the festivities, she released a letter to her people, expressing her gratitude: "I cannot rest satisfied without personally giving utterance to these sentiments. It is difficult for me on this occasion to say how truly touched and grateful I am for the spontaneous and universal outburst of loyal attachment and real affection which I have experienced on the completion of the sixtieth year of my reign. . . . It is indeed deeply gratifying after so many years of labor and anxiety for the good of my beloved country to find that my exertions have been appreciated throughout my vast empire. . . . It has given me unbounded pleasure to see so many of my subjects from all parts of the world assembled here and to find them joining in the acclamations of loyal devotion to myself, and I would wish to think them all from the depth of my grateful heart."[74]

The ceremonies had invested the elderly sovereign in black with a new resonance, the image of domestic queen replaced with a symbolic mantle that wrapped her in the accumulated glories of nineteenth-century England and the larger triumph of empire and that solidified Victoria's position as the very image of her age, her country, and her colonialism. It completed, noted Stanley Weintraub, "the metamorphosis of a stout, lame, nearly blind little lady in a bonnet, now nearly eighty, into legend." As memories of the Diamond Jubilee faded, Victoria's subjects understood that it had been the twilight of an era, with the queen "likely to be seen again only in portraits adorning drawing rooms and public offices, and on her postage stamps."[75]

EPILOGUE
The Twilight of Splendor

IN THE YEARS FOLLOWING THE DIAMOND JUBILEE, Victoria's health continued to steadily decline. Increasingly lame, she rarely walked; instead she relied on being pushed about in a wheelchair. As the world awaited the arrival of the twentieth century, the queen was nearly blind, a fragile eighty-year-old woman plagued with frequent indigestion, insomnia, and growing circulatory and breathing problems.[1] Month by month, Victoria seemed to weaken. More and more, she could not eat, and she fell asleep frequently.[2] "All about her are really anxious for the first time," Marie Mallet's husband wrote in that fall of 1900, noting the fears that "it must be the beginning of the end."[3] Still, Victoria clung tenaciously to life; her eldest son, Bertie, often joked that his mother was reluctant to die, as she would have to cede her precedence when she went to heaven.[4]

The passage of time had not only wrought physical deterioration in the queen but also brought with them tragedy. The deaths of her mother and of Prince Albert in 1861 seemed long past, but the decades had been filled with heartbreak: the deaths of two of her children, Alice and Leopold; her three favorite sons-in-law; and more than half a dozen grandchildren, including the Duke of Clarence, heir presumptive to the throne. And now there were fresh tragedies: her eldest daughter, Vicky, was dying of cancer in Berlin; her second son, Affie, died of cancer at the end of July 1900; and her grandson Prince Christian of Schleswig-Holstein died in October of malaria while fighting in Africa.

Events in Africa provided an additional, onerous burden. The Boer War had come as a shock, a crack in the carefully constructed mythology surrounding the Diamond Jubilee of a happy, united colonial empire under British rule. The open rebellion against Victoria's domination weighed heavily on her mind; stoically, she met talk of military reverses and possible negotiation with a firm, "We are not interested in the possibilities of defeat; they do not exist."[5] But such declarations flew in the face of a rapidly turning opinion. As newspapers chronicled the miseries of the internment camps the British had built, the starvation of the rebellious Boers, and the grim realities of a savage war, much of the public was horrified. Although the Boer War was not the first challenge to colonial expansion, it was the first time that Victoria saw her beloved British Empire crumbling away under the nationalistic strains that eventually tore it asunder.

On December 14, 1900, Victoria paid her customary visit to her husband's tomb in the royal mausoleum at Frogmore. It was a gray, barren winter's day, its desolation matching the queen's failing health and subdued mood. In another four days she would leave for Osborne, to once again spend Christmas in the Italianate house Albert had designed so many years before. When she had finished her prayers, Victoria once again crossed the inlaid marble floor, beneath the burnished copper dome above. When she left the mausoleum, it was for the last time; in less than two months she would return here, in her coffin, to be forever reunited with her beloved Albert.

Victoria's last Christmas at Osborne brought with it new tragedy. That holiday morning, her closest friend and confidante, Jane, Lady Churchill—who had served her as a lady-in-waiting for nearly half a century—was found dead in her bed. The queen's own health was so fragile that at first her physician, Sir James Reid, kept the news from her; finally, as night fell across the Isle of Wight, he broke the news. It proved a great shock to the queen; that night she took her last Christmas dinner, alone in her room, though she hardly ate.[6]

The new year brought no improvements to the queen's physical or mental health. As her insomnia increased and her appetite continued to fail, Victoria fell into a depression that echoed her swift decline. As the first week of January slipped toward the second, Victoria could be induced only to make feeble attempts at eating; with the loss of appetite, her remaining strength faltered, and she now found it an ordeal to leave her bed. Occasionally she would rise in the early evening and be wheeled into her sitting room, but those around her found her confused, as if she could no longer control her once-vibrant mind.[7] Victoria was suffering from physical collapse, and her heart was weakened. To everyone at Osborne it was obvious that the end was near. Quietly, without notifying anyone, officials in the household informed the Excelsior Hotel in Cimiez that the queen would not be returning for her customary spring holiday.[8]

On Thursday, January 17, Reid noted that the queen seemed more confused and her breathing labored as she passed into and out of a fitful sleep. He also saw that the right side of her face had become paralyzed as a result of a small stroke.[9] The following day, Reid decided to summon Sir Thomas Barlow, a heart specialist, to see if he could offer any treatment; Reid also dispatched cables to members of Victoria's family, warning them in guarded terms that her condition was deteriorating. Only Vicky, wasted by the cancer that would kill her in another eight months, was not told.[10]

On Saturday, January 19, the public learned for the first time of the queen's illness. The court circular announced: "The Queen has not lately been in her usual health, and is unable at present to take her customary drives. The Queen during the past year has had a great strain upon her powers, which has told rather upon Her Majesty's nervous system. It has, therefore, been thought advisable by Her Majesty's physicians that the Queen should be kept perfectly quiet in the house and should abstain for the present from transacting business."[11]

That evening, Victoria seemed to rally slightly. She asked Reid: "Am I better? I have been very ill."

"Yes," the doctor replied, "Your Majesty has been very ill, but now you are better." Still, the reassuring words failed to convince her. That same evening, she confided to Reid: "I should like to live a little longer, as I have still a few things to settle."[12]

The gravity of the situation began to settle over Victoria's subjects. At Osborne, her breathing had become labored, and, for the first time, she was given oxygen. To make caring for her easier, the large mahogany bed in her room was replaced with a smaller bed, placed beneath the chintz-hung canopy.[13] Family members had begun to make their way to Osborne, prepared for the worst. In Berlin, Arthur was attending the Bicentennial celebrations for his nephew Wilhelm II's House of Hohenzollern; when word of the queen's condition reached them, the kaiser abruptly canceled the festivities and accompanied his uncle to England.[14] No one had invited him, and members of the British royal family made little attempt to disguise their resentment. But the kaiser behaved impeccably. "My first wish," he told his English relatives, "is not to be in the light, and I will return to London if you wish. I should like to see Grandmama before she dies but if that is impossible, I shall quite understand."[15]

The kaiser arrived at Osborne on Monday, January 21, accompanied by the Prince of Wales and Prince Arthur; by now the other members of the family also had come. By this time the queen could no longer recognize her family and had to be told who was present; in one lucid moment she asked Bertie to come and kiss her.[16]

The following morning, Tuesday, January 22, 1901, Victoria sank into and out of consciousness. She asked that her white Pomeranian Turi be brought to her, but the dog was too restless to remain at its mistress's side for long, and darted into and out of the bedroom. Believing that the end was near, Reid's first bulletin that morning prepared the public for the worst: "The Queen this morning shows signs of diminishing strength, and Her Majesty's condition again assumes a more serious aspect." A second bulletin came four hours later: "There is no change for the worse in the Queen's condition since this morning's bulletin. Her Majesty has recognized the several members of the Royal Family who are here. The Queen is now asleep." As the *Times* of London informed its readers: "All day long the Angel of Death has been hovering over Osborne House. One could almost hear the beating of his wings."[17]

At Osborne, Randall Davidson, Bishop of Winchester, stood in a corner of the queen's bedroom, praying throughout the day. Victoria's family gathered around her bed, and her three daughters Helena, Louise, and

Beatrice kept repeating the names of those present so their mother would know who was with her: Bertie and Alix; Prince George and his wife, Mary; Louise and her husband; Helena; Arthur and his wife; Beatrice; Marie, the Duchess of Edinburgh; and Princesses Victoria and Maud of Wales. They pointedly ignored the kaiser, who stood in a corner of the room. Noting this rather cruel omission, Reid turned to the Prince of Wales and asked if the queen should not be told that her eldest grandson was present. "No," Bertie whispered. "It would excite her too much."[18]

Reid took this pettiness personally. That afternoon he found the kaiser and told him that he meant to take him to see the queen, for a private visit. Wilhelm was deeply touched. When Reid informed the Prince of Wales of this, Bertie gave in. Reid escorted the kaiser into the bedroom and told the queen that he had come to see her; on hearing this, Victoria smiled, and the doctor left Wilhelm alone with his grandmother. Later that afternoon, in one of her last lucid moments, Victoria whispered to Reid, "The Emperor is very kind."[19]

Then, late that afternoon, it was obvious that the queen would not last the night. At four o'clock, Reid issued an ominous bulletin: "The Queen is slowly sinking."[20] The family was again summoned to the bedroom. Reid knelt at the right side of the bed, his left arm supporting the queen, while Wilhelm knelt on the right side, with his one good arm around his grandmother. In her last conscious moment, Victoria turned her head slightly to the right, gazing with unseeing eyes toward a large painting, *The Entombment of Christ*, that hung over the chimneypiece. At exactly six-thirty, her eyes closed and her head dropped to her shoulder.[21] Queen Victoria was dead at the age of eighty-one.

A few minutes before seven that night, the last official bulletin was posted on the gates of Osborne as a crowd of reporters and the public looked on: "Her Majesty The Queen breathed her last at 6:30 P.M., surrounded by her children and grandchildren."[22] At once, the reporters and messengers on bicycles raced down York Street to East Cowes to file their reports, shouting as they went, "The queen is dead."[23] Within a few minutes, the news reached London, and the bells of St. Paul's Cathedral, where Victoria had marked her Diamond Jubilee four years earlier, began to toll, announcing to the city that she had died.[24]

The next day, all businesses were closed, and memorial editions of newspapers, ringed with thick black borders, detailed the queen's life and end. "To write the life of Queen Victoria," declared the *Times*, "is to relate the history of Great Britain during the period of great events, manifold changes and unexampled national prosperity. No reign in the annals of any country can compare with that of the Late Sovereign, the Throne is never vacant, and at the very moment of parting from our Queen, we have to proclaim our King."[25]

"London was plunged in fog and crepe," recalled one man. "Every shop window was streaked by a mourning shutter. The women, old and young, were draped with veils, and most touching was the mourning worn by the prostitutes, in whose existence the old queen had always refused to believe. Even the crossing sweepers carried crepe on their brooms. . . . It seemed as though the keystone had fallen out of the arch of heaven."[26]

The queen's large bed was moved back into place and her body laid atop it, surrounded by a thick frame of palm leaves and white lilies. Even as her body was laid out, officials were at work planning her funeral. Victoria had left several sets of written instructions detailing her last wishes. She requested that there be no formal lying in state, and that she not be embalmed. She also requested that, as head of the Royal Army, she be given a military funeral.[27] There had been no state funeral in Great Britain since the death of the Duke of Wellington in 1852, and no one knew with any certainty what precedents should be followed. It was left to the Catholic Henry Fitzalan-Howard, the fifteenth Duke of Norfolk, in his capacity as earl marshal, to arrange the ceremonies. Victoria would remain at Osborne for a week, lying in state in the dining room, before being taken to London. The queen had studied various funerary rites in crafting her own and, ironically for the woman who held the title Defender of the Faith for the Church of England, took her inspiration from Catholic rites used at papal funerals in the Vatican.[28] Her two sets of funerary instructions, written in 1897 and 1898, decreed that there was to be no black, but rather white and purple.[29] "What had become known as Victorian mourning," noted Stanley Weintraub, "was not meant for Victoria herself."[30] Her coffin would rest atop a gun carriage, banked in white flowers and drawn by eight white horses through the city in a stately procession, but she would not rest there. Instead, her body would be taken to Windsor, where her funeral would be held in St. George's Chapel, before she was interred in the royal mausoleum at Frogmore.

Mary Tuck and Sir James Reid prepared her body according to the queen's instructions, including a number of secret requests that were to be kept from her family. There were three caskets: a wooden shell lined with white satin, into which the queen's body would be placed; an outer lead casket; and finally, a elaborately carved oak outer coffin.[31] The bottom and sides of the wooden shell were lined with charcoal packed into muslin bags, atop which were placed the dressing gown Prince Albert had worn in his final illness, a cloak embroidered by Princess Alice, a number of family photographs, and plaster casts of Albert's hands concealed by a white, quilted cushion. The new king, Edward VII, along with Prince Arthur and his son, lifted the queen's body into the coffin, placing it atop this quilted cushion. Victoria was dressed in a white silk dressing gown, with the blue ribbon of the Order of the Garter across her chest and Albert's Diamond Star of the order pinned to a corner of the bodice. Her wedding veil, of white Honiton lace, was arranged around her silver hair, and her face was framed by bunches of white flowers laid into the coffin.[32] As soon as the members of the royal family left the room, Mary Tuck and Reid attended to the queen's other requests. According to her wishes, a wedding ring that had been worn by John Brown's mother was placed on her finger, next to the queen's own wedding ring; in her left hand, they placed a photograph of Brown, along with a small locket containing a cutting of his hair. Reid carefully covered these items with a bouquet of flowers from the new Queen Alexandra so that no one would notice their presence. Once the family had filed by and paid their last respects, the lids of all three coffins were affixed and screwed down, never to be removed.[33]

On Friday morning, January 25, a contingent of sailors carried the closed casket down the Grand Staircase to the dining room, which had been transformed into a *chapelle ardente*. The walls were draped with deep red, which provided a vivid contrast to the silver of the tall, standing candelabra that stood at the corners of the dais on which the coffin rested. The coffin was covered with a white silk pall, woven by the Royal School of Needlework, over which were arranged the royal standard and the queen's Garter robe, edged with ermine.[34] At each corner of the dais stood a member of the Grenadier Guard Regiment, in scarlet tunics and black bearskin hats, heads bowed and white-gloved hands folded atop the butts of their rifles in tribute.[35] The entire room resembled a somber hothouse, with a lush forest of potted palms and banks of memorial bouquets and wreaths from members of the queen's family, foreign royals, and heads of state.

One week later, on the morning of February 1, the Bishop of Winchester conducted a short service before the coffin, carried by a handful of bluejackets from the Royal Navy, was carried through the entrance hall and out into the courtyard, where it was placed atop a waiting gun carriage drawn by eight horses. Shortly after one-thirty that cold Friday afternoon, the queen left her beloved Osborne for the last time. The cortege was led by mounted grooms, followed by local officials representing Hampshire, Portsmouth, and the Isle of Wight; the massed bands of the Royal Marine Artillery and the Royal Marine Light Infantry followed, playing Chopin's "Funeral March" as they made their way down the graveled drive and beneath the bare trees.[36]

A contingent of the queen's Highland servants, led by James Campbell, the queen's pipe major, who played the "Lament" of the Black Watch, preceded the gun carriage.[37] The queen's equerries and aides-de-camp followed her coffin, with the scarlet-coated men of the queen's Company of Grenadier Guards marching slowly behind. The new king walked with his nephew Wilhelm II, both in the uniform of an admiral in the Royal Navy, followed by Prince Arthur, in the uniform of a British general, and the male members of the queen's family. Behind them came the royal women, led by the new Queen Alexandra, all in long black dresses of silk, cashmere, and crepe, with black caps and long black veils.[38] Members of Victoria's household and her domestic staff finished the procession.[39]

The entire length of the road from the gates of Osborne down the hillside to Trinity Pier in East Cowes was lined with troops, behind which stood thousands of members of the public. Trinity Pier had been draped in black; here the royal yacht *Alberta* lay at anchor. As the pipe major played a lament, grenadier guards lifted the coffin from the gun carriage and carried it aboard *Alberta*, placing it on a dais sheltered by a crimson canopy on the aft deck as the guns of the massed fleet of warships lining the Solent fired their salutes. The king and members of his family followed aboard *Victoria and Albert II*, the household aboard the Prince of Wales's yacht *Osborne*, and Kaiser Wilhelm II aboard his shining white yacht *Hohenzollern*. When he boarded the yacht, Edward VII noticed that the royal standard flying from her foremast was at half mast, and asked why this was so. "The Queen is dead, Sir," replied an official. "The King of England lives!" Edward replied, and ordered the flag raised to the top of the mast.[40]

The yachts left the Isle of Wight escorted by eight torpedo boats, slowly steaming between a double line of battleships and cruisers, their decks lined with sailors and their guns firing salutes to the dead monarch that echoed across the still water.[41] The gray skies above had cleared, and the sea was calm as the yachts proceeded in a stately procession. At five that evening, the bells of Portsmouth's churches rang out, announcing the arrival of the queen's body. The royal mourners boarded a train that carried them to London, but the queen's coffin remained on *Alberta*, which had pulled into Clarence Dock for the night.

On the following day, Saturday, February 2, the queen's coffin was carried to a special funeral train and placed atop a dais in a saloon car adorned with mourning ribbons. On arrival at Victoria Station in London, soldiers carried the coffin to a waiting gun carriage, and, at eleven-twenty that morning the cortege set out through the rainy city streets. The length of the procession, from Victoria Station through Pimlico, past Buckingham Palace and down the Mall, along Piccadilly and Hyde Park to Paddington Station, was adorned with laurel wreaths suspended from lamp standards, purple bows hung with gold ribbons, and swags of white satin that hung limply in the downpour.[42]

"The most impressive feature of the whole ceremony," recalled one witness, "was the attitude of the crowd; its size, its silence, the universal black."[43] And Mrs. Hwfa Williams remembered: "The whole route was one dense mass of people, everyone in those huge crowds in black, every one silent with grief."[44]

A contingent of troops and officials led the funeral cortege, followed by massed military bands playing funeral marches by Beethoven and Chopin.

Eight white horses, caparisoned in crimson, pulled the gun carriage. There were gasps when the coffin appeared—"almost a child's coffin," recalled one observer.[45] King Edward VII, in a dark cloak, rode behind his mother's coffin; at his side was the kaiser, atop a white horse, and the Duke of Connaught, in the uniform of a field marshal. King George I of the Hellenes and King Carlos of Portugal followed atop their own mounts, while the elderly King Leopold II of the Belgians rode in a carriage. They were followed by the crown princes of Germany, Denmark, Norway and Sweden, Greece, Romania, and Siam; Archduke Franz Ferdinand of Austria-Hungary; Grand Duke Ernst Ludwig of Hesse; Grand Duke Michael Alexandrovich of Russia; the Duke of Aosta, representing the King of Italy; and several dozen princes and grand dukes. They were followed by closed carriages containing Queen Alexandra, the other women of the royal family, and foreign princesses and grand duchesses. "How unimportant they all seemed, the kings of the earth, compared to the little packet of ashes they were honoring with bowed heads and shuffling tread," recalled one witness.[46] The clatter of hooves against the pavement, the rattle of the carriage wheels, the funereal music floating from the massed bands, the tolling of the city's church bells, and the booming of the artillery salutes in Hyde Park all added to the somber tone of the procession.

At Paddington Station, the cortege came to a halt as the strains of Beethoven's "Funeral March" filled the air. A guard of honor composed of a hundred officers from the Royal Marines stood along the edges of the crimson carpet that covered the platform. The gun carriage halted before a circular bed of evergreen boughs and white flowers, and the coffin was carried aboard a special saloon car and placed on a dais. At one-thirty-two that afternoon, the royal sovereign locomotive, adorned with the royal arms and draped in purple and white crepe garlands and wreaths, slowly steamed out of the station, carrying Victoria's body and the party of mourners out of London.[47]

A second gun carriage awaited the train's arrival at Windsor, but as the coffin was being unloaded, the restless horses bolted, snapping their traces. The early part of the procession had already begun its slow march up the steep hillside to the castle. Prince Louis of Battenberg, married to the queen's granddaughter Victoria of Hesse, suggested that a contingent of sailors man the braces and pull the gun carriage, establishing a royal tradition that continues to this day.[48] Through the intermittent sleet, the procession made its way up High Street to the Long Walk as the queen's pipers played the lament "Flowers in the Forest," continuing into the castle precincts as minute guns fired a salute of eighty-one shots, one for each year of Victoria's life.[49] That night the queen lay in state in the Albert Memorial Chapel, watched over by a guard of honor formed of members of the Life Guards Regiment; the scent from the thousands of wreaths piled around the walls was so overpowering that one of the guards fainted during his vigil.[50]

The queen's funeral was held on Sunday, February 3. Shortly after three in the afternoon, a guard of honor, composed of members of the Grenadier Guards Regiment, carried the queen's coffin up the steps to the western door of St. George's Chapel, followed by members of her family. Despite the shrunken body of the late queen within, the three coffins weighed a thousand pounds and were so heavy that the grenadier guards stumbled as they climbed the steps and nearly dropped their burden; only the rush of a few soldiers who helped hoist the coffin level and supported it as the cortege ascended to the west door saved the situation from disaster.[51]

"As the great doors were thrown open," remembered the Duchess of Marlborough, "one saw the royal cortege slowly mounting the steps; only the boom of distant guns and the clangor of swords were heard above the muffled notes of the funeral march."[52] As the white-robed choir began its long walk down the chapel, led by the Bishop of Oxford, the Dean of Windsor, and the Archbishop of Canterbury, the congregation stood. Despite the mournful occasion, the crowd inside the chapel was a sea of vivid colors: the blue and scarlet uniforms of members of the household cavalry; the knights of the Order of the Garter, in their blue velvet mantles; the military knights of Windsor, clad in scarlet and gold; and the yeomen of the guard, in their bright red coats adorned with gold and white Elizabethan ruffled collars.[53]

Victoria's coffin was placed on a purple-covered bier before the altar as her family took their places in the carved oak choir stalls. The gloom of the gray day outside barely penetrated into the chapel, which was illuminated with the eerie, flickering light from hundreds of candles. Victoria had selected all of the music: the hymn "Lord, Thou Hast Been Our Refuge" opened the service, followed by Chopin's "Funeral March" and a number of prayers. A lesson from Corinthians was followed by the Lord's Prayer, chanted by the choir, and Tchaikovsky's "How Blessed Are They That Die." After the benediction, the Norroy king at arms stepped forward and proclaimed, "It hath pleased Almighty God to take out of this transitory life into His Divine Mercy the late, Most High, Most Mighty, and Most Excellent Monarch, Victoria, by the Grace of God of the United Kingdom of Great Britain and Ireland, Queen, Defender of the Faith, Empress of India, and Sovereign of the Most Noble Order of the Garter."[54] After the proclamation of Victoria's titles, the lord great chamberlain, in his scarlet tailcoat emblazoned with gold embroidery, approached the coffin and broke his white stave of office, signifying that his service to the monarch had ended.[55] The service ended with Beethoven's "Funeral March," as the queen's coffin was carried from St. George's Chapel and back into the Albert Memorial Chapel, where it would rest overnight before being interred at Frogmore.[56]

The committal service took place the following day, Monday, February 4. The shock of the queen's death had begun to dissipate, though Frederick Ponsonby was stunned that morning to find the kaiser, the King of Portugal, and others standing in a drawing room before the final service, smoking—a sure sign that the strictures of Victoria's court had passed into history.[57]

It was, remembered Princess Marie Louise, "a bitterly cold day."[58] A few minutes before three that afternoon, the coffin was loaded onto the gun carriage drawn by eight white horses and slowly passed for the last time through the Lower and Upper wards of Windsor as church bells rang and the guns of the Royal Artillery Regiment fired their salutes. A company of the queen's grenadier guards led the cortege, followed by her personal servants, the Bishop of Winchester and the Dean of Windsor, and the lord chamberlain and the lord steward. Behind the coffin walked the royal mourners, led by the new king Edward VII, flanked by the kaiser and the Duke of Connaught and followed by a sea of uniformed princes and grand dukes; at the rear, moving slowly through the flurries of snow like a group of crows, were the royal women, clothed in long black gowns and draped in veils of black tulle and lace, followed by the members of the queen's household. The cortege passed through the George IV Gate to the Long Walk, whose length was lined with grenadier guards who stood rigidly at attention; the sound of muffled drums, tolling bells, and the strains of Chopin's "Funeral March" accompanied Victoria on her last journey.[59]

As the cortege reached the gates of Frogmore, the band of the grenadier guards fell silent and Chopin's "Funeral March" was replaced with the plaintive sound of the queen's pipers as they played "Flowers of the Forest."[60] Within the cold marble walls of the royal mausoleum, the mourners watched as the coffin was carried to the tomb, accompanied by the plaintive strains of pipers playing a last lament. The great sarcophagus lay open; Albert's oak coffin was visible inside, his sword and scabbard crossed on its dusty top. A few weeks before his death, he had told Victoria: "We don't know in what state we shall meet again; but that we shall recognize each other and be together in eternity I am perfectly certain."[61] Now that reunion had come. After the Bishop of Winchester offered a prayer, the mourners passed the coffin, sprinkling its lid with handfuls of earth from silver trays brought from the Mount of Olives in Jerusalem.[62] Once the coffin was lowered into the vault, workers affixed the recumbent, white marble effigy of Victoria, carved shortly after the prince consort's death, atop the tomb next to that of her beloved husband. As the mausoleum's great doors were closed, evening fell over the tranquil countryside and the skies above opened, covering the scene with a blanket of snow. "Queen's Weather" had given Victoria sunshine on the day of her Diamond Jubilee; now the elements again conspired, and they joined to give the queen her white funeral.

APPENDIX
The Royal Household

THE FOLLOWING LIST INCLUDES the principal officeholders in the royal household in the year covered by this book. When the Marquess of Salisbury came to power as prime minister for the third time, on July 2, 1895, certain offices considered to be political in nature, including the lord chamberlain, the lord steward, and the master of the horse, were changed. The vast majority of members of the royal household, however, were not subject to governmental jurisdiction. The royal household was always something of a fluid entity; people retired from service (a not uncommon occurrence in these years, when many members had held office for decades), existing officials were elevated, and new faces entered into the queen's employ. I have noted any such retirements or replacements for the sake of completeness.

Lord chamberlain: the Earl of Lathom, from July 1895.

Vice chamberlain: the Honorable Ailwyn Fellowes, from July 1895.

Comptroller of the lord chamberlain's department: the Honorable Sir Spencer Ponsonby-Fane.

Master of ceremonies: Colonel the Honorable W. T. Colville, from 1893.

Captain of the bodyguard of gentlemen-at-arms: Lord Henry Strutt, Baron Belper, from July 1895.

Captain of the yeomen of the guard: the Earl of Limerick, from July 1895 to his death in August 1896, replaced by the Earl Waldegrave.

Yeomanry aide-de-camp to Her Majesty: the Earl of Cork.

Gold stick-in-waiting: Viscount Wolseley.

Silver stick-in-waiting: Colonel Neeld.

Lord steward: the fourteenth Earl of Pembroke, from July 1895.

Master of the household: Lord Edward Pelham Clinton, from 1894.

Comptroller of the royal household: Lord Arthur Hill, from 1895.

Her Majesty's treasurer: Viscount Curzon.

Keeper of Her Majesty's Privy Purse: Lieutenant Colonel Sir Fleetwood Edwards, from 1895.

Assistant keepers of Her Majesty's Privy Purse: Colonel A. J. Pickard; Lieutenant Frederick Ponsonby; Lieutenant General Sir Arthur Bigge.

Lords-in-waiting: Lord Churchill (from 1895); Lord Harris (from 1895); the Earl of Kintore (from November 1895); Lord Lawrence (from 1895); the Earl of Ranfurly (from 1895 until April 1897); the Earl of Denbigh (from April 1897); the Earl Waldegrave (from 1895 until August 1896); Baron Bagot (from August 1896); the Earl of Clarendon (from 1895); and Viscount Bridport, permanent lord-in-waiting (from 1895).

Grooms-in-waiting: Admiral Sir J. E. Commerell, from 1893; Captain the Honorable Charles Harbord, from 1895; Colonel Lord William Cecil, from 1892; the Honorable Alexander (Alick) Yorke, from 1884; Colonel Henry Browne, from 1895; Captain Walter Campbell, from 1880; Captain Malcolm Drummond, from 1893; and General H. Lynedoch Gardiner, from January 1896.

Extra groom-in-waiting: General Sir Michael Biddulph, from 1895.

Master of the horse: the sixth Duke of Portland, from July 1895.

Master of the buckhounds: the ninth Earl of Coventry, from July 1895.

Crown equerry: Major General Sir Henry Ewart, from 1894.

Equerries-in-ordinary: Sir John McNeill, from 1874; Lieutenant Colonel the Honorable H. W. J. Byng, from 1874; Lieutenant Frederick Ponsonby, from 1894; Lieutenant Colonel the Honorable W. H. P. Carington, from 1882; the Honorable Henry Legge, from 1893; Lieutenant General Sir Arthur Bigge, from 1893; and Lieutenant Colonel Sir Arthur Davidson, from 1896.

Extra equerry-in-waiting: Lieutenant Colonel John Clerk, from 1892.

Her Majesty's private secretary: Lieutenant General Sir Arthur Bigge, from May 9, 1895.

Assistant private secretaries to Her Majesty: Colonel A. J. Pickard; Lieutenant Colonel Sir Fleetwood Edwards; and Lieutenant Frederick Ponsonby.

Mistress of the robes: Louisa, the Duchess of Buccleuch, from July 1896.

Ladies of the bedchamber: Jane, Baroness Churchill, from 1854; Louisa, the Countess of Antrim, from 1890; Emily, Baroness Ampthill, from 1885; Anne, Dowager Duchess of Athole, from 1854 to her death in May 1897; Viscountess Downe, from 1889; Edith, the Countess of Lytton, from 1895; Baroness Southampton, from 1878; and the Countess of Erroll, from 1873.

Extra ladies of the bedchamber: Elizabeth, Duchess of Bedford, from 1883 to her death in April 1897; Anne, Dowager Duchess of Roxburghe, from 1895.

Women of the bedchamber: Viscountess Chewton, from 1855; the Honorable Mrs. Ferguson, from 1877; the Honorable Harriet Phipps, from 1889; the Honorable Horatia Stopford, from 1877; Lady Hamilton Gordon, from 1855; the Honorable Emily Cathcart, from 1891; the Honorable Flora Macdonald, from 1874; and Lady Cust, from 1885.

Extra women of the bedchamber: the Honorable Mrs. Grant, from 1895; the Honorable Lady Ponsonby, from 1895.

Maids of honor: the Honorable Judith Harbord, from 1894; the Honorable M. Hughes, from 1891; the Honorable Aline Majendie, from 1894; the Honorable Bertha Lambart, from 1890; the Honorable Ethel Cadogan, from 1880; the Honorable E. Moore, from 1881; the Honorable Frances Drummond, from 1872; and the Honorable Mary Byng, from 1894.

Pages of honor to Her Majesty: the Honorable I. J. L. Hay; Josslyn Seymour Egerton; Alexander Wood until March 1897, when he was replaced by Harold E. Festing; and J. E. de G. Henniker Major.[1]

NOTES

INTRODUCTION

1. Kuhn, 251.
2. Eilers, 60.
3. Waddington, 177.
4. Prince Nicholas of Greece, 108–109.
5. Bell, 77–78.
6. See Homans, ch. 1, esp. 1–4.
7. Ibid., 44 passim.
8. Zeepvat, *Queen Victoria's Family*, viii.
9. Gernsheim and Gernsheim, *Victoria R*, 257.
10. Richards, 79.
11. Hamilton, 42.

PROLOGUE: LONDON, 1897

1. Jaffé, 143; Packard, *Queen and Her Court*, 159.
2. Menkes, 18, 179.
3. Strong, 24; *Sunday Times* of London, July 24, 1988.
4. Richards, 116.
5. Arnstein, 593; Packard, *Queen and Her Court*, 171.
6. St. Aubyn, *Queen Victoria*, 489; Hibbert, *Queen Victoria*, 381.
7. Hibbert, *Queen Victoria*, 379.
8. Buckle, *Letters of Queen Victoria . . . 1886 and 1901*, 3:165–166.
9. Lant, 217.
10. Weintraub, 571; Hibbert, *Queen Victoria*, 456–457; Benson, *Queen Victoria's Daughters*, 285.
11. Weintraub, 571; letter of Sir Matthew Ridley to Sir Arthur Bigge, January 22, 1897, quoted in Buckle, *Letters of Queen Victoria . . . 1886 and 1901*, 3:124–125.
12. Gardiner, 7.
13. Lant, 235.
14. Ibid., 216.
15. Ibid., 217.

16. Longford, *Queen Victoria*, 547.
17. Cited in Pope-Hennessy, 335.
18. Maxwell, 203; Chapman and Raben, 69.
19. Hibbert, *Queen Victoria*, 456–457.
20. Gardiner, 7.
21. Cornwallis-West, 118.
22. Hibbert, *Queen Victoria*, 380.
23. Lutyens, 116.
24. Maxwell, 194.
25. Maxwell, 194–195; Chapman and Raben, 65.
26. Maxwell, 197; Lant, 225.
27. Lant, 225.
28. Lutyens, 110.
29. Edwards, 104.

CHAPTER 1: THE WIDOW OF WINDSOR

1. Gore, 162.
2. Hibbert, *Queen Victoria*, 4.
3. Ibid.
4. De-La-Noy, *Queen Victoria at Home*, 2; Weintraub, 41; Benson, *Queen Victoria*, 66–67; Strachey, 9; see also Wandroper for further details.
5. Weintraub, 26.
6. Longford, *Queen Victoria*, 20.
7. Quoted in Longford, *Queen Victoria*, 24.
8. Hibbert, *Queen Victoria*, 15.
9. Ibid., 23.
10. Ibid., 31.
11. Strachey, 33.
12. Hibbert, *Queen Victoria*, 26.
13. Ibid., 22.
14. Ibid., 18.
15. Ibid., 33.
16. Quoted in St. Aubyn, *Queen Victoria*, 27.
17. Fulford, *Dearest Child*, 72–73.
18. Greville, 137–138.

19. Cited in Woodham-Smith, 133.
20. Hibbert, *Queen Victoria*, 49–50.
21. Frankland, 64.
22. Weintraub, 4; see also Staniland.
23. Prince Nicholas of Greece, 109.
24. Warwick, 63.
25. Tisdall, 167.
26. Martin, *Queen Victoria*, 70.
27. Cited in Strachey, 346.
28. Ponsonby, *Henry Ponsonby*, 70.
29. Bell, 353.
30. Fulford, *Prince Consort*, 21.
31. See James, *Prince Albert*, 28.
32. Queen Victoria, journal entry of October 11, 1839, Royal Archives, cited in James, *Prince Albert*, 81.
33. Queen Victoria, journal entry of October 15, 1839, Royal Archives, quoted in Esher, 1:268–269.
34. Gardiner, 67.
35. Queen Victoria, journal entry of February 11, 1840, Royal Archives, cited in James, *Prince Albert*, 101.
36. Quoted in Jagow, 68.
37. James, *Prince Albert*, xii.
38. Quoted in Bolitho, *Letters of Queen Victoria*, 2–3.
39. Queen Victoria to Crown Princess Victoria of Prussia, May 8, 1858, Schloss Friedrichshof Archive, Kronberg, quoted in Fulford, *Prince Consort*, 111–112.
40. Fulford, *Dearest Child*, 205.
41. Hough, *Victoria and Albert*, 148.
42. Quoted in Woodham-Smith, 231.
43. Prince Albert to Baron Stockmar, January 19, 1842, Royal Archives, Add. U2/5, cited in James, *Prince Albert*, 127.
44. Cited in Hibbert, *Queen Victoria*, 257.
45. Queen Victoria to Princess Augusta of Prussia, May 26, 1860, quoted in Bolitho, *Letters of Queen Victoria*, 109.
46. Weintraub, 274.
47. Queen Victoria to Crown Princess Victoria of Prussia, February 13, 1861, in Fulford, *Dearest Child*, 308.
48. James, *Prince Albert*, 269.
49. Hibbert, *Queen Victoria*, 275.
50. Hibbert, *Queen Victoria*, 278; Weintraub, 299; Bennett, 381.
51. James, *Prince Albert*, 272.
52. Longford, *Queen Victoria*, 298.
53. Weintraub, 298.
54. Ibid., 298–299.
55. James, *Prince Albert*, 272–273.
56. Weintraub, 299.
57. Windsor and Bolitho, 291.
58. Queen Victoria to King Leopold of the Belgians, December 20, 1861, in Benson and Esher, 3:473–474.
59. Queen Victoria to Queen Augusta of Prussia, February 4, 1862, in Bolitho, *Letters of Queen Victoria*, 120.
60. Gernsheim and Gernsheim, *Victoria R*, 165.
61. Watson, 156.
62. Ibid., 147.
63. Ibid., 156.
64. Tisdall, 54.
65. Bolitho, *Victoria: The Widow and Her Son*, 1–2.
66. Gernsheim and Gernsheim, *Victoria R*, 141; Tisdall, 54.
67. Lutyens, 17.
68. Quoted in Weintraub, 309.
69. Blake, 747.
70. See Brooks for more information.
71. Collier, 2.
72. Jaffé, 138.
73. Hibbert, *Queen Victoria*, 299.
74. Ponsonby, *Henry Ponsonby*, 73–74.
75. Ponsonby letters, quoted in Longford, *Queen Victoria*, 387.
76. *Times* of London, December 16, 1864.
77. Hibbert, *Queen Victoria*, 310.
78. Ponsonby, *Henry Ponsonby*, 72.
79. Ponsonby letters, quoted in Longford, *Queen Victoria*, 368.
80. Weintraub, 380; Hibbert, *Queen Victoria*, 322.
81. Richards, 116.
82. Erbach-Schönberg, 286.

CHAPTER 2: A FAMILY ON THE THRONE

1. Fulford, *Dearest Child*, 195–196.
2. Queen Victoria to Crown Princess Victoria of Prussia, June 15, 1858, quoted in Fulford, *Dearest Child*, 115.
3. Queen Victoria to Crown Princess Victoria of Prussia, February 22, 1865, quoted in Fulford, *Your Dear Letter*, 18.
4. Queen Victoria to Princess Augusta of Prussia, October 6, 1856, in Bolitho, *Letters of Queen Victoria*, 74.
5. James, *Prince Albert*, 244.
6. Queen Marie of Romania, 1:33; Gernsheim and Gernsheim, *Victoria R*, 158.
7. Weintraub, 226.
8. Fulford, *Beloved Mama*, 172.
9. Bolitho, *Letters of Queen Victoria*, 93.

10. Hibbert, *Queen Victoria,* 245.
11. Ibid., 385.
12. See Kohut, 22–29.
13. Marie Louise, 76.
14. Crown Princess Victoria of Prussia to Queen Victoria, June 19, 1866, quoted in Ponsonby, *Letters of Empress Frederick,* 60.
15. Weintraub, 464.
16. Kohut, 5.
17. Ibid., 33, 47.
18. Quoted in Weintraub, 505.
19. Lutyens, 60.
20. Queen Victoria to Crown Princess Victoria of Prussia, July 2, 1862, quoted in Fulford, *Dearest Mama,* 85.
21. Fulford, *Dearest Child,* 287–288.
22. Hough, *Louis and Victoria,* 155–156.
23. Sullivan, 136.
24. Ibid., 182.
25. Princess Ileana of Romania to Terrence Elsberry, in Elsberry, 62.
26. Buchanan, 34.
27. Queen Victoria to Crown Princess Victoria of Prussia, January 11, 1865, in Fulford, *Your Dear Letter,* 15.
28. Ponsonby, *Henry Ponsonby,* 87.
29. Van der Kiste, 8.
30. Sullivan, 29.
31. Buchanan, 115.
32. Eilers, 62.
33. Marie Louise, 31.
34. Fulford, *Dearest Mama,* 311.
35. St. Aubyn, *Edward VII,* 100–101.
36. Queen Victoria to Crown Princess Victoria of Prussia, September 11, 1865, in Fulford, *Your Dear Letter,* 42.
37. Queen Victoria to Crown Princess Victoria of Prussia, January 24, 1866, in Fulford, *Your Dear Letter,* 56.
38. Packard, *Victoria's Daughters,* 265; Reid, 117.
39. Reid, 106.
40. Packard, *Victoria's Daughters,* 269.
41. Marie Louise, 89.
42. Ibid., 92.
43. Channon, 515.
44. Gernsheim and Gernsheim, *Victoria R,* 150.
45. See Longford, *Darling Loosy,* 51–58.
46. Weintraub, 471.
47. Mallet, 50.
48. Queen Victoria to Princess Victoria of Hesse, September 5, 1882, in Hough, *Advice,* 40.
49. See Leslie, ch. 17.
50. Queen Victoria to Crown Princess Victoria of Prussia, April 11, 1868, in Fulford, *Your Dear Letter,* 184.
51. Queen Victoria to Empress Augusta of Germany, December 6, 1876, in Bolitho, *Letters of Queen Victoria,* 217.
52. Zeepvat, *Leopold,* 122.
53. Hibbert, *Queen Victoria,* 408.
54. Queen Victoria, journal entry of March 28, 1884, Royal Archives, cited in Hibbert, *Queen Victoria in Her Letters and Journals,* 285.
55. Duff, *Hessian Tapestry,* 186.
56. Buckle, *Letters of Queen Victoria . . . 1886 and 1901,* 1:85.
57. Lutyens, 47.
58. Ibid., 48.
59. Hibbert, *Queen Victoria,* 412.
60. Fulford, *Dearest Mama,* 144.
61. Arch and Marschner, 62.
62. Weintraub, 475.
63. Lutyens, 46–47.
64. Reid, 103.
65. See Wake, 318.
66. Letter from the Duchess of Teck, February 9, 1896, in Pope-Hennessy, 317.
67. Laver, 31.
68. Bagehot, 85–86.

CHAPTER 3: THE COURT OF ST. JAMES'S

1. Reid, 65.
2. Cannadine, 249.
3. Longford, *Louisa: Lady in Waiting,* 11.
4. Hibbert, *Queen Victoria,* 116–117.
5. Turner, 294–295; Fulford, *Prince Consort,* 61.
6. Cannadine, 247; Reid, 185.
7. Lindsay, 133.
8. Balsan, 75.
9. James and Russell, 198.
10. Packard, *Queen and Her Court,* 86.
11. Fletcher, 52.
12. Mullen and Munson, 11.
13. Lindsay, 20, 100; Lant, 59.
14. Lant, 221; Lindsay, 154.
15. Strachey, 182–183; James, *Prince Albert,* 116; Packard, *Queen and Her Court,* 85–87; Howard, 183.
16. Fletcher, 49.
17. Lutyens, 171.
18. Queen Victoria, journal entry of September 28, 1894, quoted in Nevill, 7.
19. Lindsay, 20, 26.

20. Packard, *Queen and Her Court,* 87; Howard, 183.
21. Turner, 317.
22. Mallet, 53.
23. Lindsay, 160; Bruce, Calder, and Cator, 74; Fletcher, 59.
24. Strachey, 182–183; Packard, *Queen and Her Court,* 87; James, *Prince Albert,* 116; De-La-Noy, *Windsor,* 73; Howard, 189.
25. Lindsay, 29; *Royal Mews,* 2.
26. Campbell, 35; Lutyens, 173; Howard, 189.
27. Lindsay, 29–30, 72, 83, 133; Reid, 39; Ponsonby, *Recollections,* 41, 78.
28. Laird, 83; Howard, 192; James and Russell, 86; Ponsonby, *Recollections,* 30.
29. Reid, 65; Fletcher, 22; Windsor, *Family Album,* 17.
30. Ponsonby, *Recollections,* 9, 29, 32.
31. Ibid., 93.
32. Lindsay, 20.
33. Lindsay, 27–28; Fletcher, 53.
34. Reid, 116.
35. Mallet, xvi.
36. Marie Louise, 114.
37. Mallet, xiii.
38. Emden, 402; Lindsay, 158–159; Kuhn, 236 passim.
39. Lindsay, 51; Emden, 199.
40. Reid, 163.
41. Ibid., 103.
42. Ponsonby, *Recollections,* 33; Tisdall, 136; Lindsay, 26, 94.
43. Hall, 10.
44. Longford, *Queen Victoria,* 73.
45. Watson, 23; Hibbert, *Queen Victoria,* 58.
46. Prochaska, 77.
47. Quoted in Hall, 16.
48. Coulter and Cooper, 106.
49. Cust, 76.
50. James and Russell, 87, 206.
51. Ibid., 86.
52. Lindsay, 26; Fletcher, 55–56, 60–61; Mallet, 231.
53. Fletcher, 54–55.
54. Weintraub, 508; Reid, 36; Lamont-Brown, 138–142.
55. Reid, 24–31.
56. Ibid., 36.
57. Ponsonby, *Henry Ponsonby,* 61.
58. Ibid., 60.
59. Reid, 53.
60. Ibid., 76.
61. Ibid., 77–78.
62. Ibid., 74, 84.
63. Mallet, 197.
64. Lutyens, 19.
65. Reid, 82.
66. Lamont-Brown, 131.
67. Reid, 84; Lutyens, 23, 81.
68. Ponsonby, *Recollections,* 36–38.
69. Lutyens, 147.
70. Fletcher, 52; Laird, 155.
71. Laird, 156–157; Lindsay, 95.
72. Weintraub, 499–500.
73. Longford, *Queen Victoria,* 322; Bell, 1:82.
74. Ponsonby, *Henry Ponsonby,* 46.
75. Ibid., 119; Longford, *Queen Victoria,* 343.
76. Weintraub, 213.
77. Ponsonby, *Mary Ponsonby,* 17; Reid, 55.
78. Hibbert, *Queen Victoria,* 294–295; Weintraub, 214.
79. Lindsay, 59.
80. Reynolds, 207.
81. Stoney and Weltzien, 6; De-La-Noy, *Windsor,* 74; Lutyens, 71; Watson, 17, 19.
82. Colville, 108.
83. Ibid.
84. Stoney and Weltzien, 6; Howard, 192; James and Russell, 84.
85. Reynolds, 190–191; Kuhn, 68.
86. Gosse, 327.
87. Mallet, 1.
88. Lutyens, 20–21.
89. Ponsonby, *Mary Ponsonby,* 2.
90. Reynolds, 195.
91. Longford, *Queen Victoria,* 310.
92. Lutyens, 77; Mallet, 231.
93. Ponsonby, *Mary Ponsonby,* 19.
94. Reid, 44.
95. Lutyens, 18, 177.
96. Mallet, 2.
97. See Reynolds, 202.
98. Lutyens, 12–13; Lindsay, 140.
99. Lutyens, 22.
100. Kuhn, 68; Mallet, 8.
101. Lutyens, 18; Watson, 17.
102. One of Her Majesty's Servants, 172.
103. Mallet, 4.
104. Reynolds, 199.
105. Turner, 308.
106. Lutyens, 13; Reid, 176; Hibbert, *Queen Victoria,* 350; One of Her Majesty's Servants, 174.
107. Mallet, 1.
108. Reynolds, 199.
109. Ponsonby, *Henry Ponsonby,* 58.

CHAPTER 4: SPRING AT WINDSOR

1. Windsor, *Family Album,* 4.
2. Morshead, 6–11.
3. De-La-Noy, *Windsor,* 38–39; Montgomery-Massingberd, 108; Morshead, 64–65.
4. Williams, *Royal Homes,* 24.
5. Gernsheim and Gernsheim, *Victoria R,* 49.
6. See Morshead, ch. 6, for a fuller description of Wyatville's work at Windsor Castle.
7. Morshead, 87.
8. Mackworth-Young, 30.
9. Morshead, 18–20.
10. Ibid.; see ch. 4.
11. Mackworth-Young, 81; Jaffé, 135; Tytler, 2:268–269; Homans, *Royal Representations,* 168.
12. Hibbert, *Court at Windsor,* 166.
13. Morshead, 93.
14. Hill, 4.
15. De-La-Noy, *Windsor,* 139.
16. Hill, 18.
17. Cust, 16.
18. Hill, 18.
19. De-La-Noy, *Windsor,* 38–39, 141; Hill, 16; Mackworth-Young, 47; Harris, *Queen's Windsor,* 28; Morshead, 150–152.
20. De-La-Noy, *Windsor,* 141; Stoney and Weltzien, 63–64; Hill, 15; Mackworth-Young, 71; Morshead, 162–163.
21. Hill, 12.
22. Morshead, 166.
23. Morton, 16; De-La-Noy, *Windsor,* 142; Hill, 8; Mackworth-Young, 67.
24. Hill, 8.
25. Stoney and Weltzien, 66.
26. De-La-Noy, *Windsor,* 142; Hill, 7.
27. Harris, *Queen's Windsor,* 29.
28. Nicolson, 15, 63.
29. Hibbert, *Queen Victoria,* 232.
30. Harris, *Queen's Windsor,* 29.
31. Packard, *Queen and Her Court,* 64; Nicolson, 18; De-La-Noy, *Windsor,* 139; Hill, 24, 30; Mackworth-Young, 60; Harris, *Queen's Windsor,* 30.
32. Stoney and Weltzien, 48; Hill, 20; Harris, *Queen's Windsor,* 20; Gernsheim and Gernsheim, *Victoria R,* 190.
33. Nicolson, 18, 174–176; De-La-Noy, *Windsor,* 140; Hill, 22; Mackworth-Young, 56.
34. Stoney and Weltzien, 50.
35. One of Her Majesty's Servants, 41.
36. Nicolson, 6–7, 36, 92; One of Her Majesty's Servants, 155–157.
37. Bolitho, *Reign of Queen Victoria,* 363.
38. Nicolson, 180.
39. Ibid., 29, 178, 183, 191.
40. Montgomery-Massingberd, 116.
41. Williams, *Royal Homes,* 109.
42. Nicolson, 34, 62, 194, 197; Morshead, 176.
43. Nicolson, 62.
44. Roper, 12; Morshead, 96–97; Hibbert, *Court at Windsor,* 167.
45. Morshead, 91–92.
46. Lasdun, 67.
47. Cornforth, 1370.
48. Victoria, Marchioness of Milford Haven (Princess Victoria of Hesse), "Reminiscences," unpublished manuscript, 39, cited in King, 22.
49. One of Her Majesty's Servants, 5.
50. One of Her Majesty's Servants, 138; Ponsonby, *Recollections,* 45; Morshead, 87.
51. One of Her Majesty's Servants, 6–7.
52. Watson, 156.
53. Morton, 20.
54. Richards, 100.
55. Queen Marie of Romania, 1:19.
56. Cust, 185; Gernsheim and Gernsheim, *Victoria R,* 60.
57. Queen Marie of Romania, 1:19.
58. Morton, 12; One of Her Majesty's Servants, 11–16.
59. Cornforth, 1370.
60. Morton, 12; One of Her Majesty's Servants, 11–16.
61. Morton, 14; Gernsheim and Gernsheim, *Victoria R,* 274; One of Her Majesty's Servants, 15–19.
62. Bolitho, *Reign of Queen Victoria,* 363.
63. Hibbert, *Court at Windsor,* 229; Gernsheim and Gernsheim, *Victoria R,* 285; One of Her Majesty's Servants, 17–19.
64. Gernsheim and Gernsheim, *Victoria R,* 60.
65. Quoted in Hibbert, *Queen Victoria,* 288.
66. Cited in Harris, de Bellaigue, and Millar, 240.
67. Plumb and Wheldon, 256–257.
68. Ponsonby, *Recollections,* 85.
69. Warner, 95.
70. Ibid., 130.
71. Richards, 110.
72. Cust, 16–19.
73. Roper, 11; Morshead, 66–67.
74. Windsor, *Family Album,* 9.

75. Lasdun, 93; Hibbert, *Court at Windsor,* 144.
76. Harris, *Queen's Windsor,* 83.
77. Roper, 61–62; De-La-Noy, *Windsor,* 169–170.
78. Hibbert, *Queen Victoria,* 288.
79. Weintraub, 640.
80. Jaffé, 134; Hibbert, *Queen Victoria,* 288.
81. Plumb and Wheldon, 272.
82. Jaffé, 134; Weintraub, 566–567, 640; Hibbert, *Queen Victoria,* 288; De-La-Noy, *Windsor,* 172.
83. Ames, 10.
84. Hibbert, *Court at Windsor,* 107.
85. Queen Victoria to Princess Augusta of Prussia, October 14, 1856, in Bolitho, *Letters of Queen Victoria,* 76–77.
86. Queen Victoria to Anne, Duchess of Atholl, November 3, 1886, Atholl MSS, Bundle 1647, cited in Reynolds, 190.
87. Fulford, *Beloved Mama,* 172.

CHAPTER 5: A DAY IN THE LIFE

1. Royal Archives, Add J/1591, cited in Stoney and Weltzien, 12.
2. Royal Archives, undated memorandum from Queen Victoria, RA Z 202/62, cited in Stoney and Weltzien, 11.
3. Gardiner, 67.
4. Marie Louise, 111.
5. Watson, 193–194.
6. Gernsheim and Gernsheim, *Victoria R,* 263.
7. Maurois, 10.
8. Marie Louise, 111.
9. Tschumi, 48; Ponsonby, *Recollections,* 74; Windsor, *A King's Story,* 12.
10. Erbach-Schönberg, 236.
11. Queen Marie of Romania, 1:20.
12. Stoney and Weltzien, 13.
13. Stoney and Weltzien, 13, 123; Marie Louise, 112.
14. Victoria, Marchioness of Milford Haven (Princess Victoria of Hesse), "Reminiscences," unpublished memoirs, cited in Duff, *Hessian Tapestry,* 270.
15. Ibid.
16. Longford, *Queen Victoria,* 336; see also Hibbert, *Queen Victoria in Her Letters and Journals,* 314.
17. Weintraub, 535.
18. Ponsonby, *Henry Ponsonby,* 134–135.
19. Ibid., 45; Lutyens, 15, 31.
20. Ponsonby, *Recollections,* 43.
21. Ponsonby, *Henry Ponsonby,* 45.
22. Weintraub, 493.
23. Mackenzie, 77.
24. Gernsheim and Gernsheim, *Victoria R,* 266; Queen Victoria's journal, entry of January 14, 1878, quoted in Matson, 93.
25. Lutyens, 62; Weintraub, 569.
16. One of Her Majesty's Servants, 146–147; Queen Marie of Romania, 1:20; Tooley, 256–257.
27. One of Her Majesty's Servants, 147.
28. Fulford, *Darling Child,* 185.
29. Queen Marie of Romania, 1:19.
30. Gernsheim and Gernsheim, *Victoria R,* 58.
31. One of Her Majesty's Servants, 7.
32. Reid, 35.
33. Tisdall, 112.
34. Ponsonby, *Recollections,* 67.
35. De-La-Noy, *Queen Victoria at Home,* 207.
36. Benson, *As We Were,* 33.
37. Queen Marie of Romania, 1:18.
38. Victoria, Marchioness of Milford Haven (Princess Victoria of Hesse), "Reminiscences," unpublished memoirs, cited in Duff, *Hessian Tapestry,* 188.
39. Cited in Gelardi, 28.
40. One of Her Majesty's Servants, 56; Tooley, 259; York and Stoney, *Travels with Queen Victoria,* 38; Ponsonby, *Recollections,* 35.
41. Lutyens, 25.
42. Victoria, Marchioness of Milford Haven (Princess Victoria of Hesse), "Reminiscences," unpublished memoirs, cited in Duff, *Hessian Tapestry,* 270.
43. Lutyens, 25.
44. Erbach-Schönberg, 231.
45. Ponsonby, *Recollections,* 32.
46. Tisdall, 115.
47. Tschumi, 68, 211.
48. One of Her Majesty's Servants, 84.
49. Hibbert, *Queen Victoria,* 478.
50. Ponsonby, *Recollections,* 84–85.
51. Fulford, *Your Dear Letter,* 21; Lutyens, 109.
52. Jay, 197.
53. Queen Victoria, *More Leaves from the Journal of A Life in the Highlands,* vii.
54. St. Aubyn, *Victoria,* 365.
55. Gernsheim and Gernsheim, *Victoria R,* 149.
56. Royal Archives, RA Add J/1492, cited in Stoney and Weltzien, 12; Victoria, Marchioness of Milford Haven (Princess

Victoria of Hesse), "Reminiscences," unpublished memoirs, cited in Duff, *Hessian Tapestry,* 271.

57. Menkes, 8–12.
58. Ibid., 179–180.
59. Ibid., 7.
60. Ibid., 179–180.
61. Blake, 562; Hall, 178.
62. Hall, 176; Menkes, 11–13, 179.
63. Menkes, 12, 179.
64. Jaffé, 143.
65. Menkes, 9.
66. Ibid., 180.
67. Tooley, 105.
68. Marie Louise, 111; Esher, 2:127.
69. Marie Louise, 136.
70. Mallet, 6.
71. Balsan, 86.
72. Waddington, 191.
73. Balsan, 86; Waddington, 192.
74. Hibbert, *Queen Victoria,* 465.
75. Lutyens, 121.
76. De-La-Noy, *Queen Victoria at Home,* 273.
77. Lutyens, 59.
78. Ibid., 21.
79. Erbach-Schönberg, 231.
80. Ponsonby, *Recollections,* 47, 49.
81. Tschumi, 14.
82. Waddington, 192.
83. Ponsonby, *Henry Ponsonby,* 119.
84. Ponsonby, *Recollections,* 44.
85. Waddington, 192.
86. Cornwallis-West, 180.
87. Tschumi, 82.
88. Ibid., 41.
89. Ibid., 65.
90. Ibid., 66.
91. Ibid., 45, 64.
92. Ibid., 61–62.
93. Ibid., 49, 61.
94. One of Her Majesty's Servants, 140–142, 228–229; Aga Khan, 46–47; Mallet, 5.
95. Queen Marie of Romania, 1:24.
96. One of Her Majesty's Servants, 142; Erbach-Schönberg, 237.
97. Aga Khan, 46–47.
98. Tschumi, 61.
99. Ribblesdale, 119–120.
100. Balsan, 87.
101. Waddington, 193–194.
102. Aga Khan, 47.
103. William II, 78.

104. One of Her Majesty's Servants, 190; Reid, 120.
105. One of Her Majesty's Servants, 89.
106. Ponsonby, *Recollections,* 82–83.
107. Queen Marie of Romania, 1:236.
108. Weintraub, 180–181.
109. Reid, 116.
110. One of Her Majesty's Servants, 88–89.
111. Ponsonby, *Recollections,* 84.
112. Reid, 119; Mallet, 186.
113. Lutyens, 22.
114. Ibid., 53.
115. Ibid., 34.
116. Ibid., 22.
117. Royal Archives, memorandum, RA Add J/1593, cited in Stoney and Weltzien, 12.
118. Reid, 82.
119. Ponsonby, *Recollections,* 36.
120. Victoria, Marchioness of Milford Haven (Princess Victoria of Hesse), "Reminiscences," unpublished memoirs, cited in Duff, *Hessian Tapestry,* 188.
121. Tooley, 274; Ponsonby, *Recollections,* 36.
122. Ponsonby, *Recollections,* 37.
123. Ponsonby, *Henry Ponsonby,* 87.
124. Ponsonby, *Recollections,* 38.
125. Tooley, 138.

CHAPTER 6: LIFE BELOW STAIRS

1. Tschumi, 19.
2. Gosse, 329–330.
3. Longford, *Queen Victoria,* 536.
4. Royal Archives, RA HH 1/75, November–December 1869; RA Add A 3/101, memorandum dated November 22, 1867; and RA C 64/77, memorandum dated August 1874, cited in Stoney and Weltzien, 23–24.
5. Bolitho, *My Restless Years,* 208.
6. Tschumi, 31.
7. Mallet, 215.
8. Lutyens, 62.
9. Reid, 159.
10. Bolitho, *Reign of Queen Victoria,* 51.
11. Tschumi, 70.
12. Glasheen, 160; Watson, 18, 127.
13. Chapman and Raben, 57.
14. Watson, 18.
15. Cited in Hibbert, *Queen Victoria,* 140.
16. Low and Minto, 10.
17. Strachey, 182–183; Watson, 21.
18. Strachey, 183.
19. Bennett, 104; James, *Prince Albert,* 116; Turner, 306–307.

20. Hibbert, *Queen Victoria,* 139.
21. Turner, 307; Bolitho, *Reign of Queen Victoria,* 72.
22. Watson, 238.
23. Ponsonby, *Henry Ponsonby,* 390.
24. Ibid., 359.
25. Tschumi, 70.
26. Ibid., 45, 68.
27. Roper, 30, 39.
28. One of Her Majesty's Servants, 231.
29. Roper, 30, 39; Tschumi, 45, 52.
30. Tschumi, 67.
31. One of Her Majesty's Servants, 34; Tschumi, 40.
32. One of Her Majesty's Servants, 33–34; Nicolson, 254; Stoney and Weltzien, 42; Bloomfield, 1:32.
33. Tschumi, 39–40.
34. Ibid., 40, 44.
35. Ibid., 49.
36. Chapman and Raben, 99.
37. Tschumi, 71–72.
38. Jaffé, 87; Lutyens, 61.
39. Nicolson, 40, 51, 160.
40. Roper, 30, 39.
41. One of Her Majesty's Servants, 35; Nicolson, 40, 51, 160; Watson, 82.
42. Tschumi, 15, 41, 43.
43. Ibid., 41.
44. Ibid., 66.
45. Ibid., 80.
46. One of Her Majesty's Servants, 35; Tschumi, 33.
47. Watson, 127.
48. One of Her Majesty's Servants, 64.
49. Watson, 90; Glasheen, 160.
50. Stoney and Weltzien, 78.
51. Nevill, 49.
52. Reid, 187.
53. Stoney and Weltzien, 44.
54. Royal Archives, RA Add J/1591, cited in Stoney and Weltzien, 12.
55. Watson, 22–23; Stoney and Weltzien, 10.
56. Stoney and Weltzien, 7–12.
57. Watson, 93.
58. One of Her Majesty's Servants, 96.
59. Tisdall, 54.
60. One of Her Majesty's Servants, 118; York, *Victoria and Albert,* 85.
61. Fischer and Fischer, *Monarchy and the Royal Family,* 6–7.
62. Glasheen, 160.
63. James and Russell, 86; Bruce, Calder, and Cator, 202; Watson, 51.
64. Glasheen, 160.
65. James and Russell, 73.

66. Laird, 262.
67. Ponsonby, *Henry Ponsonby,* 118.
68. De-La-Noy, *Windsor,* 113; Stoney and Weltzien, 42; Ponsonby, *Recollections,* 46.
69. Nevill, 193.
70. Tschumi, 70.
71. Fletcher, 34.
72. One of Her Majesty's Servants, 180.
73. Bloomfield, 32.
74. One of Her Majesty's Servants, 181–185.
75. Menkes, 10.
76. Fischer and Fischer, 6.
77. One of Her Majesty's Servants, 118–119; Hill, 4; Fletcher, 33; De-La-Noy, *Windsor,* 138; Maxwell, 153; Plumb and Wheldon, 209; Laird, 261–262.
78. Laird, 260–261; Roberts, 118.
79. Tschumi, 56.
80. One of Her Majesty's Servants, 120.
81. Laird, 261.
82. Ibid., 262.
83. Tschumi, 49, 61.
84. Fletcher, 34.

CHAPTER 7: THE WAYWARD HEIR

1. Hibbert, *The Royal Victorians,* 111.
2. Cited, Farago and Sinclair, 14.
3. St. Aubyn, *Edward VII,* 17.
4. Auchincloss, 63.
5. Hibbert, *Queen Victoria,* 186.
6. Quoted in Hibbert, *Edward VII,* 16.
7. Magnus, 27.
8. Fulford, *Dearest Child,* 279.
9. St. Aubyn, *Edward VII,* 51.
10. James, *Prince Albert,* 268.
11. Magnus, 59.
12. Weintraub, 322.
13. Magnus, 67.
14. Hamilton, 45.
15. Aronson, *Family of Kings,* 36.
16. Pearson, 41.
17. Queen Victoria to Crown Princess Victoria of Prussia, August 4, 1869, in Fulford, *Your Dear Letter,* 246.
18. St. Aubyn, *Edward VII,* 159–160; Cowles, 90.
19. Aronson, *King in Love,* 339.
20. Carlton, 147.
21. Hibbert, *Royal Victorians,* 177–179; Hough, *Edward and Alexandra,* 176–177.
22. Duff, *Alexandra: Princess and Queen,* 179.
23. Battiscombe, 187; Hough, *Edward and Alexandra,* 179; Aronson, *Family of*

Kings, 94; Duff, *Alexandra: Princess and Queen,* 179–180; Magnus, 234.

24. Aronson, *King in Love,* 346.
25. Magnus, 268; Hibbert, *Royal Victorians,* 254.
26. Cust, 91.
27. Fischer and Fischer, *Bertie and Alix,* 79–80.
28. Cust, 32.
29. Prince Nicholas of Greece, 101.
30. Ponsonby, *Henry Ponsonby,* 109.
31. Weintraub, 518.
32. Battiscombe, 240.
33. Ibid., 163.
34. Pope-Hennessy, 190.
35. Cust, 33.
36. Aronson, *Prince Eddy and the Homosexual Underworld,* 199.
37. See Colin Simpson, Lewis Chester, and David Leitch, *Cleveland Street Affair,* for further details.
38. Weintraub, 527.
39. Ponsonby, *Henry Ponsonby,* 45.
40. Pope-Hennessy, 222.
41. Lutyens, 61.
42. Pope-Hennessy, 278.
43. Rose, 26.
44. Leslie, 255, 257.
45. Battiscombe, 175; Hibbert, *Royal Victorians,* 205.
46. Magnus, 245; Battiscombe, 200; Pope-Hennessy, 321.
47. Aronson, *Grandmama of Europe,* 102.
48. Pope-Hennessy, 57.
49. Warwick, 272.
50. Grand Duchess George of Russia, 166.
51. Gernsheim and Gernsheim, *Edward VII and Queen Alexandra,* 66.
52. Vorres, 53.
53. Leslie, 258–260.
54. Pope-Hennessy, 279.
55. Warwick, 273.
56. Aronson, *Grandmama of Europe,* 103; St. Aubyn, *Edward VII,* 116.
57. Aronson, *Grandmama of Europe,* 103; Pope-Hennessy, 318–319.
58. Prince Nicholas of Greece, 121.
59. Cited in Gelardi, 64.
60. Greve, 1–3; Duff, *Alexandra: Princess and Queen,* 198.
61. Letter to Prince Alexander of Teck, January 8, 1896, in RA GV FF 3/458, cited in Greve, 10.
62. Pope-Hennessy, 316.
63. *Times* of London, July 23, 1896.
64. Ibid.

65. Ibid.
66. Ibid.
67. Prince Nicholas of Greece, 122.
68. *Times* of London, July 23, 1896.
69. Ibid.
70. Ibid.
71. Ibid.
72. Ibid.
73. Ibid.
74. Prince Nicholas of Greece, 122.
75. *Times* of London, July 23, 1896.
76. Maxwell, 182.
77. *Times* of London, July 23, 1896.
78. Maxwell, 182; Nevill, 168.
79. Nevill, 168.
80. Maxwell, 182.
81. *Times* of London, July 23, 1896.
82. Duff, *Alexandra: Princess and Queen,* 198.

CHAPTER 8: AUTUMN AT BALMORAL

1. Gernsheim and Gernsheim, *Victoria R,* 287.
2. Ibid., 286.
3. Garrett, 97; Allen, 10–12.
4. Garrett, 97.
5. Maxwell, 198; Allen, 10.
6. Garrett, 95.
7. Allen, 4.
8. Nevill, 114.
9. Mallet, 195.
10. Tisdall, 145.
11. Queen Victoria, *Leaves from the Journal of Our Life in the Highlands, from 1848 to 1861,* 111.
12. Clark, 20; Millar, 39.
13. Duff, *Queen Victoria's Highland Journals,* 99–100.
14. Clark, 29; see Hall, 11–12.
15. Clark, 30.
16. Ibid., 37.
17. Clark, 49; McCann, 13.
18. Jaffé, 93.
19. Clark, 30.
20. Ibid., 51.
21. Bolitho, *Reign of Queen Victoria,* 140.
22. Marie Louise, 15.
23. Millar, 60.
24. Morton, 61.
25. Millar, 67; One of Her Majesty's Servants, 210.
26. Plumb and Wheldon, 272; Windsor and Bolitho, 64; Lutyens, 17; Morton, 62; Gernsheim and Gernsheim, *Victoria R,* 57; Lichten, 28.
27. Queen Marie of Romania, 1:68.

28. Windsor and Bolitho, 72.
29. Ponsonby, *Recollections,* 35.
30. Whittle, 80.
31. Millar, 64.
32. Clark, 51.
33. Millar, 67; Ponsonby, *Recollections,* 37.
34. Stoney and Weltzien, 128; Millar, 60; Brown, 67.
35. Clark, 59; Millar, 65; Morton, 64.
36. Morton, 64.
37. Clark, 50.
38. Morton, 66.
39. Lutyens, 19.
40. Queen Victoria, *Leaves from the Journal of Our Life in the Highlands, from 1848 to 1861,* 149.
41. Clark, 59–60.
42. Brown, 87; James, *Prince Albert,* 182; Clark, 29.
43. Brown, 80; Lutyens, 17; Hibbert, *Queen Victoria,* 179; Clark, 29.
44. Windsor, *King's Story,* 24.
45. Lutyens, 35.
46. Queen Victoria to Queen Augusta of Prussia, April 23, 1862, in Bolitho, *Letters of Queen Victoria,* 123.
47. Longford, *Darling Loosy,* 147.
48. Ponsonby, *Henry Ponsonby,* 117; Reid, 46.
49. Mallet, 37.
50. Ibid., 5, 33.
51. Clark, 30.
52. Whittle, 149.
53. Ponsonby, *Henry Ponsonby,* 124.
54. Cited in Millar, 66.
55. Quoted in St. Aubyn, *Queen Victoria,* 201.
56. Hibbert, *Queen Victoria,* 181.
57. McCann, 40.
58. Lutyens, 88.
59. Windsor and Bolitho, 231.
60. Mallet, 38.
61. Tschumi, 62; Lutyens, 38.
62. Ponsonby, *Recollections,* 45.
63. Ponsonby, *Henry Ponsonby,* 122.
64. Lutyens, 18; Clark, 106.
65. Brown, 175.
66. Lutyens, 26, 120.
67. Cited in Hibbert, *Queen Victoria,* 176.
68. Ponsonby, *Henry Ponsonby,* 118; Lutyens, 18.
69. Queen Victoria, *More Leaves from the Journal of A Life in the Highlands,* 155.
70. Queen Victoria to Crown Princess Victoria of Prussia, June 15, 1865, in Fulford, *Your Dear Letter,* 30.

CHAPTER 9: "THE RUSSIAN OCCUPATION"

1. Epton, 196.
2. Hough, *Advice,* 104.
3. Ibid., 100.
4. Ibid., 42.
5. Ibid., 106.
6. Ibid., 110.
7. Almedingen, 35.
8. Ponsonby, *Henry Ponsonby,* 306.
9. Tsesarevich Nicholas to Empress Marie Feodorovna, in Bing, 63.
10. Victoria, Marchioness of Milford Haven (Princess Victoria of Hesse), "Reminiscences," unpublished memoirs, 154, cited in King, 56.
11. Marie Louise, 50.
12. Cited in Duff, *Victoria Travels,* 320.
13. Hough, *Advice,* 124–127.
14. The Prince of Wales to Lieutenant Colonel Sir Arthur Bigge, Letter of August 29, 1896, quoted in Lee, *King Edward VII,* 1:695.
15. Bolitho, "*Victoria: The Widow and Her Son,* 322.
16. Lutyens, 71.
17. Poliakoff, 121.
18. Lutyens, 71.
19. Poliakoff, 121; Benson, *King Edward VII,* 179.
20. *Times* of London, September 21 and September 23, 1896.
21. *Times* of London, September 23, 1896.
22. Lutyens, 64, 75–76.
23. *Times* of London, September 23, 1896.
24. Lutyens, 73.
25. Nicholas II to Dowager Empress Marie Feodorovna, letter of September 25, 1896, in Bing, 109.
26. *Times* of London, September 23, 1896.
27. *Times* of London, October 5, 1896.
28. Quoted in Poliakoff, 123.
29. Lutyens, 74.
30. *Times* of London, September 23, 1896.
31. Lutyens, 75.
32. Nicholas II to Dowager Empress Marie Feodorovna, letter of September 25, 1896, in Bing, 109; *Times* of London, September 23, 1896.
33. Nicholas II to Dowager Empress Marie Feodorovna, letter of September 25, 1896, in Bing, 109.
34. Reid, 124.
35. *Times* of London, September 23, 1896.
36. *Times* of London, September 23, 1896; Millar, 141; Lutyens, 76.

37. Lee, *Queen Victoria,* 411; Poliakoff, 122; Millar, 141; Lutyens, 76.
38. Duff, *Queen Victoria's Highland Journals,* 222.
39. Lutyens, 87.
40. Nicholas II to Dowager Empress Marie Feodorovna, September 25, 1896, in Bing, 109.
41. Queen Victoria to Empress Friedrich of Germany, letter of September 26, 1896, in Ramm, 195.
42. Bolitho, *Reign of Queen Victoria,* 353.
43. Queen Victoria to Empress Friedrich of Germany, September 26, 1896, in Ramm, 195.
44. Mallet, 187.
45. Nicholas II to Dowager Empress Marie Feodorovna, September 25, 1896, in Bing, 109–110.
46. Bariatinsky, 58.
47. *Times* of London, September 23, 1896.
48. Buxhoeveden, 7–8.
49. *Times* of London, September 24, 1896.
50. Lee, *King Edward VII,* 1:697.
51. Benson, *Queen Victoria,* 365.
52. Lutyens, 79–82.
53. Nicholas II to Dowager Empress Marie Feodorovna, October 2, 1896, in Bing, 110.
54. Reid, 124–125.
55. Queen Victoria, journal entry of September 23, 1896, in RA, quoted in Hibbert, *Queen Victoria in Her Letters and Journals,* 333.
56. *Times* of London, September 21, 1896; Lutyens, 77.
57. Lutyens, 83.
58. Benson, *Queen Victoria's Daughters,* 280.
59. Cited in Wynn, 58.
60. Queen Victoria, journal entry of October 3, 1896, in RA, quoted in Hibbert, *Queen Victoria in Her Letters and Journals,* 334.
61. Queen Victoria, journal entry of November 23, 1896, in RA, quoted in Hibbert, *Queen Victoria in Her Letters and Journals,* 334.

Chapter 10: Christmas at Osborne

1. McCutchan, 29; Garrett, 66.
2. Warwick, 17.
3. James, *Prince Albert,* 140.
4. Matson, 30.
5. Hall, 13.
6. Whittle, 8–12; Magnus, 358; James, *Prince Albert,* 143; Matson, 30; York, *Victoria and Albert,* 26.
7. Queen Victoria to Lord Melbourne, letter of April 23, 1845, in Benson and Esher, 2:36.
8. Jaffé, 88.
9. Girouard, 148.
10. Matson, 31.
11. Hobhouse, 377.
12. Queen Victoria, letter of May 12, 1845, in Royal Archives, RA PP/Osborne, cited in Hobhouse, 379.
13. Hobhouse, 380; Girouard, 48–50, 148–149.
14. York, *Victoria and Albert,* 29–32.
15. James, *Prince Albert,* 140.
16. Hobhouse, 380–381.
17. York, *Victoria and Albert,* 40; Girouard, 13; James, *Prince Albert,* 142; Hobhouse, 380–381.
18. Glasheen, 160.
19. York, *Victoria and Albert,* 93.
20. Hobhouse, 387; York, *Victoria and Albert,* 48, 83.
21. York, *Victoria and Albert,* 82–83.
22. Longford, *Queen Victoria,* 211; Charlton, 7; Jaffé, 90–91; James, *Prince Albert,* 141.
23. Morton, 48; Charlton, 7; Stoney and Weltzien, 32; Hobhouse, 389.
24. Whittle, 167; One of Her Majesty's Servants, 158–159.
25. Matson, 36, 123; Mallet, 126.
26. Hobhouse, 388; Girouard, 152; Charlton, 6; Morton, 46.
27. Ponsonby, *Recollections,* 41.
28. Charlton, 5.
29. One of Her Majesty's Servants, 205; Plumb and Wheldon, 269; Charlton, 8; York, *Victoria and Albert,* 44; Hobhouse, 384.
30. Charlton, 8.
31. York, *Victoria and Albert,* 44.
32. James, *Prince Albert,* 141; Jaffé, 91; Charlton, 10, and supplement, "Principal Items on View," 4.
33. Ponsonby, *Recollections,* 35.
34. Ponsonby, *Mary Ponsonby,* 56.
35. Hobhouse, 387; York, *Victoria and Albert,* 47; Charlton, 11; Girouard, 150.
36. Girouard, 152; Morton, 44; Charlton, 12, and supplement, "Principal Items on View," 6.
37. York, *Victoria and Albert,* 121.
38. Girouard, 149; Charlton, 14–15.

39. Jaffé, 92; James, *Prince Albert,* 141; Stoney and Weltzien, 8–9; Charlton, 16, and supplement, "Principal Items on View," 8; York, *Victoria and Albert,* 40.
40. James, *Prince Albert,* 141; Charlton, 16.
41. James, *Prince Albert,* 142.
42. Queen Marie of Romania, 1:21.
43. Ibid.
44. Lutyens, 127; James, *Prince Albert,* 142; Jaffé, 93; Hibbert, *Queen Victoria,* 192; Charlton, 23.
45. Queen Marie of Romania, 1:35.
46. Plumb and Wheldon, 258; Jaffé, 93; Hibbert, *Queen Victoria,* 192; Charlton, 23–24.
47. Weintraub, 201.
48. Hobhouse, 390; Matson, 65; Ponsonby, *Recollections,* 39; York, *Victoria and Albert,* 54.
49. Weintraub, 506–507.
50. Charlton, 18.
51. Charlton, 20; Whittle, 181.
52. Hibbert, *Queen Victoria,* 163.
53. York, *Victoria and Albert,* 84.
54. Garrett, 61–63.
55. Ponsonby, *Henry Ponsonby,* 389.
56. Letter of Bishop William Boyd-Carpenter to Queen Victoria, December 13, 1896, in the British Library Collection, Add. MS, 46720, ff. 85.
57. Letter of Bishop William Boyd-Carpenter to Queen Victoria, December 29, 1896, in the British Library Collection, Add. MS, 46720, ff. 85.
58. York, *Victoria and Albert,* 176; Tschumi, 72.
59. Hibbert, *Queen Victoria,* 158.
60. Hibbert, *Queen Victoria,* 158; Weintraub, 150, 592.
61. Tschumi, 74.
62. York, *Victoria and Albert,* 176.
63. Hibbert, *Queen Victoria,* 158; Weintraub, 592.
64. Reid, 110; Stoney and Weltzien, 25; Mallet, 124–125.
65. Ponsonby, *Henry Ponsonby,* 389.
66. Mallet, 126.
67. Tschumi, 47; Harris, *Queen's Windsor,* 105; Jaffé, 87; Weintraub, 285, 592.
68. Tschumi, 65, 68, 212.
69. York, *Victoria and Albert,* 196; Tschumi, 73.
70. Tschumi, 65, 213.
71. Queen Victoria to Crown Princess Victoria of Prussia, July 14, 1858, in Fulford, *Dearest Child,* 359.

CHAPTER 11: EASTER IN FRANCE

1. Lutyens, 96.
2. Duff, *Victoria Travels,* 332.
3. Mallet, 47.
4. Duff, *Victoria Travels,* 14.
5. Ponsonby, *Recollections,* 85–86.
6. Lutyens, 95; Paoli, 338; Duff, *Victoria Travels,* 336.
7. Reid, 48; Weintraub, 557, 569; Hibbert, *Queen Victoria,* 428; Paoli, 337–340; Duff, *Victoria Travels,* 14; Tooley, 249.
8. Nelson, 20, 52.
9. Fulford, *Dearest Mama,* 35; Hough, *Advice,* 35; Nelson, 20; Reid, 48; Duff, *Victoria Travels,* 335.
10. Nelson, 107.
11. Ponsonby, *Recollections,* 86.
12. Ponsonby, *Side Lights on Queen Victoria,* 1; McCutchan, 24; Garrett, 65; Rousmaniere, 63.
13. Morton, 70; McCutchan, 29; Rousmaniere, 66–68.
14. Gavin, 133.
15. Gavin, 133; Morton, 72; Rousmaniere, 68.
16. Stoney and Weltzien, 89–90; McCutchan, 24.
17. Stoney and Weltzien, 90; Lutyens, 56; McCutchan, 24; Garrett, 65; Gavin, 133.
18. Ponsonby, *Recollections,* 52–53.
19. Weintraub, 205.
20. Bloomfield, 76.
21. Ponsonby, *Recollections,* 53.
22. Kingston, 129, 136; Duff, *Victoria Travels,* 333.
23. Duff, *Victoria Travels,* 333–334.
24. Paoli, 333.
25. Lutyens, 98.
26. Duff, *Victoria Travels,* 333–334.
27. Lutyens, 95; Duff, *Victoria Travels,* 334.
28. Garrett, 99.
29. Duff, *Victoria Travels,* 334.
30. Garrett, 99.
31. Ponsonby, *Recollections,* 87.
32. Lutyens, 94.
33. Lutyens, 94; Nelson, 119.
34. Lutyens, 98; Erbach-Schönberg, 282.
35. Nelson, 119; Duff, *Victoria Travels,* 332.
36. Ponsonby, *Recollections,* 87.
37. Lutyens, 101; Pope-Hennessy, 344.
38. Lutyens, 94; Nelson, 119; Pope-Hennessy, 344.
39. Nelson, 119–120.
40. York, *Travels with Queen Victoria,* 35; Pope-Hennessy, 344.
41. Ponsonby, *Recollections,* 87.

42. Paoli, 340, 348.
43. Ibid., 340.
44. Nelson, 120.
45. Ponsonby, *Recollections,* 85–87.
46. Nelson, 119.
47. Ibid., 1.
48. Ibid., 37.
49. Erbach-Schönberg, 284; Nelson, 119.
50. Lutyens, 101.
51. Erbach-Schönberg, 283.
52. Queen Victoria to Princess Victoria of Hesse, March 21, 1882, in Hough, *Advice,* 36.
53. Paoli, 342.
54. York, *Travels with Queen Victoria,* 192.
55. Duff, *Victoria Travels,* 338–339.
56. Cited in Hibbert, *Queen Victoria,* 435.
57. Lutyens, 99.
58. Weintraub, 557.
59. Lutyens, 102; Ponsonby, *Recollections,* 64.
60. Queen Victoria, journal entry of April 22, 1897, in Hibbert, *Queen Victoria in Her Letters and Journals,* 334.
61. Ponsonby, *Recollections,* 65–66.
62. Lutyens, 104.
63. Reid, 128.
64. Reid, 129; Lutyens, 38; Hibbert, *Queen Victoria,* 446.
65. Ponsonby, *Henry Ponsonby,* 130.
66. Reid, 130; Hibbert, *Queen Victoria,* 446; Weintraub, 508–509; Lutyens, 41.
67. Queen Marie of Romania, 1:230.
68. Ponsonby, *Henry Ponsonby,* 131.
69. Pope-Hennessy, 345–346.
70. Lutyens, 42.
71. Reid, 132.
72. Ibid., 142.
73. Ibid., 143.
74. Nelson, 107.
75. Reid, 143.
76. Ponsonby, *Recollections,* 33–34.
77. Ponsonby, *Henry Ponsonby,* 131–132.
78. Reid, 144–145.
79. Ibid., 145–146.
80. Lutyens, 101, 108.
81. Queen Victoria, journal entry of January 2 1901, in Royal Archives, quoted in Duff, *Victoria Travels,* 363.

Chapter 12: Summer at Buckingham Palace

1. Queen Victoria, journal entry of January 27, 1838, in Royal Archives, cited in Lasdun, 63.
2. Robinson, 12, 18; Clifford Smith, 12–15, 19–29; Sykes, 62–69; Harris, de Bellaigue, and Millar, 21–22; Wright, 117–122, 128–129, 134–135; Mackenzie, 11.
3. Montgomery-Massingberd, 108.
4. Clifford Smith, 1; Wright, 142–143.
5. Wright, 157.
6. Robinson, 55.
7. Harris, de Bellaigue, and Millar, 31; Robinson, 80; Clifford Smith, 40, 46.
8. Clifford Smith, 40; Harris, de Bellaigue, and Millar, 31.
9. Robinson, 80; Clifford Smith, 40; Mackenzie, 15; Wright, 157.
10. Harris, de Bellaigue, and Millar, 15; Clifford Smith, 36, 47, 50.
11. Robinson, 78.
12. Clifford Smith, 52; Harris, de Bellaigue, and Millar, 36.
13. Benson and Esher, 2:38.
14. Mackenzie, 18.
15. Watson, 44, 98.
16. *The Builder*, London, August 28, 1847, 405.
17. Ibid.
18. Mackenzie, 70.
19. Packard, *Queen and Her Court,* 57; Weintraub, 151; James, *Prince Albert,* 115–116.
20. Roper, 10, 23.
21. Queen Marie of Romania, 1:49.
22. Wright, 175.
23. Clifford Smith, 62.
24. Cust, 28.
25. Morelli, 112; Clifford Smith, 129–130; Harris, de Bellaigue, and Millar, 42; Robinson, 86, 106.
26. Clifford Smith, 195, 200.
27. Ibid., 54.
28. Mallet, 30; Clifford Smith, 197; Mackenzie, 22.
29. Peacocke, 30; Robinson, 80; Clifford Smith, 198–199, 201; Harris, de Bellaigue, and Millar, 81.
30. Packard, *Queen and Her Court,* 52; Clifford Smith, 203.
31. Bolitho, *Reign of Queen Victoria,* 81, 348.
32. Clifford Smith, 51, 193.
33. Ibid., 125, 208–213.
34. Ibid., 215.
35. Ponsonby, *Henry Ponsonby,* 65.
36. Clifford Smith, 131–135.
37. Clifford Smith, 136; Peacocke, 20.
38. Robinson, 68, 73; Harris, de Bellaigue, and Millar, 46.
39. Cornforth, 1370.

40. Mackenzie, 73; Clifford Smith, 138–139; Harris, de Bellaigue, and Millar, 48.
41. Morelli, 115.
42. Clifford Smith, 142–147; Harris, de Bellaigue, and Millar, 53–54; Robinson, 68.
43. Morton, 32; Robinson, 34, 56, 101; Clifford Smith, 185; Harris, de Bellaigue, and Millar, 79.
44. Harris, de Bellaigue, and Millar, 240.
45. Cust, 29.
46. Clifford Smith, 151; Harris, de Bellaigue, and Millar, 57.
47. Robinson, 87–88.
48. Mackenzie, 17, 72.
49. Robinson, 5, 83, 87–88; Clifford Smith, 153–156; Harris, de Bellaigue, and Millar, 59.
50. Robinson, 107.
51. Mackenzie, 73.
52. Clifford Smith, 9, 158–161; Harris, de Bellaigue, and Millar, 61; Robinson, 73, 87–88; Rowse, 22.
53. Clifford Smith, 9, 162–165; Harris, de Bellaigue, and Millar, 64; Robinson, 80, 87–88.
54. Harris, de Bellaigue, and Millar, 68.
55. Clifford Smith, 167–170; Robinson, 80; Peacocke, 10.
56. Harris, de Bellaigue, and Millar, 71; Clifford Smith, 56.
57. Clifford Smith, 173.
58. Harris, de Bellaigue, and Millar, 72; Clifford Smith, 175–176; Robinson, 110–112; *The Builder*, London, May 31, 1856, 297–298.
59. Goring, 141.
60. Clifford Smith, 177–178; *The Builder*, London, May 31, 1856, 298.
61. Plumb, 124, 129; Clifford Smith, 116–118; Harris, de Bellaigue, and Millar, 87; Morton, 30.
62. Peacocke, 23.
63. Cited in Wright, 51.
64. Lasdun, 62–63.
65. Watson, 42–44.
66. Gernsheim and Gernsheim, *Victoria R,* 270.
67. Mackenzie, 18.
68. Robinson, 104; Morton, 28.
69. Packard, *Queen and Her Court,* 58.
70. Weintraub, 507.
71. Victoria, Marchioness of Milford Haven (Princess Victoria of Hesse), "Reminiscences," unpublished manuscript, 39, cited in King, 22.
72. Cust, 28.

CHAPTER 13: A DAY AT BUCKINGHAM PALACE

1. Fletcher, 52.
2. *Times* of London, May 11 1897.
3. Fletcher, 31; Turner, 320.
4. Fletcher, 52.
5. Marie Louise, 37.
6. Cannadine, 346; Fletcher, 31.
7. Waddington, 196.
8. *Times* of London, May 12, 1897.
9. *Times* of London, May 12, 1897; Marie Louise, 38.
10. Waddington, 194.
11. *Times* of London, May 11, 1897; Fletcher, 32.
12. *Times* of London, May 12, 1897; Fletcher, 32.
13. *Times* of London, May 12, 1897.
14. Brown, *Ritual of Royalty,* 46–49; Bruce, Calder, and Cator, 104; Fletcher, 37–38.
15. Brown, *Ritual of Royalty,* 51; Clifford Smith, 7; Fletcher, 34; *Times* of London, May 12, 1897.
16. *Times* of London, May 12, 1897.
17. Clifford Smith, 6; Turner, 324; Fletcher, 38; Brown, *Ritual of Royalty,* 156.
18. Watson, 190–191; Fletcher, 32.
19. Watson, 190–191; Fletcher, 32; *Times* of London, May 12, 1897.
20. Watson, 190–191.
21. *Times* of London, May 12, 1897.
22. Fletcher, 32; Turner, 321.
23. Turner, 321–323; Marie Louise, 37; Waddington, 195; Fletcher, 32.
24. Waddington, 196.
25. Fletcher, 33.
26. *Times* of London, May 7, 1874.
27. Fletcher, 31–32.
28. Turner, 320–323; Fletcher, 31.
29. Ibid.
30. Laird, 316.
31. Tooley, 146; Turner, 322.
32. Hamilton, 40.
33. Waddington, 176–177.
34. Laird, 177.
35. Cannadine, 300–301; Fletcher, 117.
36. Bruce, Calder, and Cator, 204.
37. Cornwallis-West, 180.
38. James, *Prince Albert,* 225–226.
39. Fletcher, 118; Lutyens, 158; Cannadine, 300–301.
40. Fletcher, 34.
41. Nevill, 106.
42. *Times* of London, May 17, 1897.
43. Erbach-Schönberg, 279.

44. De-La-Noy, *Windsor,* 10.
45. Bruce, Calder, and Cator, 53.
46. De-La-Noy, *Windsor,* 153.
47. Bruce, Calder, and Cator, 53; Brown, *Ritual of Royalty,* 106; Stoney and Weltzien, 48.
48. Ibid.
49. Tschumi, 51–56.

CHAPTER 14: A NIGHT AT DEVONSHIRE HOUSE

1. Tuchman, 16.
2. Cornwallis-West, 51.
3. Perrott, 24.
4. Leslie, 16.
5. Warwick, 44.
6. Leslie, 11.
7. Warwick, 41.
8. Magnus, 303.
9. Warwick, 43.
10. Cornwallis-West, 60.
11. Ibid., 51.
12. Perrott, 242–243; Tuchman, 17.
13. Leslie, 3.
14. Cornwallis-West, 53–54.
15. Ibid., 56.
16. Balsan, 76.
17. Warwick, 50.
18. Ibid., 53.
19. Ibid.
20. Hamilton, 100.
21. Marie Louise, 132.
22. Waddington, 199.
23. Tuchman, 38.
24. Devonshire, 34; Tuchman, 38.
25. Ponsonby, *Henry Ponsonby,* 265.
26. Tuchman, 39.
27. Devonshire, 37.
28. Leslie, 53.
29. Cornwallis-West, 210.
30. Tuchman, 42.
31. Ponsonby, *Recollections,* 300.
32. Lindsay, 142.
33. Quoted in Magnus, 110.
34. Warwick, 82–83.
35. Hamilton, 201.
36. Balsan, 107.
37. Widow of an American Diplomat, 227.
38. Balsan, 107.
39. Devonshire, 38; Leslie, 48; Balsan, 107.
40. Sykes, 98, 102, 270–272.
41. *Times* of London, July 3, 1897.
42. Cornwallis-West, 386.
43. *Times* of London, July 3, 1897.
44. Sykes, 311; *Times* of London, July 3, 1897.

45. Sykes, 311; *Times* of London, July 3, 1897.
46. Sykes, 311.
47. Cornwallis-West, 387.
48. *Times* of London, July 3, 1897.
49. Sykes, 311.
50. *Times* of London, July 3, 1897; *Echo,* London, July 3, 1897.
51. *Daily News,* London, July 3, 1897; *Times* of London, July 3, 1897.
52. Cornwallis-West, 388.
53. Cited in Sykes, 312.
54. *Times* of London, July 3, 1897.
55. Bentley-Cranch, 107; Williams, *It Was Such Fun,* 77.
56. *Queen,* London, July 10, 1897.
57. *Times* of London, July 3, 1897.
58. Ibid.
59. Cornwallis-West, 388; *Times* of London, July 3, 1897.
60. *Times* of London, July 3, 1897.
61. Sykes, 312.
62. *Times* of London, July 3, 1897; Sykes, 312.
63. *Times* of London, July 3, 1897.
64. Cornwallis-West, 388–389.
65. Sykes, 314.
66. *Times* of London, July 3, 1897.
67. Sykes, 312–313.
68. Balsan, 96.
69. *Times* of London, July 3, 1897.

CHAPTER 15: TRIUMPH

1. Queen Victoria, journal entry of September 23, 1896, Royal Archives, quoted in Hibbert, *Queen Victoria in Her Letters and Journals,* 333.
2. Maxwell, 197; Lant, 225.
3. Lant, 225.
4. Queen Victoria, journal entry of June 20, 1897, Royal Archives, in Buckle, *Letters of Queen Victoria . . . 1886 and 1901,* 3:172.
5. Chapman and Raben, 61; Maxwell, 199.
6. Garrett, 99.
7. Bolitho, *Reign of Queen Victoria,* 364.
8. Maxwell, 200; Sitwell, 299.
9. Queen Victoria, journal entry of June 21, 1897, Royal Archives, in Buckle, *Letters of Queen Victoria . . . 1886 and 1901,* 3:173–174.
10. Ibid., 3:174.
11. Benson, *Queen Victoria,* 367.
12. Nevill, 172.
13. Bolitho, *Reign of Queen Victoria,* 365.
14. Queen Victoria, journal entry of June 21,

1897, Royal Archives, in Buckle, *Letters of Queen Victoria . . . 1886 and 1901,* 3:174.

15. Arnstein, 597.
16. Weintraub, 581.
17. Ibid., 582.
18. Maxwell, 208; Lant, 243.
19. Lutyens, 110.
20. Maxwell, 204–205; Tuchman, 54.
21. Chapman and Raben, 52; *Daily Mail,* London, June 23, 1897; Richards, 116; Tuchman, 54–55.
22. *Daily Mail,* London, June 23, 1897.
23. Maxwell, 206.
24. Ibid., 203.
25. Chapman and Raben, 52; Maxwell, 202–205.
26. Lant, 244.
27. Maxwell, 206; Lant, 244.
28. Lant, 244.
29. Quoted in St. Aubyn, *Queen Victoria,* 547.
30. Garrett, 40.
31. Arnstein, 597.
32. Gardiner, 144; Weintraub, 582; Hibbert, *Queen Victoria,* 457–458.
33. Bolitho, *Reign of Queen Victoria,* 365.
34. Quoted in St. Aubyn, *Queen Victoria,* 547.
35. Queen Victoria, journal entry of June 22, 1897, Royal Archives, in Buckle, *Letters of Queen Victoria . . . 1886 and 1901,* 3:175–176.
36. *Times* of London, June 23, 1897.
37. Weintraub, 582; Queen Victoria, journal entry of June 22, 1897, Royal Archives, in Buckle, *Letters of Queen Victoria . . . 1886 and 1901,* 3:176.
38. *Daily Mail,* London, June 23, 1897.
39. Chapman and Raben, 52.
40. Chapman and Raben, 52; Lant, 223.
41. Maxwell, 209.
42. Holmes, 2:410.
43. Gardiner, 9; Chapman and Raben, 54.
44. Weintraub, 583.
45. Queen Victoria, journal entry of June 22, 1897, Royal Archives, in Buckle, *Letters of Queen Victoria . . . 1886 and 1901,* 3:176.
46. *Times* of London, June 23, 1897.
47. Queen Victoria, journal entry of June 22, 1897, Royal Archives, in Buckle, *Letters of Queen Victoria . . . 1886 and 1901,* 3:176.
48. Hibbert, *Queen Victoria,* 458–459.

49. T. A. Cook quoted in *Royalty Digest* 3 (April 1994) No. 34, No. 10, 305.
50. Menkes, 180.
51. Chapman and Raben, 99; Tschumi, 42.
52. Chapman and Raben, 52; Maxwell, 217–218.
53. Queen Victoria, journal entry of June 22, 1897, Royal Archives, in Buckle, *Letters of Queen Victoria . . . 1886 and 1901,* 3:176.
54. Ponsonby, *Recollections,* 59.
55. Queen Victoria, journal entry of June 23, 1897, Royal Archives, in Buckle, *Letters of Queen Victoria . . . 1886 and 1901,* 3:176–177.
56. Maxwell, 223.
57. Lant, 239–240.
58. Ponsonby, *Recollections,* 59.
59. Weintraub, 584; Queen Victoria, journal entry of June 23, 1897, Royal Archives, in Buckle, *Letters of Queen Victoria . . . 1886 and 1901,* 3:179.
60. Maxwell, 224; Chapman and Raben, 52.
61. Queen Victoria, journal entry of June 23, 1897, Royal Archives, in Buckle, *Letters of Queen Victoria . . . 1886 and 1901,* 3:183–184.
62. Weintraub, 584.
63. Maxwell, 226.
64. Ibid., 233.
65. Ibid., 234.
66. Ponsonby, *Recollections,* 62–63.
67. Lutyens, 111.
68. Weintraub, 586; Lant, 240.
69. Lutyens, 112.
70. Weintraub, 587; Lutyens, 113.
71. Ibid.
72. Lutyens, 114; Weintraub, 588.
73. Marie Louise, 116.
74. *Times* of London, July 16, 1897.
75. Weintraub, 589.

EPILOGUE: THE TWILIGHT OF SPLENDOR

1. Reid, 273.
2. Lutyens, 151.
3. Mallet, 219.
4. Weintraub, 633.
5. Bolitho, *Reign of Queen Victoria,* 372.
6. Lutyens, 151; Rennell, 56; Weintraub, 631.
7. Reid, 201, 274.
8. Weintraub, 633.
9. Reid, 274.
10. Reid, 203; Weintraub, 634.

11. *Times* of London, January 19, 1901.
12. Reid, 205.
13. Ibid., 207.
14. Lee, *Edward VII,* 1:801.
15. Ponsonby, *Recollections,* 128.
16. Reid, 209–210.
17. *Times* of London, January 23, 1901.
18. Reid, 209–210.
19. Reid, 211.
20. *Times* of London, January 23, 1901.
21. Reid, 212.
22. *Times* of London, January 23, 1901.
23. Ponsonby, *Recollections,* 129.
24. Rennell, 152.
25. *Times* of London, January 23, 1901.
26. Cited in Martin, *Jennie,* 2:270.
27. Rennell, 145.
28. Longford, *Queen Victoria,* 563.
29. Rennell, 145.
30. Weintraub, 590.
31. Rennell, 145–146.
32. Reid, 215.
33. Reid, 216–217; Lamont-Brown, 191.
34. Cust, 178.
35. Ponsonby, *Recollections,* 131.
36. Coulter and Cooper, 212–213.
37. Bruce, Calder, and Cator, 202; Holmes, 2:458.
38. Lutyens, 152.
39. Coulter and Cooper, 212–213.
40. Lee, *Edward VII,* 2:8.

41. Holmes, 2:458; Lutyens, 203; Reid, 219.
42. Garrett, 52.
43. Baring, 216.
44. Williams, *It Was Such Fun,* 78.
45. St. Aubyn, *Edward VII,* 308.
46. Cited in Martin, *Jennie,* 2:270.
47. Reid, 218; Coulter and Cooper, 232.
48. Ponsonby, *Recollections,* 137.
49. Longford, *Queen Victoria,* 564; Ponsonby, *Recollections,* 132; Hatch, 70–72.
50. Bolitho, *Reign of Queen Victoria,* 381.
51. Holmes, 2:462; Rennell, 239.
52. Balsan, 160.
53. Holmes, 2:462.
54. Lant, 255; Holmes, 2:462.
55. Bruce, Calder, and Cator, 162.
56. Holmes, 2:462.
57. Ponsonby, *Recollections,* 142.
58. Marie Louise, 92.
59. Hatch, 70–72; *King Edward VII,* 129; *Daily Graphic,* London, February 5, 1901.
60. Marie Louise, 92.
61. Bolitho, *Reign of Queen Victoria,* 382.
62. *King Edward VII,* 130.

APPENDIX: THE ROYAL HOUSEHOLD

1. Information derived from Lindsay, 20–36, and from the court circular in *Times* of London, 1896–1897.

BIBLIOGRAPHY

BOOKS

Aga Khan. *Memoirs of Aga Khan*. London: Cassell, 1954.

Allen, Cecil. *Royal Trains*. London: Ian Allen, 1953.

Almedingen, E. M. *An Unbroken Unity*. London: Hutchinson, 1960.

Ames, Winslow. *Prince Albert and Victorian Taste*. London: Chapman & Hall, 1968.

Arch, Nigel, and Joanna Marschner. *The Royal Wedding Dresses*. London: Sidgwick & Jackson, 1990.

Aronson, Theo. *A Family of Kings: The Crowned Descendants of Christian IX of Denmark*. London: Cassell, 1976.

———. *Grandmama of Europe: The Crowned Descendants of Queen Victoria*. London: John Murray, 1973.

———. *Heart of a Queen: Queen Victoria's Romantic Attachments*. London: John Murray, 1991.

———. *The King in Love*. New York: Harper & Row, 1988.

———. *Prince Eddy and the Homosexual Underworld*. London: John Murray, 1994.

Auchinloss, Louis. *Persons of Consequence: Queen Victoria and Her Circle*. New York: Random House, 1979.

Bagehot, Walter. *The English Constitution*. Cambridge, U.K.: Cambridge University Press, 2001.

Baldry, A. L. *Royal Palaces*. London: Studio, 1935.

Balsan, Consuelo Vanderbilt. *The Glitter and the Gold*. London: William Heinemann, 1953.

Bariatinsky, Princess Anatole. *My Russian Life*. London: Hutchinson, 1923.

Baring, Maurice. *The Puppet Show of Memory*. London: Cassell, 1932.

Battiscombe, Georgina. *Queen Alexandra*. Boston: Houghton Mifflin, 1969.

Bell, G. K. A. *Randall Davidson, Archbishop of Canterbury*. Oxford, U.K.: Oxford University Press, 1952.

Bennett, Daphne. *King without a Crown: Albert, Prince Consort of England, 1819–1861*. New York: J. B. Lippincott, 1977.

Benson, A. C., and Viscount Esher, eds. *The Letters of Queen Victoria: A Selection from Her Majesty's Correspondence between the Years 1837 and 1861*. 3 vols. London: John Murray, 1911.

Benson, E. F. *As We Were*. London: Longmans, 1930.

———. *King Edward VII*. London: Longmans, Green, 1933.

———. *Queen Victoria*. London: Longmans, Green, 1935.

———. *Queen Victoria's Daughters*. London: Appleton, 1938.

Bentley-Cranch, Dana. *Edward VII: Image of an Era*. London: HMSO, 1992.

Bing, Edward J., ed. *The Letters of Tsar Nicholas and Empress Marie: Being the Confidential Correspondence between Nicholas II, Last of the Tsars, and His Mother, Dowager Empress Maria Feodorovna*. London: Ivor Nicholson & Watson, 1937.

Blake, Robert. *Disraeli*. London: Eyre & Spottiswoode, 1966.

Bloomfield, Baroness Georgina. *Reminiscences of Court and Diplomatic Life*. 2 vols. London: Kegan Paul, Trench, 1883.

Bolitho, Hector. *Albert the Good and the Victorian Reign*. New York: D. Appleton, 1932.

———. *Letters of Queen Victoria from the Archives of the House of Brandenburg-Prussia*. New Haven, Conn.: Yale University Press, 1938.

———. *Victoria: The Widow and Her Son*. London: Cobden-Sanderson, 1934.

———. *The Reign of Queen Victoria*. Toronto: Collins Sons, 1948.

Brooks, Chris. *The Albert Memorial: The Prince Consort National Memorial*. New Haven, Conn.: Yale University Press, 2000.

Brown, Ivor. *Balmoral*. London: Collins, 1955.

Brown, Michelle. *Ritual of Royalty: The Ceremony and Pageantry of Britain's Monarchy*. Englewood Cliffs, N.J.: Prentice-Hall, 1983.

Bruce, Alastair, Julian Calder, and Mark Cator. *Keepers of the Kingdom*. London: Cassell, 2002.

Buchanan, Meriel. *Victorian Gallery*. London: Cassell, 1956.

Buckle, G. E., ed. *The Letters of Queen Victoria: A Selection from Her Majesty's Correspondence and Journal between the Years 1862 and 1885*. 3 vols. London: John Murray, 1928.

———. *The Letters of Queen Victoria. A Selection from Her Majesty's Correspondence and Journal between the Years 1886 and 1901*. 3 vols. London: John Murray, 1932.

Buxhoeveden, Baroness Sophie. *The Life and Tragedy of Alexandra Feodorovna, Empress of Russia*. London: Longmans, Green, 1929.

Campbell, Judith. *Royalty on Horseback*. Garden City, N.Y.: Doubleday, 1974.

Cannadine, David. *The Decline and Fall of the British Aristocracy*. New Haven, Conn.: Yale University Press, 1990.

Carlton, Charles. *Royal Mistresses*. London: Routledge, 1990.

Channon, Sir Henry. *Chips: The Diaries of Sir Henry Channon*. London: Weidenfeld & Nicolson, 1967.

Chapman, Caroline, and Paul Raben. *Debrett's Queen Victoria's Jubilees*. London: Debrett's Peerage, 1977.

Charlton, John. *Osborne House*. London: English Heritage, 1985.

Clark, Ronald W. *Balmoral: Queen Victoria's Highland Home*. New York: Thames & Hudson, 1981.

Clifford Smith, H. *Buckingham Palace: Its Furniture, Decoration, and History*. With introductory chapters on the building and site by Christopher Hussey. London: Country Life, 1931.

Collier, Richard. *The Rainbow People*. London: Weidenfeld & Nicolson, 1984.

Colville, Lady Cynthia. *Crowded Life*. London: Evans Brothers, 1963.

Cornwallis-West, Mrs. George. *The Reminiscences of Lady Randolph Churchill*. New York: Century, 1908.

Coulter, John, and John Cooper. *Queen Victoria: Her Grand Life and Glorious Reign*. Chicago: American Literary and Musical Association, 1901.

Cowles, Virginia. *Edward VII and His Circle*. London: Hamish Hamilton, 1956.

Cust, Sir Lionel. *King Edward VII and His Court*. New York: E. P. Dutton, 1930.

De-La-Noy, Michael. *Queen Victoria at Home*. New York: Carroll & Graf, 2003.

———. *Windsor Castle: Past and Present*. London: Headline, 1990.

Devonshire, Deborah, Duchess of. *The House: A Portrait of Chatsworth*. London: Macmillan, 1982.

Duff, David. *Alexandra: Princess and Queen*. London: Collins, 1980.

———. *Hessian Tapestry*. London: Frederick Muller, 1967.

———. *Queen Victoria's Highland Journals*. Exeter, U.K.: Webb & Bower, 1980.

———. *Victoria Travels*. London: Frederick Muller, 1970.

Edwards, Anne. *Matriarch: Queen Mary and the House of Windsor*. New York: William Morrow, 1984.

Eilers, Marlene. *Queen Victoria's Descendants*. Falköping, Sweden: Rosvall Royal Books, 1997.

Elsberry, Terrence. *Marie of Romania: The Intimate Life of a Twentieth-Century Queen*. New York: St. Martin's Press, 1972.

Emden, Paul. *Behind the Throne*. London: Hodder & Stoughton, 1934.

Eminent Literary Gentleman, comp. *King Edward VII*. London: R. E. King, 1910.

Epton, Nina. *Victoria and Her Daughters*. London: Weidenfeld & Nicolson, 1971.

Erbach-Schönberg, Princess Marie zu. *Reminiscences*. London: George Allen & Unwin, 1925.

Esher, Viscount, ed. *The Girlhood of Queen Victoria: A Selection from Her Majesty's Diaries between the Years 1832 and 1840*. 2 vols. London: John Murray, 1912.

Farago, Ladislas, and Andrew Sinclair. *Royal Web*. New York: McGraw-Hill, 1982.

Fisher, Graham, and Heather Fisher. *Bertie and Alix: Anatomy of a Royal Marriage*. London: Robert Hale, 1974.

———. *Monarchy and the Royal Family*. London: Robert Hale, 1979.

Fletcher, Ifan Kyrle. *The British Court: Its Traditions and Ceremonial*. New York: David McKay, 1953.

Frankland, Noble. *Witness of a Century: The Life and Times of Prince Arthur, Duke of Connaught*. London: Shepheard-Walwyn, 1993.

Fulford, Roger. *Beloved Mama: Private Correspondence of Queen Victoria and the German Crown Princess, 1878–85*. London: Evans Brothers, 1981.

———. *Darling Child: Private Correspondence of Queen Victoria and the Crown Princess of Prussia, 1871–78*. London: Evans Brothers, 1976.

———. *Dearest Child: Letters between Queen Victoria and the Princess Royal, 1858–61*. London: Evans Brothers, 1964.

———. *Dearest Mama: Private Correspondence of Queen Victoria and the Crown Princess of Prussia, 1861–64*. London: Evans Brothers, 1968.

———. *The Prince Consort*. London: Macmillan, 1966.

———. *Your Dear Letter: Private Correspondence of Queen Victoria and the Crown Princess of Prussia, 1865–71*. London: Evans Brothers, 1971.

Gardiner, Juliet. *Queen Victoria*. London: Collins & Brown, 1997.

Garrett, Richard. *Royal Travel*. New York: Sterling Publishing, 1982.

Gavin, Charles Murray. *Royal Yachts*. London: Rich & Cowan, 1932.

Gelardi, Julia. *Born to Rule*. New York: St. Martin's Press 2005.

Gernsheim, Helmut and Alison Gernsheim. *Edward VII and Queen Alexandra*. London: Frederick Muller, 1962.

———. *Victoria R.* New York: G. P. Putnam's Sons, 1959.

Girouard, Mark. *The Victorian Country House*. Rev. ed. New Haven, Conn.: Yale University Press, 1990.

Glasheen, Joan. *The Secret People of the Palaces: The Royal Household from the Plantaganets to Queen Victoria*. London: Batsford, 1998.

Gore, John, ed. *A Selection of Letters and Papers of Thomas Creevey*. London: John Murray, 1949.

Goring, O. G. *From Goring House to Buckingham Palace*. London: Ivor Nicholson & Watson, 1937.

Greece, Prince Nicholas of. *My Fifty Years: The Memoirs of Prince Nicholas of Greece*. Annotated and edited by Arturo Beéche. Oakland, Calif.: Eurohistory.com, 2006.

Greve, Tim. *Haakon VII of Norway*. New York: Hippocrene Books, 1983.

Greville, Charles. *The Diaries of Charles Greville*. London: Vintage, 2005.

Hall, Phillip. *Royal Fortune: Tax, Money, and the Monarchy*. London: Bloomsbury, 1992.

Hamilton, Lord Frederic. *The Days Before Yesterday*. New York: George H. Doran, 1920.

Harris, John, Geoffrey de Bellaigue, and Oliver Millar. *Buckingham Palace and Its Treasures*. New York: Viking, 1968.

Harris, Marion. *The Queen's Windsor*. Bourne End, U.K.: Kensal Press, 1985.

Hatch, Alden. *The Mountbattens*. New York: Random House, 1965.

Hibbert, Christopher. *The Court of St. James's*. London: Weidenfeld & Nicolson, 1979.

———. *The Court at Windsor*. London: Longmans, 1964.

———. *Edward VII: A Portrait*. London: Allen Lane, 1976.

———. *Queen Victoria: A Personal History*. London: HarperCollins, 2000.

———. *Queen Victoria in Her Letters and Journals*. London: John Murray, 1984.

———. *The Royal Victorians*. Philadelphia: J. B. Lippincott, 1976.

Hill, B. J. W. *The History and Treasures of Windsor Castle*. London: Pitkin, 1970.

Hobhouse, Hermione. *Thomas Cubitt, Master Builder*. London: Macmillan, 1971.

Holmes, Sir Richard. *Edward VII: His Life and Times*. 2 vols. London: Carmelite House, 1910.

Homans, Margaret. *Royal Representations: Queen Victoria and British Culture, 1837–1876*. Chicago: University of Chicago Press, 1998.

Hough, Richard. *Louis and Victoria: The First Mountbattens*. London: Hutchinson, 1974.

———, ed. *Advice to My Granddaughter: Letters from Queen Victoria to Princess Victoria of Hesse*. New York: Simon & Schuster, 1975.

———. *Edward and Alexandra*. New York: St. Martin's Press, 1992.

———. *Victoria and Albert*. London: Richard Cohen, 1996.

Howard, Philip. *The British Monarchy in the Twentieth Century*. London: Hamish Hamilton, 1977.

Jagow, Kurt, ed. *Letters of the Prince Consort*. New York: E. P. Dutton, 1938.

Jaffé, Deborah. *Victoria: A Celebration of Queen and Empire*. London: Carlton Books, 2000.

James, Paul, and Peter Russell. *At Her Majesty's Service*. London: William Collins, 1986.

James, Robert Rhodes. *Prince Albert: A Biography*. New York: Alfred A. Knopf, 1984.

King, Greg. *The Last Empress: The Life and Times of Alexandra Feodorovna, Tsarina of Russia*. New York: Carol, 1994.

Kingston, Patrick. *Royal Trains*. London: Spring Books, 1989.

Kohut, Thomas. *Wilhelm II and the Germans: A Study in Leadership*. Oxford, U.K.: Oxford University Press, 1991.

Kuhn, William M. *Henry and Mary Ponsonby: Life at the Court of Queen Victoria*. London: Duckworth, 2002.

Laird, Dorothy. *How the Queen Reigns*. London: Hodder & Stoughton, 1959.

Lamont-Brown, Raymond. *Royal Poxes and Potions: The Lives of Court Physicians, Surgeons, and Apothecaries*. Stroud, U.K.: Sutton, 2001.

Lant, Jeffrey L. *Insubstantial Pageant: Ceremony and Confusion at Queen Victoria's Court*. New York: Taplinger, 1980.

Lasdun, Susan. *Victorians at Home*. New York: Viking Press, 1981.

Laver, James. *Manners and Morals in the Age of Optimism, 1848–1914.* New York: Harper & Row, 1966.

Lee, Sir Sidney. *Edward VII.* 2 vols. London: Macmillan, 1925.

———. *Queen Victoria.* London: Smith, Elder, 1904.

Leslie, Anita. *The Marlborough House Set.* Garden City, N.Y.: Doubleday, 1973.

Lichten, Frances. *Decorative Art of Victoria's Era.* New York: Charles Scribner's Sons, 1950.

Lindsay, W. A. *The Royal Household.* London: Kegan Paul, 1898.

Longford, Elizabeth, ed. *Darling Loosy: Letters to Princess Louise, 1856–1939.* London: Weidenfeld & Nicolson, 1991.

———. *Louisa: Lady in Waiting.* London: Jonathan Cape, 1979.

———. *Queen Victoria: Born to Succeed.* New York: Harper & Row, 1964.

Low, Craig, and Lucy Minto. *Royal Life.* London: Handbook, 1997.

Lutyens, Mary, ed. *Lady Lytton's Court Diary.* London: Rupert Hart-Davis, 1961.

Mackenzie, Compton. *The Queen's House: A History of Buckingham Palace.* London: Hutchinson, 1952.

Mackworth-Young, Robin. *The History and Treasures of Windsor Castle.* London: Pitkin Pictorials, 1988.

Magnus, Philip. *King Edward the Seventh.* London: John Murray, 1964.

Mallet, Victor, ed. *Life with Queen Victoria: Marie Mallet's Letters from Court, 1887–1901.* Boston: Houghton Mifflin, 1968.

Marie Louise, Princess. *My Memories of Six Reigns.* London: Evans Brothers, 1956.

Martin, Ralph G. *Jennie: The Life of Lady Randolph Churchill.* 2 vols. Englewood Cliffs, N.J.: Prentice-Hall, 1971.

Martin, Sir Theodore. *Queen Victoria as I Knew Her.* London: William Blackwood & Son, 1908.

Matson, John. *Dear Osborne.* London: Hamish Hamilton, 1978.

Maurois, Andre. *The Edwardian Era.* New York: Appleton, 1933.

Maxwell, Sir Herbert. *Sixty Years a Queen: The Story of Her Majesty's Reign.* London: Harmsworth Brothers, 1897.

McCann, Nick. *Balmoral: Highland Retreat of the Royal Family.* Derby, U.K.: Heritage House, 2004.

McCutchan, Philip. *Great Yachts.* New York: Crown Publishers, 1979.

Menkes, Suzy. *The Royal Jewels.* London: Grafton Books, 1988.

Millar, Delia. *Queen Victoria's Life in the Scottish Highlands.* London: Philip Wilson, 1985.

Montgomery-Massingberd, Hugh. *Royal Palaces of Europe.* New York: Vendome, 1983.

Morelli, Marcello, ed. *Royal Palaces.* New York: Barnes & Noble, 1999.

Morshead, Sir Owen. *Windsor Castle.* London: Phaidon, 1971.

Morton, Theresa-Mary. *Royal Residences of the Victorian Era.* London: Royal Collection, 1991.

Mullen, Richard, and James Munson. *Victoria: Portrait of a Queen.* London: BBC, 1987.

Nelson, Michael. *Queen Victoria and the Discovery of the Riviera.* Foreword by Asa Briggs. London: I. B. Tauris, 2001.

Nevill, Barry St.-John, ed. *Life at the Court of Queen Victoria, 1861–1901.* Exeter, U.K.: Webb & Bower, 1984.

Nicolson, Adam. *Restoration: The Rebuilding of Windsor Castle.* London: Michael Joseph, 1997.

One of Her Majesty's Servants. *The Private Life of Queen Victoria.* London: C. Arthur Pearson, 1901.

Packard, Jerrold. *The Queen and Her Court.* New York: Charles Scribner's Sons, 1981.

———. *Victoria's Daughters.* New York: St. Martin's Press, 1998.

Paoli, Xavier. *My Royal Clients*. London: Hodder & Stoughton, 1910.

Peacocke, Marguerite. *The Story of Buckingham Palace and the Royal Household*. London: Pitkin, 1950.

Pearson, John. *Edward the Rake*. New York: Harcourt Brace Jovanovich, 1975.

Perrott, Roy. *The Aristocrats*. New York: Macmillan, 1968.

Plumb, J. H. *Royal Heritage: The Reign of Elizabeth II*. London: Peerage Books, 1981.

Plumb, J. H., and Huw Wheldon. *Royal Heritage: The Treasures of the British Crown*. New York: Harcourt Brace Jovanovich, 1977.

Poliakoff, Vladimir. *The Tragic Bride: The Story of the Empress Alexandra of Russia*. New York: Appleton, 1927.

Ponsonby, Arthur. *Henry Ponsonby: Queen Victoria's Private Secretary: His Life from His Letters*. New York: Macmillan, 1943.

Ponsonby, Sir Frederick, ed. *The Letters of the Empress Frederick*. London: Macmillan, 1929.

———. *Recollections of Three Reigns*. New York: E. P. Dutton, 1952.

———. *Side Lights on Queen Victoria*. New York: Sears, 1930.

Ponsonby, Magadalen. *Mary Ponsonby: A Memoir, Some Letters, and a Journal*. London: John Murray, 1927.

Pope-Hennessy, James. *Queen Mary*. London: George Allen & Unwin, 1959.

Prochaska, Frank. *Royal Bounty: The Making of a Welfare Monarchy*. New Haven, Conn.: Yale University Press, 1995.

Ramm, Agatha, ed. *Beloved and Darling Child: Last Letters between Queen Victoria and Her Eldest Daughter, 1886–1901*. Stroud, U.K.: Sutton, 1990.

Reid, Michaela. *Ask Sir James*. New York: Viking, 1989.

Rennell, Tony. *Last Days of Glory: The Death of Queen Victoria*. New York: St. Martin's Press, 2000.

Reynolds, K. D. *Aristocratic Women and Political Society in Victorian Britain*. Oxford, U.K.: Clarendon Press, 1998.

Ribblesdale, Thomas, Baron. *Impressions and Memoirs*. London: Cassell, 1927.

Roberts, Jane. *Royal Artists*. London: Grafton, 1987.

Robinson, John Martin. *Buckingham Palace: The Official Illustrated History*. London: Royal Collection, 2000.

Romania, Marie, Queen of. *The Story of My Life*. 2 vols. New York: Charles Scribner's Sons, 1934.

Roper, Lanning. *Royal Gardens*. London: W. H. and L. Collingridge, 1953.

Rose, Kenneth. *King George V*. New York: Alfred A. Knopf, 1984.

Rousmaniere, John. *The Luxury Yachts*. Alexandria, Va.: Time-Life, 1981.

Rowse, A. L. *Royal Homes*. London: Odhams Press, 1953.

The Royal Mews, Buckingham Palace: The Queen's Horses and Carriages. London: Pitkin, 1989.

Russia, Grand Duchess George of. *A Romanov Diary*. New York: Atlantic International, 1988.

St. Aubyn, Giles. *Edward VII: Prince and King*. New York: Athenaeum, 1979.

———. *Queen Victoria: A Portrait*. London: Sinclair Stevenson, 1991.

Simpson, Colin, Lewis Chester, and David Leitch. *The Cleveland Street Affair*. Boston: Little, Brown, 1976.

Sitwell, Edith. *Victoria of England*. London: Faber & Faber, 1936.

Staniland, Kay. *In Royal Fashion: The Clothes of Princess Charlotte of Wales and Queen Victoria*. London: Museum of London, 1997.

Stoney, Benita, and Heinrich C. Weltien. *My Mistress the Queen: The Letters of Frieda Arnold, Dresser to Queen Victoria*. London: Weidenfeld & Nicolson, 1994.

Strachey, Lytton. *Queen Victoria*. New York: Harcourt, Brace, 1921.

Strong, Roy. *Cecil Beaton: The Royal Portraits*. New York: Simon & Schuster, 1988.

Sullivan, Michael John. *A Fatal Passion*. New York: Random House, 1997.

Sykes, Christopher Simon. *Private Palaces: Life in the Great London Houses*. New York: Viking, 1986.

Tisdall, E. E. P. *Queen Victoria's Private Life*. New York: John Day, 1961.

Tooley, Sarah. *Personal Life of Queen Victoria*. London: Hodder & Stoughton, 1897.

Tschumi, Gabriel. *Royal Chef*. London: William Kimber, 1954.

Tuchman, Barbara. *The Proud Tower*. New York: Macmillan, 1966.

Turner, E. S. *The Court of St. James's*. New York: St. Martin's Press, 1959.

Tytler, Sarah. *Life of Her Most Gracious Majesty the Queen*. London: Virtue & Co., 1901.

Van der Kiste, John. *Princess Victoria Melita*. Stroud, U.K.: Sutton, 1988.

Victoria, Queen of Great Britain. *Leaves from the Journal of Our Life in the Highlands, from 1848 to 1861*. Edited by Arthur Helps. London: Smith, Elder, 1868.

———. *More Leaves from the Journal of A Life in the Highlands*. London: Smith, Elder, 1884.

Vorres, Ian. *The Last Grand Duchess*. London: Hutchinson, 1964.

Waddington, Mary King. *Letters of a Diplomat's Wife*. New York: Charles Scribner's Sons, 1903.

Wake, Jehanne. *Princess Louise: Queen Victoria's Unconventional Daughter*. London: Collins, 1988.

Wandroper, John. *Wicked Ernst: An Extraordinary Life Revealed*. London: Shelfmark, 2001.

Warner, Marina. *Queen Victoria's Sketchbook*. London: Macmillan, 1979.

Warwick, Frances, Countess of. *Discretions*. New York: Charles Scribner's Sons, 1931.

Watson, Vera. *A Queen at Home: An Intimate Account of the Social and Domestic Life of Queen Victoria's Court*. London: W. H. Allen, 1952.

Weintraub, Stanley. *Victoria: An Intimate Biography*. New York: Dutton, 1987.

Whittle, Tyler. *Victoria and Albert at Home*. London: Routledge & Kegan Paul, 1980.

Widow of an American Diplomat. *Intimacies of Court and Society*. New York: Dodd, Mead, 1912.

William II, Emperor of Germany. *My Early Life*. London: Doran, 1926.

Williams, Mrs. Hwfa. *It Was Such Fun*. London: Hutchinson, 1935.

Williams, Neville. *Royal Homes*. London: Lutterworth, 1971.

Windsor, Dean of, and Hector Bolitho, eds. *Letters of Lady Augusta Stanley: A Young Lady at Court, 1849–1863*. London: Gerald Howe, 1927.

Windsor, the Duke of. *A King's Story*. New York: G. P. Putnam's Sons, 1951.

———. *A Family Album*. London: Cassell, 1960.

Woodham-Smith, Cecil. *Queen Victoria: Her Life and Times*. London: Hamish Hamilton, 1972.

Wright, Patricia. *The Strange History of Buckingham Palace*. Stroud, U.K.: Sutton, 1996.

York, H.R.H., the Duchess of. *Victoria and Albert: A Family Life at Osborne House*. New York: Prentice Hall, 1991.

———. *Queen Victoria's Family: A Century of Photographs*. Stroud, U.K.: Sutton, 2001.

York, H.R.H., the Duchess of, and Benita Stoney. *Travels with Queen Victoria*. London: Weidenfeld & Nicolson, 1993.

Zeepvat, Charlotte. *Prince Leopold*. Stroud, U.K.: Sutton, 1998.

ARTICLES

Arnstein, Walter L. "Queen Victoria's Diamond Jubilee." *American Scholar* 66, no. 4 (Fall 1997).

Cornforth, John. "Queen Victoria at Home." *Country Life* (May 26 and June 9, 1977).

Gosse, Edmund. "The Character of Queen Victoria." *Quarterly Review* 193 (April 1901).

Homans, Margaret. "To the Queen's Private Apartments: Royal Family Portraiture and the Construction of Victoria's Sovereign Obedience." *Victorian Studies* 37, no. 1 (1993).

Jay, Elisabeth. "'Mrs. Brown,' by Windsor's Other Widow." *Women's History Review* 6, no. 2 (1999).

Richards, T. "The Image of Victoria in the Years of Jubilee." *Victorian Studies* 3, no. 1 (1987).

Wynn, Marion. "What Am I Supposed to Do?" *Royalty Digest Quarterly* 1 (2006).

NEWSPAPERS AND PERIODICALS

Dates are referenced in the individual citations in the notes.
The Builder, London
Daily Graphic, London
Daily Mail, London
Daily News, London
Echo, London
Queen, London
Royalty Digest, Ticehurst, U.K.
Times, London

ARCHIVES

The letters of Bishop William Boyd Carpenter in the British Library, Additional Manuscripts Collection, 46720.

INDEX